Matthew Arnold's
ESSAYS IN CRITICISM
FIRST SERIES

Matthew Arnold's
ESSAYS IN CRITICISM
FIRST SERIES

—◆—

A Critical Edition

Edited, with an Introduction and Notes

by

SISTER THOMAS MARION HOCTOR, S.S.J.

THE UNIVERSITY OF CHICAGO PRESS

CHICAGO AND LONDON

Library of Congress Catalog Card Number: 64–17580
The University of Chicago Press, Chicago 60637
The University of Chicago Press, Ltd., London W.C. 1

Published 1968. Manufactured in the United States of America
by H. Wolff, New York

ACKNOWLEDGMENTS

In preparing this volume the editor has received valuable assistance from fellow enthusiasts of Matthew Arnold. She wishes to express her gratitude first to her mentors at Cornell University: to Professor Robert A. Donovan for guiding the work through its initial stages as a doctoral dissertation; to Professors Francis E. Mineka and M. H. Abrams for their interest and advice; and to Professor George H. Healey for his ingenuity in securing needed early texts.

Further acknowledgment is due Professor R. H. Super for a careful reading and commendation of the manuscript in its first form, and to Professors William E. Buckler, Fraser Neiman, and William B. Guthrie, each of whom generously shared his own knowledge on perplexing points.

Finally, grateful thanks are extended to Mother M. Gerardine, S.H.C.J., for her tireless proofreading; to Miss Katherine Fitzgerald for indexing; to Gerald Barrett for special assistance; and to the Sisters of St. Joseph of Rochester, because they believed in the book.

INTRODUCTION

Matthew Arnold's first series of *Essays in Criticism,* published near the end of his career as Professor of Poetry in the University of Oxford, is an extraordinary kind of anthology. Brought out by the Macmillan Company, probably at Arnold's behest, early in February of 1865, this first collection of Arnold's prose was a slim brown volume containing nine essays and a thirteen page preface especially composed for the occasion.[1] To a reader examining the volume for the first time, the most striking feature of the book is its unusual combination of subjects. Confidently independent of traditional notions of the critic's business, it expresses Arnold's own triumph, at once academic and personal, during the decade of his professorship. For the Essays are the measure of Arnold's success as an innovator. In his own way, in the language really used by men of his era, he addressed himself not to the "dead bones" of an academic audience, but to the live issues of a society in perpetual motion.[2]

When Arnold assumed the Professorship of Poetry in Oxford in 1857, he also accepted the responsibility of delivering a lecture each term to the university audience. This was a fortunate arrangement, since it rendered fairly certain a regular contribution to literature and the criticism of literature from Arnold's mind and pen.[3] At the same time it assured Arnold of the professional status he would require in order to launch the "new criticism" he was determined to inaugurate. The first years of

---

[1] "A Persian Passion Play" did not appear in the series until 1875.

[2] See Arnold's letter to his mother of June 16, 1863. It was Arnold who initiated the practice of delivering these lectures in English.

[3] For a virtually complete listing of Arnold's lectures as Professor of Poetry, see R. H. Super, "Arnold's Oxford Lectures on Poetry," *Modern Language Notes,* LXX (1955), 581–84. Super notes that "Arnold was expected to give three lectures a year, and at least once [in 1865] was fined for his failure" (p. 582). On this point, see Arnold's letter to his brother-in-law William Forster, dated September 30, 1865.

his Professorship he devoted to a series of lectures on classical topics treated with a characteristically modern twist: his inaugural lecture, "On the Modern Element in Literature," defined "those ages which are called modern" by examining "the age of Pericles" and "the Rome of Cicero and Augustus," while a subsequent series of lectures entitled *On Translating Homer* left him with a fair degree of popularity and a number of enemies for life.[4] What is important, however, is that in these lectures Arnold was drawing out certain notions about poetry which he had begun to consider in the Preface of 1853, reformulating them into fundamental tenets of criticism which until his very last *sorties* into print he continued energetically to promote.

First of all, in "The Function of Criticism at the Present Time," Arnold thoroughly demonstrates the intimate connection between the task of the poet and that of the critic, a connection hinted at as early as the Preface of 1853. But Arnold's position in the later essay is a clearer presentation of the things he had been thinking for at least a decade. In the 1853 Preface he had attacked the superficiality of contemporary literary critics whose effect upon the current state of English poetry he regarded as disastrous. "The eternal objects of poetry," he had insisted, are "actions, human actions, possessing an inherent interest in themselves, and which are to be communicated in an interesting manner by the art of the poet." [5] "What a Greek critic demanded," he continued, "and what a Greek poet endeavored to effect," was the illumination of an action, "a terrible old mythic story," in all its timelessness:

> then came the poet, embodying outlines, developing situations . . . stroke upon stroke, the drama proceeded: the light deepened upon the group; more and more it revealed itself to the riveted gaze of the spectator: until, at last, when the final words were spoken, it stood before him in broad sunlight, a model of immortal beauty.[6]

[4] One of these was Francis Newman, brother of Cardinal Newman whom Arnold very much admired. Newman's overly ambitious translation of the *Iliad* provoked some of Arnold's most entertaining and insulting "vivacities," though in the end it was the luckless Ichabod Charles Wright who was mauled by Arnold's puppy-like "apologies" in the 1865 Preface. Arnold's inaugural lecture, "On the Modern Element in Literature," as well as the Homer lectures are reprinted in R. H. Super, ed., *The Complete Prose Works of Matthew Arnold*, 6 vols. (Ann Arbor: University of Michigan Press, 1960-67), vol. 1, *On the Classical Tradition* (1960).

[5] Super, *Complete Prose Works*, I, 3. For the evolution of Arnold's poetic theory before 1853, see his letters to Clough, especially those of February, 1849, emphasizing "form," and October 28, 1852, emphasizing "contents." See also the first chapter of Lionel Trilling's *Matthew Arnold* (New York: Columbia University Press, 1949).

[6] Super, *Complete Prose Works*, I, 6. One notices Arnold's fondness for images of sight and of light in connection with poetry and the poet. Cf. "Resignation," line 198, and the well-known description of Sophocles in "To A Friend." At the end of the second Homer lecture Arnold speaks of "simple lucidity of mind" as a necessary quality in the translator of Homer (Super, *Complete Prose Works*, I, 140-41).

In the Homer lectures Arnold's statements about poetry became more concise: "The noble and profound application of ideas to life is the most essential part of poetic greatness," he affirmed, in comparing the qualities of Homer and Milton.[7] By June of 1863, when Arnold delivered his lecture on Heinrich Heine, poetry had become "simply the most beautiful, impressive, and widely effective mode of saying things," while by November of the same year, in the "Joubert" lecture, he had closed the gap completely by declaring that poetry is a "criticism of life."[8] Arnold's introductory essay in the 1865 volume, then, takes the assertions from the 1853 Preface a long way forward. The poet is, in a real sense, a particular kind of critic: he directs his current of fresh insights (Arnold calls them "ideas") not toward literary offenders, Philistines, or champions of evolution and of dogma, but toward that mystery which is life. The "critic of life" is a Sophocles, who "saw life steadily and saw it whole," and a Shakespeare, whose "victorious brow" is paradoxically both enigma and revelation to "the foil'd searching of mortality."[9]

Another important proposition in Arnold's introductory essay, this one originating in the Homer lectures, was Arnold's conception of the "critical spirit" itself:

> Of the literature of France and Germany, as of the intellect of Europe in general, the main effort, for now many years, has been a critical effort; the endeavour, in all branches of knowledge, theology, philosophy, history, art, science, to see the object as in itself it really is.[10]

In "The Function of Criticism at the Present Time," Arnold supplies ample ammunition for his accusation that the critical spirit in England is at "low ebb." One of the most amusing and yet forceful of these projectiles is his observation about the "critical hit in the religious literature of England," Dr. Colenso's absurd assessment of the problems in the Pentateuch, in contrast to the efforts in higher criticism by Strauss in Germany, and Renan in France. The writings of Bishop Colenso are

---

[7] Super, *Complete Prose Works,* I, 211-12.

[8] A similar "definition" of poetry appears in the "Wordsworth" essay of 1879: poetry is "the most perfect speech of man, that in which he comes nearest to being able to utter the truth." "The Study of Poetry" (1880) is, of course, an elaborate exposition of Arnold's notions about poetry as a "criticism of life."

[9] In Arnold's next set of lectures, those on Celtic literature, he supplies additional clues as to the meaning of his expression "criticism of life" as it applies to poetry. "The grand business of modern poetry" is "a moral interpretation from an independent point of view of man and the world" (Super, *Complete Prose Works,* III, 380); "the inevitable task for the modern poet henceforth is . . . to interpret human life afresh, and to supply a new spiritual basis to it" (Super, *Complete Prose Works,* III, 381).

[10] This passage occurs in the concluding paragraph of the second of Arnold's lectures on Homer (Super, *Complete Prose Works,* I, 140).

raucous and unenlightened, according to Arnold, while those of Strauss and Renan succeed because of their greater objectivity.

This notion of objectivity, which can be shown to derive not only from Wordsworth's Preface (1800), but from attitudes of Sainte-Beuve, Goethe, and Cardinal Newman as well, surfaces as Arnold's famous dictum of "disinterestedness" in "The Function of Criticism at the Present Time." [11] This essay, aptly styled Arnold's critical manifesto, is a cry for freedom from any kind of "national and provincial partiality," factionalism, or thickheaded dogmatism. In it, Arnold argues for an enormously extended definition of criticism. As an "intellectual and spiritual activity," criticism is generic, having for its object nothing less than "things in general"—theology, philosophy, history, art, science, or any of a hundred other interests of the modern mind.[12] For the critical spirit operates whenever a mind is functioning disinterestedly upon any subject, that is, when it is searching for "the best that is known and thought in the world" upon that subject. This involves honest critical evaluation of innumerable possible ideas, some adequate and some inadequate, upon the matter, and discovery of the best ideas to be had. *Literary* criticism, therefore, as we understand it, is not Arnold's concern in this collection. Literary criticism constitutes only a single species under the genus "criticism"; it is the critical spirit of mind at work in the endeavor to see the *literary* "object as in itself it really is." [13]

The charge that Arnold did not succeed in practicing anything like the degree of disinterestedness which he preached is not a new one. E. K. Brown developed this thesis at book-length.[14] R. H. Super, however,

---

[11] For a convenient note on Arnold's derivation of "disinterestedness" from Sainte-Beuve and from Goethe, see Super, *Complete Prose Works*, III, 477.

[12] It is worth noting that Arnold does mention the field of "science" here. In a letter to Thomas Henry Huxley, with whom Arnold enjoyed a most cordial relationship, Arnold insisted, in reply to Huxley's charges in "Science and Culture," that while he had no intention of "entering into controversy" with Huxley, he wished to affirm that "the dictum about knowing 'the best that has been known and said in the world' was meant to include knowing what has been said in science and art as well as letters. I remembered changing the word *said* to the word *uttered*, because I was dissatisfied with the formula for seeming not to include art, and a picture or a statue may be called an utterance though it cannot be called a saying; however, I went back to *said* for the base reason that the formula runs so much easier off the tongue with the shorter word. But I never doubted that the formula included science." See Arnold's letter dated October 17, 1880; W. H. G. Armytage, "Matthew Arnold and Thomas Henry Huxley: Some New Letters: 1870-80," *Review of English Studies*, n.s., IV (1953), 352.

[13] Geoffrey Tillotson points out that whenever Arnold "speaks of literary criticism or of the literary critic, he prefixes, like Keble, Newman and Ruskin, a derogative and speaks of 'mere' literary criticism, the 'mere' literary critic." See his essay, "Matthew Arnold: The Critic and the Advocate" in *Criticism and the Nineteenth Century* (London: University of London, Athlone Press, 1951), p. 44.

[14] E. K. Brown, *Matthew Arnold: A Study in Conflict* (Hamden, Conn.: Archon

describes Brown's book as "curiously uncertain in its central conception," and William Robbins insists that whereas "Brown's thesis of a heavily damaging psychological fracture maintains that this conflict, productive of irritations and contradictions, crippled the critic in his efforts to be disinterested and objective," Arnold rather succeeded to some degree in achieving "a fruitful interplay among ideas, a philosophic polarity of attitudes" which made for "continuing vitality and relevance." [15] Brown, however, contends that at times Arnold was "truly disinterested in disposition" and other times too "eager to win his readers to a moral or intellectual opinion." He concludes that Arnold had devised a deliberate and clever strategy, proceeding on some occasions "in the belief that an air of total disinterestedness will be a powerful instrument toward the accomplishment of his aim" and on others discarding it as "useless." Arnold's "disinterestedness" Brown chooses to define as his "principle of abstaining from specific proposals." [16] Arnold, of course, meant something like this. In *A French Eton* (1864), for example, he vehemently protested that "I have no pet scheme to press, no crochet to gratify, no fanatical zeal for giving this or that particular shape to the public establishment of our secondary instruction," while in the present volume his studied indifference to the notion of establishing an English Academy, his blunt reservations about Ruskin's "pugnacious political economy," about Carlyle's "furious raids" into politics, and the ordinary man's weakness, as soon as he has "an idea, or half an idea," for "running out with it into the street and trying to make it rule there," fortify his position.

In his chapter on *Essays in Criticism,* First Series, Brown furnishes some useful insights into Arnold's "rhetoric of irony"; but Arnold's techniques are treated with far greater finesse by John Holloway in *The Victorian Sage.* Brown, one feels, is inclined to make something approaching a moral issue out of Arnold's "strategy of disinterestedness" and to create a convenient dichotomy between the poles of "disinterestedness" (represented by *Essays in Criticism,* First Series) and "practical criticism" (represented by *Culture and Anarchy*).[17] Holloway, on the

---

Books, reprint, 1966). The book was originally published by the University of Chicago Press in 1948.

[15] Super, *Complete Prose Works,* III, 403; William Robbins, *The Ethical Idealism of Matthew Arnold* (Toronto: University of Toronto Press, 1959), p. 159.

[16] Brown, *Matthew Arnold,* pp. 22 and 82. See also pp. 90, 95, and 104 for other "definitions."

[17] *Ibid.,* p. 141. See also pp. 61-65 and 96-104. By "practical criticism" Brown means the offering of solutions to specific problems. But see, on this point, Fitzjames Stephen's essay, "Mr. Matthew Arnold and His Countrymen," beginning at p. 325 below.

other hand, appears to enjoy Arnold's "lethal innocence," and presents a careful study of Arnold's techniques of argument, concluding that Arnold is out subtly to convey "a certain temper of mind by example, rather than description." [18] Whereas Brown does suggest helpful "definitions" of disinterestedness (such as a "tone" which "enables the writer to insinuate his criticism without seeming to care passionately or fervently about his beliefs or the beliefs of others"), he is guilty of wielding such definitions like a sledgehammer against Arnold's stance, a rather indelicate critical approach at best.[19] The fairer method would be less a priori.

Arnold himself had a good deal to say about his penchant for irony, all of which sheds light on the problem being considered. In a letter of December 5, 1867, Arnold remarked on how "effective" a "weapon" irony had proved to be in "a confused, loud-talking, clap-trappy country like this," and commended it as delicacy of understatement.[20] Three years earlier, at the very time when he was composing the original preface to the *Essays in Criticism,* Arnold had referred to his "sinuous, easy, unpolemical mode of proceeding" as something deliberately adopted as "the best way of proceeding if one wants to get at, and keep with, truth" and gain access for one's ideas in mid-Victorian England. He had said much the same thing a year earlier than this, in a letter which assured his mother that "everything turns upon one's exercising the power of *persuasion, of charm,*" for "even in one's ridicule one must preserve a sweetness and good-humor" in order not to lose one's "chance of *getting at* the English public." [21] Shortly thereafter he remarked to Mrs. Forster that his aim was to "charm the wild beast of Philistinism while I am trying to convert him." Finally, having in 1866 turned his energies to the "sheer disquisition" of the Celtic literature series, he expressed enormous relief at this opportunity "to leave irony and the Philistines,"

[18] John Holloway, *The Victorian Sage* (New York, Norton Library reprint, 1965), pp. 235, 243. F. J. W. Harding, in *Matthew Arnold the Critic and France* (Geneva, 1964), describes the difference between Arnold's kind of disinterestedness and Sainte-Beuve's: "The literary tact of Sainte-Beuve tended to become irony and raillery with Arnold," who was "too sensitive to religious and social problems to give an equal impression of detachment" (p. 94). An interesting if exaggerated variation on Brown's theme is Gaylord C. Le Roy's rather frenetic article, "Ambivalence in Matthew Arnold's Prose Criticism," *College English,* XIII (1952), 432-38. Le Roy traces the tensions in Arnold to his ambivalence toward "what he believed the dominant tendency of his own time—the continuation of the work of the French Revolution" (p. 434).

[19] Brown, *Matthew Arnold,* p. 104. Other useful discussions of the question of disinterestedness in Arnold's criticism include the articles by Fitzjames Stephen included in this volume, Geoffrey Tillotson's "Matthew Arnold: The Critic and the Advocate," and N. N. Feltes, "Matthew Arnold and the Modern Spirit: A Reassessment," *University of Toronto Quarterly,* XXXII (1962), 27-36 (*passim*).

[20] This excerpt is quoted by Super, *Complete Prose Works,* V, 414.

[21] See Arnold's letters of December 7, 1864, and October 29, 1863.

while one reads with interest a statement made in quite a different kind of context, revealing Arnold's delight that a teacher whose school he had recently inspected had commended his disposition to be " 'always gentle and patient with the children': The great thing is *humanity, after all.*" [22]

Arnold's irony is not, in fact, nearly so vicious as Brown represents it to be. On the contrary, Arnold's dramatic sense combined with his sense of humor create a vein of comic irony which pervades the *Essays in Criticism,* First Series. Arnold's substantial deletions from the original version of his preface deprive the reader of an enormous amount of sheer comedy. Arnold thoroughly enjoyed the "vivacities" of the original preface, though his family apparently did not. "My Essays are nearly printed," he wrote to his mother on January 21, 1865, "but until I have finally got the Preface to stand as I like, I shall not feel that the book is off my hands. The Preface will make you laugh." His enjoyment is even more evident in a slightly later description of himself reading the preface to a brother and sister, "who received it in such solemn silence that I began to tremble." In reconsidering the total value of some of the "lighter parts of the preface and notes," he decided to omit them for any subsequent edition, "for the Essays are of too grave a character to tack" such material "permanently to them." [23]

In assessing the extent to which Arnold actually succeeded in being "disinterested," one must bear in mind this comic element, which he employed as a calculated risk. The comic stance creates a certain kind of detachment, as Walpole's maxim reminds us, but in the end Arnold's detachment is not the kind of which Brown really approves. One can best understand what Arnold is doing by seeing it as artistic, not personal, role-playing. Arnold saw himself as the suave, omniscient intelligence observing from the periphery the frenzy of the forum, in the tradition of Horace, Chaucer, and the *Spectator* essayists. [24]

---

[22] See Arnold's letters of November 14, 1863, March 24, 1866, and December 14, 1867.

[23] See Arnold's letter to Lady de Rothschild, February, 11, 1865. The second excerpt is from a letter of mid-March, 1865, quoted by Super, *Complete Prose Works,* III, 483. A similar statement occurs in Arnold's letter to Lady de Rothschild of April 3, 1865.

[24] Geoffrey Tillotson ("Matthew Arnold: The Critic and the Advocate") argues that because Arnold's essays are "criticisms of literature and life together," he could not succeed in being disinterested, "though he did not cease to claim to be disinterested" (p. 44). Tillotson suggests that two defects of temperament which inclined Arnold toward the role of "advocate" rather than "critic" by his own definition were that he was a "satirist" and that he was an "egotist" (pp. 55-56). Arnold distinguishes the "critic" from the "advocate" in the second of his lectures on Celtic literature (Super, *Complete Prose Works,* III, 328-29).

Not everyone, however, took Arnold's audacity amiss, as some notices of the 1865 edition of *Essays in Criticism* indicate. One reviewer expressed great satisfaction with the highly entertaining preface, a thirteen-page tirade against the vagaries of incompetent critics which masqueraded as an apology for former "vivacities." He styled it "a small quiverful of stinging, if not absolutely poisoned arrows, shot right and left at reviewers, system-mongers, and the fat-headed, respectable public in general," while another writer commended it as "a striking example of the intelligent amiability which animates his style." [25] Doubtless, Arnold's fencing was applauded more enthusiastically by those in a position to observe it at a safe distance, for the same preface was characterized by yet another critic as "a wanton outrage upon the amenities of literary warfare" demonstrating at once "how sensitive is the author himself, and yet how indifferent to the feelings of others." Yet another protested with a magnificent gesture: "Admiring him as we do, we can forgive him, but how can he forgive himself?" [26] Far from admitting a need to "forgive himself," Arnold rather congratulated himself: "The best justification of the Preface is the altered tone of the *Saturday*," he crowed.[27] Nevertheless, for the second edition Arnold deleted five long sections, directing the reader's attention much more sharply to his design in writing it as a determination to dissociate from the University of Oxford all responsibility for the arrogance of "her unworthy son." Every subsequent edition included the preface exactly as Arnold had worded it in 1869.

Arnold's revision of "The Literary Influence of Academies" also indicates very clearly his growing recognition of the importance of disinterestedness. As long as he continued to harbor the imp of comic irony in his critical writing, so long would an undiscriminating public fail to grasp the essentials of his critical scheme. Alienation of sensitive readers had proved the price of indulging an irrepressible sense of humor. Reviews of the 1865 edition told Arnold quite plainly that his public could not always decide how sharply his thrusts were aimed. Arnold's revisions here, therefore, reveal a growing regard for urbanity of spirit, as is evidenced by the softening of tone in his description of Alexander Kinglake. In most of the succeeding essays there is similar evidence that

---

[25] See "Belles Lettres," *Westminister Review*, n. s., XXVII (1865), 634-35, and "Arnold's *Essays in Criticism*," *North American Review*, CI (1865), 207.

[26] See the notices of *Essays in Criticism* in the *British Quarterly Review*, 41 (1865): 544; and the *North British Review*, XLII (1865), 182.

[27] See Arnold's letter to his mother, March 3, 1865.

Arnold's keen critical tact told him when a position was too costly to defend.[28]

The initial essay in the series, "The Function of Criticism at the Present Time," besides being the source of Arnold's first discussion of disinterestedness, is the only instance in which Arnold openly legislated upon the critic's business.[29] The other nine essays which make up this volume, and subsequent essays as well, provide illustrations to apply and reinforce the conception of criticism developed in this key introductory essay. In examining a copy of the first series of *Essays in Criticism* as it appeared from the press, Arnold remarked on "the admirable riches of human nature that are brought to light in the group of persons whom they treat, and the sort of unity that as a book to stimulate the better humanity in us the volume has." [30] Literature, Arnold like Sainte-Beuve believed, is inseparable from humanity, and from the cultural perfection of human life.[31] This explains why, in the *Essays in Criticism,* Arnold holds up literary personalities, and not isolated works of literature, as his subjects. Each writer is judged by Arnold's criteria for the ideal literary personality; the man himself is analyzed for some outstanding trait which will account for the individual quality of his work. With Maurice de Guérin it is "natural magic"; with his sister, Eugénie, "distinction"; with Joubert, a certain lightsomeness energized by a "passion for perfection"; with Cardinal Newman, that rare quality of "urbanity."

In his preface Arnold cites a maxim of Goethe's which is to recur frequently in his critical estimates in the volume. Goethe had praised Schiller highly for his ability "to have left miles out of sight behind him . . . the bondage of *was uns alle bändigt,* DAS GEMEINE!" *"Das Gemeine,"* extremely expressive in German, is difficult to render adequately in English. Arnold terms it vulgarity in the last sentence of "The Literary Influence of Academies," when he speaks of a self-conceit and self-complacency "vulgar" and "retarding" in the British culture of his day. Later, in the lectures on Celtic literature, he refers to "the

---

[28] See the textual notes to the present edition.

[29] Unless one wishes to stretch a point, citing "The Study of Poetry" as legislation about the poet as "critic of life" and his "business."

[30] See Arnold's letter to his mother, January 21, 1865.

[31] In his *Encyclopedia Britannica* article (1886) on Sainte-Beuve, Arnold speaks of French critics who, unlike German ones, "reviewed one another as gentlemen" rather than as enemies, and attributes this to "the higher social development of France" and "the closer relationships of literature with life there." French literature, Arnold continues, "more than any modern literature" has been "in the most intimate correspondence with the social life and development of the nation." Arnold contributed this article to the ninth edition of the *Britannica.*

humdrum, the plain and ugly, the ignoble: in a word, *das Gemeine, die Gemeinheit,* that curse of Germany, against which Goethe was all his life fighting." [32] Once the importance of this notion is sensed, one has discovered the real center of the *Essays.* For each of Arnold's victims here has in some fashion indulged that "vulgarity" which sins against the light of the truth, goodness, and beauty which belongs to our "humanity proper." Bishop Colenso and his book on the Pentateuch distort religious truth with mathematical calculations; Miss Cobbe's *Religious Duty* obscures the "more grandiose, noble, or beautiful character [which] properly belongs to religious constructions"; and both Heinrich Heine and his idol Byron stand in need of a "moral deliverance." [33]

Arnold's admiration, on the other hand, is directed toward figures who have contributed something to the development of "humanity proper," however modest their contribution to the field of letters alone. Hence the essays on Maurice and Eugénie de Guérin, on Joubert with his "delightful and edifying genius," on Heine, the German-French internationalist who initiated the "intellectual deliverance" of Germany. Hence, too, those on Spinoza and Marcus Aurelius, with their impeccable lives, the former possessed of keen critical tact and eminently flexible mind in Scriptural criticism, the latter endowed with the inestimable power to heighten moral precepts with religious feeling. These are the personalities of *Essays in Criticism,* whose presence in the volume evokes no surprise once Arnold's notion of the "critic's business" is understood. [34]

Despite its unusual combination of subjects, one is struck, as Arnold

---

[32] The passage occurs in the first paragraph of Lecture 4 (Super, *Complete Prose Works,* III, 341).

[33] Arnold's preoccupation with religious questions and values in this volume is noteworthy; nearly all of the essays discuss them in one form or another. Arnold was still chastising Miss Cobbe fifteen years later. See his letter to M. Fontanès, March 25, 1881.

[34] E. K. Brown labors to relate Arnold's unusual choice of subjects here to his "conflict" over the desire to be disinterested. On the one hand, Brown cites Maurice de Guérin, Joubert, and Marcus Aurelius as "examples of that disposition of disinterestedness which Arnold had sought and praised" (*Matthew Arnold,* p. 90), and on the other he suggests that the lesser-known subjects make it easier for "the personality of the critic," Arnold, to be "properly" and "naturally repressed" (*ibid.,* pp. 98-99). F. J. W. Harding and Iris Sells tend to be more concrete in their suggestions about the reasons behind Arnold's choice of subjects for his lectures and essays; the former cites the influence of Sainte-Beuve, adding that these authors "were also quite closely linked with Arnold's own personality and aims" (*Matthew Arnold,* p. 93), while the latter suggests that Arnold's "arbitrary preference for nobodies like the de Guérins" originated "in the days of his first revelation of French literature, from the oracular lips of George Sand" (Iris Sells, *Matthew Arnold and France* [Cambridge, 1935], p. xiii).

himself was, by the kind of unity which nevertheless does characterize the book. As a reviewer of the volume for the short-lived literary periodical, *The Reader,* remarked in the spring of 1865 in one of his less uncomplimentary moments:

> The subjects have no obvious connexion with each other. Yet the book leaves on the reader's mind an impression of completeness and unity which is equally rare and delightful. The opening essay in part explains the secret. Mr. Arnold desires to reform English criticism. Every one of his articles has been written to illustrate his conception of its true nature. Each one, therefore, helps to interpret the rest; the greater the diversity of topics, the more they conduce to the general object. . . . Mr. Arnold's style is so graceful, so perfect, that it has all the appearance of being the most natural and spontaneous expression of his thoughts.[35]

Actually, had this reviewer known what any student of Arnold now knows about the order in which the various essays had been composed and, in most instances, delivered in Oxford, as well as something about the directions Arnold's thinking had been taking in the 1850's and early 1860's, he would surely have realized that "The Function of Criticism at the Present Time" was Arnold's attempt to theorize about ideas introduced into the essays which had preceded it chronologically. The Spinoza series and the essays on Heine and Joubert are especially illuminating when read in this perspective. [36]

Still, the question of the kind of unity which the *Essays* do possess, like the question of Arnold's "disinterestedness," is a complex one. Therefore, one must again guard against a similar temptation to deny the volume some other kind of unity instead of granting it Arnold's own kind. With this in mind, one can weigh the elements involved.

Robert A. Donovan's intelligent and perceptive study of Arnold's "method" in the 1865 collection argues that the unity is fourfold: "The lectures, culminating in 'The Influence of Academies on National Spirit and Literature' and 'The Functions of Criticism at the Present Time' [Arnold's original titles] represent collectively Arnold's paeon of praise

---

[35] See p. 337. The review is unsigned, but its author is probably J. M. Ludlow, the "modern critic" whom Arnold attacked in his 1853 Preface. See H. W. Garrod, "Matthew Arnold's 1853 Preface," *Review of English Studies,* XVII (1941), 311 and 318. Other possible authors would be David Masson or George Henry Lewes. Professor Houghton's *Index* of Victorian Periodicals does not include *The Reader.*

[36] For a thorough examination of Arnold's set of three Colenso essays in *Macmillan's Magazine* for 1863, see Sidney M. B. Coulling, "The Background of 'The Function of Criticism at the Present Time,'" *Philological Quarterly,* XLII (1963), 36-54. Coulling concludes that Arnold did not republish the Colenso essays chiefly "to avoid further hurting the feelings of his victim" since " 'The Function of Criticism at the Present Time' " really "had said virtually all that the other two essays had said, and said it better" (p. 54). Professor Super reprints these essays in the third volume of the *Complete Prose Works.*

for France, and they form the substance of the 1865 volume." [37] He then proceeds to demonstrate that of the three essays which originated as articles and not as lectures, "Eugénie de Guérin," "Spinoza and the Bible," and "Marcus Aurelius," even the unlikely last two are "germane" to the "plan of the *Essays in Criticism*," rather than "the random interpolations which they at first seem," for all the essays, without exception, constitute Arnold's attacks on "British provincialism or Philistinism, British smugness and complacency." Mr. Donovan concludes:

> The volume is united by a common source of its inspiration [France], by a common theme [Philistinism], . . . by a common method [Arnold's "comparative method" or dialectic] . . . and by a common aim [to inculcate the notion of literature as a "great intellectual force"].[38]

On the other hand, William E. Buckler, drawing upon evidence not available to Mr. Donovan in 1956, contends that Mr. Donovan has given the *Essays*, and Arnold himself, credit for a greater degree of intellectual subtlety than either deserves. The truth of the matter is, according to Mr. Buckler, that Arnold was prompted by a certain amount of financial duress to put something on the market in the mid-1860's, a crass fact which detracts somewhat from Mr. Donovan's preoccupation with Arnold's "agile intelligence":

> I think that as much as we can say concerning the order and coherence of the first edition of *Essays in Criticism, First Series*, is this: It was a collection of the principal essays written by Arnold during 1863 and 1864, having, naturally, like critical themes and critical methods; "The Function of Criticism at the Present Time" was intentionally written as the intro-

---

[37] Robert A. Donovan, "The Method of Arnold's *Essays in Criticism*," *PMLA*, LXXI (1956), 925.

[38] *Ibid.*, pp. 925, 930. Mr. Donovan admits that he has some difficulty in accounting for "A Persian Passion Play," which Arnold added for the third edition (1875), but suggests that the dissimilarity of this last essay to the earlier ones can be traced to an "enormous change" which took place in Arnold between 1865 and 1875. Even in 1870, he feels, Arnold "had become disillusioned with the French character, had turned his back on his French master, Sainte-Beuve, and was proclaiming the virtues, not of intelligence, but of conduct as 'three-fourths, at the very least, of human life'" (p. 931).
At least two other critics of Arnold suggest something similar. E. K. Brown believed that "a conviction of crisis in English civilization took possession of Matthew Arnold" after 1865 (*Matthew Arnold*, p. 83), while N. N. Feltes locates the change a decade later, contending that "the religious essays of the seventies" are "a watershed separating the period of Arnold's approval of the workings of the modern spirit from that of his fear of its evil effects" ("Matthew Arnold and the Modern Spirit: A Reassessment," *University of Toronto Quarterly*, XXXII [1962], 27). Lionel Trilling associates this change in Arnold with his changing attitude toward "middle-class liberalism"; see also Gaylord C. Le Roy on Arnold's "ambivalence" with respect to the French Revolution and its political and social consequences ("Ambivalence in Matthew Arnold's Prose Criticism").

duction, and in the individual essays Arnold offered to the public "attempts" at or "specimens" of criticism.[39]

Arnold himself had something to say about all this, and Mr. Buckler's final sentence is an allusion to this. In his letter to Alexander Macmillan of July 26, 1864, Arnold remarked: "I have enough already, and more than enough, to make a volume . . . only I must write an introduction, and this I will do sometime in the course of the autumn. . . . What to call the volume is not easily settled. I had thought of 'Essays of Criticism' in the old sense of the word *Essay—attempt—specimen;* but perhaps this would hardly do. What do you think of 'Essays *in* Criticism'?" [40] Arnold's design is reflected in the title he finally devised for the collection. If *Essays in Criticism* immediately recalls Pope's masterpiece of neoclassic criticism, it does so only in order to shift the emphasis. Arnold's essays, after the first one, are not mere "essays *on* criticism," establishing strict literary canons and defining the boundaries of literary endeavor. Rather, they are "attempts," in the French sense, to illustrate clearly and effectively the sense which Arnold was determined to convey by that much-worried term "criticism."

Perhaps, then, one ought to associate with Arnold's choice of a title, not Pope at all, but the two contemporary French critics whom Arnold read devoutly and, as devoutly, imitated. Lewis F. Mott was the first to point out that Arnold owed to Renan, as well as to Sainte-Beuve, a heavy debt, in this first collection of essays. Like Renan, Arnold was publishing a collection of essays which had already appeared in journals, essays which thus had "instead of a formal unity of subject-matter, a more abstract unity of tendency and motive." [41] In her ill-tempered treatment of Arnold as critic, Ruth Temple suggests that Arnold is guilty of something close to plagiarism in his debts to Sainte-Beuve; it should be noted, however, that Arnold disagrees entirely with Sainte-Beuve's estimate of Eugénie de Guérin, and builds a rather complicated parallel with Coleridge into the Joubert essay.[42]

[39] William E. Buckler, "Studies in Three Arnold Problems," sec. 3, *PMLA,* LXXIII (1958), 268-69.

[40] William E. Buckler, *Matthew Arnold's Books,* (Geneva: Librarie E. Droz, 1958) pp.66-67. In preparing the lecture "The Functions of Criticism at the Present Time" for publication in this collection, Arnold added for the 1865 edition the paragraph on p. 30 describing the "unity" of the collection.

[41] Lewis F. Mott, "Renan and Matthew Arnold," *Modern Language Notes,* 33 (1918): 68. Mott further notes several interesting parallels between the prefaces to the two collections. See also Super, *Collected Prose Works,* III, 482, 490-91.

[42] Ruth Temple, *The Critic's Alchemy: A Study of the Introduction of French Symbolism into England* (New Haven, Conn.: College and University Press reprint, n.d.), p. 56.

Sol Liptzin cites Saint-René Taillander's article in the *Revue des deux mondes*

Still, a study of Arnold's debts in the 1865 series of *Essays in Criticism* provides valuable insights into Arnold's estimate of himself as a thinker. For Arnold's "critical spirit," as a mentality, comprises certain elements, certain "habits, methods, ruling ideas" which in a letter to Cardinal Newman, written in 1872, Arnold acknowledged having learned from Goethe, Wordsworth, Sainte-Beuve, and Newman himself.[43] Following a very simple scheme, one might associate with Goethe Arnold's notion of the *zeitgeist* or "modern spirit," as he was more inclined to call it, the notion in particular of "intellectual deliverance" from the bondage of received traditions and accredited dogmas which have outlived their usefulness: with Wordsworth, contemplation, or an honest effort to "see the object as in itself it really is"; with Sainte-Beuve, "curiosity," or "a desire after the things of the mind for their own sake," manifesting itself in "disinterested love of a free play of the mind"; and finally, with Newman himself, "urbanity," "criticism's right tone and temper of mind," "a miracle of intellectual delicacy" which holds ideas easily and is ever alert for true modifications of those ideas.[44] A delicate fusion of all these qualities is what prepares the critic to meet the thrusts and counterthrusts of an "epoch of expansion." Arnold describes the process in a quotation from Burke which stood as a motto for the *Essays* in 1865:

> Our antagonist is our helper. This amicable conflict with difficulty obliges us to an intimate acquaintance with our object, and compels us to consider it in all its relations. It will not suffer us to be superficial.

---

for April 1, 1852, as a source for both "Heine's Grave" and the Oxford lecture. See "Heine, the Continuator of Goethe: A Mid-Victorian Legend," *Journal of English and Germanic Philology,* XLIII (1944), 322.

[43] Arnold Whitridge, ed., *Unpublished Letters of Matthew Arnold* (New Haven: Yale University Press, 1923), pp. 65-66.

[44] Yet, Arnold's notion of "disinterestedness" and the contemplation of "the object as in itself it really is" owes something too to his reading of the *Bhagavad-Gita,* as his celebration of "the Indian virtue of detachment" in "The Function of Criticism at the Present Time" reminds us. And W. S. Knickerbocker asserts that while Arnold was at Balliol, Benjamin Jowett's "passion for the Hegelian *zeitgeist* was too infectious for young Arnold to resist." See "Matthew Arnold at Oxford," *Sewanee Review,* XXXV (1927), 413.

Arnold's essay on Emerson, reprinted in the *Discourses in America,* cites "four voices" in the air of Oxford during his undergraduate years, those of Newman, Carlyle, Goethe, and Emerson. David J. De Laura devotes a lengthy article to assessing the extent of Arnold's largely unacknowledged debt to Carlyle in "Arnold and Carlyle," *PMLA,* LXXIX (1964), 104-29, though as Professor Super points out, De Laura exaggerates Arnold's "fixed need to depreciate Carlyle" (Super, *Complete Prose Works,* V, 414). See also De Laura's excellent monograph on the influence of Newman's writings on Arnold: "Matthew Arnold and John Henry Newman: The 'Oxford Sentiment' and the Religion of the Future," *Texas Studies in Literature and Language,* VI, supplement (1965), 571-702.

This "simple scheme," however, though convenient, is not quite accurate. A careful examination of Arnold's "ruling ideas" indicates that they derive from not one but all four of the figures named in his letter to Newman. For example, the idea of "disinterestedness," as suggested earlier, comes most immediately from the concluding paragraph of Sainte-Beuve's original preface to *Chateaubriand et son groupe littéraire sous l'Empire* (1849), conveniently reprinted in Professor Super's notes to "The Function of Criticism at the Present Time." Professor Super regards Arnold's use of the term, as well as the idea which it represents, as Arnold's "principal debt to Sainte-Beuve." [45] But Arnold is not simply seizing upon an idea of Sainte-Beuve's alone. Goethe too was of this mind. And surely Wordsworth's early declaration of the importance of keeping the eye upon the subject, in his preface to the second edition of the *Lyrical Ballads* (1800), underlies Arnold's notion of disinterestedness, which is only another term for the critic's endeavor "to see the object as in itself it really is." Finally, Arnold shared with Cardinal Newman the ideal of liberal education represented by the University of Oxford, "to see things as they are, to go right to the point." [46] Thus, it is surely more valid to conclude that Arnold did not "derive" his "ruling ideas" from one source or another, but instead that he discovered his own affinities with the minds which helped to form his, and savored their expression of ideas and attitudes which, in Coleridge's phrase, could "find" him.[47] In one sense, Arnold is simply illustrating his own conception of the "critic's business" by stocking his mind with what, for him at least, represents the best that is known and thought in the world.

Another instance of this same intellectual "eclecticism" in Arnold can be seen in the derivation of his concept of "culture." As Helen C. White

[45] Super, *Complete Prose Works*, III, 477. He notes also Goethe's expression for the same idea, *uneigennützigkeit* (*Dichtung und Warheit*, bk. XIV), which Goethe sees as a characteristic excellence in Spinoza. Arnold's introduction to Spinoza doubtless came through Goethe.

[46] C. F. Harrold, ed., *The Idea of A University* (New York: Longmans, 1947), p. 157. Thomas Arnold's choice of the University of Oxford for his sons was a deliberate move to expose them to exactly this kind of intellectual discipline and atmosphere, by way of "arming them in a manner for whatever may happen to them." See Warren D. Anderson's informative first chapter ("The Student Years") in *Matthew Arnold and the Classical Tradition* (Ann Arbor: University of Michigan Press, 1965), p. 10. Dr. Arnold's influence in this area, therefore, should not be overlooked.

[47] What Iris Sells asserts of Arnold's selection of reading in French authors could readily be generalized in an effort to describe Arnold's intellectual formation: "Arnold's deep sense of affinity with his sources impelled him from the outset; he read where his sympathies lay." See her *Matthew Arnold and France*, p. xii. Likewise, J. W. Angell accounts for Arnold's debt to Renan by the evident resemblances to Arnold's own bent of thought; see "Matthew Arnold's Indebtedness to Renan's *Essais de morale et de critique*," *Revue de littérature comparée*, XIV (1934), 714-33.

long ago pointed out, culture was Goethe's "favorite word." [48] Arnold's citing of Goethe's "reproach" against the French Revolution, in "The Function of Criticism at the Present Time," because it had "thrown quiet culture back" is a characteristic example. J. B. Orrick, however, has an extremely conservative estimate of Goethe's influence on Arnold's intellectual formation:

> That Matthew Arnold has learnt no habits and methods from Goethe is, I think, fairly obvious. . . . Whether Arnold has learnt any ruling ideas from Goethe must depend on one's definition of a ruling idea. He has acquired some of his theories and opinions from that source, and received for others a reinforcement [but only] after proceeding from a biased interpretation of Goethe's ideas.

Goethe's influence, he concludes, was not a "primary influence," because "it was fundamental only where it corresponded to certain preconceived attitudes in Matthew Arnold." In other words, "Matthew Arnold's conception of Goethe . . . did not influence his mode of thought quite so much as his mode of thought influenced his conception of Goethe." [49] Nevertheless, Arnold did regard Goethe's concern over the condition of German "culture" as a salutary warning for his nation as well.

But the word "culture" is also Newman's, as the opening paragraphs of the discourse "Knowledge Viewed in Relation to Learning" demonstrates. In casting about for a suitable term to describe the effect which a liberal education should have upon a sensitive mind, Newman discards

[48] "Matthew Arnold and Goethe," *PMLA,* XXXVI (1921), 442. Miss White also contends that "in the principle that all literary effort should be directed and judged by the standard of the excellent, in the conception of that excellent, in the teaching that that ideal was best to be found in the masterpieces of classical antiquity, Arnold found his literary program in Goethe" (p. 452). This is, of course, nothing else than Arnold's famous "touchstone" method from "The Study of Poetry" (1880), a method which several of the essays in the 1865 collection anticipate. Warren Anderson's description of the Winchester School institution of the "Standing-Up" which was "solemnized periodically throughout the school year" points out that "boys would publicly recite from memory massive quantities of Greek or Latin verse" (*Matthew Arnold,* pp. 5-6). This academic performance doubtless also contributes something to Arnold's convictions about the value of poetic "touchstones." Once again, therefore, Dr. Arnold's attention to the schools his sons attended must be cited in relation to Arnold's poetic development.

[49] *Matthew Arnold and Goethe* (London: Publications of the English Goethe Society, no. 4, n. s., 1928), pp. 50-52. Orrick's objection to Arnold's estimate of Goethe is simply that "Goethe was not primarily a thinker, as Matthew Arnold supposed [in "A French Critic on Goethe"] but an artist, a liver of the creative life" on not nearly so moralistic a basis as Arnold liked to think (pp. 47, 50). F. J. W. Harding makes the same point with respect to Arnold's attitude toward Sainte-Beuve: "Sainte-Beuve was not so sure as Arnold about the necessary connection between the study of the classics and the pursuit of '*la morale*'" (*Matthew Arnold the Critic and France,* pp. 94-95). Arnold did find, of course, a considerable moral sense in Renan, particularly in *Essais de morale et de critique* (Paris, 1889). See, for example, Renan's preface, p. vii.

in turn such unsatisfactory expressions as "wisdom," "knowledge," "taste," "talent," or "judgment," in his search for an intellectual equivalent for the physical state of "health" and the moral state of "virtue." [50] In "The Literary Influence of Academies" Arnold praises a later work of Newman's, his *Apologia pro Vita Sua* (1864-65), which does not discuss but rather demonstrates the degree of culture which Arnold admired. Writing to his mother on March 11, 1865, Arnold remarks that he had sent a copy of the *Essays* to Newman, inscribed "From one of his old hearers," as well as one to John Keble, his godfather and predecessor as Professor of Poetry at Oxford (1831-42). He had, of course, also given a copy to Sainte-Beuve.

The next sources, chronologically, upon which Arnold drew for affirmation of his own instincts about the importance of culture were the contemporary French critics Sainte-Beuve and Renan. Two passages from "The Literary Influence of Academies" in which Arnold is concerned with the effects of the Academy upon French literature and culture link the names of these critics, whose essays on the French Academy Arnold had freely used in writing his own. "M. Sainte-Beuve and M. Renan are, both of them, very keen-sighted critics; and they show it signally by seizing and putting prominently forward this character of the French Academy," Arnold observes, referring to Renan's statement that an Academy has a special power of "creating a form of intellectual *culture which shall impose itself on all around.*" A few pages later, in his discussion of the contrast between the "urbanity" of France and the "provinciality" of the "bulk of the intellectual work of a nation which has no center, no intellectual metropolis like an academy, like M. Sainte-Beuve's 'sovereign organ of opinion,' like M. Renan's 'recognised authority in matters of tone and taste,'" Arnold emphasizes the fact that "to get rid of provinciality is a certain stage of culture."

Whether or not Ruth Temple and Irving Babbitt are correct in suggesting that Arnold's "dogmatism" takes him closer in critical practice to Edmond Scherer than to Renan and Sainte-Beuve, it is Arnold's conscious

---

[50] Harrold, *Idea*, pp. 110-11. Newman finally settles for the expression "intellectual culture." David J. De Laura illustrates in some detail how "Arnold's doctrine of criticism and culture, especially in its characteristic dualism, levied extensively upon Newman's thought"; he sees "The Function of Criticism at the Present Time" in particular as "suffused with Newmanesque thinking" (p. 607). See his "Matthew Arnold and John Henry Newman: The 'Oxford Sentiment' and the Religion of the Future," in *Texas Studies in Language and Literature,* VI supplement (1965), 573-702. Part 3 of this monograph considers Newman's influence on the *Essays in Criticism* (1865), arguing that Newman's *Apologia,* "appearing as it did at the precise moment of Arnold's most intensive concern over his own critical stance and tone, represented in itself a highly distinguished example of a public controversial manner" (p. 601).

debt to these critics which is of interest here.[51] Arnold's debts to Renan
have been carefully studied at least three times, by Lewis F. Mott, by
J. W. Angell, and, more recently, by Sidney M. B. Coulling. Each treatment amplifies the one preceding.[52] Aside from Arnold's extensive use
of Renan's essay on the French Academy, his greatest debt is to Renan's
treatment of Celtic poetry in the same collection. Ruth Temple, who
cannot forgive Arnold for his sweeping dismissal of French poetry,
charges that Arnold "never publicly acknowledged Renan as he did
Sainte-Beuve." As a matter of fact, Arnold regularly acknowledges his
borrowings from Renan as they occur. It is simply that he is conscious of
a greater debt to Sainte-Beuve.

Arnold's estimate of Sainte-Beuve, "the first of living critics," as
Arnold styled him to Sainte-Beuve's embarrassment, is worth examining.
If the later series of Celtic literature lectures owes its inspiration to
Renan, the earlier series comprising the present volume of lectures is
obviously heavily indebted to Sainte-Beuve. Four of these essays draw
upon earlier essays published by the French critics, "The Literary Influence of Academies," the two Guérin essays, and the one on Joubert.
Mrs. Temple's suggestion that the hectic pace of Arnold's life caused
him to pilfer from Sainte-Beuve as "shortcuts to copy" underestimates
both the man and the critic in Arnold.[53] A simpler and more likely
explanation is that Arnold saw himself as the channel of continental
thought into England. His introductory essay in this collection makes
the point quite clearly. The value of his selection of such minor figures
as the Guérins and Joubert is, of course, a separate question.

Arnold composed formal essays on Sainte-Beuve for two occasions.
The first appeared, at the editor's request, in *The Academy* for November
13, 1869, a month after Sainte-Beuve's death. The death had deeply
affected Arnold, whose letter to his mother on October 16, 1869, indicates real reluctance to undertake the task of a memoir quite so soon.
But write it he did, utilizing a number of Sainte-Beuve's own sayings
as compliments: *"la plus grande gloire du critique est dans l'approbation*

---

[51] Temple, *The Critic's Alchemy*, pp. 67-70. See also Irving Babbitt, *Masters of Modern French Criticism* (New York, 1912), pp. 202-11.

[52] Mott, "Renan and Matthew Arnold," 65-73; J. W. Angell, "Matthew Arnold's Indebtedness to Renan's *Essais de morale et de critique*," *Revue de littérature comparée*, XIV (1934), 714-33; Sidney M. B. Coulling, "Renan's Influence on Matthew Arnold's Literary and Social Criticism," *Florida State University Studies*, V (1952).

[53] Temple, *The Critic's Alchemy*, pp. 61, 56. Had Mrs. Temple studied Arnold's essays on Sainte-Beuve more carefully, she would have discovered, as F. J. W. Harding notes, that "Sainte-Beuve sold Arnold a good deal short on French poetry" (*Matthew Arnold the Critic and France*, p. 91).

et dans l'estime des bons esprits." [54] Arnold concludes with a tribute to Sainte-Beuve's exercise of "curiosity, the desire to know things as they really are," arguing that to have done this much is "to have served well one need of his age." [55] But Arnold's masterpiece is the article on Sainte-Beuve which Arnold contributed to the ninth edition of the *Encyclopedia Britannica* in 1886. Sainte-Beuve's merits cover a long list: "good sense, tact, and finesse" inherited evidently from his mother, combined with "mental independence, industry, measure and lucidity," as well as the "happy temper and disposition" which combined to make Sainte-Beuve "the most notable critic of our time" and one of the "foremost literary men of France." [56]

Less formal acknowledgments of Sainte-Beuve's excellences, and his own conscious debt to those excellences, occur in scattered places, chiefly in the letters which Arnold wrote to Sainte-Beuve. [57] Arnold's letter of January 6, 1854, which accompanied a presentation copy of the 1853 *Poems,* confessed that "since the death of Goethe you have remained, in my opinion, the sole guide and sole hope of those who love above all else the truth in the arts and in literature." [58] Two other letters, both written during the first half of the year 1863, describe more explicitly the virtues which Arnold was attempting to imitate. On January 28, 1863, Arnold wrote:

Vous seul avez la souplesse, la finesse, la curiosité désinteressée, qui donnent la pénétration et qui font en critique, le veritable maître.

[54] R. H. Super reprints this essay in vol. V of the *Complete Prose Works* (pp. 304-309). The quotation appears on p. 305.

[55] *Ibid.,* p. 309. For Arnold's discussion of "curiosity" see "The Function of Criticism at the Present Time," and the first chapter of *Culture and Anarchy,* entitled "Sweetness and Light."

[56] Arnold does exaggerate Sainte-Beuve's merits in his final paragraph, in which he aligns Sainte-Beuve as literary critic with the poets Homer and Shakespeare and with the philosophers Plato and Voltaire as "spokesmen for the human race." For a solid discussion of Sainte-Beuve's position in modern literary criticism see René Wellek, *A History of Modern Criticism* (New Haven: Yale University Press, 1965), III, 34-72.

[57] See R. H. Super, "Documents in the Matthew Arnold-Sainte-Beuve Relationship," *Modern Philology,* LX (1963), 206-10; Arnold Whitridge (Arnold's grandson), "Matthew Arnold and Sainte-Beuve," *PMLA,* LII (1938), 303-13; and Jean Bonnerot, *Matthew Arnold, poëte: essai de biographie psychologique* (Paris, 1947). Bonnerot's appendix (pp. 517-38) reprints the texts of nine letters which Arnold wrote to Sainte-Beuve between 1854 and 1964.

[58] Bonnerot, *Matthew Arnold, poëte,* pp. 518-19. In a letter to his mother, October 16, 1869, Arnold spoke feelingly of Sainte-Beuve's death, and continued: "When George Sand and Newman go, there will be no writers left living from whom I have received a strong influence; they will all have departed." This excerpt is quoted in Super, *Complete Prose Works,* V, 465.

And a few months later, on May 19, 1863, Arnold produced the following assessment of the merits of Sainte-Beuve:

> Mais c'est surtout comme critique que vous vivrez: faut-il vous en plaindre? Je ne le pense pas. Les grands critiques (et vous en êtes) ont de tout temps été plus rares que même les grands poëtes; dans un grand critique il y a toujours, selon moi, un grand poëte; un peu supprimé. Notre siècle est celui de la critique; vous y trouverez votre compte; tout le monde regarde du côté où vous êtes, du côté où l'esprit français (lequel est bien aussi le vôtre) se deploie librement, et retrouve tous ses avantages. En fait de poëtes, aucun pays, dans ce moment, n'en a que de second ordre; en fait de critiques, la France seule peut se vanter d'en avoir un de premier ordre:—c'est vous.[59]

Even so brief an examination of the backgrounds of Arnold's thinking makes it quite clear that he did, in fact, search the best minds he had met in an effort to find ways of crystallizing and anchoring his own insights, and that he did not disguise his debts. Therefore, such judgments as those of Lewis F. Mott, that Arnold's "chief literary and critical guides" were "Goethe in thought and Sainte-Beuve in critical method," and of Arnold Whitridge, that "Arnold's literary fame owes more to Sainte-Beuve than to any other one man," bear closer scrutiny.[60] Above all, one must not neglect Arnold's famous father and his eldest son's ambivalent relationship to Dr. Arnold.

The academic diffidence and elegant dandyism of his Oxford years is transparently the young man's declaration of independence from all that Dr. Arnold symbolized. W. S. Knickerbocker states that Arnold "entered public life under the handicap" of his father's early influence over him, but this is somewhat redeemed by Iris Sells' initial chapter which capably demonstrates that "it was from his father that the son acquired his taste" for foreign languages (since Rugby was the only public school in Arnold's day which furnished instruction in French), "together with others, which included a strong fondness for foreign travel." [61] Arnold's cosmopolitanism, as well as his historical sense, both conspicuous in the 1865 *Essays,* are traceable to Dr. Arnold. J. B. Orrick suggests that in Arnold's estimate of Voltaire's "fame as a great man," that it is "equivocal," we "seem to hear Dr. Arnold." One might extend this suggestion to cover Arnold's estimates of Coleridge ("he had

---

[59] Bonnerot, *Matthew Arnold, poëte,* pp. 531-33, 535. See also Super, *Complete Prose Works,* III, 380, on the adequacy of German poetry.

[60] Mott, "Renan and Matthew Arnold," p. 65; and Whitridge, "Matthew Arnold and Sainte-Beuve," p. 303.

[61] W. S. Knickerbocker, "Matthew Arnold at Oxford: The Natural History of a Father and Son," *Sewanee Review,* XXXV (1927), 399; and Sells, *Matthew Arnold and France,* pp. xii-xiii, p. 1.

no morals") and Heine (who required a "moral deliverance") as well.[62] Arnold's description of his father as the "mighty oak" and of the family bereaved "lacking the shelter of thee," in "Rugby Chapel" hints at the sense he had of his father's strength and the value he placed upon it. A passage in a letter written to his mother on Christmas Day, 1867, further reveals this positive side of Arnold's attitude to his father:

> At this time of year, and with my birthday reminding me how much of my term is spent, I like to bring before my mind the course and scope of his labours, and to try and connect my own with them. Perhaps the change of times and modes of action being allowed for, my scope is not so different from his as you and I often think.

W. S. Knickerbocker, who has devoted a good deal of attention to this relationship, suggests that Arnold's awareness of the inherited cardiac weakness on his father's side of the family accounts in large part for the tragic, or at least melancholy, quality of much of the poetry. As for the criticism, he argues that in *Culture and Anarchy, St. Paul and Protestantism, Literature and Dogma, God and the Bible,* and the *Last Essays,* Arnold was "deliberately turning to complete the unfinished work of his father, reinterpreting, *mutatis mutandis,* the latter's religious and political philosophy for the special needs of the Victorian era." [63]

Arnold's relationship to Newman is worth recalling in this connection. Alan Harris states that "as an undergraduate, he could recommend his father's sermons to a High Church friend, while he himself went off to St. Mary's to hear Newman purely for the sensation." Arnold's brother Thomas maintained that Matt's interest in Newman's preaching was purely stylistic, but one wonders whether the profound and lifelong admiration in which Arnold held Newman could have been founded upon aesthetic considerations alone.[64] One feels that there must have been something deeper. Harris's remark suggests that Newman was, in some fashion or other, a kind of substitute or alternate "father-figure" for Arnold in his Oxford days, though this is not to deny Arnold's consciousness of intellectual debts to his own father. Writing to his mother on February 20, 1869, of the mentions of Dr. Arnold which he had come upon in reading J. T. Coleridge's *Memoir* of John Keble, he affirmed: "My one feeling when I close the book is of papa's immense superiority to all the set, mainly because, owing to his historic sense, he was so wonderfully, for his nation, time, and profession, European, and thus

[62] Orrick, *Matthew Arnold and Goethe,* p. 13.
[63] Knickerbocker, "Matthew Arnold at Oxford," pp. 401, 417-18.
[64] See Mrs. Humphrey Ward, *A Writer's Recollections* (London, 1918), p. 11.

so got himself out of the narrow medium in which, after all, all his English friends lived." In any case, Knickerbocker's insistence that "though he lacked Newman's facility and grace in logic, Dr. Arnold did not suffer from Newman's fatal mental defect, the tendency to substitute poetry for fact," takes on a new coloring when one recalls the passage with which Arnold introduces his essay "The Study of Poetry":

> Our religion has materialised itself in the fact, in the supposed fact; it has attached its emotion to the fact, and now the fact is failing it. But for poetry the idea is everything; the rest is a world of illusion, of divine illusion. Poetry attaches its emotion to the idea; the idea *is* the fact. The strongest part of our religion to-day is its unconscious poetry.[65]

Those among the orthodox who have found this passage offensive, largely because they have failed to understand that it is a compliment to poetry rather than an attack upon religion, might be surprised to discover that it owes a good deal to Arnold's admiration for Newman. And it would probably not really have scandalized Dr. Arnold.

Finally, some attempt to estimate Arnold's real stature as a critic, including the question of his abandonment of the role of poet for that of critic, would be in order. As has already been demonstrated, for Arnold the roles of poet and critic were not, as we are inclined to think, completely separate roles. One of the most telling passages in *Culture and Anarchy* is a section in the very first chapter in which Arnold, asserting that "culture is of a like spirit with poetry, follows one law with poetry," confronts the inadequacy of certain middle-class religious attitudes with the insistence that the persons and organizations concerned "can only be reached by the criticism which culture, like poetry, speaking a language not to be sophisticated, and resolutely testing these organizations by the ideal of a human perfection complete on all sides, applies to them." [66] The critic of society, the "critic of life," the critic of the "critic of life," all are engaged in the same basic activity, all are endowed with the same basic capacities.

For Arnold, the critic, like the poet, is not a "doctor" but an "explorer," a "mere solitary wanderer in search of the light," who must talk "an

---

[65] Knickerbocker, "Matthew Arnold at Oxford," p. 405. Arnold's introductory passage is actually quoted from his own introduction to the first volume of *The Hundred Greatest Men* (London, 1879). Its context in "The Study of Poetry," however, is the more familiar one.

[66] Super, *Complete Prose Works,* V, 101-2. See Arnold's much later expression of the same position, in his letter to M. Fontanès, March 25, 1881: "Whoever treats of religion and religious discussions, questions of churches and sects as absorbing, is not in vital sympathy with the movement of men's minds at present."

artless, unstudied, everyday, familiar language." [67] His obligation is threefold: (1) to "learn and propagate the best that is known and thought in the world"; (2) to maintain at all times while exercising his function as critic a "fair and clear mind" open to fresh knowledge; and (3) to communicate this fresh knowledge in all the judgments which he forms and the estimates of literary master-currents which he makes, allowing his own judgments to slip almost imperceptibly into this knowledge and to pass along to his reader "as a sort of companion and clue, not as an abstract lawgiver." In other words, he must exercise in some degree a creative activity akin to that of the literary artist with whom he deals.

This intimacy between the creative and the critical powers is no accident in Arnold's critical scheme. On the contrary, it is the psychological basis for the assertion that "poetry is a criticism of life." In "Joubert" Arnold distinguishes the orders of poets: "The criticism of life which the men of genius pass upon human life is permanently acceptable to mankind; the criticism which the men of ability pass upon human life is transitorily acceptable." The "men of genius," Arnold continues, are the "great abiding fountains of truth, whose criticism of life is a source of illumination and joy to the whole human race forever." Some kind of ideational content is postulated here for poetry, while Arnold's use of the expression "pass upon" in connection with the "criticism of life" implies that the poet is exercising an almost juridical power. Yet this power in poetry operates by indirection; its efficacy is in the process, in the "profound and beautiful application of ideas to life."

While he himself was actually writing poetry, Arnold thought of it as a serious and demanding occupation of mind, and not merely a distraction, a "superior amusement" in Eliot's phrase. Upon the appearance of a two-volume edition of his *Poems* in 1869, Arnold looked back upon his poetic achievement with great satisfaction. In a letter to his mother at this time he attempted an estimate of that achievement:

> My poems represent the main movement of mind of the last quarter of a century, and thus they will probably have their day as people become conscious to themselves of what that movement of mind is, and interested in the literary productions which reflect it. It might be fairly urged that I have less poetical sentiment than Tennyson, and less intellectual vigour and abundance than Browning yet, because I have perhaps more of a fusion of the two than either of them, and have more regularly applied that fusion

[67] Arnold speaks in a prefatory note to his lecture "On the Modern Element in Literature" of his abandonment of the position of "doctor" for that of "explorer"; see Super, *Complete Prose Works,* I, 18. The other two phrases appeared in a note to "The Function of Criticism at the Present Time" in the 1865 edition only.

to the main line of modern development, I am likely enough to have my
turn, as they have had theirs.[68]

The "movement of mind" to which Arnold refers is the "modern spirit,"
the critical spirit, which attempts to replace dissolving traditions with
the solace derived from "the best that is known and thought in the world"
on the problems of human life. Just as it is the function of criticism to
create a current of true and fresh ideas gleaned from the very best the
human mind has ever produced, it is the function of poetry as a "criticism
of life" to apply the fruits of criticism—the best ideas—most beautifully
to the business of living.[69] It is the poet's privilege, according to Arnold,
to exercise the critical function "under the conditions fixed for such a
criticism by the laws of poetic truth and poetic beauty."

It is frequently alleged that Arnold abandoned poetry for criticism,
that his poetic power deteriorated under the pressure of an interminable
round of mundane occupations. This may or may not be true as a partial
explanation; it is certainly not the whole story. Writing to his friend
Madame Blaze de Bury, who had complimented him on the article
"Anarchy and Authority," his last Oxford lecture which was subsequently
reprinted in the *Cornhill Magazine,* Arnold remarked:

> I am very glad you like my Cornhill disquisition; when I see my criticisms
> of various kinds beginning to take hold here and there in England I often
> think of your having insisted on my critical qualities years ago.[70]

This suggests that Arnold had very early become conscious that his poetic
talents were of a particular kind; the 1853 Preface, with its staunch
classical assumptions and postulates vying with the incurably romantic
qualities of Arnold's own practice, is an attempt to correct theoretically
the mistakes of his poetic attempts. In an article discussing this preface,
H. W. Garrod concludes that Arnold's real mistakes were not the ones
he himself was ever aware of. His greatest mistake was his repudiation
of Keats and the romantic "influences which had gone to make his best
poem," the "Scholar-Gipsy." [71] Iris Sells too sees the transition as one

---

[68] See Arnold's letter to his mother, June 5, 1869.

[69] To select only two instances in Arnold's own poetry, his sonnet "The Better
Part" applies the idea of the essential dignity of human nature to the problems of
current religious doubt, while "East London" considers the idea of the inexhaustible
resources of the human spirit in relation to inevitable sieges of discouragement.
They are not, of course, very good poems.

[70] This excerpt is quoted by Iris Sells in *Matthew Arnold and France* (pp. 270-71).

[71] See "Matthew Arnold's 1853 Preface," *Review of English Studies,* XVII (1941),
310-21. It is significant, of course, that Arnold's complaint about the poem could
be expressed in the form of the question: "What does it *do* for you?" In this respect
it was as useless as "Empedocles on Etna."

between the romantic and the classical phases of Arnold's career:

> After 1860 Arnold, like Sainte-Beuve, began to devote himself to criticism rather than to poetical writing, an evolution naturally determined by the intellectual quality of his genius. . . . As the fire of his youth and sentimental experiences sank lower, he turned less often to the sources that had kept it bright and living in the past. . . . Henceforth he would write little poetry with the pure spontaneous beauty of his first poems. *The critical and intellectual instincts had triumphed in him.*[72]

A. Dwight Culler takes this insight a little further in raising a philosophic question. Why a poet ceases to write is always a mystery, he maintains, but

> in Arnold's case we can see that certain changes in philosophic outlook accompanied the change from poetry to prose, and we may believe that the changes were in some way related. The philosophic change was a movement from a predominantly subjective view of the world to a predominantly objective view of the world, and it seems to have been accomplished by a deliberate process of self-discipline.[73]

This is a more complex way of approaching the romantic-classical dichotomy in Arnold; it is also a simple enough statement about the process of Arnold's maturing.

In *Matthew Arnold: The Poet as Humanist,* G. Robert Stange offers an intelligent analysis of Arnold's poetic achievement and of his transition from poetry to criticism. "For Arnold," Stange contends "aesthetic and ethical ideas are ultimately the same," so that "his poetry is philosophical" and "engaged in expressing a highly cosmopolitan ethical conviction." "Beginning with an impression and ending with a moral lesson," Stange concludes, "is what Arnold thought the experience of genuine poetry to be."[74]

The question of Arnold's adoption of the role of literary critic is treated in Stange's introduction. While Arnold was writing poetry, "he

---

[72] Sells, *Matthew Arnold and France,* pp. 255-56 (italics mine). On this point, too, E. K. Brown promotes his fundamental thesis about Arnold. He sees as one of many possible reasons "for Arnold's turning from verse to prose the inconsistency of the ideal of the disinterested disposition with success in the kinds of poetry which he believed a modern poet should attempt" (Brown, *Matthew Arnold: A Study in Conflict,* p. 52).

[73] *The Poetry and Criticism of Matthew Arnold,* ed. A. Dwight Culler (Boston: Houghton Mifflin, 1961), p. xvi. Of the 1853 Preface, Culler affirms that "that document is the turning point in Arnold's critical development, for he there turns his back upon his period of *Sturm und Drang* and lays the foundations of an Olympian personality."

[74] G. Robert Stange, *Matthew Arnold: The Poet as Humanist* (Princeton, N. J.: Princeton University Press, 1967), pp. 16, 108, 115. It is interesting to compare the passage quoted from Stange with that quoted from Culler above.

made his poems serve the great critical effort which he felt was requisite to the best creation." But Arnold also "knew, better than anyone else, that his poems did not fulfill his own criteria; his job was to avoid false poetic practice and to aspire toward the ideal of excellence he had defined." [75] What happened next is well described by A. Dwight Culler in *Imaginative Reason:*

> He has saved himself—now he must save others along with himself, and for this the instrument is prose. It has always been something of a problem why Arnold turned from poetry to prose, and the answer may be given in various ways. But one way of stating it is simply to say that the task of the poetry was done.[76]

In other words, it is possible to argue that Arnold, experimenting with poetry and prose in turn as media for the critical spirit, found prose criticism more effective. It is worth mentioning, however, that he did not find it easier to write. In a well-known letter to Clough, written shortly after he had completed the 1853 Preface, Arnold exclaimed: "How difficult it is to write prose." The reason he gives is not a particularly original one, it is true, but it says something about the emphasis which was beginning to concern Arnold more: "Why? Because of the *articulations of the discourse:* one leaps these over in Poetry . . . but in prose this will not do." [77] Discursive thinking militates against lyric intensity. The poet must make his choice.

From the outset, the response to Arnold as a critic was divided. On one count only was there a kind of unanimity; whether they enjoyed him or despised him, Arnold's public received him with vehemence. Indifference was simply not a characteristic reaction.

Favorable estimates usually commended perceptive literary judgments clothed in beauty of diction and masterful style, or admired the courage, if not the convictions, of the writer. Analysis of the opposition shows that either or both of two basic objections found their way into every attack upon Arnold's criticism: either his opponents could make very little out of what he had to say, or they were sorely offended at the manner in which he chose to say it.[78] Charges of "intellectual audacity,"

---

[75] *Ibid.,* pp. 4-5.

[76] A. Dwight Culler, *Imaginative Reason: The Poetry of Matthew Arnold* (New Haven, Conn.: Yale University Press, 1966), pp. 285-86. Walter Raleigh had much the same idea. To Arnold, Raleigh states, "the critic seemed no less than the Saviour of Society" (p. 301). In a subsequent estimate of Arnold he playfully remarks that "his invincible air of superiority has interfered somewhat with his efficiency as an evangelist" (p. 309).

[77] Howard Foster Lowry, ed., *The Letters of Matthew Arnold to Arthur Hugh Clough* (London: Oxford University Press, 1932), p. 144.

[78] Arnold immensely enjoyed the consternation he created in certain quarters with

an "invincible air of superiority," "foppery," "arrogance," and "affectation" abound in reviews of Arnold and his work, charges couched in such adjectives as "ethereal," "aristocratic," "esoteric," "common-herd-compassionating," and "enormously insulting." As early as 1861, Arnold's archenemy on the *Saturday Review,* Fitzjames Stephen, scored the "bitterly contemptuous" and "insulting" language of Arnold's recently published Homer lectures, as well as the "outrageous self-conceit" of their author: *"Das grosse ich* reigns from one end [of the lectures] to the other," he complained.[79] Arnold could indeed be coolly annoying when he chose, and it is this trait which Chesterton has memorialized in his description of Arnold, wearing "a smile of heart-broken forbearance, as of the teacher in an idiot school." [80]

Twentieth century estimates of Arnold have reflected the same range of disagreements: from E. K. Brown, who has called Arnold "the greatest critic of his age," and Lionel Trilling, who thinks of him as "the most influential critic of his age," to T. S. Eliot, who regards Arnold not as a critic at all, but as a mere "propagandist for criticism." [81] Arnold has won allies and alienated as easily. There is little that one can think of as middle ground. Still, the establishment in the University of Oxford of a critical journal designed to give the "harrassed mad world" the example of Arnold's critical virtues of "intellectual clarity, spiritual integrity, and social conscience" in dedication to "a more than literary discipline," is in itself a demonstration of the validity of Arnold's contribution to the history of criticism.[82] And when such eminent literary

such phrases as "the grand style." In the fourth of his Homer lectures, he offered an elaborate explanation of the term in deference to the "sincere" perplexity of some of his critics.

[79] Fitzjames Stephen, "Homeric Translators and Critics," *Saturday Review,* XII (July 27, 1861), 95-96.

[80] G. K. Chesterton, *The Victorian Age in Literature* (New York: Henry Holt, 1913), p. 13.

[81] Brown, *Matthew Arnold: A Study in Conflict,* p. 5; Trilling, *Matthew Arnold,* p. 190, and *Beyond Culture* (London, 1955), pp. 211, 213, 219, 225; T. S. Eliot, "The Perfect Critic," *The Sacred Wood* (London, 1948), p. 1. Variations on Eliot's famous remark are Lewis F. Mott's description of Arnold as "the partisan of non-partisanship, the prophet of the dogma of the undogmatic" ("Renan and Matthew Arnold," *Modern Language Quarterly, XXXIII* [1918], 73); and René Wellek's statement that Arnold is a "very important apologist for criticism" (*A History of Modern Criticism,* IV, 156). Arnold Whitridge called Arnold "the greatest English critic of his generation," but then Arnold Whitridge was Matthew Arnold's grandson (see "Matthew Arnold and Sainte-Beuve," *PMLA,* LIII [1938], 311). But for Henry James, Arnold was "one of the two or three best English prose writers" of his day ("Matthew Arnold," *Literary Essays and Reviews,* ed. Albert Mordell [New York: Vista House, 1957], p. 351).

[82] F. W. Bateson, "The Function of Criticism at the Present Time," *Essays in Criticism,* III (1953), 2. It is interesting to compare Mr. Bateson's objectives with

critics of the moment as C. S. Lewis, Douglas Bush, and Northrop Frye find themselves instinctively turning to Arnold for inspiration or authoritative support, one cannot help feeling that he has somehow remained a vital influence.[83] In fact, with a few minor exceptions, it is the single figure of T. S. Eliot who stands between Arnold and a quite passable reputation at the present time. R. P. Blackmur, in an essay aptly entitled "In the Hope of Straightening Things Out," observes that for Eliot "the fight with, and use of, Matthew Arnold is lifelong." [84] The truth of this statement is worth the demonstration.

David J. DeLaura's remark about the alleged ambivalence of Arnold himself toward Carlyle is, *mutatis mutandis,* far more appropriate as a description of Eliot's stance toward Arnold:

> At the heart of Arnold's attitude to Carlyle is a persistent ambivalence, one half of it a remarkable bulk of conscious and half-conscious borrowing of ideas and key expressions, the other a seemingly fixed need to depreciate Carlyle, combined with something very close to concealment of his influence.[85]

A passage in Eliot's Introduction to *The Sacred Wood* is one of the most convincing evidences of Eliot's uneasiness about his own attitudes toward Arnold:

> To anyone who is at all capable of experiencing the pleasures of justice, it is gratifying to be able to make amends to a writer whom one has

those described by T. S. Eliot in the founding of the *Criterion:* "In starting this review, I had the aim of bringing together the best in new thinking and new writing in its time, from all the countries of Europe that had anything to contribute to the common good" (*Notes Toward the Definition of Culture* [New York, 1949], p. 118). Mr. Bateson is, of course, closer to Arnold's view of the comprehensiveness of criticism than is Mr. Eliot.

[83] C. S. Lewis, *An Experiment in Criticism* (Cambridge: Cambridge University Press, 1962), chap. 11; Douglas Bush, "Keats and His Ideas," *English Romantic Poets,* ed. M. H. Abrams (New York: Oxford University Press, 1960), p. 327; Northrop Frye, *Anatomy of Criticism* (Princeton: Princeton University Press, 1957), pp. 3, 9-10, 21-22.

[84] R. P. Blackmur, "In the Hope of Straightening Things Out," in *T. S. Eliot: A Collection of Critical Essays,* ed. Hugh Kenner (Englewood Cliffs, N. J.: Prentice-Hall, Inc., 1962), p. 136. An excellent chapter on Arnold and Eliot in John H. Raleigh's *Matthew Arnold and American Culture* (Berkeley and Los Angeles: University of California Press, 1961) surveys this relationship in some detail, but without suggesting the nature and extent of Eliot's debt to Arnold.

One should also notice the ill-tempered essay of Geoffrey Carnall enitled "Matthew Arnold's 'Great Critical Effort' " (*Essays in Criticism,* VII [1958], 256-68), as well as Ruth Temple's "inescapable" if "unorthodox" conclusion that "Arnold on his own terms or any others was not a great literary critic" (*Critic's Alchemy,* p. 71).

[85] David J. De Laura, "Arnold and Carlyle," *PMLA,* LXXIX (1964), 104. See also Super, *Complete Prose Works,* V, 414. Vincent Buckley's estimate of the relationship is kinder when he remarks that "Eliot has maintained a stance of rigorous dissent from Arnold's influence while conceding his greatness" (*Poetry and Morality,* [London: Chatto and Windus, 1959] p. 88).

vaguely depreciated for some years. The faults and foibles of Matthew Arnold are no less evident to me now than twelve years ago, after my first admiration for him; but I hope that now, on re-reading some of his prose with more care, I can better appreciate his position.[86]

Readers of Eliot's first and second essays on Milton will recognize the innocent dexterity in Eliot's retractions, if they are that, about both Arnold and Milton.[87] Eliot's "vague depreciation" is masterly in its understatement, as any student of Eliot's criticism is well aware. Besides the four largely uncomplimentary essays which take Arnold's notion of the critic as a starting point ("The Function of Criticism," 1923; "Arnold and Pater," 1930; "Matthew Arnold" and "The Modern Mind" in *The Use of Poetry and The Use of Criticism,* 1933), Eliot's Introduction to *The Sacred Wood* (1920), as well as his essays on "The Perfect Critic" and "Imperfect Critics," level unmistakable brickbats at Arnold.[88] Eliot draws Arnold also into the essay on F. H. Bradley, ostensibly for stylistic reasons only, but he does not neglect to mention Bradley's assault upon Arnold in the "Concluding Remarks" of his *Ethical Studies* (1876), which "knocked the bottom out of *Literature and Dogma"* by demonstrating that "the greatest weakness of Arnold's culture was his weakness in philosophical training." [89] The introduction to Eliot's next new series of essays, *The Use of Poetry and the Use of Criticism,* gives full marks to Arnold's original sin of making "the doctrine of 'art for art's sake' " possible in the first place.[90] Finally, Eliot's determined effort to replace Arnold's *Culture and Anarchy* with a more valid statement about man

---

[86] *The Sacred Wood,* Introduction, (1920), p. xi.

[87] The first (1936) and second (1947) Milton essays are both reprinted in Eliot's *On Poetry and Poets* (New York, 1957). In the introductory paragraph to the second essay Eliot designates the essay "my apology," admitting that certain "errors and prejudices," presumably judgments about Milton, "have been associated with my own name . . . and no one can correct an error with better authority than the person who has been held responsible for it" (p. 165). He clarifies this further along by noting that "the reproach against Milton, that his technical influence has been bad, appears to have been made by no one more positively than by myself" (p. 171). Eliot's failing memory is noticeable also in "The Frontiers of Criticism" in the same volume, where he ingenuously "cannot recall a single book or essay, or the name of a single critic, as representative of the kind of impressionistic criticism which aroused my ire thirty-three years ago" (p. 113).

[88] Eliot gallantly does not make Arnold the subject of his essay "Imperfect Critics." In fact, Arnold is named among the "notable English critics" and indirectly complimented as intelligent: "Matthew Arnold was intelligent, and by so much difference as the presence of one intelligent man makes, our age is inferior to that of Arnold" (*The Sacred Wood* [London, 1948], pp. 39, 45-46).

[89] Eliot cites the Bradley passage, noting that it represents "the identical weapon of Arnold, sharpened to a razor edge and turned against Arnold" (*Selected Essays,* [London: Faber and Faber, 1932] p. 412).

[90] T. S. Eliot, *The Use of Poetry and the Use of Criticism* (London: Faber and Faber, 1933), p. 26.

in society produced not one book but two: *The Idea of A Christian Society* (1939) and *Notes Toward the Definition of Culture* (1949).[91]

The latter book abounds in what David De Laura termed "half-conscious borrowing of ideas and key expressions" from, particularly, "The Function of Criticism at the Present Time." Running throughout are Arnold's "key expressions" with no indication of the fact that they are Arnold's. In describing his early objectives for *The Criterion,* for example, Eliot remarks that at least one such "network of independent reviews" is needed "in every capital of Europe" in order to ensure "the transmission of ideas—and to make possible the circulation of ideas while they are still fresh," as he laments the absence of a social situation in which "we could take for granted an interest, a delight, in ideas for their own sake, in the free play of intellect." [92] Eliot's express admiration for Goethe's notions about art, as well as his appendix to the lectures entitled "On the Unity of European Culture," described as "a series of talks about the unity of European culture from the point of view of a man of letters," are so obvious as to warrant the merest mention.[93]

Eliot's ambivalence toward Arnold is manifest in the curious combination of left-handed praise and genteel insults which characterize the essays under consideration. On the one hand, Eliot can commend Arnold because he "had real taste" and his work "will always have been good sense." [94] Arnold's evaluation of the Romantic poets too seems to have some merit in Eliot's judgment.[95] And at least an illusion of compliment

---

[91] Eliot discusses *Culture and Anarchy* in "Arnold and Pater" (*The Use of Poetry,* pp. 394-99) as well as in *Notes Toward the Definition of Culture* (New York: Harcourt, Brace, 1949), which states as its aim "to help define a word, the word culture" (p. 1) and declares quite emphatically that "no culture can appear or develop except in relation to a religion" (p. 26). In Eliot's work, religion takes entire precedence over "culture" (cf. Super, *Complete Prose Works,* V, 99-107). In other respects too, Eliot's work is different from Arnold's: it is not satiric, but rather quite theoretical (even academic); Eliot adopts the stance of "scientist" (pp. 20, 83, 124, 126); and the book reflects twentieth-century developments in the areas of politics, communication, education, and intellectual exchange. See also the concluding paragraph of "Matthew Arnold" (*The Use of Poetry,* p. 119).

[92] *Notes Toward the Definition of Culture,* pp. 119, 121. Note also Eliot's use of the expressions "the best known and thought in the world" (p. 118) and the "higher culture" (p. 124).

[93] *Ibid.,* p. 115. Additional illustrations include Eliot's comment on our knowledge of the "dead writers" in "Tradition and the Individual Talent," as well as sections 3 and 4 of "The Function of Criticism" (*Selected Essays,* pp. 16, 29-31).

[94] "Matthew Arnold," *The Use of Poetry,* p. 118; and "The Perfect Critic," *The Sacred Wood,* p. 1.

[95] *The Use of Poetry,* pp. 110, 122. See also Eliot's earlier statement about Arnold and the Romantics in his introduction to *The Sacred Wood,* p. xii. A careful assessment of the extent to which Arnold's judgment here reflects current opinion in Victorian literary periodicals is presented by R. G. Cox, "Victorian Criticism of Poetry: The Minority Tradition," *Scrutiny,* XVIII (1951-52), 2-17.

is created by Eliot's statement on the influence of *Culture and Anarchy*. Comparing it with Carlyle's *Past and Present* and Ruskin's *Unto This Last,* Eliot concludes that

> its ideas are really no clearer—one reason why Arnold, Carlyle and Ruskin were so influential, for precision and completeness of thought do not always make for influence. (Arnold, it is true, gave something else: he produced a kind of illusion of precision and clarity; that is, he maintained these qualities as ideals of style.) [96]

Eliot mellows enough in following years to concede eventually that "even if the delight we get from Arnold's writings, prose and verse, be moderate, yet he is in some respects the most satisfactory man of letters of his age," protesting that "however well-nourished we may be on previous literature and previous culture, we cannot afford to neglect Arnold." [97]

Yet, most of the "neglect" which Arnold has actually suffered can be attributed to the climate which Eliot's damaging and largely exaggerated generalizations about Arnold have created. In the introduction to *The Use of Poetry and the Use of Criticism,* Eliot quickly transforms what begins as a compliment into a forthright statement of what really bothers him about Arnold's ideas, couched as a refined description of Arnold's rank among English poets:

> For a long time the poet is the priest; there are still, I believe, people who imagine that they draw religious aliment from Browning or Meredith. But the next stage is best exemplified by Matthew Arnold. Arnold was too temperate and too reasonable a man to maintain exactly that religious instruction is best conveyed by poetry, and himself had very little to convey; but he discovered a new formula: poetry is not religion but it is a capital substitute for religion.

Further on in the same volume, of course, Eliot gives vent to his annoyance at "this conjuring trick" of Arnold's, announcing in no uncertain terms that "nothing in this world or the next is a substitute for anything else; and if you find that you must do without something, such as religious faith or philosophic belief, then you must just do without it." [98] The tone of this, nevertheless, is at least more restrained than Eliot's earlier treatment of the same matter. In "Arnold and Pater" he had condemned

---

[96] "Arnold and Pater," *Selected Essays,* p. 395.

[97] "Matthew Arnold," *The Use of Poetry,* pp. 104, 105. In commenting on Arnold's idea of the poet's greatness in this essay, Eliot remarks that Arnold's was "not a happy way of putting it, as if ideas were a lotion for the inflamed skin of suffering humanity" (p. 112). René Wellek comments in the same amusing vein, chiding Arnold for thinking that "ideas" can be "applied like plasters" (*A History of Modrn Criticism,* IV, 166).

[98] *The Use of Poetry,* pp. 26, 113-14.

Arnold's malicious influence: "the degredation of philosophy and religion, skilfully initiated by Arnold, is competently continued by Pater," he declares. What responsibility Arnold has for the "birth of Humanism" Eliot can merely guess at, but "Arnold could father something apparently quite different,—the view of life of Walter Pater," since " 'art for art's sake' is the offspring of Arnold's Culture." [99] Still, Eliot is no better pleased by Arnold's dutiful efforts to moralize about poetry, for he lashes out in several instances at the absurdity of calling poetry a "criticism of life." [100] In this respect Arnold has been fathering something at least as dangerous as Pater's aestheticism, and this is I. A. Richards' absurd notion that "poetry is capable of saving us." [101]

Quite reprehensible, therefore, in one who has so little that is not insulting to say of Arnold, are Eliot's solemn pronouncements of positions and ideas which come nearly verbatim from sources in Arnold. Eliot's estimate of Chaucer in the essay "What Is A Classic?" (itself modeled on Arnold's "On the Modern Element in Literature" and "The Study of Poetry"), together with his somewhat pompous declaration of what he means by the expression "provincial," are fairly recent examples. [102] A more amusing, because more apparent, illustration is the passage in the third paragraph of "The Function of Criticism":

> I thought of literature then, as I think of it now, of the literature of the world, of the literature of Europe, of the literature of a single country, not as a collection of the writings of individuals, but as "organic wholes," as systems in relation to which, and only in relation to which, individual works of literary art, and the works of individual artists, have their significance. [103]

And for all Eliot's superiority to the "touchstone" theory, one smiles at his remark in the 1928 preface to *The Sacred Wood*:

[99] *Selected Essays*, pp. 399, 396, 401. In the last passage Eliot continues that "we can hardly venture to say that [" art for art's sake"] is even a perversion of Arnold's doctrine, considering how very vague and ambiguous that doctrine is."

[100] See *The Sacred Wood*, pp. ix and 43, and *The Use of Poetry*, p. 122. Arnold, it might be noted, was rather too "dutiful" in his efforts to produce very good poetry.

[101] See Leonard Brown, "Arnold's Succession: 1850-1914," *Sewanee Review*, XLII (1934), 158-79. Brown sees as Arnold's successors not Pater and Richards but Hardy and Housman in poetry. Eliot himself elsewhere designates Arnold's "successors" as Pater, Arthur Symons, Addington Symonds, Leslie Stephen, F. W. H. Myers, George Saintsbury: "all the more eminent critical names of the time bear witness" to "the criticism of Arnold" ("The Modern Mind," in *The Use of Poetry*, p. 123). Vincent Buckley's *Poetry and Morality*, ironically enough, sees Eliot himself as in the tradition of Arnold.

[102] *On Poetry and Poets*, pp. 61, 71. In "Arnold and Pater," Eliot had acknowledged Arnold's use of the expression, declaring that "in his books dealing with Christianity he seems bent upon illustrating in himself the provincialisms which he rebuked in others" (*Selected Essays*, p. 397).

[103] *Selected Essays*, pp. 23-24.

Hence, in criticising poetry, we are right if we begin, with what sensibility and what knowledge of other poetry we possess, with poetry as excellent words in excellent arrangement and excellent metre.[104]

Finally, the thesis of Eliot's "What Is A Classic?" (itself somewhat indebted to Sainte-Beuve), that "the word *maturity*" suggests "the maximum of what I mean by the term 'a classic,' " can hardly fail to recall something to any reader of Arnold's inaugural lecture at Oxford:

> An intellectual deliverance is the peculiar demand of those ages which are called modern. . . . The deliverance consists in man's comprehension of this present and past. It begins when our mind begins to enter into possession of the general ideas which are the law of this vast multitude of facts. . . . What distinguishes certain epochs in the history of the human race, and our own amongst the number, [is] on the one hand, the presence of a significant spectacle to contemplate; on the other hand, the desire to find the true point of view from which to contemplate this spectacle. He who has found that point of view, he who adequately comprehends this spectacle, has risen to the comprehension of his age: he who communicates that point of view to his age, he who interprets to it that spectacle, is one of his age's intellectual deliverers.[105]

As one continues reading the same section of this essay, one is struck by its remarkable similarities with the central idea of Eliot's "Tradition and the Individual Talent":

> The spectacle, the facts, presented for the comprehension of the present age, are indeed immense. The facts consist of the events, the institutions, the sciences, the arts, the literatures, in which human life has manifested itself up to the present time: the spectacle is the collective life of humanity. And everywhere there is connexion, everywhere there is illustration: no single event, no single literature, is adequately comprehended except in its relation to other events, to other literatures.[106]

In the two overt essays on Arnold, Eliot indulges very generously in that "vague depreciation" he had confessed to. The earlier one, "Arnold and Pater," maintains that "Arnold had little gift for consistency or for definition. Nor had he the power of connected reasoning at any length: his flights are either short flights or circular flights." His estimate here of Arnold's value to the twentieth century is equally unenthusiastic: "To us . . . Arnold is rather a friend than a leader. He was a champion of 'ideas' most of whose ideas we no longer take seriously." But it is in "Matthew Arnold" that both of Eliot's major irritations at Arnold's ideas are apparent. He describes Arnold's criticism as "his sermon to the British public"

---

[104] *The Sacred Wood,* p. ix.
[105] *On Poetry and Poets,* p. 54; Super, *Complete Prose Works,* I, 19-20.
[106] Super, *Complete Prose Works,* I, 20-21.

and severely reprimands him for the facile "conjuring trick" by which he attempted to substitute poetry for religion.[107] In fact, Eliot's apparent objections to Arnold are two: overly moralistic literary theory which Arnold's own poetry is so unsuccessful in vindicating, and the fatal substitution already mentioned, which let loose the excesses of Pater and I. A. Richards.[108] But the more one reads of Eliot's literary criticism, the more one realizes that other objections are moving beneath the surface.

Eliot's militant anti-romanticism, enunciated in "Tradition and the Individual Talent," explains much of Eliot's antipathy for Arnold's thought and writing. N. N. Feltes has stated the central problem well when he observes that "the temper of Matthew Arnold's later criticism is given by the concept of God, an Eternal not ourselves, the State of 'our best self,' and a literature judged in relation to touchstones." [109] The high degree of "inwardness" which Arnold's conceptions embody grate upon a man who professes to be an Anglo-Catholic in religion, a Tory in politics, and a classicist in literary theory, and who gaily styles himself in another place as an "Inner Deaf Mute." Secondly, it is apparent that Eliot resists the possibility that a man of intelligence and sensitivity could renounce his Christianity, or at least the formal practice of it.[110] Eliot's determination to redo Arnold's social criticism with heavy emphasis upon the importance of religion has already been described: "Arnold's prose

[107] *Selected Essays*, pp. 393, 395-96; *The Use of Poetry*, pp. 110, 113. In his introduction to *The Sacred Wood*, Eliot had described Arnold as "a critic tempted outside criticism," who succumbed to the temptation "to put literature into the corner until he cleaned up the whole country first," a task which could have been done as well "by some disciple (had there been one) in an editorial position on a newspaper" (pp. xii-xiv).

[108] See Vincent Buckley, *Poetry and Morality*, p. 149. Eliot chides Arnold for demanding too much "affirmation" from poetry, but Buckley suggests in turn that Eliot "expects almost too little affirmation" himself. Eliot's essay "Religion and Literature," of course, argues that theology and ethics "complete" art and criticism, but must remain separate from them. M. L. S. Loring takes issue with Eliot on the question of the "absurdity" of Arnold's "religious beliefs," as does Leonard Brown on Eliot's "most unjust" judgment that Arnold's is "a counsel to get all the emotional kick out of Christianity one can, without the bother of believing it." See Loring, "T. S. Eliot on Matthew Arnold," *Sewanee Review*, XLIII (1935), 483; and Brown, "Arnold's Succession: 1850-1914," *Sewanee Review*, XLII (1934), 158.

[109] "Matthew Arnold and the Modern Spirit: A Reassessment," *University of Toronto Quarterly*, XXXII (1962), 35.

[110] See "The Function of Criticism" in *Selected Essays*, p. 30. Eliot is here referring to John Middleton Murry's statement that the English writer inherits from the past a sense of "the inner voice" (p. 27). In "Arnold and Pater," Eliot seems to identify "aestheticism" with "insincerity" (p. 402).

In a letter to Mrs. Forster, dated January 4, 1868, Arnold makes a statement about the quality of his Christian thought: "However different the interpretation we put on much of the facts and history of Christianity, we may unite in the bond of this call [to live not "in the flesh" but "to the will of God"], which is true for all of us." For a critique of Eliot's "dogmatism" see M. L. S. Loring, "T. S. Eliot on Matthew Arnold," *Sewanee Review*, XLIII (1935), 484.

writings fall into two parts," Eliot contends, "those on culture and those on religion; and the books about Christianity seem only to say again and again—merely that the Christian faith is of course impossible to the man of culture." And a little later, he insists that "the total effect of Arnold's philosophy is to set up Culture in the place of Religion, and to leave Religion to be laid waste by the anarchy of feeling." [111] Yet, it is possible that Mr. Eliot has himself underestimated the extent to which Arnold was simply sketching a world exactly as it was going. One cannot help thinking of Prufrock as one reads in Arnold's 1853 Preface a statement about modern times, in which "the calm, the cheerfulness, the disinterested objectivity have disappeared; the dialogue of the mind with itself has commenced; modern problems have presented themselves; we hear already the doubts, we witness the discouragement, of Hamlet and of Faust." Nor can one deny the importance of Leonard Brown's statement that "the sole attitude which made it possible for Mr. Eliot to write his very fine poem *The Wasteland* rather than another sheaf of lyrics on trees was Arnold's." [112]

But it is, finally, Eliot's pseudo-attack upon Arnold's "far too bluntly" distinguished powers of criticism and creativity which, instead of turning the tables on Arnold, actually reveals the nature of Eliot's uncertainty in the face of Arnold's attitudes. In an amusing note to "Matthew Arnold," Eliot describes Arnold as often "an inferior poet [who] faggoted his verses as they fell," instead of indulging in judicious deletions. Thus, "we cannot be blamed for forming a low opinion of his capacity for self-criticism. He need not have printed them." [113] One is somewhat puzzled by the several contexts in which Eliot acts as though Arnold had never suggested, as in fact he does in the final paragraphs of "The Function of Criticism at the Present Time," that criticism "may have, in no contemptible measure, a joyful sense of creative activity." [114] But two other passages in *The Sacred Wood* seem to furnish the key to Eliot's uneasiness. Speaking of Arnold as "the critic tempted outside of criticism," he com-

---

[111] "Arnold and Pater," *Selected Essays*, pp. 396, 398. Eliot's concluding paragraph in "Matthew Arnold," on Arnold's "inner uncertainty" and "lack of faith" is surely a thinly disguised comment on Arnold's religious attitudes (*The Use of Poetry*, p. 119).

[112] Super, *Complete Prose Works*, I, 1; Leonard Brown, "Arnold's Succession: 1850-1914," *Sewanee Review*, XLII (1934), 160.

[113] *The Use of Poetry*, p. 111, n.

[114] See "The Function of Criticism" (sec. 4); Eliot's introduction to *The Use of Poetry;* and *Notes Toward the Definition of Culture (passim)*. Vincent Buckley's statement on this matter is perceptive: "Eliot plainly sees poetry as a liberation not only from the oppression of emotion but also from the eccentricity of ideas. It is in this sense, I think, that he insists that the use of the critical faculty is necessary to creativity" (*Poetry and Morality*, p. 121).

ments on "men who ought to preserve their critical ability for the improvement of their own creative work," since "the great bulk of the work of criticism could be done by minds of the second order . . . necessary for the rapid circulation of ideas." And in "The Perfect Critic," in a passage on Swinburne, he suggests that Swinburne "is one man in his poetry and a different man in his criticism" and concludes that "Swinburne found an adequate outlet for the creative impulse in his poetry; and none of it was forced back and out through his critical prose." [115] Thus, it becomes clear that Eliot finds Arnold a threat to his own stance as poet-critic, even as he finds him a threat to his own commitment to Christian orthodoxy.

Nevertheless, Arnold's real importance to the twentieth century is, ironically enough, aptly discovered by T. S. Eliot in a passage from "Arnold and Pater": "Arnold is in the end, I believe, at his best in satire and apologetics for literature, in his defense and enunciation of a needed attitude." [116] Eliot does not specify the kind of "attitude" he is commending, and recommending, here, but one can conclude certain things from the fact that he emphasizes a qualitative, not a quantitative, value in Arnold's criticism. Whether or not Arnold succeeded in realizing in himself his own ideal for the critic, one must admit that he set the standards high. "Criticism" is neither an entity nor a code, not a set of value judgments nor a body of reading techniques. It is an "attitude," a spirit, a habit of mind opening out upon all areas of human endeavor, an "attitude" of honest critical evaluation based upon a true idea (or at least upon the most "adequate ideas" available), and not upon mere practical exigencies of whatever kind. He urged that the "critical spirit" might well prove a solution to many of the dilemmas of the Victorians. But it is quite clear that he was not addressing himself to advocates of conventional criticism, for he refused to be bound by any but his own "definition" of criticism and its functions: "Well, then, am I to alter my definition of criticism, in order to meet the requirements of a number of practicing English critics, who, after all, are free in their choice of a business?" he demanded, adding under his breath, no doubt, "If this be treason, make the most of it!" Whatever his failings, it is entirely clear what he was about. He had determined to set a new pace in English

---

[115] *The Sacred Wood*, pp. xiv (Introduction), 5-6 ("The Perfect Critic," section on Swinburne). Eliot's judgments of Arnold as critic in "Matthew Arnold" stands in significant contrast to his statement about the enormous effect of the "great poet" (see *The Use of Poetry*, p. 109, and *Notes Toward the Definition of Culture*, p. 118).

[116] *Selected Essays*, p. 395 ("Arnold and Pater"). See also Leonard Brown, who remarks that "Arnold's noblest bequest to succeeding generations was not his opinions but his attitude" ("Arnold's Succession: 1850-1914," p. 59).

criticism by deflecting its tone and temper away from dogmatic disputation and ill-natured, captious wrangling. He was bent upon substituting a good-humored "bantering of the world on the irrationality of its ways without losing temper with it." [117] His counsel was for warfare, delicately conducted, against utilitarian platitudes and shallow Victorian optimism, for the triumph of intelligence over stock notions and half-assimilated, inadequate, uncritical ideas.

[117] See Arnold's letter to his mother, November 8, 1867. Much later Arnold revealed the almost philosophical consideration underlying his attitude toward irony: "Tragedy breasts the pressure of life. Comedy eludes it, half liberates itself by irony." Liberation from irrational, unnecessary "pressures" was Arnold's goal. See Leon Gottfried, *Matthew Arnold and the Romantics* (London: Routledge and Kegan Paul, 1963), p. 114. In his *Encyclopedia Britannica* (1886) article on Sainte-Beuve, Arnold suggests another relevant point: "Goethe long ago noticed that, whereas Germans reviewed one another as enemies whom they hated, the critics of the *Globe* reviewed one another as gentlemen. This arose from the higher social development of France, and from the closer relations of literature with life there."

CONTENTS

————◄◆►————

ESSAYS IN CRITICISM

FIRST SERIES

by

MATTHEW ARNOLD

1875

PREFACE

(1875)

———————◆———————

Several of the Essays which are here collected and reprinted had the good or the bad fortune to be much criticised at the time of their first appearance. I am not now going to inflict upon the reader a reply to those criticisms; for one or two explanations which are desirable, I shall elsewhere, perhaps, be able some day to find an opportunity; but, indeed, it is not in my nature,—some of my critics would rather say, not in my power,—to dispute on behalf of any opinion, even my own, very obstinately. To try and approach truth on one side after another, not to strive or cry, nor to persist in pressing forward, on any one side, with violence and self-will,— it is only thus, it seems to me, that mortals may hope to gain any vision of the mysterious Goddess, whom we shall never see except in outline, but only thus even in outline. He who will do nothing but fight impetuously towards her on his own, one, favourite, particular line, is inevitably destined to run his head into the folds of the black robe in which she is wrapped.

So it is not to reply to my critics that I write this Preface, but to prevent

10

a misunderstanding, of which certain phrases that some of them use make me apprehensive. Mr. Wright, one of the many translators of Homer, has published a Letter to the Dean of Canterbury, complaining of some remarks of mine, uttered now a long while ago, on his version of the Iliad. One cannot be always studying one's own works, and I was really under the impression, till I saw Mr. Wright's complaint, that I had spoken of him with all respect. The reader may judge of my astonishment, therefore, at finding, from Mr. Wright's pamphlet, that I had 'declared with much solemnity that there is not any proper reason for his existing.' That I never said; but, on looking back at my Lectures on translating Homer, I find that I did say, not that Mr. Wright, but that Mr. Wright's version of the Iliad, repeating in the main the merits and defects of Cowper's version, as Mr. Sotheby's repeated those of Pope's version, had, if I might be pardoned for saying so, no proper reason for existing. Elsewhere I expressly spoke of the merit of his version; but I confess that the phrase, qualified as I have shown, about its want of a proper reason for existing, I used. Well, the phrase had, perhaps, too much vivacity; we have all of us a right to exist, we and our works; an unpopular author should be the last person to call in question this right. So I gladly withdraw the offending phrase, and I am sorry for having used it; Mr. Wright, however, would perhaps be more indulgent to my vivacity, if he considered that we are none of us likely to be lively much longer. My vivacity is but the last sparkle of flame before we are all in the dark, the last glimpse of colour before we all go into drab,—the drab of the earnest, prosaic, practical, austerely literal future. Yes, the world will soon be the Philistines'! and then, with every voice, not of thunder, silenced, and the whole earth filled and ennobled every morning by the magnificent roaring of the young lions of the *Daily Telegraph,* we shall all yawn in one another's faces with the dismallest, the most unimpeachable gravity.

But I return to my design in writing this Preface. That design was, after apologising to Mr. Wright for my vivacity of five years ago, to beg him and others to let me bear my own burdens, without saddling the great and famous University to which I have the honour to belong with any portion of them. What I mean to deprecate is such phrases as, 'his professorial assault,' 'his assertions issued *ex cathedra,*' 'the sanction of his name as the representative of poetry,' and so on. Proud as I am of my connection with the University of Oxford,[1] I can truly say, that knowing how unpopular a task one is undertaking when one tries to pull out a few more stops

---

[1] When the above was written the author had still the Chair of Poetry at Oxford, which he has since vacated.

in that powerful but at present somewhat narrow-toned organ, the modern Englishman, I have always sought to stand by myself, and to compromise others as little as possible. Besides this, my native modesty is such, that I have always been shy of assuming the honourable style of Professor, because this is a title I share with so many distinguished men,—Professor Pepper, Professor Anderson, Professor Frickel, and others,—who adorn it, I feel, much more than I do.

However, it is not merely out of modesty that I prefer to stand alone, and to concentrate on myself, as a plain citizen of the republic of letters, and not as an office-bearer in a hierarchy, the whole responsibility for all I write; it is much more out of genuine devotion to the University of Oxford, for which I feel, and always must feel, the fondest, the most reverential attachment. In an epoch of dissolution and transformation, such as that on which we are now entered, habits, ties, and associations are inevitably broken up, the action of individuals becomes more distinct, the shortcomings, errors, heats, disputes, which necessarily attend individual action, are brought into greater prominence. Who would not gladly keep clear, from all these passing clouds, an august institution which was there before they arose, and which will be there when they have blown over?

It is true, the *Saturday Review* maintains that our epoch of transformation is finished; that we have found our philosophy; that the British nation has searched all anchorages for the spirit, and has finally anchored itself, in the fulness of perfected knowledge, on Benthamism. This idea at first made a great impression on me; not only because it is so consoling in itself, but also because it explained a phenomenon which in the summer of last year had, I confess, a good deal troubled me. At that time my avocations led me to travel almost daily on one of the Great Eastern Lines,—the Woodford Branch. Every one knows that the murderer, Müller, perpetrated his detestable act on the North London Railway, close by. The English middle-class, of which I am myself a feeble unit, travel on the Woodford Branch in large numbers. Well, the demoralisation of our class,—the class which (the newspapers are constantly saying it, so I may repeat it without vanity) has done all the great things which have ever been done in England,—the demoralisation, I say, of our class, caused by the Bow tragedy, was something bewildering. Myself a transcendentalist (as the *Saturday Review* knows), I escaped the infection; and, day after day, I used to ply my agitated fellow-travellers with all the consolations which my transcendentalism would naturally suggest to me. I reminded them how Caesar refused to take precautions against assassination, because life was not worth having at the price of an ignoble solicitude for it. I reminded them

what insignificant atoms we all are in the life of the world. 'Suppose the
worst to happen,' I said, addressing a portly jeweller from Cheapside;
'suppose even yourself to be the victim; *il n'y a pas d'homme nécessaire.*
We should miss you for a day or two upon the Woodford Branch; but the
great mundane movement would still go on, the gravel walks of your villa
would still be rolled, dividends would still be paid at the Bank, omnibuses   10
would still run, there would still be the old crush at the corner of Fenchurch Street.' All was of no avail. Nothing could moderate, in the
bosom of the great English middle-class, their passionate, absorbing,
almost blood-thirsty clinging to life. At the moment I thought this over-
concern a little unworthy; but the *Saturday Review* suggests a touching
explanation of it. What I took for the ignoble clinging to life of a comfortable worldling, was, perhaps, only the ardent longing of a faithful Benthamite, traversing an age still dimmed by the last mists of transcendentalism, to be spared long enough to see his religion in the full and final
blaze of its triumph. This respectable man, whom I imagined to be going   11
up to London to serve his shop, or to buy shares, or to attend an Exeter
Hall meeting, or to assist at the deliberations of the Marylebone Vestry,
was even, perhaps, in real truth, on a pious pilgrimage, to obtain from
Mr. Bentham's executors a sacred bone of his great, dissected master.

And yet, after all, I cannot but think that the *Saturday Review* has
here, for once, fallen a victim to an idea,—a beautiful but deluding idea,—
and that the British nation has not yet, so entirely as the reviewer seems
to imagine, found the last word of its philosophy. No, we are all seekers
still! seekers often make mistakes, and I wish mine to redound to my own
discredit only, and not to touch Oxford. Beautiful city! so venerable, so   12
lovely, so unravaged by the fierce intellectual life of our century, so serene!
        'There are our young barbarians, all at play!'
And yet, steeped in sentiment as she lies, spreading her gardens to the
moonlight, and whispering from her towers the last enchantments of the
Middle Age, who will deny that Oxford, by her ineffable charm, keeps
ever calling us nearer to the true goal of all of us, to the ideal, to perfection,—to beauty, in a word, which is only truth seen from another side?—
nearer, perhaps, than all the science of Tübingen. Adorable dreamer,
whose heart has been so romantic! who hast given thyself so prodigally,
given thyself to sides and to heroes not mine, only never to the Philistines!   13
home of lost causes, and forsaken beliefs, and unpopular names, and
impossible loyalties! what example could ever so inspire us to keep down
the Philistine in ourselves, what teacher could ever so save us from that
bondage to which we are all prone, that bondage which Goethe, in his

incomparable lines on the death of Schiller, makes it his friend's highest praise (and nobly did Schiller deserve the praise) to have left miles out of sight behind him;—the bondage of '*was uns alle bändigt,* DAS GE-MEINE!' She will forgive me, even if I have unwittingly drawn upon her a shot or two aimed at her unworthy son; for she is generous, and the cause in which I fight is, after all, hers. Apparitions of a day, what is our puny war- [140] fare against the Philistines, compared with the warfare which this queen of romance has been waging against them for centuries, and will wage after we are gone?

THE FUNCTION OF CRITICISM
AT THE PRESENT TIME

—————◄◆►—————

Many objections have been made to a proposition which, in some remarks of mine on translating Homer, I ventured to put forth; a proposition about criticism, and its importance at the present day. I said: 'Of the literature of France and Germany, as of the intellect of Europe in general, the main effort, for now many years, has been a critical effort; the endeavour, in all branches of knowledge, theology, philosophy, history, art, science, to see the object as in itself it really is.' I added, that owing to the operation in English literature of certain causes, 'almost the last thing for which one would come to English literature is just that very thing which now Europe most desires,—criticism;' and that the power and value of English literature was thereby impaired. More than one rejoinder declared that the importance I here assigned to criticism was excessive, and asserted the inherent superiority of the creative effort of the human spirit over its critical effort. And the other day, having been led by a Mr. Shairp's excellent notice of Wordsworth [1] to turn again to his biography, I found, in

[1] I cannot help thinking that a practice, common in England during the last cen-

8

the words of this great man, whom I, for one, must always listen to with
the profoundest respect, a sentence passed on the critic's business, which
seems to justify every possible disparagement of it. Wordsworth says in
one of his letters:—

'The writers in these publications' (the Reviews), 'while they prosecute   20
their inglorious employment, cannot be supposed to be in a state of mind
very favourable for being affected by the finer influences of a thing so pure
as genuine poetry.'

And a trustworthy reporter of his conversation quotes a more elaborate
judgment to the same effect:—

'Wordsworth holds the critical power very low, infinitely lower than the
inventive; and he said to-day that if the quantity of time consumed in
writing critiques on the works of others were given to original composition,
of whatever kind it might be, it would be much better employed; it would
make a man find out sooner his own level, and it would do infinitely less   30
mischief. A false or malicious criticism may do much injury to the minds
of others; a stupid invention, either in prose or verse, is quite harmless.'

It is almost too much to expect of poor human nature, that a man capable of producing some effect in one line of literature, should, for the
greater good of society, voluntarily doom himself to impotence and
obscurity in another. Still less is this to be expected from men addicted to
the composition of the 'false or malicious criticism,' of which Wordsworth
speaks. However, everybody would admit that a false or malicious criticism had better never have been written. Everybody, too, would be willing
to admit, as a general proposition, that the critical faculty is lower than the   40
inventive. But is it true that criticism is really, in itself, a baneful and
injurious employment; is it true that all time given to writing critiques on
the works of others would be much better employed if it were given to
original composition, of whatever kind this may be? Is it true that Johnson
had better have gone on producing more *Irenes* instead of writing his
Lives of the Poets; nay, is it certain that Wordsworth himself was better
employed in making his Ecclesiastical Sonnets, than when he made his
celebrated Preface, so full of criticism, and criticism of the works of

---

tury, and still followed in France, of printing a notice of this kind,—a notice by a
competent critic,—to serve as an introduction to an eminent author's works, might
be revived among us with advantage. To introduce all succeeding editions of Wordsworth, Mr. Shairp's notice might, it seems to me, excellently serve; it is written from
the point of view of an admirer, nay, of a disciple, and that is right; but then the
disciple must be also, as in this case he is, a critic, a man of letters, not, as too often
happens, some relation or friend with no qualification for his task except affection
for his author.

others? Wordsworth was himself a great critic, and it is to be sincerely regretted that he has not left us more criticism; Goethe was one of the greatest of critics, and we may sincerely congratulate ourselves that he has left us so much criticism. Without wasting time over the exaggeration which Wordsworth's judgment on criticism clearly contains, or over an attempt to trace the causes,—not difficult I think to be traced,—which may have led Wordsworth to this exaggeration, a critic may with advantage seize an occasion for trying his own conscience, and for asking himself of what real service, at any given moment, the practice of criticism either is, or may be made, to his own mind and spirit, and to the minds and spirits of others.

The critical power is of lower rank than the creative. True; but in assenting to this proposition, one or two things are to be kept in mind. It is undeniable that the exercise of a creative power, that a free creative activity, is the highest function of man; it is proved to be so by man's finding in it his true happiness. But it is undeniable, also, that men may have the sense of exercising this free creative activity in other ways than in producing great works of literature or art; if it were not so, all but a very few men would be shut out from the true happiness of all men. They may have it in well-doing, they may have it in learning, they may have it even in criticising. This is one thing to be kept in mind. Another is, that the exercise of the creative power in the production of great works of literature or art, however high this exercise of it may rank, is not at all epochs and under all conditions possible; and that therefore labour may be vainly spent in attempting it, which might with more fruit be used in preparing for it, in rendering it possible. This creative power works with elements, with materials; what if it has not those materials, those elements, ready for its use? In that case it must surely wait till they are ready. Now in literature,—I will limit myself to literature, for it is about literature that the question arises,—the elements with which the creative power works are ideas; the best ideas, on every matter which literature touches, current at the time. At any rate we may lay it down as certain that in modern literature no manifestation of the creative power not working with these can be very important or fruitful. And I say *current* at the time, not merely accessible at the time; for creative literary genius does not principally show itself in discovering new ideas; that is rather the business of the philosopher. The grand work of literary genius is a work of synthesis and exposition, not of analysis and discovery; its gift lies in the faculty of being happily inspired by a certain intellectual and spiritual atmosphere, by a certain order of ideas, when it finds itself in them; of dealing divinely with these

50

60

70

80

ideas, presenting them in the most effective and attractive combinations,—
making beautiful works with them, in short. But it must have the atmos-   90
phere, it must find itself amidst the order of ideas, in order to work freely;
and these it is not so easy to command. This is why great creative epochs
in literature are so rare, this is why there is so much that is unsatisfactory
in the productions of many men of real genius;—because, for the creation
of a master-work of literature two powers must concur, the power of the
man and the power of the moment, and the man is not enough without the
moment; the creative power has, for its happy exercise, appointed elements, and those elements are not in its own control.

Nay, they are more within the control of the critical power. It is the
business of the critical power, as I said in the words already quoted, 'in   100
all branches of knowledge, theology, philosophy, history, art, science, to
see the object as in itself it really is.' Thus it tends, at last, to make an intellectual situation of which the creative power can profitably avail itself. It
tends to establish an order of ideas, if not absolutely true, yet true by comparison with that which it displaces; to make the best ideas prevail. Presently these new ideas reach society, the touch of truth is the touch of life,
and there is a stir and growth everywhere; out of this stir and growth come
the creative epochs of literature.

Or, to narrow our range, and quit these considerations of the general
march of genius and of society, considerations which are apt to become too   110
abstract and impalpable,—every one can see that a poet, for instance,
ought to know life and the world before dealing with them in poetry; and
life and the world being, in modern times, very complex things, the creation of a modern poet, to be worth much, implies a great critical effort
behind it; else it must be a comparatively poor, barren, and short-lived
affair. This is why Byron's poetry had so little endurance in it, and
Goethe's so much; both Byron and Goethe had a great productive power,
but Goethe's was nourished by a great critical effort providing the true
materials for it, and Byron's was not; Goethe knew life and the world, the
poet's necessary subjects, much more comprehensively and thoroughly   120
than Byron. He knew a great deal more of them, and he knew them much
more as they really are.

It has long seemed to me that the burst of creative activity in our literature, through the first quarter of this century, had about it, in fact, something premature; and that from this cause its productions are doomed,
most of them, in spite of the sanguine hopes which accompanied and do
still accompany them, to prove hardly more lasting than the productions of
far less splendid epochs. And this prematureness comes from its having

proceeded without having its proper data, without sufficient materials to
work with. In other words, the English poetry of the first quarter of this
century, with plenty of energy, plenty of creative force, did not know
enough. This makes Byron so empty of matter, Shelley so incoherent,
Wordsworth even, profound as he is, yet so wanting in completeness and
variety. Wordsworth cared little for books, and disparaged Goethe. I
admire Wordsworth, as he is, so much that I cannot wish him different;
and it is vain, no doubt, to imagine such a man different from what he is,
to suppose that he *could* have been different. But surely the one thing
wanting to make Wordsworth an even greater poet than he is,—his
thought richer, and his influence of wider application,—was that he should
have read more books, among them, no doubt, those of that Goethe whom
he disparaged without reading him.

But to speak of books and reading may easily lead to a misunderstanding here. It was not really books and reading that lacked to our poetry, at
this epoch; Shelley had plenty of reading, Coleridge had immense reading.
Pindar and Sophocles—as we all say so glibly, and often with so little
discernment of the real import of what we are saying—had not many
books; Shakspeare was no deep reader. True; but in the Greece of Pindar
and Sophocles, in the England of Shakspeare, the poet lived in a current
of ideas in the highest degree animating and nourishing to the creative
power; society was, in the fullest measure, permeated by fresh thought,
intelligent and alive. And this state of things is the true basis for the creative power's exercise, in this it finds its data, its materials, truly ready for
its hand; all the books and reading in the world are only valuable as they
are helps to this. Even when this does not actually exist, books and reading
may enable a man to construct a kind of semblance of it in his own mind, a
world of knowledge and intelligence in which he may live and work. This
is by no means an equivalent, to the artist, for the nationally diffused life
and thought of the epochs of Sophocles or Shakspeare; but, besides that
it may be a means of preparation for such epochs, it does really constitute,
if many share in it, a quickening and sustaining atmosphere of great value.
Such an atmosphere the many-sided learning and the long and widely-
combined critical effort of Germany formed for Goethe, when he lived and
worked. There was no national glow of life and thought there, as in the
Athens of Pericles, or the England of Elizabeth. That was the poet's weakness. But there was a sort of equivalent for it in the complete culture and
unfettered thinking of a large body of Germans. That was his strength. In
the England of the first quarter of this century, there was neither a national
glow of life and thought, such as we had in the age of Elizabeth, nor yet

a culture and a force of learning and criticism, such as were to be found in
Germany. Therefore the creative power of poetry wanted, for success in   170
the highest sense, materials and a basis; a thorough interpretation of the
world was necessarily denied to it.

At first sight it seems strange that out of the immense stir of the French
Revolution and its age should not have come a crop of works of genius
equal to that which came out of the stir of the great productive time of
Greece, or out of that of the Renascence with its powerful episode the
Reformation. But the truth is that the stir of the French Revolution took
a character which essentially distinguished it from such movements as
these. These were, in the main, disinterestedly intellectual and spiritual
movements; movements in which the human spirit looked for its satisfac-   180
tion in itself and in the increased play of its own activity. The French Revolution took a political, practical character. The movement which went on
in France under the old *régime,* from 1700 to 1789, was far more really
akin than that of the Revolution itself to the movement of the Renascence;
the France of Voltaire and Rousseau told far more powerfully upon the
mind of Europe than the France of the Revolution. Goethe reproached
this last expressly with having 'thrown quiet culture back.' Nay, and the
true key to how much in our Byron, even in our Wordsworth, is this!—
that they had their source in a great movement of feeling, not in a great
movement of mind. The French Revolution, however,—that object of so   190
much blind love and so much blind hatred,—found undoubtedly its
motive-power in the intelligence of men and not in their practical sense;—
this is what distinguishes it from the English Revolution of Charles the
First's time. This is what makes it a more spiritual event than our Revolution, an event of much more powerful and world-wide interest, though
practically less successful;—it appeals to an order of ideas which are universal, certain, permanent. 1789 asked of a thing, Is it rational? 1642
asked of a thing, Is it legal? or, when it went furthest, Is it according to
conscience? This is the English fashion; a fashion to be treated, within its
own sphere, with the highest respect; for its success, within its own sphere,   200
has been prodigious. But what is law in one place, is not law in another; what
is law here to-day, is not law even here to-morrow; and as for conscience,
what is binding on one man's conscience is not binding on another's. The old
woman who threw her stool at the head of the surpliced minister in St.
Giles's Church at Edinburgh obeyed an impulse to which millions of the
human race may be permitted to remain strangers. But the prescriptions of
reason are absolute, unchanging, of universal validity; *to count by tens is
the easiest way of counting,*—that is a proposition of which every one,

from here to the Antipodes, feels the force; at least, I should say so, if we did not live in a country where it is not impossible that any morning we may find a letter in the *Times* declaring that a decimal coinage is an absurdity. That a whole nation should have been penetrated with an enthusiasm for pure reason, and with an ardent zeal for making its prescriptions triumph, is a very remarkable thing, when we consider how little of mind, or anything so worthy and quickening as mind, comes into the motives which alone, in general, impel great masses of men. In spite of the extravagant direction given to this enthusiasm, in spite of the crimes and follies in which it lost itself, the French Revolution derives from the force, truth, and universality of the ideas which it took for its law, and from the passion with which it could inspire a multitude for these ideas, a unique and still living power; it is,—it will probably long remain,—the greatest, the most animating event in history. And, as no sincere passion for the things of the mind, even though it turn out in many respects an unfortunate passion, is ever quite thrown away and quite barren of good, France has reaped from hers one fruit,—the natural and legitimate fruit, though not precisely the grand fruit she expected; she is the country in Europe where *the people* is most alive.

But the mania for giving an immediate political and practical application to all these fine ideas of the reason was fatal. Here an Englishman is in his element: on this theme we can all go on for hours. And all we are in the habit of saying on it has undoubtedly a great deal of truth. Ideas cannot be too much prized in and for themselves, cannot be too much lived with; but to transport them abruptly into the world of politics and practice, violently to revolutionise this world to their bidding,—that is quite another thing. There is the world of ideas and there is the world of practice; the French are often for suppressing the one and the English the other; but neither is to be suppressed. A member of the House of Commons said to me the other day: 'That a thing is an anomaly, I consider to be no objection to it whatever.' I venture to think he was wrong; that a thing is an anomaly *is* an objection to it, but absolutely and in the sphere of ideas: it is not necessarily, under such and such circumstances, or at such and such a moment, an objection to it in the sphere of politics and practice. Joubert has said beautifully: 'C'est la force et le droit qui règlent toutes choses dans le monde; la force en attendant le droit.' (Force and right are the governors of this world; force till right is ready.) *Force till right is ready;* and till right is ready, force, the existing order of things, is justified, is the legitimate ruler. But right is something moral, and implies inward recognition, free assent of the will; we are not ready for right,—*right,* so far as we are concerned, *is not ready,*—until we have attained this sense of seeing it and willing it. The way in which for us it may change and transform force, the existing order of things, and become, in its turn, the legitimate ruler of the world, should depend on the way in which, when our time comes, we see it and will it. Therefore for other people enamoured of their own newly discerned right, to attempt to impose it upon us as ours, and violently to substitute their right for our force, is an act of tyranny, and to be resisted. It sets at nought the second great half of our maxim, *force till right is ready.* This was the grand error of the French Revolution; and its movement of ideas, by quitting the intellectual sphere and rushing furiously into the political sphere, ran, indeed, a prodigious and memorable course, but produced no such intellectual fruit as the movement of ideas of the Renascence, and created, in opposition to itself, what I may call an *epoch of concentration.* The great force of that epoch of concentration was England; and the great voice of that epoch of concentration was Burke. It is the fashion to treat Burke's writings on the French Revolution as superannuated and conquered by the event; as the eloquent but unphilosophical tirades of bigotry and prejudice. I will not deny that they are often disfigured by the violence and passion of the moment, and that in some directions Burke's view was bounded, and his observation therefore at fault. But on the whole, and for those who can make the needful corrections, what distinguishes these writings is their profound, permanent, fruitful, philosophical truth. They contain the true philosophy of an epoch of concentration, dissipate the heavy atmosphere which its own nature is apt to engender round it, and make its resistance rational instead of mechanical.

But Burke is so great because, almost alone in England, he brings thought to bear upon politics, he saturates politics with thought. It is his accident that his ideas were at the service of an epoch of concentration, not of an epoch of expansion; it is his characteristic that he so lived by ideas, and had such a source of them welling up within him, that he could float even an epoch of concentration and English Tory politics with them. It does not hurt him that Dr. Price and the Liberals were enraged with him; it does not even hurt him that George the Third and the Tories were enchanted with him. His greatness is that he lived in a world which neither English Liberalism nor English Toryism is apt to enter;—the world of ideas, not the world of catchwords and party habits. So far is it from being really true of him that he 'to party gave up what was meant for mankind,' that at the very end of his fierce struggle with the French Revolution, after all his invectives against its false pretensions, hollowness, and madness, with his sincere conviction of its mischievousness, he can close a memorandum on the best means of combating it, some of the last pages he ever wrote,—the *Thoughts on French Affairs,* in December 1791,—with these striking words:— 290

'The evil is stated, in my opinion, as it exists. The remedy must be where power, wisdom, and information, I hope, are more united with good intentions than they can be with me. I have done with this subject, I believe, for ever. It has given me many anxious moments for the last two years. *If a great change is to be made in human affairs, the minds of men will be fitted to it; the general opinions and feelings will draw that way. Every fear, every hope will forward it; and then they who persist in opposing this mighty current in human affairs, will appear rather to resist the decrees* 300 *of Providence itself, than the mere designs of men. They will not be resolute and firm, but perverse and obstinate.'*

That return of Burke upon himself has always seemed to me one of the finest things in English literature, or indeed in any literature. That is what I call living by ideas: when one side of a question has long had your earnest support, when all your feelings are engaged, when you hear all round you no language but one, when your party talks this language like a steam-engine and can imagine no other,—still to be able to think, still to be irresistibly carried, if so it be, by the current of thought to the opposite side of the question, and, like Balaam, to be unable to speak anything 310 *but what the Lord has put in your mouth.* I know nothing more striking, and I must add that I know nothing more un-English.

For the Englishman in general is like my friend the Member of Parliament, and believes, point-blank, that for a thing to be an anomaly is absolutely no objection to it whatever. He is like the Lord Auckland of Burke's day, who, in a memorandum on the French Revolution, talks of 'certain miscreants, assuming the name of philosophers, who have presumed themselves capable of establishing a new system of society.' The Englishman has been called a political animal, and he values what is political and practical so much that ideas easily become objects of dislike in his 320 eyes, and thinkers 'miscreants,' because ideas and thinkers have rashly meddled with politics and practice. This would be all very well if the dislike and neglect confined themselves to ideas transported out of their own sphere, and meddling rashly with practice; but they are inevitably extended to ideas as such, and to the whole life of intelligence; practice is everything, a free play of the mind is nothing. The notion of the free play of the mind upon all subjects being a pleasure in itself, being an object of desire, being an essential provider of elements without which a nation's spirit, whatever compensations it may have for them, must, in the long run, die of inanition, hardly enters into an Englishman's thoughts. It is notice- 330 able that the word *curiosity,* which in other languages is used in a good sense, to mean, as a high and fine quality of man's nature, just this disin- terested love of a free play of the mind on all subjects, for its own sake,— it is noticeable, I say, that this word has in our language no sense of the kind, no sense but a rather bad and disparaging one. But criticism, real criticism, is essentially the exercise of this very quality. It obeys an instinct prompting it to try to know the best that is known and thought in the world, irrespectively of practice, politics, and everything of the kind; and to value knowledge and thought as they approach this best, without the intrusion of any other considerations whatever. This is an instinct for 340 which there is, I think, little original sympathy in the practical English nature, and what there was of it has undergone a long benumbing period of blight and suppression in the epoch of concentration which followed the French Revolution.

But epochs of concentration cannot well endure for ever; epochs of expansion, in the due course of things, follow them. Such an epoch of expansion seems to be opening in this country. In the first place all danger of a hostile forcible pressure of foreign ideas upon our practice has long disappeared; like the traveller in the fable, therefore, we begin to wear our cloak a little more loosely. Then, with a long peace, the ideas of Europe 350 steal gradually and amicably in, and mingle, though in infinitesimally small quantities at a time, with our own notions. Then, too, in spite of all that is said about the absorbing and brutalising influence of our passionate mate- rial progress, it seems to me indisputable that this progress is likely, though not certain, to lead in the end to an apparition of intellectual life; and that man, after he has made himself perfectly comfortable and has now to determine what to do with himself next, may begin to remember that he has a mind, and that the mind may be made the source of great pleasure. I grant it is mainly the privilege of faith, at present, to discern this end to our railways, our business, and our fortune-making; but we shall see if, 360 here as elsewhere, faith is not in the end the true prophet. Our ease, our travelling, and our unbounded liberty to hold just as hard and securely as we please to the practice to which our notions have given birth, all tend to beget an inclination to deal a little more freely with these notions them- selves, to canvass them a little, to penetrate a little into their real nature. Flutterings of curiosity, in the foreign sense of the word, appear amongst us, and it is in these that criticism must look to find its account. Criticism first; a time of true creative activity, perhaps,—which, as I have said, must inevitably be preceded amongst us by a time of criticism,—hereafter, when criticism has done its work.   370

It is of the last importance that English criticism should clearly discern what rule for its course, in order to avail itself of the field now opening to it, and to produce fruit for the future, it ought to take. The rule may be summed up in one word,—*disinterestedness*. And how is criticism to show disinterestedness? By keeping aloof from what is called 'the practical view of things;' by resolutely following the law of its own nature, which is to be a free play of the mind on all subjects which it touches. By steadily refusing to lend itself to any of those ulterior, political, practical considerations about ideas, which plenty of people will be sure to attach to them, which perhaps ought often to be attached to them, which in this country at any   380
rate are certain to be attached to them quite sufficiently, but which criticism has really nothing to do with. Its business is, as I have said, simply to know the best that is known and thought in the world, and by in its turn making this known, to create a current of true and fresh ideas. Its business is to do this with inflexible honesty, with due ability; but its business is to do no more, and to leave alone all questions of practical consequences and applications, questions which will never fail to have due prominence given to them. Else criticism, besides being really false to its own nature, merely continues in the old rut which it has hitherto followed in this country, and will certainly miss the chance now given to it. For what is at pres-   390
ent the bane of criticism in this country? It is that practical considerations cling to it and stifle it. It subserves interests not its own. Our organs of criticism are organs of men and parties having practical ends to serve, and with them those practical ends are the first thing and the play of mind the second; so much play of mind as is compatible with the prosecution of those practical ends is all that is wanted. An organ like the *Revue des Deux Mondes,* having for its main function to understand and utter the best that is known and thought in the world, existing, it may be said, as just an organ for a free play of the mind, we have not. But we have the
Edinburgh Review, existing as an organ of the old Whigs, and for as much   400
play of the mind as may suit its being that; we have the *Quarterly Review,* existing as an organ of the Tories, and for as much play of mind as may suit its being that; we have the *British Quarterly Review,* existing as an organ of the political Dissenters, and for as much play of mind as may suit its being that; we have the *Times,* existing as an organ of the common, satisfied, well-to-do Englishman, and for as much play of mind as may suit

its being that. And so on through all the various fractions, political and religious, of our society; every fraction has, as such, its organ of criticism, but the notion of combining all fractions in the common pleasure of a free disinterested play of mind meets with no favour. Directly this play of mind wants to have more scope, and to forget the pressure of practical considerations a little, it is checked, it is made to feel the chain. We saw this the other day in the extinction, so much to be regretted, of the *Home and Foreign Review*. Perhaps in no organ of criticism in this country was there so much knowledge, so much play of mind; but these could not save it. The *Dublin Review* subordinates play of mind to the practical business of English and Irish Catholicism, and lives. It must needs be that men should act in sects and parties, that each of these sects and parties should have its organ, and should make this organ subserve the interests of its action; but it would be well, too, that there should be a criticism, not the minister of these interests, not their enemy, but absolutely and entirely independent of them. No other criticism will ever attain any real authority or make any real way towards its end,—the creating a current of true and fresh ideas.

It is because criticism has so little kept in the pure intellectual sphere, has so little detached itself from practice, has been so directly polemical and controversial, that it has so ill accomplished, in this country, its best spiritual work; which is to keep man from a self-satisfaction which is retarding and vulgarising, to lead him towards perfection, by making his mind dwell upon what is excellent in itself, and the absolute beauty and fitness of things. A polemical practical criticism makes men blind even to the ideal imperfection of their practice, makes them willingly assert its ideal perfection, in order the better to secure it against attack; and clearly this is narrowing and baneful for them. If they were reassured on the practical side, speculative considerations of ideal perfection they might be brought to entertain, and their spiritual horizon would thus gradually widen. Sir Charles Adderley says to the Warwickshire farmers:—

'Talk of the improvement of breed! Why, the race we ourselves represent, the men and women, the old Anglo-Saxon race, are the best breed in the whole world. . . . The absence of a too enervating climate, too unclouded skies, and a too luxurious nature, has produced so vigorous a race of people, and has rendered us so superior to all the world.'
Mr. Roebuck says to the Sheffield cutlers:—

'I look around me and ask what is the state of England? Is not property safe? Is not every man able to say what he likes? Can you not walk from one end of England to the other in perfect security? I ask you

whether, the world over or in past history, there is anything like it? Nothing. I pray that our unrivalled happiness may last.'
Now obviously there is a peril for poor human nature in words and thoughts of such exuberant self-satisfaction, until we find ourselves safe in   450
the streets of the Celestial City.

> 'Das wenige verschwindet leicht dem Blicke
> Der vorwärts sieht, wie viel noch übrig bleibt—'

says Goethe; 'the little that is done seems nothing when we look forward and see how much we have yet to do.' Clearly this is a better line of reflection for weak humanity, so long as it remains on this earthly field of labour and trial.

But neither Sir Charles Adderley nor Mr. Roebuck are by nature inaccessible to considerations of this sort. They only lose sight of them owing to the controversial life we all lead, and the practical form which all specu-   460
lation takes with us. They have in view opponents whose aim is not ideal, but practical; and in their zeal to uphold their own practice against these innovators, they go so far as even to attribute to this practice an ideal perfection. Somebody has been wanting to introduce a six-pound franchise, or to abolish church-rates, or to collect agricultural statistics by force, or to diminish local self-government. How natural, in reply to such proposals, very likely improper or ill-timed, to go a little beyond the mark, and to say stoutly, 'Such a race of people as we stand, so superior to all the world! The old Anglo-Saxon race, the best breed in the whole world! I pray that our unrivalled happiness may last! I ask you whether, the world   470
over or in past history, there is anything like it!' And so long as criticism answers this dithyramb by insisting that the old Anglo-Saxon race would be still more superior to all others if it had no church-rates, or that our unrivalled happiness would last yet longer with a six-pound franchise, so long will the strain, 'The best breed in the whole world!' swell louder and louder, everything ideal and refining will be lost out of sight, and both the assailed and their critics will remain in a sphere, to say the truth, perfectly unvital, a sphere in which spiritual progression is impossible. But let criticism leave church-rates and the franchise alone, and in the most candid spirit, without a single lurking thought of practical innovation, confront   480
with our dithyramb this paragraph on which I stumbled in a newspaper immediately after reading Mr. Roebuck:—

'A shocking child murder has just been committed at Nottingham. A girl named Wragg left the workhouse there on Saturday morning with her young illegitimate child. The child was soon afterwards found dead on Mapperly Hills, having been strangled. Wragg is in custody.'

Nothing but that; but, in juxtaposition with the absolute eulogies of Sir Charles Adderley and Mr. Roebuck, how eloquent, how suggestive are those few lines! 'Our old Anglo-Saxon breed, the best in the whole world!' —how much that is harsh and ill-favoured there is in this best! *Wragg!*   490 If we are to talk of ideal perfection, of 'the best in the whole world,' has any one reflected what a touch of grossness in our race, what an original shortcoming in the more delicate spiritual perceptions, is shown by the natural growth amongst us of such hideous names,—Higginbottom, Stiggins, Bugg! In Ionia and Attica they were luckier in this respect than 'the best race in the world;' by the Ilissus there was no Wragg, poor thing! And 'our unrivalled happiness;'—what an element of grimness, bareness, and hideousness mixes with it and blurs it; the workhouse, the dismal Mapperly Hills,—how dismal those who have seen them will remember; —the gloom, the smoke, the cold, the strangled illegitimate child! 'I ask   500 you whether, the world over or in past history, there is anything like it?' Perhaps not, one is inclined to answer; but at any rate, in that case, the world is very much to be pitied. And the final touch,—short, bleak, and inhuman: *Wragg is in custody.* The sex lost in the confusion of our unrivalled happiness; or (shall I say?) the superfluous Christian name lopped off by the straightforward vigour of our old Anglo-Saxon breed! There is profit for the spirit in such contrasts as this; criticism serves the cause of perfection by establishing them. By eluding sterile conflict, by refusing to remain in the sphere where alone narrow and relative conceptions have any worth and validity, criticism may diminish its momentary   510 importance, but only in this way has it a chance of gaining admittance for those wider and more perfect conceptions to which all its duty is really owed. Mr. Roebuck will have a poor opinion of an adversary who replies to his defiant songs of triumph only by murmuring under his breath, *Wragg is in custody;* but in no other way will these songs of triumph be induced gradually to moderate themselves, to get rid of what in them is excessive and offensive, and to fall into a softer and truer key.

It will be said that it is a very subtle and indirect action which I am thus prescribing for criticism, and that by embracing in this manner the Indian virtue of detachment and abandoning the sphere of practical life, it con-   520 demns itself to a slow and obscure work. Slow and obscure it may be, but it is the only proper work of criticism. The mass of mankind will never have any ardent zeal for seeing things as they are; very inadequate ideas will always satisfy them. On these inadequate ideas reposes, and must repose, the general practice of the world. That is as much as saying that whoever sets himself to see things as they are will find himself one of a very small circle; but it is only by this small circle resolutely doing its own work that adequate ideas will ever get current at all. The rush and roar of practical life will always have a dizzying and attracting effect upon the most collected spectator, and tend to draw him into its vortex; most of all will 530 this be the case where that life is so powerful as it is in England. But it is only by remaining collected, and refusing to lend himself to the point of view of the practical man, that the critic can do the practical man any service; and it is only by the greatest sincerity in pursuing his own course, and by at last convincing even the practical man of his sincerity, that he can escape misunderstandings which perpetually threaten him.

For the practical man is not apt for fine distinctions, and yet in these distinctions truth and the highest culture greatly find their account. But it is not easy to lead a practical man,—unless you reassure him as to your practical intentions, you have no chance of leading him,—to see that a 540 thing which he has always been used to look at from one side only, which he greatly values, and which, looked at from that side, quite deserves, perhaps, all the prizing and admiring which he bestows upon it,—that this thing, looked at from another side, may appear much less beneficent and beautiful, and yet retain all its claims to our practical allegiance. Where shall we find language innocent enough, how shall we make the spotless purity of our intentions evident enough, to enable us to say to the political Englishman that the British Constitution itself, which, seen from the practical side, looks such a magnificent organ of progress and virtue, seen from the speculative side,—with its compromises, its love of facts, its horror of 550 theory, its studied avoidance of clear thoughts,—that, seen from this side, our august Constitution sometimes looks,—forgive me, shade of Lord Somers!—a colossal machine for the manufacture of Philistines? How is Cobbett to say this and not be misunderstood, blackened as he is with the smoke of a life-long conflict in the field of political practice? how is Mr. Carlyle to say it and not be misunderstood, after his furious raid into this field with his *Latter-day Pamphlets?* how is Mr. Ruskin, after his pugnacious political economy? I say, the critic must keep out of the region of immediate practice in the political, social, humanitarian sphere, if he wants to make a beginning for that more free speculative treatment of 560 things, which may perhaps one day make its benefits felt even in this sphere, but in a natural and thence irresistible manner.

Do what he will, however, the critic will still remain exposed to frequent misunderstandings, and nowhere so much as in this country. For here people are particularly indisposed even to comprehend that without this free disinterested treatment of things, truth and the highest culture are out of the question. So immersed are they in practical life, so accustomed to take all their notions from this life and its processes, that they are apt to think that truth and culture themselves can be reached by the processes of this life, and that it is an impertinent singularity to think of reaching them in any other. 'We are all *terrae filii*,' cries their eloquent advocate; 'all Philistines together. Away with the notion of proceeding by any other course than the course dear to the Philistines; let us have a social movement, let us organise and combine a party to pursue truth and new thought, let us call it *the liberal party*, and let us all stick to each other, and back each other up. Let us have no nonsense about independent criticism, and intellectual delicacy, and the few and the many. Don't let us trouble ourselves about foreign thought; we shall invent the whole thing for ourselves as we go along. If one of us speaks well, applaud him; if one of us speaks ill, applaud him too; we are all in the same movement, we are all liberals, we are all in pursuit of truth.' In this way the pursuit of truth becomes really a social, practical, pleasurable affair, almost requiring a chairman, a secretary, and advertisements; with the excitement of an occasional scandal, with a little resistance to give the happy sense of difficulty overcome; but, in general, plenty of bustle and very little thought. To act is so easy, as Goethe says; to think is so hard! It is true that the critic has many temptations to go with the stream, to make one of the party of movement, one of these *terrae filii;* it seems ungracious to refuse to be a *terrae filius,* when so many excellent people are; but the critic's duty is to refuse, or, if resistance is vain, at least to cry with Obermann: *Périssons en résistant.*

How serious a matter it is to try and resist, I had ample opportunity of experiencing when I ventured some time ago to criticise the celebrated first volume of Bishop Colenso.[1] The echoes of the storm which was then raised I still, from time to time, hear grumbling round me. That storm arose out of a misunderstanding almost inevitable. It is a result of no little culture to

---

[1] So sincere is my dislike to all personal attack and controversy, that I abstain from reprinting, at this distance of time from the occasion which called them forth, the essays in which I criticised Dr. Colenso's book; I feel bound, however, after all that has passed, to make here a final declaration of my sincere impenitence for having published them. Nay, I cannot forbear repeating yet once more, for his benefit and that of his readers, this sentence from my original remarks upon him: *There is truth of science and truth of religion; truth of science does not become truth of religion till it is made religious.* And I will add: Let us have all the science there is from the men of science; from the men of religion let us have religion.

attain to a clear perception that science and religion are two wholly different things. The multitude will for ever confuse them; but happily that is of
no great real importance, for while the multitude imagines itself to live by
its false science, it does really live by its true religion. Dr. Colenso, how-   600
ever, in his first volume did all he could to strengthen the confusion,[2] and
to make it dangerous. He did this with the best intentions, I freely admit,
and with the most candid ignorance that this was the natural effect of what
he was doing; but, says Joubert, 'Ignorance, which in matters of morals
extenuates the crime, is itself, in intellectual matters, a crime of the first
order.' I criticised Bishop Colenso's speculative confusion. Immediately
there was a cry raised: 'What is this? here is a liberal attacking a liberal.
Do not you belong to the movement? are not you a friend of truth? Is not
Bishop Colenso in pursuit of truth? then speak with proper respect of his
book. Dr. Stanley is another friend of truth, and you speak with proper   610
respect of his book; why make these invidious differences? both books are
excellent, admirable, liberal; Bishop Colenso's perhaps the most so,
because it is the boldest, and will have the best practical consequences for
the liberal cause. Do you want to encourage to the attack of a brother liberal his, and your, and our implacable enemies, the *Church and State
Review* or the *Record,*—the High Church rhinoceros and the Evangelical
hyaena? Be silent, therefore; or rather speak, speak as loud as ever you
can! and go into ecstasies over the eighty and odd pigeons.'
   But criticism cannot follow this coarse and indiscriminate method. It is
unfortunately possible for a man in pursuit of truth to write a book which   620
reposes upon a false conception. Even the practical consequences of a
book are to genuine criticism no recommendation of it, if the book is, in
the highest sense, blundering. I see that a lady who herself, too, is in pursuit of truth, and who writes with great ability, but a little too much, perhaps, under the influence of the practical spirit of the English liberal
movement, classes Bishop Colenso's book and M. Renan's together, in her
survey of the religious state of Europe, as facts of the same order, works,
both of them, of 'great importance;' 'great ability, power, and skill;' Bishop
Colenso's, perhaps, the most powerful; at least, Miss Cobbe gives special
expression to her gratitude that to Bishop Colenso 'has been given the   630
strength to grasp, and the courage to teach, truths of such deep import.'
In the same way, more than one popular writer has compared him to
Luther. Now it is just this kind of false estimate which the critical spirit is,

---

[2] It has been said I make it 'a crime against literary criticism and the higher culture to attempt to inform the ignorant.' Need I point out that the ignorant are not
informed by being confirmed in a confusion?

it seems to me, bound to resist. It is really the strongest possible proof of
the low ebb at which, in England, the critical spirit is, that while the critical hit in the religious literature of Germany is Dr. Strauss's book, in that
of France M. Renan's book, the book of Bishop Colenso is the critical hit
in the religious literature of England. Bishop Colenso's book reposes on a
total misconception of the essential elements of the religious problem, as
that problem is now presented for solution. To criticism, therefore, which   640
seeks to have the best that is known and thought on this problem, it is,
however well meant, of no importance whatever. M. Renan's book
attempts a new synthesis of the elements furnished to us by the Four Gospels. It attempts, in my opinion, a synthesis, perhaps premature, perhaps
impossible, certainly not successful. Up to the present time, at any rate, we
must acquiesce in Fleury's sentence on such recastings of the Gospel story:
Quiconque s'imagine la pouvoir mieux écrire, ne l'entend pas. M. Renan
had himself passed by anticipation a like sentence on his own work, when
he said: 'If a new presentation of the character of Jesus were offered to
me, I would not have it; its very clearness would be, in my opinion, the   650
best proof of its insufficiency.' His friends may with perfect justice rejoin
that at the sight of the Holy Land, and of the actual scene of the Gospel-
story, all the current of M. Renan's thoughts may have naturally changed,
and a new casting of that story irresistibly suggested itself to him; and that
this is just a case for applying Cicero's maxim: Change of mind is not
inconsistency—*nemo doctus unquam mutationem consilii inconstantiam
dixit esse.* Nevertheless, for criticism, M. Renan's first thought must still be
the truer one, as long as his new casting so fails more fully to commend
itself, more fully (to use Coleridge's happy phrase about the Bible) to
find us. Still M. Renan's attempt is, for criticism, of the most real interest   660
and importance, since, with all its difficulty, a fresh synthesis of the New
Testament *data,*—not a making war on them, in Voltaire's fashion, not a
leaving them out of mind, in the world's fashion, but the putting a new
construction upon them, the taking them from under the old, traditional,
conventional point of view and placing them under a new one,—is the very
essence of the religious problem, as now presented; and only by efforts in
this direction can it receive a solution.

Again, in the same spirit in which she judges Bishop Colenso, Miss
Cobbe, like so many earnest liberals of our practical race, both here and in
America, herself sets vigorously about a positive reconstruction of religion,   670
about making a religion of the future out of hand, or at least setting about
making it. We must not rest, she and they are always thinking and saying,
in negative criticism, we must be creative and constructive; hence, we have

such works as her recent *Religious Duty,* and works still more considerable, perhaps, by others, which will be in every one's mind. These works
often have much ability; they often spring out of sincere convictions, and
a sincere wish to do good; and they sometimes, perhaps, do good. Their
fault is (if I may be permitted to say so) one which they have in common
with the British College of Health, in the New Road. Every one knows the
British College of Health; it is that building with the lion and the statue of   680
the Goddess Hygeia before it; at least, I am sure about the lion, though I
am not absolutely certain about the Goddess Hygeia. This building does
credit, perhaps, to the resources of Dr. Morrison and his disciples; but it
falls a good deal short of one's idea of what a British College of Health
ought to be. In England, where we hate public interference and love individual enterprise, we have a whole crop of places like the British College
of Health; the grand name without the grand thing. Unluckily, creditable
to individual enterprise as they are, they tend to impair our taste by making us forget what more grandiose, noble, or beautiful character properly
belongs to a public institution. The same may be said of the religions of the   690
future of Miss Cobbe and others. Creditable, like the British College of
Health, to the resources of their authors, they yet tend to make us forget
what more grandiose, noble, or beautiful character properly belongs to
religious constructions. The historic religions, with all their faults, have had
this; it certainly belongs to the religious sentiment, when it truly flowers,
to have this; and we impoverish our spirit if we allow a religion of the
future without it. What then is the duty of criticism here? To take the practical point of view, to applaud the liberal movement and all its works,—its
New Road religions of the future into the bargain,—for their general utility's sake? By no means; but to be perpetually dissatisfied with these   700
works, while they perpetually fall short of a high and perfect ideal.

For criticism, these are elementary laws; but they never can be popular,
and in this country they have been very little followed, and one meets with
immense obstacles in following them. That is a reason for asserting them
again and again. Criticism must maintain its independence of the practical
spirit and its aims. Even with well-meant efforts of the practical spirit it
must express dissatisfaction, if in the sphere of the ideal they seem impov-
erishing and limiting. It must not hurry on to the goal because of its practical importance. It must be patient, and know how to wait; and flexible,
and know how to attach itself to things and how to withdraw from them. It   710
must be apt to study and praise elements that for the fulness of spiritual
perfection are wanted, even though they belong to a power which in the
practical sphere may be maleficent. It must be apt to discern the spiritual

shortcomings or illusions of powers that in the practical sphere may be beneficent. And this without any notion of favouring or injuring, in the practical sphere, one power or the other; without any notion of playing off, in this sphere, one power against the other. When one looks, for instance, at the English Divorce Court,—an institution which perhaps has its practical conveniences, but which in the ideal sphere is so hideous; an institution which neither makes divorce impossible nor makes it decent, which allows a man to get rid of his wife, or a wife of her husband, but makes them drag one another first, for the public edification, through a mire of unutterable infamy,—when one looks at this charming institution, I say, with its crowded trials, its newspaper-reports, and its money-compensations, this institution in which the gross unregenerate British Philistine has indeed stamped an image of himself,—one may be permitted to find the marriage-theory of Catholicism refreshing and elevating. Or when Protestantism, in virtue of its supposed rational and intellectual origin, gives the law to criticism too magisterially, criticism may and must remind it that its pretensions, in this respect, are illusive and do it harm; that the Reformation was a moral rather than an intellectual event; that Luther's theory of grace no more exactly reflects the mind of the spirit than Bossuet's philosophy of history reflects it; and that there is no more antecedent probability of the Bishop of Durham's stock of ideas being agreeable to perfect reason than of Pope Pius the Ninth's. But criticism will not on that account forget the achievements of Protestantism in the practical and moral sphere; nor that, even in the intellectual sphere, Protestantism, though in a blind and stumbling manner, carried forward the Renascence, while Catholicism threw itself violently across its path.

I lately heard a man of thought and energy contrasting the want of ardour and movement which he now found amongst young men in this country with what he remembered in his own youth, twenty years ago. 'What reformers we were then!' he exclaimed; 'what a zeal we had! how we canvassed every institution in Church and State, and were prepared to remodel them all on first principles!' He was inclined to regret, as a spiritual flagging, the lull which he saw. I am disposed rather to regard it as a pause in which the turn to a new mode of spiritual progress is being accomplished. Everything was long seen, by the young and ardent amongst us, in inseparable connection with politics and practical life. We have pretty well exhausted the benefits of seeing things in this connection, we have got all that can be got by so seeing them. Let us try a more disinterested mode of seeing them; let us betake ourselves more to the serener life of the mind and spirit. This life, too, may have its excesses and dangers;

but they are not for us at present. Let us think of quietly enlarging our
stock of true and fresh ideas, and not, as soon as we get an idea or half an
idea, be running out with it into the street, and trying to make it rule there.
Our ideas will, in the end, shape the world all the better for maturing a
little. Perhaps in fifty years' time it will in the English House of Commons
be an objection to an institution that it is an anomaly, and my friend the
Member of Parliament will shudder in his grave. But let us in the mean-   76
while rather endeavour that in twenty years' time it may, in English literature, be an objection to a proposition that it is absurd. That will be a
change so vast, that the imagination almost fails to grasp it. *Ab integro
saeclorum nascitur ordo.*

If I have insisted so much on the course which criticism must take where
politics and religion are concerned, it is because, where these burning matters are in question, it is most likely to go astray. I have wished, above all,
to insist on the attitude which criticism should adopt towards things in general; on its right tone and temper of mind. But then comes another question
as to the subject-matter which literary criticism should most seek. Here, in   77
general, its course is determined for it by the idea which is the law of its
being; the idea of a disinterested endeavour to learn and propagate the
best that is known and thought in the world, and thus to establish a current
of fresh and true ideas. By the very nature of things, as England is not all
the world, much of the best that is known and thought in the world cannot
be of English growth, must be foreign; by the nature of things, again, it is
just this that we are least likely to know, while English thought is streaming in upon us from all sides, and takes excellent care that we shall not be
ignorant of its existence. The English critic of literature, therefore, must
dwell much on foreign thought, and with particular heed on any part of it,   78
which, while significant and fruitful in itself, is for any reason specially
likely to escape him. Again, judging is often spoken of as the critic's one
business; and so in some sense it is; but the judgment which almost
insensibly forms itself in a fair and clear mind, along with fresh knowledge,
is the valuable one; and thus knowledge, and ever fresh knowledge, must
be the critic's great concern for himself. And it is by communicating fresh
knowledge, and letting his own judgment pass along with it,—but insensibly, and in the second place, not the first, as a sort of companion and
clue, not as an abstract lawgiver,—that the critic will generally do most
good to his readers. Sometimes, no doubt, for the sake of establishing an   79
author's place in literature, and his relation to a central standard (and if
this is not done, how are we to get at our *best in the world*?) criticism
may have to deal with a subject-matter so familiar that fresh knowledge is

out of the question, and then it must be all judgment; an enunciation and detailed application of principles. Here the great safeguard is never to let oneself become abstract, always to retain an intimate and lively consciousness of the truth of what one is saying, and, the moment this fails us, to be sure that something is wrong. Still, under all circumstances, this mere judgment and application of principles is, in itself, not the most satisfactory work to the critic; like mathematics, it is tautological, and cannot well give us, like fresh learning, the sense of creative activity.

But stop, some one will say; all this talk is of no practical use to us whatever; this criticism of yours is not what we have in our minds when we speak of criticism; when we speak of critics and criticism, we mean critics and criticism of the current English literature of the day; when you offer to tell criticism its function, it is to this criticism that we expect you to address yourself. I am sorry for it, for I am afraid I must disappoint these expectations. I am bound by my own definition of criticism: *a disinterested endeavour to learn and propagate the best that is known and thought in the world.* How much of current English literature comes into this 'best that is known and thought in the world?' Not very much, I fear; certainly less, at this moment, than of the current literature of France or Germany. Well, then, am I to alter my definition of criticism, in order to meet the requirements of a number of practising English critics, who, after all, are free in their choice of a business? That would be making criticism lend itself just to one of those alien practical considerations, which, I have said, are so fatal to it. One may say, indeed, to those who have to deal with the mass—so much better disregarded—of current English literature, that they may at all events endeavour, in dealing with this, to try it, so far as they can, by the standard of the best that is known and thought in the world; one may say, that to get anywhere near this standard, every critic should try and possess one great literature, at least, besides his own; and the more unlike his own, the better. But, after all, the criticism I am really concerned with,—the criticism which alone can much help us for the future, the criticism which, throughout Europe, is at the present day meant, when so much stress is laid on the importance of criticism and the critical spirit, —is a criticism which regards Europe as being, for intellectual and spiritual purposes, one great confederation, bound to a joint action and working to a common result; and whose members have, for their proper outfit, a knowledge of Greek, Roman, and Eastern antiquity, and of one another. Special, local, and temporary advantages being put out of account, that modern nation will in the intellectual and spiritual sphere make most progress, which most thoroughly carries out this programme. And what is that but saying that we too, all of us, as individuals, the more thoroughly we carry it out, shall make the more progress?

There is so much inviting us!—what are we to take? what will nourish us in growth towards perfection? That is the question which, with the immense field of life and of literature lying before him, the critic has to answer; for himself first, and afterwards for others. In this idea of the critic's business the essays brought together in the following pages have had their origin; in this idea, widely different as are their subjects, they have, perhaps, their unity. 84

I conclude with what I said at the beginning: to have the sense of creative activity is the great happiness and the great proof of being alive, and it is not denied to criticism to have it; but then criticism must be sincere, simple, flexible, ardent, ever widening its knowledge. Then it may have, in no contemptible measure, a joyful sense of creative activity; a sense which a man of insight and conscience will prefer to what he might derive from a poor, starved, fragmentary, inadequate creation. And at some epochs no other creation is possible. 85

Still, in full measure, the sense of creative activity belongs only to genuine creation; in literature we must never forget that. But what true man of letters ever can forget it? It is no such common matter for a gifted nature to come into possession of a current of true and living ideas, and to produce amidst the inspiration of them, that we are likely to underrate it. The epochs of Æschylus and Shakspeare make us feel their pre-eminence. In an epoch like those is, no doubt, the true life of a literature; there is the promised land, towards which criticism can only beckon. That promised land it will not be ours to enter, and we shall die in the wilderness; but to have desired to enter it, to have saluted it from afar, is already, perhaps, 86 the best distinction among contemporaries; it will certainly be the best title to esteem with posterity,

THE LITERARY INFLUENCE
OF ACADEMIES

———————◄◆►———————

It is impossible to put down a book like the history of the French Academy, by Pellisson and D'Olivet, which M. Charles Livet has lately re-edited, without being led to reflect upon the absence, in our own country, of any institution like the French Academy, upon the probable causes of this absence, and upon its results. A thousand voices will be ready to tell us that this absence is a signal mark of our national superiority; that it is in great part owing to this absence that the exhilarating words of Lord Macaulay, lately given to the world by his very clever nephew, Mr. Trevelyan, are so profoundly true: 'It may safely be said that the literature now extant in the English language is of far greater value than all the literature which three hundred years ago was extant in all the languages of the world together.' I daresay this is so; only, remembering Spinoza's maxim that the two great banes of humanity are self-conceit and the laziness coming from self-conceit, I think it may do us good, instead of resting in our pre-eminence with perfect security, to look a little more closely why this is so, and whether it is so without any limitations.

10

31

But first of all I must give a very few words to the outward history of
the French Academy. About the year 1629, seven or eight persons in
Paris, fond of literature, formed themselves into a sort of little club to meet
at one another's houses and discuss literary matters. Their meetings got   2
talked of, and Cardinal Richelieu, then minister and all powerful, heard of
them. He himself had a noble passion for letters, and for all fine culture;
he was interested by what he heard of the nascent society. Himself a man
in the grand style, if ever man was, he had the insight to perceive what
a potent instrument of the grand style was here to his hand. It was the
beginning of a great century for France, the seventeenth; men's minds
were working, the French language was forming. Richelieu sent to ask the
members of the new society whether they would be willing to become a
body with a public character, holding regular meetings. Not without a
little hesitation,—for apparently they found themselves very well as they   3
were, and these seven or eight gentlemen of a social and literary turn were
not perfectly at their ease as to what the great and terrible minister could
want with them,—they consented. The favours of a man like Richelieu are
not easily refused, whether they are honestly meant or no; but this favour
of Richelieu's was meant quite honestly. The Parliament, however, had its
doubts of this. The Parliament had none of Richelieu's enthusiasm about
letters and culture; it was jealous of the apparition of a new public body in
the state; above all, of a body called into existence by Richelieu. The
King's letters patent, establishing and authorizing the new society, were
granted early in 1635; but, by the old constitution of France, these letters   4
patent required the verification of the Parliament. It was two years and a
half,—towards the autumn of 1637,—before the Parliament would give
it; and it then gave it only after pressing solicitations, and earnest assurances of the innocent intentions of the young Academy. Jocose people
said that this society, with its mission to purify and embellish the language,
filled with terror a body of lawyers like the French Parliament, the stronghold of barbarous jargon and of chicane.

This improvement of the language was in truth the declared grand aim
for the operations of the Academy. Its statutes of foundation, approved
by Richelieu before the royal edict establishing it was issued, say   5
expressly: 'The Academy's principal function shall be to work with all the
care and all the diligence possible at giving sure rules to our language, and
rendering it pure, eloquent, and capable of treating the arts and sciences.'
This zeal for making a nation's great instrument of thought,—its language,—correct and worthy, is undoubtedly a sign full of promise, a
weighty earnest of future power. It is said that Richelieu had it in his mind

that French should succeed Latin in its general ascendency, as Latin had succeeded Greek; if it was so, even this wish has to some extent been fulfilled. But, at any rate, the *ethical* influences of style in language,—its close relations, so often pointed out, with character,—are most important. Richelieu, a man of high culture, and, at the same time, of great character, felt them profoundly; and that he should have sought to regularise, strengthen, and perpetuate them by an institution for perfecting language, is alone a striking proof of his governing spirit and of his genius.

This was not all he had in his mind, however. The new Academy, now enlarged to a body of forty members, and meant to contain all the chief literary men of France, was to be a *literary tribunal*. The works of its members were to be brought before it previous to publication, were to be criticised by it, and finally, if it saw fit, to be published with its declared approbation. The works of other writers, not members of the Academy, might also, at the request of these writers themselves, be passed under the Academy's review. Besides this, in essays and discussions the Academy examined and judged works already published, whether by living or dead authors, and literary matters in general. The celebrated opinion on Corneille's *Cid,* delivered in 1637 by the Academy at Richelieu's urgent request, when this poem, which strongly occupied public attention, had been attacked by M. de Scudéry, shows how fully Richelieu designed his new creation to do duty as a supreme court of literature, and how early it in fact began to exercise this function. One [1] who had known Richelieu declared, after the Cardinal's death, that he had projected a yet greater institution than the Academy, a sort of grand European college of art, science, and literature, a Prytaneum, where the chief authors of all Europe should be gathered together in one central home, there to live in security, leisure, and honour;—that was a dream which will not bear to be pulled about too roughly. But the project of forming a high court of letters for France was no dream; Richelieu in great measure fulfilled it. This is what the Academy, by its idea, really is; this is what it has always tended to become; this is what it has, from time to time, really been; by being, or tending to be this, far more than even by what it has done for the language, it is of such importance in France. To give the law, the tone to literature, and that tone a high one, is its business. 'Richelieu meant it,' says M. Sainte-Beuve, 'to be a *haut jury*,'—a jury the most choice and authoritative that could be found on all important literary matters in question before the public; to be, as it in fact became in the latter half of the eighteenth century, 'a sovereign organ of opinion.' 'The duty of the Acad-

[1] La Mesnardière.

emy is,' says M. Renan, '*maintenir la délicatesse de l'esprit français*'—to keep the fine quality of the French spirit unimpaired; it represents a kind of '*maîtrise en fait de bon ton*'—the authority of a recognised master in matters of tone and taste. 'All ages,' says M. Renan again, 'have had their inferior literature; but the great danger of our time is that this inferior literature tends more and more to get the upper place. No one has the same advantage as the Academy for fighting against this mischief;' the Academy, which, as he says elsewhere, has even special facilities for 'creating a form of intellectual culture *which shall impose itself on all around.*' M. Sainte-Beuve and M. Renan are, both of them, very keen-sighted critics; and they show it signally by seizing and putting so prominently forward this character of the French Academy.

Such an effort to set up a recognised authority, imposing on us a high standard in matters of intellect and taste, has many enemies in human nature. We all of us like to go our own way, and not be forced out of the atmosphere of commonplace habitual to most of us;—'*was uns alle bändigt,*' says Goethe, '*DAS GEMEINE.*' We like to be suffered to lie comfortably in the old straw of our habits, especially of our intellectual habits, even though this straw may not be very clean and fine. But if the effort to limit this freedom of our lower nature finds, as it does and must find, enemies in human nature, it finds also auxiliaries in it. Out of the four great parts, says Cicero, of the *honestum,* or good, which forms the matter on which *officium,* or human duty, finds employment, one is the fixing of a *modus* and an *ordo,* a measure and an order, to fashion and wholesomely constrain our action, in order to lift it above the level it keeps if left to itself, and to bring it nearer to perfection. Man alone of living creatures, he says, goes feeling after '*quid sit* ordo, *quid sit quod* deceat, *in factis dictisque qui* modus—the discovery of an *order,* a law of *good taste,* a *measure* for his words and actions.' Other creatures submissively follow the law of their nature; man alone has an impulse leading him to set up some other law to control the bent of his nature.

This holds good, of course, as to moral matters, as well as intellectual matters: and it is of moral matters that we are generally thinking when we affirm it. But it holds good as to intellectual matters too. Now, probably, M. Sainte-Beuve had not these words of Cicero in his mind when he made, about the French nation, the assertion I am going to quote; but, for all that, the assertion leans for support, one may say, upon the truth conveyed in those words of Cicero, and wonderfully illustrates and confirms them. 'In France,' says M. Sainte-Beuve, 'the first consideration for us is not whether we are amused and pleased by a work of art or mind, nor is it whether we are touched by it. What we seek above all to learn is, whether *we were right* in being amused with it and in applauding it, and in being moved by it.' Those are very remarkable words, and they are, I believe, in the main quite true. A Frenchman has, to a considerable degree, what one may call a conscience in intellectual matters; he has an active belief that there is a right and a wrong in them, that he is bound to honour and obey the right, that he is disgraced by cleaving to the wrong. All the world has, or professes to have, this conscience in moral matters. The word *conscience* has become almost confined, in popular use, to the moral sphere, because this lively susceptibility of feeling is, in the moral sphere, so far more common than in the intellectual sphere; the livelier, in the moral sphere, this susceptibility is, the greater becomes a man's readiness to admit a high standard of action, an ideal authoritatively correcting his everyday moral habits; here, such willing admission of authority is due to sensitiveness of conscience. And a like deference to a standard higher than one's own habitual standard in intellectual matters, a like respectful recognition of a superior ideal, is caused, in the intellectual sphere, by sensitiveness of intelligence. Those whose intelligence is quickest, openest, most sensitive, are readiest with this deference; those whose intelligence is less delicate and sensitive are less disposed to it. Well, now we are on the road to see why the French have their Academy and we have nothing of the kind.

What are the essential characteristics of the spirit of our nation? Not, certainly, an open and clear mind, not a quick and flexible intelligence. Our greatest admirers would not claim for us that we have these in a preeminent degree; they might say that we had more of them than our detractors gave us credit for; but they would not assert them to be our essential characteristics. They would rather allege, as our chief spiritual characteristics, energy and honesty; and, if we are judged favorably and positively, not invidiously and negatively, our chief characteristics are, no doubt, these:—energy and honesty, not an open and clear mind, not a quick and flexible intelligence. Openness of mind and flexibility of intelligence were very signal characteristics of the Athenian people in ancient times; everybody will feel that. Openness of mind and flexibility of intelligence are remarkable characteristics of the French people in modern times; at any rate, they strikingly characterise them as compared with us; I think everybody, or almost everybody, will feel that. I will not now ask what more the Athenian or the French spirit has than this, nor what shortcomings either of them may have as a set-off against this; all I want

now to point out is that they have this, and that we have it in a much
lesser degree.

Let me remark, however, that not only in the moral sphere, but also in
the intellectual and spiritual sphere, energy and honesty are most important and fruitful qualities; that, for instance, of what we call genius energy
is the most essential part. So, by assigning to a nation energy and honesty
as its chief spiritual characteristics,—by refusing to it, as at all eminent
characteristics, openness of mind and flexibility of intelligence,—we do not
by any means, as some people might at first suppose, relegate its importance and its power of manifesting itself with effect from the intellectual
to the moral sphere. We only indicate its probable special line of successful activity in the intellectual sphere, and, it is true, certain imperfections
and failings to which, in this sphere, it will always be subject. Genius is
mainly an affair of energy, and poetry is mainly an affair of genius; therefore, a nation whose spirit is characterised by energy may well be eminent
in poetry;—and we have Shakspeare. Again, the highest reach of science
is, one may say, an inventive power, a faculty of divination, akin to the
highest power exercised in poetry; therefore, a nation whose spirit is characterised by energy may well be eminent in science;—and we have Newton. Shakspeare and Newton: in the intellectual sphere there can be no
higher names. And what that energy, which is the life of genius, above
everything demands and insists upon, is freedom; entire independence of
all authority, prescription, and routine,—the fullest room to expand as it
will. Therefore, a nation whose chief spiritual characteristic is energy, will
not be very apt to set up, in intellectual matters, a fixed standard, an
authority, like an academy. By this it certainly escapes certain real inconveniences and dangers, and it can, at the same time, as we have seen,
reach undeniably splendid heights in poetry and science. On the other
hand, some of the requisites of intellectual work are specially the affair
of quickness of mind and flexibility of intelligence. The form, the method
of evolution, the precision, the proportions, the relations of the parts to
the whole, in an intellectual work, depend mainly upon them. And these
are the elements of an intellectual work which are really most communicable from it, which can most be learned and adopted from it, which
have, therefore, the greatest effect upon the intellectual performance of
others. Even in poetry, these requisites are very important; and the poetry
of a nation, not eminent for the gifts on which they depend, will, more or
less, suffer by this shortcoming. In poetry, however, they are, after all,
secondary, and energy is the first thing; but in prose they are of first-rate
importance. In its prose literature, therefore, and in the routine of intel-

lectual work generally, a nation with no particular gifts for these will not be so successful. These are what, as I have said, can to a certain degree be learned and appropriated, while the free activity of genius cannot. Academies consecrate and maintain them, and, therefore, a nation with an eminent turn for them naturally establishes academies. So far as routine and authority tend to embarrass energy and inventive genius, academies may be said to be obstructive to energy and inventive genius, and, to this extent, to the human spirit's general advance. But then this evil is so much compensated by the propagation, on a large scale, of the mental aptitudes and demands which an open mind and a flexible intelligence naturally engender, genius itself, in the long run, so greatly finds its account in this propagation, and bodies like the French Academy have such power for promoting it, that the general advance of the human spirit is perhaps, on the whole, rather furthered than impeded by their existence.

How much greater is our nation in poetry than prose! how much better, in general, do the productions of its spirit show in the qualities of genius than in the qualities of intelligence! One may constantly remark this in the work of individuals; how much more striking, in general, does any Englishman,—of some vigour of mind, but by no means a poet,—seem in his verse than in his prose! His verse partly suffers from his not being really a poet, partly, no doubt, from the very same defects which impair his prose, and he cannot express himself with thorough success in it. But how much more powerful a personage does he appear in it, by dint of feeling, and of originality and movement of ideas, than when he is writing prose! With a Frenchman of like stamp, it is just the reverse: set him to write poetry, he is limited, artificial, and impotent; set him to write prose, he is free, natural, and effective. The power of French literature is in its prose-writers, the power of English literature is in its poets. Nay, many of the celebrated French poets depend wholly for their fame upon the qualities of intelligence which they exhibit,—qualities which are the distinctive support of prose; many of the celebrated English prose-writers depend wholly for their fame upon the qualities of genius and imagination which they exhibit,—qualities which are the distinctive support of poetry. But, as I have said, the qualities of genius are less transferable than the qualities of intelligence; less can be immediately learned and appropriated from their product; they are less direct and stringent intellectual agencies, though they may be more beautiful and divine. Shakspeare and our great Elizabethan group were certainly more gifted writers than Corneille and his group; but what was the sequel to this great literature, this literature of genius, as we may call it, stretching from Marlow to Milton? What did it

lead up to in English literature? To our provincial and second-rate literature of the eighteenth century. What, on the other hand, was the sequel to
the literature of the French 'great century,' to this literature of intelligence,
as, by comparison with our Elizabethan literature, we may call it; what did
it lead up to? To the French literature of the eighteenth century, one of
the most powerful and pervasive intellectual agencies that have ever
existed,—the greatest European force of the eighteenth century. In science, again, we had Newton, a genius of the very highest order, a type of
genius in science, if ever there was one. On the continent, as a sort of
counterpart to Newton, there was Leibnitz; a man, it seems to me (though
on these matters I speak under correction), of much less creative energy
of genius, much less power of divination than Newton, but rather a man
of admirable intelligence, a type of intelligence in science, if ever there was
one. Well, and what did they each directly lead up to in science? What was
the intellectual generation that sprang from each of them? I only repeat
what the men of science have themselves pointed out. The man of genius
was continued by the English analysts of the eighteenth century, comparatively powerless and obscure followers of the renowned master. The
man of intelligence was continued by successors like Bernouilli, Euler,
Lagrange, and Laplace, the greatest names in modern mathematics.

What I want the reader to see is, that the question as to the utility of
academies to the intellectual life of a nation is not settled when we say, for
instance: 'Oh, we have never had an academy, and yet we have, con-
fessedly, a very great literature.' It still remains to be asked: 'What sort
of a great literature? a literature great in the special qualities of genius,
or great in the special qualities of intelligence?' If in the former, it is by no
means sure that either our literature, or the general intellectual life of our
nation, has got already, without academies, all that academies can give.
Both the one and the other may very well be somewhat wanting in those
qualities of intelligence out of a lively sense for which a body like the
French Academy, as I have said, springs, and which such a body does a
great deal to spread and confirm. Our literature, in spite of the genius
manifested in it, may fall short in form, method, precision, proportions,
arrangement,—all of them, I have said, things where intelligence proper
comes in. It may be comparatively weak in prose, that branch of literature
where intelligence proper is, so to speak, all in all. In this branch it may
show many grave faults to which the want of a quick, flexible intelligence,
and of the strict standard which such an intelligence tends to impose,
makes it liable; it may be full of hap-hazard, crudeness, provincialism,
eccentricity, violence, blundering. It may be a less stringent and effective

intellectual agency, both upon our own nation and upon the world at large, than other literatures which show less genius, perhaps, but more intelligence.

The right conclusion certainly is that we should try, so far as we can, to make up our shortcomings; and that to this end, instead of always fixing our thoughts upon the points in which our literature, and our intellectual life generally, are strong, we should, from time to time, fix them upon those in which they are weak, and so learn to perceive clearly what we have to amend. What is our second great spiritual characteristic,—our honesty,—good for, if it is not good for this? But it will,—I am sure it will,—more and more, as time goes on, be found good for this.

Well, then, an institution like the French Academy,—an institution owing its existence to a national bent towards the things of the mind, towards culture, towards clearness, correctness, and propriety in thinking and speaking, and, in its turn, promoting this bent,—sets standards in a number of directions, and creates, in all these directions, a force of educated opinion, checking and rebuking those who fall below these standards, or who set them at nought. Educated opinion exists here as in France; but in France the Academy serves as a sort of centre and rallying-point to it, and gives it a force which it has not got here. Why is all the *journeyman-work* of literature, as I may call it, so much worse done here than it is in France? I do not wish to hurt any one's feelings; but surely this is so. Think of the difference between our books of reference and those of the French, between our biographical dictionaries (to take a striking instance) and theirs; think of the difference between the translations of the classics turned out for Mr. Bohn's library and those turned out for M. Nisard's collection! As a general rule, hardly any one amongst us, who knows French and German well, would use an English book of reference when he could get a French or German one; or would look at an English prose translation of an ancient author when he could get a French or German one. It is not that there do not exist in England, as in France, a number of people perfectly well able to discern what is good, in these things, from what is bad, and preferring what is good; but they are isolated, they form no powerful body of opinion, they are not strong enough to set a standard, up to which even the journeyman work of literature must be brought, if it is to be vendible. Ignorance and charlatanism in work of this kind are always trying to pass off their wares as excellent, and to cry down criticism as the voice of an insignificant, over-fastidious minority; they easily persuade the multitude that this is so when the minority is scattered about as it is here; not so easily when it is banded together as in the French

Academy. So, again, with freaks in dealing with language; certainly all such freaks tend to impair the power and beauty of language; and how far more common they are with us than with the French! To take a very familiar instance. Every one has noticed the way in which the *Times* chooses to spell the word 'diocese;' it always spells it dioce*ss*,[1] deriving it, I suppose, from *Zeus* and *census*. The *Journal des Débats* might just as well write 'diocess' instead of 'diocèse,' but imagine the *Journal des Débats* doing so! Imagine an educated Frenchman indulging himself in an orthographical antic of this sort, in face of the grave respect with which the Academy and its dictionary invest the French language! Some people will say these are little things; they are not; they are of bad example. They tend to spread the baneful notion that there is no such thing as a high, correct standard in intellectual matters; that every one may as well take his own way; they are at variance with the severe discipline necessary for all real culture; they confirm us in habits of wilfulness and eccentricity, which hurt our minds, and damage our credit with serious people. The late Mr. Donaldson was certainly a man of great ability, and I, who am not an Orientalist, do not pretend to judge his *Jashar:* but let the reader observe the form which a foreign Orientalist's judgment of it naturally takes. M. Renan calls it a *tentative malheureuse,* a failure, in short; this it may be, or it may not be; I am no judge. But he goes on: 'It is astonishing that a recent article' (in a French periodical, he means) 'should have brought forward as the last word of German exegesis a work like this, composed by a doctor of the University of Cambridge, and universally condemned by German critics.' You see what he means to imply: an extravagance of this sort could never have come from Germany, where there is a great force of critical opinion controlling a learned man's vagaries, and keeping him straight; it comes from the native home of intellectual eccentricity of all kinds,[2]—from England, from a doctor of the University of Cambridge;—and I daresay he would not expect much better things from a doctor of the University of Oxford. Again, after speaking of what Germany and France have done for the history of Mahomet: 'America and England,' M. Renan goes on, 'have also occupied themselves with Mahomet.' He mentions Washington Irving's 'Life of Mahomet,' which does not, he says, evince much of an historical sense, a *sentiment his-*

---

1 The *Times* has now (1868) abandoned this spelling and adopted the ordinary one.

2 A critic declares I am wrong in saying that M. Renan's language implies this. I still think that there is a shade, a *nuance* of expression, in M. Renan's language, which does imply this; but, I confess, the only person who can really settle such a question is M. Renan himself.

torique fort élevé; 'but,' he proceeds, 'this book shows a real progress,   370
when one thinks that in 1829 Mr. Charles Forster published two thick volumes, which enchanted the English *reverends,* to make out that Mahomet
was the little horn of the he-goat that figures in the eighth chapter of Daniel, and that the Pope was the great horn. Mr. Forster founded on this
ingenious parallel a whole philosophy of history, according to which the
Pope represented the Western corruption of Christianity, and Mahomet
the Eastern; thence the striking resemblances between Mahometanism and
Popery.' And in a note M. Renan adds: 'This is the same Mr. Charles
Forster who is the author of a mystification about the Sinaitic inscriptions,
in which he declares he finds the primitive language.' As much as to say: 380
'It is an Englishman, be surprised at no extravagance.' If these innuendoes
had no ground, and were made in hatred and malice, they would not be
worth a moment's attention; but they come from a grave Orientalist, on his
own subject, and they point to a real fact;—the absence, in this country,
of any force of educated literary and scientific opinion, making aberrations like those of the author of *The One Primeval Language* out of the
question. Not only the author of such aberrations, often a very clever man,
suffers by the want of check, by the not being kept straight, and spends
force in vain on a false road, which, under better discipline, he might have
used with profit on a true one; but all his adherents, both 'reverends' and   390
others, suffer too, and the general rate of information and judgment is in
this way kept low.

In a production which we have all been reading lately, a production
stamped throughout with a literary quality very rare in this country, and
of which I shall have a word to say presently,—*urbanity;* in this production, the work of a man never to be named by any son of Oxford without
sympathy, a man who alone in Oxford of his generation, alone of many
generations, conveyed to us in his genius that same charm, that same
ineffable sentiment, which this exquisite place itself conveys,—I mean Dr.
Newman,—an expression is frequently used which is more common in   400
theological than in literary language, but which seems to me fitted to be of
general service; the *note* of so and so, the note of catholicity, the note of
antiquity, the note of sanctity, and so on. Adopting this expressive word, I
say that in the bulk of the intellectual work of a nation which has no
centre, no intellectual metropolis like an academy, like M. Sainte-Beuve's
'sovereign organ of opinion,' like M. Renan's 'recognised authority in matters of tone and taste,'—there is observable a *note of provinciality.* Now
to get rid of provinciality is a certain stage of culture; a stage the positive
result of which we must not make of too much importance, but which is,

nevertheless, indispensable; for it brings us on to the platform where alone the best and highest intellectual work can be said fairly to begin. Work done after men have reached this platform is *classical;* and that is the only work which, in the long run, can stand. All the *scoriae* in the work of men of great genius who have not lived on this platform, are due to their not having lived on it. Genius raises them to it by moments, and the portions of their work which are immortal are done at these moments; but more of it would have been immortal if they had not reached this platform at moments only, if they had had the culture which makes men live there.

The less a literature has felt the influence of a supposed centre of correct information, correct judgment, correct taste, the more we shall find in it this note of provinciality. I have shown the note of provinciality as caused by remoteness from a centre of correct information. Of course, the note of provinciality from the want of a centre of correct taste is still more visible, and it is also still more common. For here great,—even the greatest,—powers of mind most fail a man. Great powers of mind will make him inform himself thoroughly, great powers of mind will make him think profoundly, even with ignorance and platitude all round him; but not even great powers of mind will keep his taste and style perfectly sound and sure, if he is left too much to himself, with no 'sovereign organ of opinion,' in these matters near him. Even men like Jeremy Taylor and Burke suffer here. Take this passage from Taylor's funeral sermon on Lady Carbery:—

'So have I seen a river, deep and smooth, passing with a still foot and a sober face, and paying to the *fiscus,* the great exchequer of the sea, a tribute large and full; and hard by it, a little brook, skipping and making a noise upon its unequal and neighbour bottom; and after all its talking and bragged motion, it paid to its common audit no more than the revenues of a little cloud or a contemptible vessel: so have I sometimes compared the issues of her religion to the solemnities and famed outsides of another's piety.'

That passage has been much admired, and, indeed, the genius in it is undeniable. I should say, for my part, that genius, the ruling divinity of poetry, had been too busy in it, and intelligence, the ruling divinity of prose, not busy enough. But can any one, with the best models of style in his head, help feeling the note of provinciality there, the want of simplicity, the want of measure, the want of just the qualities that make prose classical? If he does not feel what I mean, let him place beside the passage of Taylor this passage from the Panegyric of St. Paul, by Taylor's contemporary, Bossuet:—

'Il ira, cet ignorant dans l'art de bien dire, avec cette locution rude,

avec cette phrase qui sent l'étranger, il ira en cette Grèce polie, la mère   ₄₅₀
des philosophes et des orateurs; et malgré la résistance du monde, il y
établira plus d'Eglises que Platon n'y a gagné de disciples par cette élo-
quence qu'on a crue divine.'

There we have prose without the note of provinciality,—classical prose,
prose of the centre.

Or take Burke, our greatest English prose-writer, as I think; take expressions like this:—

'Blindfold themselves, like bulls that shut their eyes when they push,
they drive, by the point of their bayonets, their slaves, blindfolded, indeed,
no worse than their lords, to take their fictions for currencies, and to swal-   ₄₆₀
low down paper pills by thirty-four millions sterling at a dose.'

Or this:—

'They used it' (the royal name) 'as a sort of navel-string, to nourish
their unnatural offspring from the bowels of royalty itself. Now that the
monster can purvey for its own subsistence, it will only carry the mark
about it, as a token of its having torn the womb it came from.'

Or this:—

'Without one natural pang, he' (Rousseau) 'casts away, as a sort of
offal and excrement, the spawn of his disgustful amours, and sends his children to the hospital of foundlings.'   ₄₇₀

Or this:—

'I confess I never liked this continual talk of resistance and revolution,
or the practice of making the extreme medicine of the constitution its daily
bread. It renders the habit of society dangerously valetudinary; it is taking
periodical doses of mercury sublimate, and swallowing down repeated
provocatives of cantharides to our love of liberty.'

I say that is extravagant prose; prose too much suffered to indulge its
caprices; prose at too great a distance from the centre of good taste; prose,
in short, with the note of provinciality. People may reply, it is rich and
imaginative; yes, that is just it, it is *Asiatic* prose, as the ancient critics   ₄₈₀
would have said; prose somewhat barbarously rich and over-loaded. But
the true prose is Attic prose.

Well, but Addison's prose is Attic prose. Where, then, it may be asked,
is the note of provinciality in Addison? I answer, in the commonplace of
his ideas.[1] This is a matter worth remarking. Addison claims to take lead-

---

[1] A critic says this is paradoxical, and urges that many second-rate French academicians have uttered the most commonplace ideas possible. I agree that many second-rate French academicians have uttered the most commonplace ideas possible; but
Addison is not a second-rate man. He is a man of the order, I will not say of Pascal,

ing rank as a moralist. To do that, you must have ideas of the first order on your subject,—the best ideas, at any rate, attainable in your time,—as well as be able to express them in a perfectly sound and sure style. Else you show your distance from the centre of ideas by your matter; you are provincial by your matter, though you may not be provincial by your style. It is comparatively a small matter to express oneself well, if one will be content with not expressing much, with expressing only trite ideas; the problem is to express new and profound ideas in a perfectly sound and classical style. He is the true classic, in every age, who does that. Now Addison has not, on his subject of morals, the force of ideas of the moralists of the first class,—the classical moralists; he has not the best ideas attainable in or about his time, and which were, so to speak, in the air then, to be seized by the finest spirits; he is not to be compared for power, searchingness, or delicacy of thought, to Pascal, or La Bruyère, or Vauvenargues; he is rather on a level, in this respect, with a man like Marmontel. Therefore, I say, he has the note of provinciality as a moralist; he is provincial by his matter, though not by his style.

To illustrate what I mean by an example. Addison, writing as a moralist on fixedness in religious faith, says:—

'Those who delight in reading books of controversy do very seldom arrive at a fixed and settled habit of faith. The doubt which was laid revives again, and shows itself in new difficulties; and that generally for this reason,—because the mind, which is perpetually tossed in controversies and disputes, is apt to forget the reasons which had once set it at rest, and to be disquieted with any former perplexity when it appears in a new shape, or is started by a different hand.'

It may be said, that is classical English, perfect in lucidity, measure, and propriety. I make no objection; but, in my turn, I say that the idea expressed is perfectly trite and barren, and that it is a note of provinciality in Addison, in a man whom a nation puts forward as one of its great moralists, to have no profounder and more striking idea to produce on this great subject. Compare, on the same subject, these words of a moralist really of the first order, really at the centre by his ideas,—Joubert:—

---

but at any rate of La Bruyère and Vauvenargues; why does he not equal them? I say, because of the medium in which he finds himself, the atmosphere in which he lives and works; an atmosphere which tells unfavourably, or rather *tends* to tell unfavourably (for that is the truer way of putting it) either upon style or else upon ideas; tends to make even a man of great ability either a Mr. Carlyle or else a Lord Macaulay.

It is to be observed, however, that Lord Macaulay's style has in its turn suffered by his failure in ideas, and this cannot be said of Addison's.

'L'expérience de beaucoup d'opinions donne à l'esprit beaucoup de flexibilité et l'affermit dans celles qui'il croit les meilleures.' 520

With what a flash of light that touches the subject! how it sets us thinking! what a genuine contribution to moral science it is!

In short, where there is no centre like an academy, if you have genius and powerful ideas, you are apt not to have the best style going; if you have precision of style and not genius, you are apt not to have the best ideas going.

The provincial spirit, again, exaggerates the value of its ideas for want of a high standard at hand by which to try them. Or rather, for want of such a standard, it gives one idea too much prominence at the expense of others; it orders its ideas amiss; it is hurried away by fancies; it likes and dislikes 530 too passionately, too exclusively. Its admiration weeps hysterical tears, and its disapprobation foams at the mouth. So we get the *eruptive* and the *aggressive* manner in literature; the former prevails most in our criticism, the latter in our newspapers. For, not having the lucidity of a large and centrally placed intelligence, the provincial spirit has not its graciousness; it does not persuade, it makes war; it has not urbanity, the tone of the city, of the centre, the tone which always aims at a spiritual and intellectual effect, and not excluding the use of banter, never disjoins banter itself from politeness, from felicity. But the provincial tone is more violent, and seems to aim rather at an effect upon the blood and senses than upon the 540 spirit and intellect; it loves hard-hitting rather than persuading. The newspaper, with its party spirit, its thorough-goingness, its resolute avoidance of shades and distinctions, its short, highly-charged, heavy-shotted, articles, its style so unlike that style *lenis minimèque pertinax*—easy and not too violently insisting,—which the ancients so much admired, is its true literature; the provincial spirit likes in the newspaper just what makes the newspaper such bad food for it,—just what made Goethe say, when he was pressed hard about the immorality of Byron's poems, that, after all, they were not so immoral as the newspapers. The French talk of the *brutalité des journaux anglais*. What strikes them comes from the necessary inherent 550 tendencies of newspaper-writing not being checked in England by any centre of intelligent and urbane spirit, but rather stimulated by coming in contact with a provincial spirit. Even a newspaper like the *Saturday Review,* that old friend of all of us, a newspaper expressly aiming at an immunity from the common newspaper-spirit, aiming at being a sort of organ of reason,—and, by thus aiming, it merits great gratitude and has done great good,—even the *Saturday Review,* replying to some foreign criticism on our precautions against invasion, falls into a strain of this kind:—

'To do this' (to take these precautions) 'seems to us eminently worthy of a great nation, and to talk of it as unworthy of a great nation, seems to us eminently worthy of a great fool.'

There is what the French mean when they talk of the *brutalité des journaux anglais;* there is a style certainly as far removed from urbanity as possible,—a style with what I call the note of provinciality. And the same note may not unfrequently be observed even in the ideas of this newspaper, full as it is of thought and cleverness: certain ideas allowed to become fixed ideas, to prevail too absolutely. I will not speak of the immediate present, but, to go a little while back, it had the critic who so disliked the Emperor of the French; it had the critic who so disliked the subject of my present remarks—academies; it had the critic who was so fond of the German element in our nation, and, indeed, everywhere; who ground his teeth if one said *Charlemagne* instead of *Charles the Great,* and, in short, saw all things in Teutonism, as Malebranche saw all things in God. Certainly any one may fairly find faults in the Emperor Napoleon or in academies, and merit in the German element; but it is a note of the provincial spirit not to hold ideas of this kind a little more easily, to be so devoured by them, to suffer them to become crotchets.

In England there needs a miracle of genius like Shakspeare's to produce balance of mind, and a miracle of intellectual delicacy like Dr. Newman's to produce urbanity of style. How prevalent all round us is the want of balance of mind and urbanity of style! How much, doubtless, it is to be found in ourselves,—in each of us! but, as human nature is constituted, every one can see it clearest in his contemporaries. There, above all, we should consider it, because they and we are exposed to the same influences; and it is in the best of one's contemporaries that it is most worth considering, because one then most feels the harm it does, when one sees what they would be without it. Think of the difference between Mr. Ruskin exercising his genius, and Mr. Ruskin exercising his intelligence; consider the truth and beauty of this:—

'Go out, in the spring-time, among the meadows that slope from the shores of the Swiss lakes to the roots of their lower mountains. There, mingled with the taller gentians and the white narcissus, the grass grows deep and free; and as you follow the winding mountain paths, beneath arching boughs all veiled and dim with blossom,—paths that for ever droop and rise over the green banks and mounds sweeping down in scented undulation, steep to the blue water studded here and there with new-mown heaps, filling all the air with fainter sweetness,—look up towards the higher hills, where the waves of everlasting green roll silently into their long inlets among the shadows of the pines. . . . . .'

There is what the genius, the feeling, the temperament in Mr. Ruskin, the original and incommunicable part, has to do with; and how exquisite it is! All the critic could possibly suggest, in the way of objection, would be, perhaps, that Mr. Ruskin is there trying to make prose do more than it can perfectly do; that what he is there attempting he will never, except in poetry, be able to accomplish to his own entire satisfaction: but he accomplishes so much that the critic may well hesitate to suggest even this. Place beside this charming passage another,—a passage about Shakspeare's names, where the intelligence and judgment of Mr. Ruskin, the acquired, trained, communicable part in him, are brought into play,—and see the difference:—

'Of Shakspeare's names I will afterwards speak at more length; they are curiously—often barbarously—mixed out of various traditions and languages. Three of the clearest in meaning have been already noticed. Desdemona—"δυσδαιμονία," *miserable fortune*—is also plain enough. Othello is, I believe, "the careful"; all the calamity of the tragedy arising from the single flaw and error in his magnificently collected strength. Ophelia, "serviceableness," the true, lost wife of Hamlet, is marked as having a Greek name by that of her brother, Laertes; and its signification is once exquisitely alluded to in that brother's last word of her, where her gentle preciousness is opposed to the uselessness of the churlish clergy:— "A *ministering* angel shall my sister be, when thou liest howling." Hamlet is, I believe, connected in some way with "homely," the entire event of the tragedy turning on betrayal of home duty. Hermione (ἕρμα), "pillar-like" (ἣ εἶδος ἔχε χρυσῆς Ἀφροδίτης); Titania (τιτήνη), "the queen"; Benedict and Beatrice, "blessed and blessing"; Valentine and Proteus, "enduring or strong" (*valens*), and "changeful." Iago and Iachimo have evidently the same root—probably the Spanish Iago, Jacob, "the supplanter." '

Now, really, what a piece of extravagance all that is! I will not say that the meaning of Shakspeare's names (I put aside the question as to the correctness of Mr. Ruskin's etymologies) has no effect at all, may be entirely lost sight of; but to give it that degree of prominence is to throw the reins to one's whim, to forget all moderation and proportion, to lose the balance of one's mind altogether. It is to show in one's criticism, to the highest excess, the note of provinciality.

Again, there is Mr. Palgrave, certainly endowed with a very fine critical tact; his *Golden Treasury* abundantly proves it. The plan of arrangement

which he devised for that work, the mode in which he followed his plan
out, nay, one might even say, merely the juxtaposition, in pursuance of it,
of two such pieces as those of Wordsworth and Shelley which form the
285th and 286th in his collection, show a delicacy of feeling in these matters which is quite indisputable and very rare. And his notes are full of
remarks which show it too. All the more striking, conjoined with so much
justness of perception, are certain freaks and violences in Mr. Palgrave's
criticism, mainly imputable, I think, to the critic's isolated position in this
country, to his feeling himself too much left to take his own way, too much
without any central authority representing high culture and sound judgment, by which he may be, on the one hand, confirmed as against the
ignorant, on the other, held in respect when he himself is inclined to take
liberties. I mean such things as this note on Milton's line,—

'The great Emathian conqueror bade spare' . . .

'When Thebes was destroyed, Alexander ordered the house of Pindar to
be spared. *He was as incapable of appreciating the poet as Louis XIV.
of appreciating Racine; but even the narrow and barbarian mind of
Alexander could understand the advantage of a showy act of homage to
poetry.*' A note like that I call a freak or a violence; if this disparaging
view of Alexander and Louis XIV., so unlike the current view, is wrong,—
if the current view is, after all, the truer one of them,—the note is a freak.
But, even if its disparaging view is right, the note is a violence; for, abandoning the true mode of intellectual action—persuasion, the instilment of
conviction,—it simply astounds and irritates the hearer by contradicting
without a word of proof or preparation, his fixed and familiar notions;
and this is mere violence. In either case, the fitness, the measure, the cen-
trality, which is the soul of all good criticism, is lost, and the note of
provinciality shows itself.

Thus in the famous *Handbook,* marks of a fine power of perception are
everywhere discernible, but so, too, are marks of the want of sure balance,
of the check and support afforded by knowing one speaks before good and
severe judges. When Mr. Palgrave dislikes a thing, he feels no pressure
constraining him either to try his dislike closely or to express it moder-
ately; he does not mince matters, he gives his dislike all its own way; both
his judgment and his style would gain if he were under more restraint.
'The style which has filled London with the dead monotony of Gower or
Harley Streets, or the pale commonplace of Belgravia, Tyburnia and Ken-
sington; which has pierced Paris and Madrid with the feeble frivolities of
the Rue Rivoli and the Strada de Toledo.' He dislikes the architecture of

the Rue Rivoli, and he puts it on a level with the architecture of Belgravia and Gower Street; he lumps them all together in one condemnation, he loses sight of the shade, the distinction, which is everything here; the distinction, namely, that the architecture of the Rue Rivoli expresses show, splendour, pleasure,—unworthy things, perhaps, to express alone and for their own sakes, but it expresses them; whereas the architecture of Gower Street and Belgravia merely expresses the impotence of the architect to express anything. Then, as to style: 'sculpture which stands in a contrast with Woolner hardly more shameful than diverting.' . . . 'passing from Davy or Faraday to the art of the mountebank or the science of the spirit-rapper.' . . . 'it is the old, old story with Marochetti, the frog, trying to blow himself out to bull dimensions. He may puff and be puffed, but he will never do it.' We all remember that shower of amenities on poor M. Marochetti. Now, here Mr. Palgrave himself enables us to form a contrast which lets us see just what the presence of an academy does for style; for he quotes a criticism by M. Gustave Planche on this very M. Marochetti. M. Gustave Planche was a critic of the very first order, a man of strong opinions, which he expressed with severity; he, too, condemns M. Marochetti's work, and Mr. Palgrave calls him as a witness to back what he has himself said; certainly Mr. Palgrave's translation will not exaggerate M. Planche's urbanity in dealing with M. Marochetti, but, even in this translation, see the difference in sobriety, in measure, between the critic writing in Paris and the critic writing in London:—

'These conditions are so elementary, that I am at a perfect loss to comprehend how M. Marochetti has neglected them. There are soldiers here like the leaden playthings of the nursery: it is almost impossible to guess whether there is a body beneath the dress. We have here no question of style, not even of grammar; it is nothing beyond mere matter of the alphabet of art. To break these conditions is the same as to be ignorant of spelling.'

That is really more formidable criticism than Mr. Palgrave's, and yet in how perfectly temperate a style! M. Planche's advantage is, that he feels himself to be speaking before competent judges, that there is a force of cultivated opinion for him to appeal to. Therefore, he must not be extravagant, and he need not storm; he must satisfy the reason and taste,—that is his business. Mr. Palgrave, on the other hand, feels himself to be speaking before a promiscuous multitude, with the few good judges so scattered through it as to be powerless; therefore, he has no calm confidence and no self-control; he relies on the strength of his lungs; he knows that big words impose on the mob, and that, even if he is outrageous, most of his audience are apt to be a great deal more so.[1]

Again, the first two volumes of Mr. Kinglake's *Invasion of the Crimea* were certainly among the most successful and renowned English books of our time. Their style was one of the most renowned things about them, and yet how conspicuous a fault in Mr. Kinglake's style is this over-charge of which I have been speaking! Mr. James Gordon Bennett, of the *New York Herald,* says, I believe, that the highest achievement of the human intellect is what he calls 'a good editorial.' This is not quite so; but, if it were so, on what a height would these two volumes by Mr. Kinglake stand! I have already spoken of the Attic and the Asiatic styles; besides these, there is the Corinthian style. That is the style for 'a good editorial,' and Mr. Kinglake has really reached perfection in it. It has not the warm glow, blithe movement, and soft pliancy of life, as the Attic style has; it has not the over-heavy richness and encumbered gait of the Asiatic style; it has glitter without warmth, rapidity without ease, effectiveness without charm. Its characteristic is, that it has no *soul;* all it exists for, is to get its ends, to make its points, to damage its adversaries, to be admired, to triumph. A style so bent on effect at the expense of soul, simplicity, and delicacy; a style so little studious of the charm of the great models; so far from classic truth and grace, must surely be said to have the note of provinciality. Yet Mr. Kinglake's talent is a really eminent one, and so in harmony with our intellectual habits and tendencies, that, to the great bulk of English people, the faults of his style seem its merits; all the more needful that criticism should not be dazzled by them.

We must not compare a man of Mr. Kinglake's literary talent with French writers like M. de Bazancourt. We must compare him with M. Thiers. And what a superiority in style has M. Thiers from being formed in a good school, with severe traditions, wholesome restraining influences! Even in this age of Mr. James Gordon Bennett, his style has nothing Corinthian about it, its lightness and brightness make it almost Attic. It is not quite Attic, however; it has not the infallible sureness of Attic taste. Sometimes his head gets a little hot with the fumes of patriotism, and then he crosses the line, he loses perfect measure, he declaims, he raises a momentary smile. France condemned 'a être l'effroi du monde *dont elle pourrait être l'amour,*'—Caesar, whose exquisite simplicity M. Thiers so much admires, would not have written like that. There is, if I may be

---

[1] When I wrote this I had before me the first edition of Mr. Palgrave's *Handbook.* I am bound to say that in the second edition much strong language has been expunged, and what remains, softened.

allowed to say so, the slightest possible touch of fatuity in such language,— of that failure in good sense which comes from too warm a self-satisfaction. But compare this language with Mr. Kinglake's Marshal St. Arnaud— 'dismissed from the presence' of Lord Raglan or Lord Stratford, 'cowed and pressed down' under their 'stern reproofs,' or under 'the majesty of the great Elchi's Canning brow and tight, merciless lips!' The failure in good sense and good taste there reaches far beyond what the French mean by *fatuity;* they would call it by another word, a word expressing blank defect of intelligence, a word for which we have no exact equivalent in English,— *bête.* It is the difference between a venial, momentary, good-tempered excess, in a man of the world, of an amiable and social weakness,—vanity; and a serious, settled, fierce, narrow, provincial misconception of the whole relative value of one's own things and the things of others. So baneful to the style of even the cleverest man may be the total want of checks.

In all I have said, I do not pretend that the examples given prove my rule as to the influence of academies; they only illustrate it. Examples in plenty might very likely be found to set against them; the truth of the rule depends, no doubt, on whether the balance of all the examples is in its favour or not; but actually to strike this balance is always out of the question. Here, as everywhere else, the rule, the idea, if true, commends itself to the judicious, and then the examples make it clearer still to them. This is the real use of examples, and this alone is the purpose which I have meant mine to serve. There is also another side to the whole question,— as to the limiting and prejudicial operation which academies may have; but this side of the question it rather behoves the French, not us, to study.

The reader will ask for some practical conclusion about the establishment of an Academy in this country, and perhaps I shall hardly give him the one he expects. But nations have their own modes of acting, and these modes are not easily changed; they are even consecrated, when great things have been done in them. When a literature has produced Shakspeare and Milton, when it has even produced Barrow and Burke, it cannot well abandon its traditions; it can hardly begin, at this late time of day, with an institution like the French Academy. I think academies with a limited, special, scientific scope, in the various lines of intellectual work,—academies like that of Berlin, for instance,—we with time may, and probably shall, establish. And no doubt they will do good; no doubt the presence of such influential centres of correct information will tend to raise the standard amongst us for what I have called the *journeyman-work* of literature, and to free us from the scandal of such biographical dictionaries as Chalmers's, or such translations as a recent one of Spinoza, or perhaps, such philological freaks

760

770

780

790

as Mr. Forster's about the one primeval language. But an academy quite like the French Academy, a sovereign organ of the highest literary opinion, a recognised authority in matters of intellectual tone and taste, we shall hardly have, and perhaps we ought not to wish to have it. But then every one amongst us with any turn for literature will do well to remember to what shortcomings and excesses, which such an academy tends to correct, we are liable; and the more liable, of course, for not having it. He will do well constantly to try himself in respect of these, steadily to widen his culture, severely to check in himself the provincial spirit; and he will do this the better the more he keeps in mind that all mere glorification by ourselves of ourselves or our literature, in the strain of what, at the beginning of these remarks, I quoted from Lord Macaulay, is both vulgar, and, besides being vulgar, retarding.

MAURICE DE GUÉRIN

I will not presume to say that I now know the French language well; but at a time when I knew it even less well than at present,—some fifteen years ago,—I remember pestering those about me with this sentence, the rhythm of which had lodged itself in my head, and which, with the strangest pronunciation possible, I kept perpetually declaiming: *'Les dieux jaloux ont enfoui quelque part les témoignages de la descendance des choses; mais au bord de quel Océan ont-ils roulé la pierre qui les couvre, ô Macarée!'*

These words come from a short composition called the *Centaur,* of which the author, Georges-Maurice de Guérin, died in the year 1839, at the age of twenty-eight, without having published anything. In 1840, 10 Madame Sand brought out the *Centaur* in the *Revue des Deux Mondes,* with a short notice of its author, and a few extracts from his letters. A year or two afterwards she reprinted these at the end of a volume of her novels; and there it was that I fell in with them. I was so much struck with the *Centaur* that I waited anxiously to hear something more of its author, and of what he had left; but it was not till the other day—twenty years after the first publication of the *Centaur* in the *Revue des Deux Mondes,* that my anxiety was satisfied. At the end of 1860 appeared two volumes with the title, *Maurice de Guérin, Reliquiae,* containing the *Centaur,* several poems of Guérin, his journals, and a number of his letters, collected and edited by a devoted friend, M. Trebutien, and preceded by a notice of Guérin by the first of living critics, M. Sainte-Beuve.

The grand power of poetry is its interpretative power; by which I mean, not a power of drawing out in black and white an explanation of the mystery of the universe, but the power of so dealing with things as to awaken in us a wonderfully full, new, and intimate sense of them, and of our relations with them. When this sense is awakened in us, as to objects without us, we feel ourselves to be in contact with the essential nature of those objects, to be no longer bewildered and oppressed by them, but to have their secret, and to be in harmony with them; and this feeling calms and satisfies us as no other can. Poetry, indeed, interprets in another way besides this; but one of its two ways of interpreting, of exercising its highest power, is by awakening this sense in us. I will not now inquire whether this sense is illusive, whether it can be proved not to be illusive, whether it does absolutely make us possess the real nature of things; all I say is, that poetry can awaken it in us, and that to awaken it is one of the highest powers of poetry. The interpretations of science do not give us this intimate sense of objects as the interpretations of poetry give it; they appeal to a limited faculty, and not to the whole man. It is not Linnaeus, or Cavendish, or Cuvier who gives us the true sense of animals, or water, or plants, who seizes their secret for us, who makes us participate in their life; it is Shakspeare, with his

> 'daffodils
> That come before the swallow dares, and take
> The winds of March with beauty;'

it is Wordsworth, with his

> 'voice . . . heard
> In spring-time from the cuckoo-bird,
> Breaking the silence of the seas
> Among the farthest Hebrides,'

it is Keats, with his

> 'moving waters at their priestlike task
> Of cold ablution round Earth's human shores;'

it is Châteaubriand, with his *'cîme indéterminée des forêts;'* it is Senancour, with his mountain birch-tree: *'Cette écorce blanche, lisse et crevassée; cette tige agreste; ces branches qui s'inclinent vers la terre; la mobilité des feuilles, et tout cet abandon, simplicité de la nature, attitude des déserts.'*

Eminent manifestations of this magical power of poetry are very rare and very precious: the compositions of Guérin manifest it, I think, in singular eminence. Not his poems, strictly so called,—his verse,—so much as his prose; his poems in general take for their vehicle that favourite metre of French poetry, the Alexandrine; and, in my judgment, I confess they have thus, as compared with his prose, a great disadvantage to start with. In prose, the character of the vehicle for the composer's thoughts is not determined beforehand; every composer has to make his own vehicle; and who has ever done this more admirably than the great prose-writers of France,—Pascal, Bossuet, Fénelon, Voltaire? But in verse the composer has (with comparatively narrow liberty of modification) to accept his vehicle ready-made; it is therefore of vital importance to him that he should find at his disposal a vehicle adequate to convey the highest matters of poetry. We may even get a decisive test of the poetical power of a language and nation by ascertaining how far the principal poetical vehicle which they have employed, how far (in plainer words) the established national metre for high poetry, is adequate or inadequate. It seems to me that the established metre of this kind in France,—the Alexandrine,—is inadequate; that as a vehicle for high poetry it is greatly inferior to the hexameter or to the iambics of Greece (for example), or to the blank verse of England. Therefore the man of genius who uses it is at a disadvantage as compared with the man of genius who has for conveying his thoughts a more adequate vehicle, metrical or not. Racine is at a disadvantage as compared with Sophocles or Shakspeare, and he is likewise at a disadvantage as compared with Bossuet.

The same may be said of our own poets of the eighteenth century, a century which gave them as the main vehicle for their high poetry a metre inadequate (as much as the French Alexandrine, and nearly in the same way) for this poetry,—the ten-syllable couplet. It is worth remarking, that the English poet of the eighteenth century whose compositions wear best and give one the most entire satisfaction,—Gray,—hardly uses that couplet at all: this abstinence, however, limits Gray's productions to a few short compositions, and (exquisite as these are) he is a poetical nature repressed and without free issue. For English poetical production on a great scale, for an English poet deploying all the forces of his genius, the ten-syllable couplet was, in the eighteenth century, the established, one may almost say the inevitable, channel. Now this couplet, admirable (as Chaucer uses it) for story-telling not of the epic pitch, and often admirable for a few lines even in poetry of a very high pitch, is for continuous use in poetry of this latter kind, inadequate. Pope, in his *Essay on Man,* is thus at a disadvantage compared with Lucretius in his poem on Nature: Lucretius has an adequate vehicle, Pope has not. Nay, though Pope's genius for didactic poetry was not less than that of Horace, while his satirical power was certainly greater, still one's taste receives, I cannot but think, a certain satisfaction when one reads the Epistles and Satires of Horace, which it fails to receive when one reads the Satires and Epistles of Pope. Of such avail is the superior adequacy of the vehicle used to compensate even an inferiority of genius in the user! In the same way Pope is at a disadvantage as compared with Addison. The best of Addison's composition (the 'Coverley Papers' in the *Spectator,* for instance) wears better than the best of Pope's, because Addison has in his prose an intrinsically better vehicle for his genius than Pope in his couplet. But Bacon has no such advantage over Shakspeare; nor has Milton, writing prose (for no contemporary English prose-writer must be matched with Milton except Milton himself), any such advantage over Milton writing verse: indeed, the advantage here is all the other way.

It is in the prose remains of Guérin,—his journals, his letters, and the striking composition which I have already mentioned, the *Centaur,*—that his extraordinary gift manifests itself. He has a truly interpretative faculty; the most profound and delicate sense of the life of Nature, and the most exquisite felicity in finding expressions to render that sense. To all who love poetry, Guérin deserves to be something more than a name; and I shall try, in spite of the impossibility of doing justice to such a master of expression by translations, to make English readers see for themselves how gifted an organisation his was, and how few artists have received from Nature a more magical faculty of interpreting her.

In the winter of the year 1832 there was collected in Brittany, around the well-known Abbé Lamennais, a singular gathering. At a lonely place, La Chênaie, he had founded a religious retreat, to which disciples, attracted by his powers or by his reputation, repaired. Some came with the intention of preparing themselves for the ecclesiastical profession; others merely to profit by the society and discourse of so distinguished a master. Among the inmates were men whose names have since become known to all Europe,—Lacordaire and M. de Montalembert; there were others, who have acquired a reputation, not European, indeed, but considerable,—the Abbé Gerbet, the Abbé Rohrbacher; others, who have never quitted the shade of private life. The winter of 1832 was a period of crisis in the religious world of France: Lamennais's rupture with Rome, the condemnation of his opinions by the Pope, and his revolt against that condemnation, were imminent. Some of his followers, like Lacordaire, had already resolved not to cross the Rubicon with their leader, not to go into rebellion against Rome; they were preparing to separate from him. The society of La Chênaie was soon to dissolve; but, such as it is shown to us for a moment, with its voluntary character, its simple and severe life in common, its mixture of lay and clerical members, the genius of its chiefs, the sincerity of its disciples,—above all, its paramount fervent interest in matters of spiritual and religious concernment,—it offers a most instructive spectacle. It is not the spectacle we most of us think to find in France, the France we have imagined from common English notions, from the streets of Paris, from novels; it shows us how, wherever there is greatness like that of France, there are, as its foundation, treasures of fervour, pure-mindedness, and spirituality somewhere, whether we know of them or not;—a store of that which Goethe calls *Halt;*—since greatness can never be founded upon frivolity and corruption.

On the evening of the 18th of December in this year 1832, M. de Lamennais was talking to those assembled in the sitting-room of La Chênaie of his recent journey to Italy. He talked with all his usual animation; 'but,' writes one of his hearers, a Breton gentleman, M. de Marzan, 'I soon became inattentive and absent, being struck with the reserved attitude of a young stranger some twenty-two years old, pale in face, his black hair already thin over his temples, with a southern eye, in which brightness and melancholy were mingled. He kept himself somewhat aloof, seeming to avoid notice rather than to court it. All the old faces of friends which I found about me at this my re-entry into the circle of La Chênaie failed to occupy me so much as the sight of this stranger, looking on, listening, observing, and saying nothing.'

The unknown was Maurice de Guérin. Of a noble but poor family, having lost his mother at six years old, he had been brought up by his father, a man saddened by his wife's death, and austerely religious, at the château of Le Cayla, in Languedoc. His childhood was not gay; he had not the society of other boys; and solitude, the sight of his father's gloom, and the habit of accompanying the curé of the parish on his rounds among the sick and dying, made him prematurely grave and familiar with sorrow. He went to school at first at Toulouse, then at the Collège Stanislas at Paris, with a temperament almost as unfit as Shelley's for common school life. His youth was ardent, sensitive, agitated, and unhappy. In 1832 he procured admission to La Chênaie to brace his spirit by the teaching of Lamennais, and to decide whether his religious feelings would determine themselves into a distinct religious vocation. Strong and deep religious feelings he had, implanted in him by nature, developed in him by the circumstances of his childhood; but he had also (and here is the key to his character) that temperament which opposes itself to the fixedness of a religious vocation, or of any vocation of which fixedness is an essential attribute; a temperament mobile, inconstant, eager, thirsting for new impressions, abhorring rules, aspiring to a 'renovation without end;' a temperament common enough among artists, but with which few artists, who have it to the same degree as Guérin, unite a seriousness and a sad intensity like his. After leaving school, and before going to La Chênaie, he had been at home at Le Cayla with his sister Eugénie (a wonderfully gifted person, whose genius so competent a judge as M. Sainte-Beuve is inclined to pronounce even superior to her brother's) and his sister Eugénie's friends. With one of these friends he had fallen in love,—a slight and transient fancy, but which had already called his poetical powers into exercise; and his poems and fragments, in a certain green note-book (*le Cahier Vert*) which he long continued to make the depository of his thoughts, and which became famous among his friends, he brought with him to La Chênaie. There he found among the younger members of the Society several who, like himself, had a secret passion for poetry and literature; with these he became intimate, and in his letters and journal we find him occupied, now with a literary commerce established with these friends, now with the fortunes, fast coming to a crisis, of the Society, and now with that for the sake of which he came to La Chênaie,—his religious progress and the state of his soul.

On Christmas-day, 1832, having been then three weeks at La Chênaie, he writes thus of it to a friend of his family, M. de Bayne:—

'La Chênaie is a sort of oasis in the midst of the steppes of Brittany. In front of the château stretches a very large garden cut in two by a terrace with a lime avenue, at the end of which is a tiny chapel. I am extremely fond of this little oratory, where one breathes a twofold peace,—the peace of solitude and the peace of the Lord. When spring comes we shall walk to prayers between two borders of flowers. On the east side, and only a few yards from the château, sleeps a small mere between two woods, where the birds in warm weather sing all day long; and then,—right, left, on all sides, —woods, woods, everywhere woods. It looks desolate just now that all is bare and the woods are rust-colour, and under this Brittany sky, which is always clouded and so low that it seems as if it were going to fall on your head; but as soon as spring comes the sky raises itself up, the woods come to life again, and everything will be full of charm.'

Of what La Chênaie will be when spring comes he has a foretaste on the 3rd of March.

'To-day' (he writes in his journal) 'has enchanted me. For the first time for a long while the sun has shown himself in all his beauty. He has made the buds of the leaves and flowers swell, and he has waked up in me a thousand happy thoughts. The clouds assume more and more their light and graceful shapes, and are sketching, over the blue sky, the most charming fancies. The woods have not yet got their leaves, but they are taking an indescribable air of life and gaiety, which gives them quite a new physiognomy. Everything is getting ready for the great festival of Nature.'

Storm and snow adjourn this festival a little longer. On the 11th of March he writes:—

'It has snowed all night. I have been to look at our primroses; each of them had its small load of snow, and was bowing its head under its burden. These pretty flowers, with their rich yellow colour, had a charming effect under their white hoods. I saw whole tufts of them roofed over by a single block of snow; all these laughing flowers thus shrouded and leaning one upon another, made one think of a group of young girls surprised by a shower, and sheltering under a white apron.'

The burst of spring comes at last, though late. On the 5th of April we find Guérin 'sitting in the sun to penetrate himself to the very marrow with the divine spring.' On the 3rd of May, 'one can actually *see* the progress of the green; it has made a start from the garden to the shrubberies, it is getting the upper hand all along the mere; it leaps, one may say, from tree to tree, from thicket to thicket, in the fields and on the hill-sides; and I can see it already arrived at the forest edge and beginning to spread itself over the broad back of the forest. Soon it will have overrun everything as far as the eye can reach, and all those wide spaces between here and the horizon will be moving and sounding like one vast sea, a sea of emerald.'

Finally, on the 16th of May, he writes to M. de Bayne that 'the gloomy and bad days,—bad because they bring temptation by their gloom,—are, thanks to God and the spring, over; and I see approaching a long file of shining and happy days, to do me all the good in the world. This Brittany of ours,' he continues, 'gives one the idea of the greyest and most wrinkled old woman possible suddenly changed back by the touch of a fairy's wand into a girl of twenty, and one of the loveliest in the world; the fine weather has so decked and beautified the dear old country.' He felt, however, the cloudiness and cold of the 'dear old country' with all the sensitiveness of a child of the South. 'What a difference,' he cries, 'between the sky of Brittany, even on the finest day, and the sky of our South! Here the summer has, even on its highdays and holidays, something mournful, overcast, and stinted about it. It is like a miser who is making a show; there is a niggardliness in his magnificence. Give me our Languedoc sky, so bountiful of light, so blue, so largely vaulted!' And somewhat later, complaining of the short and dim sunlight of a February day in Paris, 'What a sunshine,' he exclaims, 'to gladden eyes accustomed to all the wealth of light of the South!—*aux larges et libérales effusions de lumière du ciel du Midi.*'

In the long winter of La Chênaie his great resource was literature. One has often heard that an educated Frenchman's reading seldom goes much beyond French and Latin, and that he makes the authors in these two languages his sole literary standard. This may or may not be true of Frenchmen in general, but there can be no question as to the width of the reading of Guérin and his friends, and as to the range of their literary sympathies. One of the circle, Hippolyte la Morvonnais,—a poet who published a volume of verse, and died in the prime of life,—had a passionate admiration for Wordsworth, and had even, it is said, made a pilgrimage to Rydal Mount to visit him; and in Guérin's own reading I find, besides the French names of Bernardin de St. Pierre, Châteaubriand, Lamartine, and Victor Hugo, the names of Homer, Dante, Shakspeare, Milton, and Goethe; and he quotes both from Greek and from English authors in the original. His literary tact is beautifully fine and true. 'Every poet,' he writes to his sister, 'has his own art of poetry written on the ground of his own soul; there is no other. Be constantly observing Nature in her smallest details, and then write as the current of your thoughts guides you;—that is all.' But with all this freedom from the bondage of forms and rules, Guérin marks with perfect precision the faults of the *free* French literature of his time,—the *littérature facile,*—and judges the romantic school and its prospects like a master: 'that youthful literature which has put forth all its blossom prematurely, and has left itself a helpless prey to the returning frost, stimulated as it has been by the burning sun of our century, by this atmosphere charged with a perilous heat, which has over-hastened every sort of development, and will most likely reduce to a handful of grains the harvest of our age.' And the popular authors,—those 'whose name appears once and disappears for ever, whose books, unwelcome to all serious people, welcome to the rest of the world, to novelty-hunters and novel-readers, fill with vanity these vain souls, and then, falling from hands heavy with the languor of satiety, drop for ever into the gulf of oblivion;' and those, more noteworthy, 'the writers of books celebrated, and, as works of art, deserving celebrity, but which have in them not one grain of that hidden manna, not one of those sweet and wholesome thoughts which nourish the human soul and refresh it when it is weary,'—these he treats with such severity that he may in some sense be described, as he describes himself, as 'invoking with his whole heart a classical restoration.' He is best described, however, not as a partisan of any school, but as an ardent seeker for that mode of expression which is the most natural, happy, and true. He writes to his sister Eugénie:—

'I want you to reform your system of composition; it is too loose, too vague, too Lamartinian. Your verse is too sing-song; it does not *talk* enough. Form for yourself a style of your own, which shall be your real expression. Study the French language by attentive reading, making it your care to remark constructions, turns of expression, delicacies of style, but without ever adopting the manner of any master. In the works of these masters we must learn our language, but we must use it each in our own fashion.' [1]

It was not, however, to perfect his literary judgment that Guérin came to La Chênaie. The religious feeling, which was as much a part of his essence as the passion for Nature and the literary instinct, shows itself at moments jealous of these its rivals, and alarmed at their predominance. Like all powerful feelings, it wants to exclude every other feeling and to be absolute. One Friday in April, after he has been delighting himself with the shapes of the clouds and the progress of the spring, he suddenly bethinks himself that the day is Good Friday, and exclaims in his diary:—

'My God, what is my soul about that it can thus go running after such fugitive delights on Good Friday, on this day all filled with thy death and our redemption? There is in me I know not what damnable spirit, that awakens in me strong discontents, and is for ever prompting me to rebel against the holy exercises and the devout collectedness of soul which are the meet preparation for these great solemnities of our faith. Oh how well can I trace here the old leaven, from which I have not yet perfectly cleared my soul!'

And again, in a letter to M. de Marzan: 'Of what, my God, are we made,' he cries, 'that a little verdure and a few trees should be enough to rob us of our tranquillity and to distract us from thy love?' And writing, three days after Easter Sunday, in his journal, he records the reception at La Chênaie of a fervent neophyte, in words which seem to convey a covert blame of his own want of fervency:—

'Three days have passed over our heads since the great festival. One

---

[1] Part of these extracts date from a time a little after Guérin's residence at La Chênaie; but already, amidst the readings and conversations of La Chênaie, his literary judgment was perfectly formed.

anniversary the less for us yet to spend of the death and resurrection of our Saviour! Every year thus bears away with it its solemn festivals; when will the everlasting festival be here? I have been witness of a most touching sight; François has brought us one of his friends whom he has gained to the faith. This neophyte joined us in our exercises during the Holy week, and on Easter-day he received the communion with us. François was in raptures. It is a truly good work which he has thus done. François is quite young, hardly twenty years old; M. de la M. is thirty, and is married. There is something most touching and beautifully simple in M. de la M. letting himself thus be brought to God by quite a young man; and to see friendship, on François's side, thus doing the work of an Apostle, is not less beautiful and touching.'

Admiration for Lamennais worked in the same direction with this feeling. Lamennais never appreciated Guérin; his combative, rigid, despotic nature, of which the characteristic was energy, had no affinity with Guérin's elusive, undulating, impalpable nature, of which the characteristic was delicacy. He set little store by his new disciple, and could hardly bring himself to understand what others found so remarkable in him, his own genuine feeling towards him being one of indulgent compassion. But the intuition of Guérin, more discerning than the logic of his master, instinctively felt what there was commanding and tragic in Lamennais's character, different as this was from his own; and some of his notes are among the most interesting records of Lamennais which remain.

' "Do you know what it is," M. Féli [1] said to us on the evening of the day before yesterday, "which makes man the most suffering of all creatures? It is that he has one foot in the finite and the other in the infinite, and that he is torn asunder, not by four horses, as in the horrible old time, but between two worlds." Again he said to us as we heard the clock strike: "If that clock knew that it was to be destroyed the next instant, it would still keep striking its hour until that instant arrived. My children, be as the clock; whatever may be going to happen to you, strike always your hour." '

Another time Guérin writes,

'To-day M. Féli startled us. He was sitting behind the chapel, under the two Scotch firs; he took his stick and marked out a grave on the turf, and said to Elie, "It is there I wish to be buried, but no tombstone! only a simple hillock of grass. Oh, how well I shall be there!" Elie thought he had a presentiment that his end was near. This is not the first time he has been visited by such a presentiment; when he was setting out for Rome,

---

[1] The familiar name given to M. de Lamennais by his followers at La Chênaie.

he said to those here: "I do not expect ever to come back to you; you must [370]
do the good which I have failed to do." He is impatient for death.'

Overpowered by the ascendency of Lamennais, Guérin, in spite of his
hesitations, in spite of his confession to himself that, 'after a three weeks'
close scrutiny of his soul, in the hope of finding the pearl of a religious
vocation hidden in some corner of it,' he had failed to find what he sought,
took, at the end of August, 1833, a decisive step. He joined the religious
order which Lamennais had founded. But at this very moment the deep-
ening displeasure of Rome with Lamennais determined the Bishop of
Rennes to break up, in so far as it was a religious congregation, the Society
of La Chênaie, to transfer the novices to Ploërmel, and to place them under [380]
other superintendence. In September, Lamennais, 'who had not yet ceased,'
writes M. de Marzan, a fervent Catholic, 'to be a Christian and a priest,
took leave of his beloved colony of La Chênaie, with the anguish of a general who disbands his army down to the last recruit, and withdraws annihilated from the field of battle.' Guérin went to Ploërmel. But here, in the
seclusion of a real religious house, he instantly perceived how alien to a
spirit like his,—a spirit which, as he himself says somewhere, 'had need of
the open air, wanted to see the sun and the flowers,'—was the constraint
and monotony of a monastic life, when Lamennais's genius was no longer
present to enliven this life for him. On the 7th of October he renounced [390]
the novitiate, believing himself a partisan of Lamennais in his quarrel with
Rome, reproaching the life he had left with demanding passive obedience
instead of trying 'to put in practice the admirable alliance of order with
liberty, and of variety with unity,' and declaring that, for his part, he preferred taking the chances of a life of adventure to submitting himself to
be *garotté par un réglement,*—tied hand and foot by a set of rules.' In real
truth, a life of adventure, or rather a life free to wander at its own will, was
that to which his nature irresistibly impelled him.

For a career of adventure, the inevitable field was Paris. But before this
career began, there came a stage, the smoothest, perhaps, and the most [400]
happy in the short life of Guérin. M. la Morvonnais, one of his La Chênaie
friends,—some years older than Guérin, and married to a wife of singular
sweetness and charm,—had a house by the seaside at the mouth of one of
the beautiful rivers of Brittany, the Arguenon. He asked Guérin, when he
left Ploërmel, to come and stay with him at this place, called Le Val de
l'Arguenon, and Guérin spent the winter of 1833–4 there. I grudge every
word about Le Val and its inmates which is not Guérin's own, so charming
is the picture he draws of them, so truly does his talent find itself in its best
vein as he draws it.

'How full of goodness' (he writes in his journal of the 7th of December) 'is Providence to me! For fear the sudden passage from the mild and temperate air of a religious life to the torrid clime of the world should be too trying for my soul, it has conducted me, after I have left my sacred shelter, to a house planted on the frontier between the two regions, where, without being in solitude, one is not yet in the world; a house whose windows look on the one side towards the plain where the tumult of men is rocking, on the other towards the wilderness where the servants of God are chanting. I intend to write down the record of my sojourn here, for the days here spent are full of happiness, and I know that in the time to come I shall often turn back to the story of these past felicities. A man, pious, and a poet; a woman, whose spirit is in such perfect sympathy with his that you would say they had but one being between them; a child, called Marie like her mother, and who sends, like a star, the first rays of her love and thought through the white cloud of infancy; a simple life in an old-fashioned house; the ocean, which comes morning and evening to bring us its harmonies; and lastly, a wanderer who descends from Carmel and is going on to Babylon, and who has laid down at this threshold his staff and his sandals, to take his seat at the hospitable table;—here is matter to make a biblical poem of, if I could only describe things as I can feel them!'

Every line written by Guérin during this stay at Le Val is worth quoting, but I have only room for one extract more:—

'Never' (he writes, a fortnight later, on the 20th of December), 'never have I tasted so inwardly and deeply the happiness of home-life. All the little details of this life which in their succession make up the day, are to me so many stages of a continuous charm carried from one end of the day to the other. The morning greeting, which in some sort renews the pleasure of the first arrival, for the words with which one meets are almost the same, and the separation at night, through the hours of darkness and uncertainty, does not ill represent longer separations; then breakfast, during which you have the fresh enjoyment of having met together again; the stroll afterwards, when we go out and bid Nature good-morning; the return and setting to work in an old panelled chamber looking out on the sea, inaccessible to all the stir of the house, a perfect sanctuary of labour; dinner, to which we are called, not by a bell, which reminds one too much of school or a great house, but by a pleasant voice; the gaiety, the merriment, the talk flitting from one subject to another and never dropping so long as the meal lasts; the crackling fire of dry branches to which we draw our chairs directly afterwards, the kind words that are spoken round the warm flame which sings while we talk; and then, if it is fine, the walk by

the seaside, when the sea has for its visitors a mother with her child in her 450
arms, this child's father and a stranger, each of these two last with a stick
in his hand; the rosy lips of the little girl, which keep talking at the same
time with the waves,—now and then tears shed by her and cries of childish
fright at the edge of the sea; our thoughts, the father's and mine, as we
stand and look at the mother and child smiling at one another, or at the
child in tears and the mother trying to comfort it by her caresses and
exhortations; the Ocean, going on all the while rolling up his waves and
noises; the dead boughs which we go and cut, here and there, out of the
copse-wood, to make a quick and bright fire when we get home,—this
little taste of the woodman's calling which brings us closer to Nature and 460
makes us think of M. Féli's eager fondness for the same work; the hours
of study and poetical flow which carry us to supper-time; this meal, which
summons us by the same gentle voice as its predecessor, and which is
passed amid the same joys, only less loud, because evening sobers everything, tones everything down; then our evening, ushered in by the blaze of
a cheerful fire, and which with its alternations of reading and talking brings
us at last to bed-time:—to all the charms of a day so spent add the dreams
which follow it, and your imagination will still fall far short of these home-
joys in their delightful reality.'

I said the foregoing should be my last extract, but who could resist this 470
picture of a January evening on the coast of Brittany?—

'All the sky is covered over with grey clouds just silvered at the edges.
The sun, who departed a few minutes ago, has left behind him enough
light to temper for awhile the black shadows, and to soften down, as it
were, the approach of night. The winds are hushed, and the tranquil ocean
sends up to me, when I go out on the doorstep to listen, only a melodious
murmur, which dies away in the soul like a beautiful wave on the beach.
The birds, the first to obey the nocturnal influence, make their way
towards the woods, and you hear the rustle of their wings in the clouds.
The copses which cover the whole hill-side of Le Val, which all the day- 480
time are alive with the chirp of the wren, the laughing whistle of the woodpecker,[1] and the different notes of a multitude of birds, have no longer
any sound in their paths and thickets, unless it be the prolonged high call
of the blackbirds at play with one another and chasing one another, after
all the other birds have their heads safe under their wings. The noise of
man, always the last to be silent, dies gradually out over the face of the
fields. The general murmur fades away, and one hears hardly a sound

---

[1] 'The woodpecker *laughs*,' says White of Selborne; and here is Guérin, in Brittany,
confirming his testimony.

except what comes from the villages and hamlets, in which, up till far into the night, there are cries of children and barking of dogs. Silence wraps me round; everything seeks repose except this pen of mine, which perhaps disturbs the rest of some living atom asleep in a crease of my note-book, for it makes its light scratching as it puts down these idle thoughts. Let it stop, then! for all I write, have written, or shall write, will never be worth setting against the sleep of an atom.'

On the 1st of February we find him in a lodging at Paris. 'I enter the world' (such are the last words written in his journal at Le Val) 'with a secret horror.' His outward history for the next five years is soon told. He found himself in Paris, poor, fastidious, and with health which already, no doubt, felt the obscure presence of the malady of which he died,—consumption. One of his Brittany acquaintances introduced him to editors, tried to engage him in the periodical literature of Paris; and so unmistakeable was Guérin's talent, that even his first essays were immediately accepted. But Guérin's genius was of a kind which unfitted him to get his bread in this manner. At first he was pleased with the notion of living by his pen; '*je n'ai qu'à écrire,*' he says to his sister,—'I have only got to write.' But to a nature like his, endued with the passion for perfection, the necessity to produce, to produce constantly, to produce whether in the vein or out of the vein, to produce something good or bad or middling, as it may happen, but at all events *something,*—is the most intolerable of tortures. To escape from it he betook himself to that common but most perfidious refuge of men of letters, that refuge to which Goldsmith and poor Hartley Coleridge had betaken themselves before him,—the profession of teaching. In September, 1834, he procured an engagement at the Collège Stanislas, where he had himself been educated. It was vacation-time, and all he had to do was to teach a small class composed of boys who did not go home for the holidays,—in his own words, 'scholars left like sick sheep in the fold, while the rest of the flock are frisking in the fields.' After the vacation he was kept on at the Collège as a supernumerary. 'The master of the fifth class has asked for a month's leave of absence; I am taking his place, and by this work I get one hundred francs (£4.). I have been looking about for pupils to give private lessons to, and I have found three or four. Schoolwork and private lessons together fill my day from half-past seven in the morning till half-past nine at night. The college dinner serves me for breakfast, and I go and dine in the evening at twenty-four *sous,* as a young man beginning life should.' To better his position in the hierarchy of public teachers it was necessary that he should take the degree of *agrégé ès-lettres,* corresponding to our degree of Master of Arts; and to his heavy work in teaching, there was thus added that of preparing for a severe examination. The drudgery of this life was very irksome to him, although less insupportable than the drudgery of the profession of letters; inasmuch as to a sensitive man, like Guérin, to silence his genius is more tolerable than to hackney it. Still the yoke wore him deeply, and he had moments of bitter revolt; he continued, however, to bear it with resolution, and on the whole with patience, for four years. On the 15th of November, 1838, he married a young Creole lady of some fortune, Mademoiselle Caroline de Gervain, 'whom,' to use his own words, 'Destiny, who loves these surprises, has wafted from the farthest Indies into my arms.' The marriage was happy; and it ensured to Guérin liberty and leisure; but now 'the blind Fury with the abhorred shears' was hard at hand. Consumption declared itself in him: 'I pass my life,' he writes with his old playfulness and calm, to his sister, on the 8th of April, 1839, 'within my bed curtains, and wait patiently enough, thanks to Caro's [1] goodness, books, and dreams, for the recovery which the sunshine is to bring with it.' In search of this sunshine he was taken to his native country, Languedoc, but in vain. He died at Le Cayla on the 19th of July, 1839.

The vicissitudes of his inward life during these five years were more considerable. His opinions and tastes underwent great, or what seem to be great, changes. He came to Paris the ardent partisan of Lamennais: even in April, 1834, after Rome had finally condemned Lamennais,—'To-night there will go forth from Paris,' he writes, 'with his face set to the west, a man whose every step I would fain follow, and who returns to the desert for which I sigh. M. Féli departs this evening for La Chênaie.' But in October, 1835,—'I assure you,' he writes to his sister, 'I am at last weaned from M. de Lamennais; one does not remain a babe and suckling for ever; I am perfectly freed from his influence.' There was a greater change than this. In 1834 the main cause of Guérin's aversion to the literature of the French romantic school, was that this literature, having had a religious origin, had ceased to be religious: 'it has forgotten,' he says, 'the house and the admonitions of its Father.' But his friend, M. de Marzan, tells us of a 'deplorable revolution' which, by 1836, had taken place in him. Guérin had become intimate with the chiefs of this very literature; he no longer went to church; 'the bond of a common faith, in which our friendship had its birth, existed between us no longer.' Then, again, 'this interregnum was not destined to last.' Reconverted to his old faith by suffering and by the pious efforts of his sister Eugénie, Guérin died a Catholic. His feelings about society underwent a like change. After 'entering the world

[1] His wife.

with a secret horror,' after congratulating himself when he had been some months at Paris on being 'disengaged from the social tumult, out of the reach of those blows which, when I live in the thick of the world, bruise me, irritate me, or utterly crush me,' M. Sainte-Beuve tells us of him, two years afterwards, appearing in society 'a man of the world, elegant, even fashionable; a talker who could hold his own against the most brilliant talkers of Paris.'

In few natures, however, is there really such essential consistency as in Guérin's. He says of himself, in the very beginning of his journal: 'I owe everything to poetry, for there is no other name to give to the sum total of my thoughts; I owe to it whatever I now have pure, lofty, and solid in my soul; I owe to it all my consolations in the past; I shall probably owe to it my future.' Poetry, the poetical instinct, was indeed the basis of his nature; but to say so thus absolutely is not quite enough. One aspect of poetry fascinated Guérin's imagination and held it prisoner. Poetry is the interpretress of the natural world, and she is the interpretress of the moral world; it was as the interpretress of the natural world that she had Guérin for her mouthpiece. To make magically near and real the life of Nature, and man's life only so far as it is a part of that Nature, was his faculty; a faculty of naturalistic, not of moral interpretation. This faculty always has for its basis a peculiar temperament, an extraordinary delicacy of organisation and susceptibility to impressions; in exercising it the poet is in a great degree passive (Wordsworth thus speaks of a *wise passiveness*); he aspires to be a sort of human Æolian-harp, catching and rendering every rustle of Nature. To assist at the evolution of the whole life of the world is his craving, and intimately to feel it all:

> . . 'the glow, the thrill of life,
> Where, where do these abound

is what he asks: he resists being riveted and held stationary by any single impression, but would be borne on for ever down an enchanted stream. He goes into religion and out of religion, into society and out of society, not from the motives which impel men in general, but to feel what it is all like; he is thus hardly a moral agent, and, like the passive and ineffectual Uranus of Keats's poem, he may say:

> . . . . 'I am but a voice;
> My life is but the life of winds and tides;
> No more than winds and tides can I avail.'

He hovers over the tumult of life, but does not really put his hand to it.

No one has expressed the aspirations of this temperament better than Guérin himself. In the last year of his life he writes:—

'I return, as you see, to my old brooding over the world of Nature, that line which my thoughts irresistibly take; a sort of passion which gives me enthusiasm, tears, bursts of joy, and an eternal food for musing; and yet I am neither philosopher, nor naturalist, nor anything learned whatsoever. There is one word which is the God of my imagination, the tyrant, I ought rather to say, that fascinates it, lures it onward, gives it work to do without ceasing, and will finally carry it I know not where; the word *life*.' And in one place in his journal he says:—

'My imagination welcomes every dream, every impression, without attaching itself to any, and goes on for ever seeking something new.'

And again, in another:—

'The longer I live, and the clearer I discern between true and false in society, the more does the inclination to live, not as a savage or a misanthrope, but as a solitary man on the frontiers of society, on the outskirts of the world, gain strength and grow in me. The birds come and go and make nests around our habitations, they are fellow-citizens of our farms and hamlets with us; but they take their flight in a heaven which is boundless, but the hand of God alone gives and measures to them their daily food, but they build their nests in the heart of the thick bushes, or hang them in the height of the trees. So would I, too, live, hovering round society, and having always at my back a field of liberty vast as the sky.'

In the same spirit he longed for travel. 'When one is a wanderer,' he writes to his sister, 'one feels that one fulfils the true condition of humanity.' And the last entry in his journal is—'The stream of travel is full of delight. Oh, who will set me adrift on this Nile!'

Assuredly it is not in this temperament that the active virtues have their rise. On the contrary, this temperament, considered in itself alone, indisposes for the discharge of them. Something morbid and excessive, as manifested in Guérin, it undoubtedly has. In him, as in Keats, and as in another youth of genius, whose name, but the other day unheard of, Lord Houghton has so gracefully written in the history of English poetry,—David Gray,— the temperament, the talent itself, is deeply influenced by their mysterious malady; the temperament is *devouring;* it uses vital power too hard and too fast, paying the penalty in long hours of unutterable exhaustion and in premature death. The intensity of Guérin's depression is described to us by Guérin himself with the same incomparable touch with which he describes happier feelings; far oftener than any pleasurable sense of his gift he has 'the sense profound, near, immense, of my misery, of my inward poverty.' And again: 'My inward misery gains upon me; I no longer dare look within.' And on another day of gloom he does look within, and here is the terrible analysis:—

'Craving, unquiet, seeing only by glimpses, my spirit is stricken by all those ills which are the sure fruit of a youth doomed never to ripen into manhood. I grow old and wear myself out in the most futile mental strainings, and make no progress. My head seems dying, and when the wind blows I fancy I feel it, as if I were a tree, blowing through a number of withered branches in my top. Study is intolerable to me, or rather it is quite out of my power. Mental work brings on, not drowsiness, but an irritable and nervous disgust which drives me out, I know not where, into the streets and public places. The Spring, whose delights used to come every year stealthily and mysteriously to charm me in my retreat, crushes me this year under a weight of sudden hotness. I should be glad of any event which delivered me from the situation in which I am. If I were free I would embark for some distant country where I could begin life anew.'

Such is the temperament in the frequent hours when the sense of its own weakness and isolation crushes it to the ground. Certainly it was not for Guérin's happiness, or for Keats's, as men count happiness, to be as they were. Still the very excess and predominance of their temperament has given to the fruits of their genius an unique brilliancy and flavour. I have said that poetry interprets in two ways; it interprets by expressing with magical felicity the physiognomy and movement of the outward world, and it interprets by expressing, with inspired conviction, the ideas and laws of the inward world of man's moral and spiritual nature. In other words, poetry is interpretative both by having *natural magic* in it, and by having *moral profundity*. In both ways it illuminates man; it gives him a satisfying sense of reality; it reconciles him with himself and the universe. Thus Æschylus's 'δράσαντι παθεῖν' and his 'ἀνήριθμον γέλασμα' are alike interpretative. Shakspeare interprets both when he says,

> 'Full many a glorious morning have I seen,
> Flatter the mountain-tops with sovran eye;'

and when he says,

> 'There's a divinity that shapes our ends,
> Rough-hew them as we will.'

These great poets unite in themselves the faculty of both kinds of interpretation, the naturalistic and the moral. But it is observable that in the poets who unite both kinds, the latter (the moral) usually ends by making itself the master. In Shakspeare the two kinds seem wonderfully to balance one another; but even in him the balance leans; his expression tends to become too little sensuous and simple, too much intellectualised. The same thing may be yet more strongly affirmed of Lucretius and of Wordsworth. In Shelley there is not a balance of the two gifts, nor even a co-existence of them, but there is a passionate straining after them both, and this is what makes Shelley, as a man, so interesting: I will not now inquire how much Shelley achieves as a poet, but whatever he achieves, he in general fails to achieve natural magic in his expression; in Mr. Palgrave's charming *Treasury* may be seen a gallery of his failures.[1] But in Keats and Guérin, in whom the faculty of naturalistic interpretation is overpoweringly predominant, the natural magic is perfect; when they speak of the world they speak like Adam naming by divine inspiration the creatures; their expression corresponds with the thing's essential reality. Even between Keats and Guérin, however, there is a distinction to be drawn. Keats has, above all, a sense of what is pleasureable and open in the life of Nature; for him she is the *Alma Parens:* his expression has, therefore, more than Guérin's, something genial, outward, and sensuous. Guérin has above all a sense of what there is adorable and secret in the life of Nature; for him she is the *Magna Parens;* his expression has, therefore, more than Keats's, something mystic, inward, and profound.

So he lived like a man possessed; with his eye not on his own career, not on the public, not on fame, but on the Isis whose veil he had uplifted. He published nothing: 'There is more power and beauty,' he writes, 'in the well-kept secret of one's-self and one's thoughts, than in the display of a whole heaven that one may have inside one.' 'My spirit,' he answers the friends who urge him to write, 'is of the home-keeping order, and has no fancy for adventure; literary adventure is above all distasteful to it; for this, indeed (let me say so without the least self-sufficiency), it has a contempt. The literary career seems to me unreal, both in its own essence and in the rewards which one seeks from it, and therefore fatally marred by a secret absurdity.' His acquaintances, and among them distinguished men of letters, full of admiration for the originality and delicacy of his talent laughed at his self-depreciation, warmly assured him of his powers. He received their assurances with a mournful incredulity, which contrasts curiously with the self-assertion of poor David Gray, whom I just now men-

[1] Compare, for example, his 'Lines Written in the Euganean Hills,' with Keats's 'Ode to Autumn' (*Golden Treasury,* pp. 256, 284). The latter piece *renders* Nature; the former *tries to render* her. I will not deny, however, that Shelley has natural magic in his rhythm; what I deny is, that he has it in his language. It always seems to me that the right sphere for Shelley's genius was the sphere of music, not of poetry; the medium of sounds he can master, but to master the more difficult medium of words he has neither intellectual force enough nor sanity enough.

tioned. 'It seems to me intolerable,' he writes, 'to appear to men other than
one appears to God. My worst torture at this moment is the overestimate
which generous friends form of me. We are told that at the last judgment
the secret of all consciences will be laid bare to the universe; would that
mine were so this day, and that every passer-by could see me as I am!'
'High above my head,' he says at another time, 'far, far away, I seem to
hear the murmur of that world of thought and feeling to which I aspire so
often, but where I can never attain. I think of those of my own age who
have wings strong enough to reach it, but I think of them without jealousy,
and as men on earth contemplate the elect and their felicity.' And, criticising his own composition, 'When I begin a subject, my self-conceit' (says
this exquisite artist) 'imagines I am doing wonders; and when I have
finished, I see nothing but a wretched made-up imitation, composed of
odds and ends of colour stolen from other people's palettes, and tastelessly
mixed together on mine.' Such was his *passion for perfection,* his disdain
for all poetical work not perfectly adequate and felicitous. The magic of
expression to which by the force of this passion he won his way, will make
the name of Maurice de Guérin remembered in literature.

I have already mentioned the *Centaur,* a sort of prose poem by Guérin,
which Madame Sand published after his death. The idea of this composition came to him, M. Sainte-Beuve says, in the course of some visits which
he made with his friend, M. Trebutien, a learned antiquarian, to the
Museum of Antiquities in the Louvre. The free and wild life which the
Greeks expressed by such creations as the Centaur had, as we might well
expect, a strong charm for him; under the same inspiration he composed
a *Bacchante,* which was meant by him to form part of a prose poem on
the adventures of Bacchus in India. Real as was the affinity which Guérin's
nature had for these subjects, I doubt whether, in treating them, he would
have found the full and final employment of his talent. But the beauty of
his *Centaur* is extraordinary; in its whole conception and expression this
piece has in a wonderful degree that natural magic of which I have said
so much, and the rhythm has a charm which bewitches even a foreigner.
An old Centaur on his mountain is supposed to relate to Melampus, a
human questioner, the life of his youth. Untranslateable as the piece is,
I shall conclude with some extracts from it:—

THE CENTAUR

'I had my birth in the caves of these mountains. Like the stream of this
valley, whose first drops trickle from some weeping rock in a deep cavern,

the first moment of my life fell in the darkness of a remote abode, and without breaking the silence. When our mothers draw near to the time of their delivery, they withdraw to the caverns, and in the depth of the lone-liest of them, in the thickest of its gloom, bring forth, without uttering a plaint, a fruit silent as themselves. Their puissant milk makes us surmount, without weakness or dubious struggle, the first difficulties of life; and yet we leave our caverns later than you your cradles. The reason is that we have a doctrine that the early days of existence should be kept apart and enshrouded, as days filled with the presence of the gods. Nearly the whole term of my growth was passed in the darkness where I was born. The recesses of my dwelling ran so far under the mountain, that I should not have known on which side was the exit, had not the winds, when they sometimes made their way through the opening, sent fresh airs in, and a sudden trouble. Sometimes, too, my mother came back to me, having about her the odours of the valleys, or streaming from the waters which were her haunt. Her returning thus, without a word said of the valleys or the rivers, but with the emanations from them hanging about her, troubled my spirit, and I moved up and down restlessly in my darkness. "What is it," I cried, "this outside world whither my mother is borne, and what reigns there in it so potent as to attract her so often?" At these moments my own force began to make me unquiet. I felt in it a power which could not remain idle; and betaking myself either to toss my arms or to gallop backwards and forwards in the spacious darkness of the cavern, I tried to make out from the blows which I dealt in the empty space, or from the transport of my course through it, in what direction my arms were meant to reach, or my feet to bear me. Since that day, I have wound my arms round the bust of Centaurs, and round the body of heroes, and round the trunk of oaks; my hands have assayed the rocks, the waters, plants without number, and the subtlest impressions of the air,—for I uplift them in the dark and still nights to catch the breaths of wind, and to draw signs whereby I may augur my road; my feet,—look, O Melampus, how worn they are! And yet, all benumbed as I am in this extremity of age, there are days when, in broad sunlight, on the mountain-tops, I renew these gallopings of my youth in the cavern, and with the same object, brandishing my arms and employing all the fleetness which yet is left to me.

760

770

780

790

*   *   *   *

'O Melampus, thou who wouldst know the life of the Centaurs, where-fore have the gods willed that thy steps should lead thee to me, the oldest and most forlorn of them all? It is long since I have ceased to practise any part of their life. I quit no more this mountain summit, to which age has confined me. The point of my arrows now serves me only to uproot some tough-fibred plant; the tranquil lakes know me still, but the rivers have forgotten me. I will tell thee a little of my youth; but these recollections, issuing from a worn memory, come like the drops of a niggardly libation poured from a damaged urn.

'The course of my youth was rapid and full of agitation. Movement was my life, and my steps knew no bound. One day when I was following the course of a valley seldom entered by the Centaurs, I discovered a man making his way up the stream-side on the opposite bank. He was the first whom my eyes had lighted on: I despised him. "Behold," I cried, "at the utmost but the half of what I am! How short are his steps! and his movement how full of labour! Doubtless he is a Centaur overthrown by the gods, and reduced by them to drag himself along thus."

*   *   *   *

'Wandering along at my own will like the rivers, feeling wherever I went the presence of Cybele, whether in the bed of the valleys, or on the height of the mountains, I bounded whither I would, like a blind and chainless life. But when Night, filled with the charm of the gods, overtook me on the slopes of the mountain, she guided me to the mouth of the caverns, and there tranquillised me as she tranquillises the billows of the sea. Stretched across the threshold of my retreat, my flanks hidden within the cave, and my head under the open sky, I watched the spectacle of the dark. The sea-gods, it is said, quit during the hours of darkness their palaces under the deep; they seat themselves on the promontories, and their eyes wander over the expanse of the waves. Even so I kept watch, having at my feet an expanse of life like the hushed sea. My regards had free range, and travelled to the most distant points. Like sea-beaches which never lose their wetness, the line of mountains to the west retained the imprint of gleams not perfectly wiped out by the shadows. In that quarter still survived, in pale clearness, mountain-summits naked and pure. There I beheld at one time the god Pan descend, ever solitary; at another, the choir of the mystic divinities; or I saw pass some mountain-nymph charm-struck by the night. Sometimes the eagles of Mount Olympus traversed the upper sky, and were lost to view among the far-off constellations, or in the shade of the dreaming forests.

'Thou pursuest after wisdom, O Melampus, which is the science of the will of the gods; and thou roamest from people to people like a mortal driven by the destinies. In the times when I kept my night-watches before the caverns, I have sometimes believed that I was about to surprise the thought of the sleeping Cybele, and that the mother of the gods, betrayed by her dreams, would let fall some of her secrets; but I have never made out more than sounds which faded away in the murmur of night, or words inarticulate as the bubbling of the rivers.

' "O Macareus," one day said the great Chiron to me, whose old age I tended; "we are, both of us, Centaurs of the mountain; but how different are our lives! Of my days all the study is (thou seest it) the search for plants; thou, thou art like those mortals who have picked up on the waters or in the woods, and carried to their lips, some pieces of the reed-pipe thrown away by the god Pan. From that hour these mortals, having caught from their relics of the god of passion for wild life, or perhaps smitten with some secret madness, enter into the wilderness, plunge among the forests, follow the course of the streams, bury themselves in the heart of the mountains, restless, and haunted by an unknown purpose. The mares beloved of the winds in the farthest Scythia are not wilder than thou, nor more cast down at nightfall, when the North Wind has departed. Seekest thou to know the gods, O Macareus, and from what source men, animals, and the elements of the universal fire have their origin? But the aged Ocean, the father of all things, keeps locked within his own breast these secrets; and the nymphs, who stand around, sing as they weave their eternal dance before him, to cover any sound which might escape from his lips half-opened by slumber. The mortals, dear to the gods for their virtue, have received from their hands lyres to give delight to man, or the seeds of new plants to make him rich; but from their inexorable lips, nothing!"

    *   *   *   *

'Such were the lessons which the old Chiron gave me. Waned to the very extremity of life, the Centaur yet nourished in his spirit the most lofty discourse.

    *   *   *   *

'For me, O Melampus, I decline into my last days, calm as the setting of the constellations. I still retain enterprise enough to climb to the top of the rocks, and there I linger late, either gazing on the wild and restless clouds, or to see come up from the horizon the rainy Hyades, the Pleiades, or the great Orion; but I feel myself perishing and passing quickly away, like a snow-wreath floating on the stream; and soon shall I be mingled with the waters which flow in the vast bosom of Earth.'

EUGÉNIE DE GUÉRIN

———————⊷◆⊶———————

Who that had spoken of Maurice de Guérin could refrain from speaking of his sister Eugénie, the most devoted of sisters, one of the rarest and most beautiful of souls? 'There is nothing fixed, no duration, no vitality in the sentiments of women towards one another; their attachments are mere pretty knots of ribbon, and no more. In all the friendships of women I observe this slightness of the tie. I know no instance to the contrary, even in history. Orestes and Pylades have no sisters.' So she herself speaks of the friendships of her own sex. But Electra can attach herself to Orestes, if not to Chrysothemis. And to her brother Maurice, Eugénie de Guérin was Pylades and Electra in one.

The name of Maurice de Guérin,—that young man so gifted, so attractive, so careless of fame, and so early snatched away; who died at twenty-nine; who, says his sister, 'let what he did be lost with a carelessness so unjust to himself, set no value on any of his own productions, and departed hence without reaping the rich harvest which seemed his due;' who, in spite of his immaturity, in spite of his fragility, exercised such a charm, 'fur-

76

nished to others so much of that which all live by,' that some years after
his death his sister found in a country-house where he used to stay, in the
journal of a young girl who had not known him, but who heard her family
speak of him, his name, the date of his death, and these words, *'il était leur* **20**
vie' (he was their life); whose talent, exquisite as that of Keats, with much
less of sunlight, abundance, inventiveness, and facility in it than that of
Keats, but with more of distinction and power, had 'that winning, delicate,
and beautifully happy turn of expression' which is the stamp of the master,
—is beginning to be well known to all lovers of literature. This establishment of Maurice's name was an object for which his sister Eugénie passionately laboured. While he was alive, she placed her whole joy in the
flowering of this gifted nature; when he was dead, she had no other thought
than to make the world know him as she knew him. She outlived him nine
years, and her cherished task for those years was to rescue the fragments **30**
of her brother's composition, to collect them, to get them published. In
pursuing this task she had at first cheering hopes of success; she had at
last baffling and bitter disappointment. Her earthly business was at an end;
she died. Ten years afterwards, it was permitted to the love of a friend,
M. Trebutien, to effect for Maurice's memory what the love of a sister had
failed to accomplish. But those who read, with delight and admiration, the
journal and letters of Maurice de Guérin, could not but be attracted and
touched by this sister Eugénie, who met them at every page. She seemed
hardly less gifted, hardly less interesting, than Maurice himself. And presently M. Trebutien did for the sister what he had done for the brother. **40**
He published the journal of Mdlle. Eugénie de Guérin, and a few (too few,
alas!) of her letters.[1] The book has made a profound impression in France;
and the fame which she sought only for her brother now crowns the sister
also.

Parts of Mdlle. de Guérin's journal were several years ago printed for
private circulation, and a writer in the *National Review* had the good fortune to fall in with them. The bees of our English criticism do not often
roam so far afield for their honey, and this critic deserves thanks for
having flitted in his quest of blossom to foreign parts, and for having settled
upon a beautiful flower found there. He had the discernment to see that **50**
Mdlle. de Guérin was well worth speaking of, and he spoke of her with
feeling and appreciation. But that, as I have said, was several years ago;
even a true and feeling homage needs to be from time to time renewed,
if the memory of its object is to endure; and criticism must not lose the

---

[1] A volume of these, also, has just been brought out by M. Trebutien. One good
book, at least, in the literature of the year 1865!

occasion offered by Mdlle. de Guérin's journal being for the first time published to the world, of directing notice once more to this religious and beautiful character.

Eugénie de Guérin was born in 1805, at the château of Le Cayla, in Languedoc. Her family, though reduced in circumstances, was noble; and even when one is a saint one cannot quite forget that one comes of the stock of the Guarini of Italy, or that one counts among one's ancestors a Bishop of Senlis, who had the marshalling of the French order of battle on the day of Bouvines. Le Cayla was a solitary place, with its terrace looking down upon a stream-bed and valley; 'one may pass days there without seeing any living thing but the sheep, without hearing any living thing but the birds.' M. de Guérin, Eugénie's father, lost his wife when Eugénie was thirteen years old, and Maurice seven; he was left with four children,—Eugénie, Marie, Erembert, and Maurice,—of whom Eugénie was the eldest, and Maurice was the youngest. This youngest child, whose beauty and delicacy had made him the object of his mother's most anxious fondness, was commended by her in dying to the care of his sister Eugénie. Maurice at eleven years old went to school at Toulouse; then he went to the Collège Stanislas at Paris; then he became a member of the religious society which M. de Lamennais had formed at La Chênaie in Brittany; afterwards he lived chiefly at Paris, returning to Le Cayla, at the age of twenty-nine, to die. Distance, in those days, was a great obstacle to frequent meetings of the separated members of a French family of narrow means. Maurice de Guérin was seldom at Le Cayla after he had once quitted it, though his few visits to his home were long ones; but he passed five years,—the period of his sojourn in Brittany, and of his first settlement in Paris,—without coming home at all. In spite of the check from these absences, in spite of the more serious check from a temporary alteration in Maurice's religious feelings, the union between the brother and sister was wonderfully close and firm. For they were knit together, not only by the tie of blood and early attachment, but also by the tie of a common genius. 'We were,' says Eugénie, 'two eyes looking out of one head.' She, on her part, brought to her love for her brother the devotedness of a woman, the intensity of a recluse, almost the solicitude of a mother. Her home duties prevented her from following the wish, which often arose in her, to join a religious sisterhood. There is a trace,—just a trace,—of an early attachment to a cousin; but he died when she was twenty-four. After that, she lived for Maurice. It was for Maurice that, in addition to her constant correspondence with him by letter, she began in 1834 her journal, which was sent to him by portions as it was finished. After his death she tried to continue it, addressing it 'to Maurice in heaven.' But the effort was beyond her strength; gradually the entries became rarer and rarer; and on the last day of December, 1840, the pen dropped from her hand: the journal ends.

Other sisters have loved their brothers, and it is not her affection for Maurice, admirable as this was, which alone could have made Eugénie de Guérin celebrated. I have said that both brother and sister had genius: M. Sainte-Beuve goes so far as to say that the sister's genius was equal, if not superior, to her brother's. No one has a more profound respect for M. Sainte-Beuve's critical judgments than I have; but it seems to me that this particular judgment needs to be a little explained and guarded. In Maurice's special talent, which was a talent for interpreting nature, for finding words which incomparably render the subtlest impressions which nature makes upon us, which bring the intimate life of nature wonderfully near to us, it seems to me that his sister was by no means his equal. She never, indeed, expresses herself without grace and intelligence; but her words, when she speaks of the life and appearances of nature, are in general but intellectual signs; they are not like her brother's—symbols equivalent with the thing symbolised. They bring the notion of the thing described to the mind, they do not bring the feeling of it to the imagination. Writing from the Nivernais, that region of vast woodlands in the centre of France: 'It does one good,' says Eugénie, 'to be going about in the midst of this enchanting nature, with flowers, birds, and verdure all round one, under this large and blue sky of the Nivernais. How I love the gracious form of it, and those little white clouds here and there, like cushions of cotton, hung aloft to rest the eye in this immensity!' It is pretty and graceful, but how different from the grave and pregnant strokes of Maurice's pencil! 'I have been along the Loire, and seen on its banks the plains where nature is puissant and gay; I have seen royal and antique dwellings, all marked by memories which have their place in the mournful legend of humanity,— Chambord, Blois, Amboise, Chenonceaux; then the towns on the two banks of the river,—Orléans, Tours, Saumur, Nantes; and, at the end of it all, the Ocean rumbling. From these I passed back into the interior of the country, as far as Bourges and Nevers, a region of vast woodlands, in which murmurs of an immense range and fulness' (*ce beau torrent de rumeurs,* as, with an expression worthy of Wordsworth, he elsewhere calls them) 'prevail and never cease.' Words whose charm is like that of the sounds of the murmuring forest itself, and whose reverberations, like theirs, die away in the infinite distance of the soul.

Maurice's life was in the life of nature, and the passion for it consumed him; it would have been strange if his accent had not caught more of the soul of nature than Eugénie's accent, whose life was elsewhere. 'You will find in him,' Maurice says to his sister of a friend whom he was recommending to her, 'you will find in him that which you love, and which suits you better than anything else,—*l'onction, l'effusion, la mysticité.*' Unction, the pouring out of the soul, the rapture of the mystic, were dear to Maurice also; but in him the bent of his genius gave even to those a special direction of its own. In Eugénie they took the direction most native and familiar to them; their object was the religious life.

And yet, if one analyses this beautiful and most interesting character quite to the bottom, it is not exactly as a saint that Eugénie de Guérin is remarkable. The ideal saint is a nature like Saint François de Sales or Fénelon; a nature of ineffable sweetness and serenity, a nature in which struggle and revolt is over, and the whole man (so far as is possible to human infirmity) swallowed up in love. Saint Theresa (it is Mdlle. de Guérin herself who reminds us of it) endured twenty years of unacceptance and of repulse in her prayers; yes, but the Saint Theresa whom Christendom knows is Saint Theresa repulsed no longer! it is Saint Theresa accepted, rejoicing in love, radiant with ecstasy. Mdlle. de Guérin is not one of these saints arrived at perfect sweetness and calm, steeped in ecstasy; there is something primitive, indomitable in her, which she governs, indeed, but which chafes, which revolts. Somewhere in the depths of that strong nature there is a struggle, an impatience, an inquietude, an ennui, which endures to the end, and which leaves one, when one finally closes her journal, with an impression of profound melancholy. 'There are days,' she writes to her brother, 'when one's nature rolls itself up, and becomes a hedgehog. If I had you here at this moment, here close by me, how I should prick you! how sharp and hard!' 'Poor soul, poor soul,' she cries out to herself another day, 'what is the matter, what would you have? Where is that which will do you good? Everything is green, everything is in bloom, all the air has a breath of flowers. How beautiful it is! well, I will go out. No, I should be alone, and all this beauty, when one is alone, is worth nothing. What shall I do then? Read, write, pray, take a basket of sand on my head like that hermit-saint, and walk with it? Yes, work, work! keep busy the body which does mischief to the soul! I have been too little occupied to-day, and that is bad for one, and it gives a certain ennui which I have in me time to ferment.'

A certain ennui which I have in me: her wound is there. In vain she follows the counsel of Fénelon: 'If God tires you, *tell him that he tires you.*' No doubt she obtained great and frequent solace and restoration from prayer: 'This morning I was suffering; well, at present I am calm, and this I owe to faith, simply to faith, to an act of faith. I can think of death and eternity without trouble, without alarm. Over a deep of sorrow there floats a divine calm, a suavity which is the work of God only. In vain have I tried other things at a time like this: nothing human comforts the soul, nothing human upholds it:—

> "A l'enfant il faut sa mère,
> A mon âme il faut mon Dieu." '

Still the ennui reappears, bringing with it hours of unutterable forlornness, and making her cling to her one great earthly happiness,—her affection for her brother,—with an intenseness, an anxiety, a desperation in which there is something morbid, and by which she is occasionally carried into an irritability, a jealousy, which she herself is the first, indeed, to censure, which she severely represses, but which nevertheless leaves a sense of pain.

Mdlle. de Guérin's admirers have compared her to Pascal, and in some respects the comparison is just. But she cannot exactly be classed with Pascal, any more than with Saint François de Sales. Pascal is a man, and the inexhaustible power and activity of his mind leave him no leisure for ennui. He has not the sweetness and serenity of the perfect saint; he is, perhaps, 'der strenge, kranke Pascal—*the severe, morbid Pascal,*'—as Goethe (and, strange to say, Goethe at twenty-three, an age which usually feels Pascal's charm most profoundly) calls him. But the stress and movement of the lifelong conflict waged in him between his soul and his reason keep him full of fire, full of agitation, and keep his reader, who witnesses this conflict, animated and excited; the sense of forlornness and dejected weariness which clings to Eugénie de Guérin does not belong to Pascal. Eugénie de Guérin is a woman, and longs for a state of firm happiness, for an affection in which she may repose. The inward bliss of Saint Theresa or Fénelon would have satisfied her; denied this, she cannot rest satisfied with the triumphs of self-abasement, with the sombre joy of trampling the pride of life and of reason underfoot, of reducing all human hope and joy to insignificance; she repeats the magnificent words of Bossuet, words which both Catholicism and Protestantism have uttered with indefatigable iteration: 'On trouve au fond de tout le vide et le néant—*at the bottom of everything one finds emptiness and nothingness,*'—but she feels, as every one but the true mystic must ever feel, their incurable sterility.

She resembles Pascal, however, by the clearness and firmness of her intelligence, going straight and instinctively to the bottom of any matter she is dealing with, and expressing herself about it with incomparable precision; never fumbling with what she has to say, never imperfectly seizing or imperfectly presenting her thought. And to this admirable precision she joins a lightness of touch, a feminine ease and grace, a flowing facility which are her own. 'I do not say,' writes her brother Maurice, an excellent judge, 'that I find in myself a dearth of expression; but I have not this abundance of yours, this productiveness of soul which streams forth, which courses along without ever failing, and always with an infinite charm.' And writing to her of some composition of hers, produced after her religious scruples had for a long time kept her from the exercise of her talent: 'You see, my dear Tortoise,' he writes, 'that your talent is no illusion, since after a period, I know not how long, of poetical inaction,—a trial to which any half-talent would have succumbed,—it rears its head again more vigorous than ever. It is really heart-breaking to see you repress and bind down, with I know not what scruples, your spirit, which tends with all the force of its nature to develop itself in this direction. Others have made it a case of conscience for you to resist this impulse, and I make it one for you to follow it.' And she says of herself, on one of her freer days: 'It is the instinct of my life to write, as it is the instinct of the fountain to flow.' The charm of her expression is not a sensuous and imaginative charm like that of Maurice, but rather an intellectual charm; it comes from the texture of the style rather than from its elements; it is not so much in the words as in the turn of the phrase, in the happy cast and flow of the sentence. Recluse as she was, she had a great correspondence: every one wished to have letters from her; and no wonder.

To this strength of intelligence and talent of expression she joined a great force of character. Religion had early possessed itself of this force of character, and reinforced it: in the shadow of the Cevennes, in the sharp and tonic nature of this region of southern France, which has seen the Albigensians, which has seen the Camisards, Catholicism too is fervent and intense. Eugénie de Guérin was brought up amidst strong religious influences, and they found in her a nature on which they could lay firm hold. I have said that she was not a saint of the order of Saint François de Sales or Fénelon; perhaps she had too keen an intelligence to suffer her to be this, too forcible and impetuous a character. But I did not mean to imply the least doubt of the reality, the profoundness, of her religious life. She was penetrated by the power of religion; religion was the master-influence of her life; she derived immense consolations from religion, she earnestly strove to conform her whole nature to it; if there was an element in her which religion could not perfectly reach, perfectly transmute, she groaned over this element in her, she chid it, she made it bow. Almost every thought in her was brought into harmony with religion; and what few thoughts were not thus brought into harmony were brought into subjection.

Then she had her affection for her brother; and this, too, though perhaps there might be in it something a little over-eager, a little too absolute, a little too susceptible, was a pure, a devoted affection. It was not only passionate, it was tender. It was tender, pliant, and self-sacrificing to a degree that not in one nature out of a thousand,—of natures with a mind and will like hers,—is found attainable. She thus united extraordinary power of intelligence, extraordinary force of character, and extraordinary strength of affection; and all these under the control of a deep religious feeling.

This is what makes her so remarkable, so interesting. I shall try and make her speak for herself, that she may show us the characteristic sides of her rare nature with her own inimitable touch.

It must be remembered that her journal is written for Maurice only; in her lifetime no eye but his ever saw it. *'Ceci n'est pas pour le public,'* she writes; *'c'est de l'intime, c'est de l'âme, c'est pour un.'* 'This is not for the public; it contains my inmost thoughts, my very soul; it is for *one.*' And Maurice, this *one,* was a kind of second self to her. 'We see things with the same eyes; what you find beautiful, I find beautiful; God has made our souls of one piece.' And this genuine confidence in her brother's sympathy gives to the entries in her journal a naturalness and simple freedom rare in such compositions. She felt that he would understand her, and be interested in all that she wrote.

One of the first pages of her journal relates an incident of the home-life of Le Cayla, the smallest detail of which Maurice liked to hear; and in relating it she brings this simple life before us. She is writing in November, 1834:—

'I am furious with the grey cat. The mischievous beast has made away with a little half-frozen pigeon, which I was trying to thaw by the side of the fire. The poor little thing was just beginning to come round; I meant to tame him; he would have grown fond of me; and there is my whole scheme eaten up by a cat! This event, and all the rest of to-day's history, has passed in the kitchen. Here I take up my abode all the morning and a part of the evening, ever since I am without Mimi.[1] I have to superintend the cook; sometimes papa comes down, and I read to him by the oven, or by the fireside, some bits out of the *Antiquities of the Anglo-Saxon Church.* This book struck Pierril[2] with astonishment. "Que de mouts aqui dédins! What a lot of words there are inside it!" This boy is a real original. One evening

---

[1] The familiar name of her sister Marie.
[2] A servant-boy at Le Cayla.

he asked me if the soul was immortal; then afterwards, what a philosopher was? We had got upon great questions, as you see. When I told him that a philosopher was a person who was wise and learned: "Then, mademoiselle, you are a philosopher." This was said with an air of simplicity and sincerity which might have made even Socrates take it as a compliment; but it made me laugh so much that my gravity as catechist was gone for that evening. A day or two ago Pierril left us, to his great sorrow: his time with us was up on Saint Brice's day. Now he goes about with his little dog, truffle-hunting. If he comes this way I shall go and ask him if he still thinks I look like a philosopher.'

Her good sense and spirit made her discharge with alacrity her household tasks in this patriarchal life of Le Cayla, and treat them as the most natural thing in the world. She sometimes complains, to be sure, of burning her fingers at the kitchen-fire. But when a literary friend of her brother expresses enthusiasm about her and her poetical nature: 'The poetess,' she says, 'whom this gentleman believes me to be, is an ideal being, infinitely removed from the life which is actually mine—a life of occupations, a life of household-business, which takes up all my time. How could I make it otherwise? I am sure I do not know; and, besides, my duty is in this sort of life, and I have no wish to escape from it.'

Among these occupations of the patriarchal life of the châtelaine of Le Cayla intercourse with the poor fills a prominent place:—

'To-day,' she writes on the 9th of December, 1834, 'I have been warming myself at every fireside in the village. It is a round which Mimi and I often make, and in which I take pleasure. To-day we have been seeing sick people, and holding forth on doses and sick-room drinks. "Take this, do that;" and they attend to us just as if we were the doctor. We prescribed shoes for a little thing who was amiss from having gone barefoot; to the brother, who, with a bad headache, was lying quite flat, we prescribed a pillow; the pillow did him good, but I am afraid it will hardly cure him. He is at the beginning of a bad feverish cold; and these poor people live in the filth of their hovels like animals in their stable; the bad air poisons them. When I come home to Le Cayla I seem to be in a palace.'

She had books, too; not in abundance, not for the fancying them; the list of her library is small, and it is enlarged slowly and with difficulty. The *Letters of Saint Theresa,* which she had long wished to get, she sees in the hands of a poor servant girl, before she can procure them for herself. 'What then?' is her comment: 'very likely she makes a better use of them than I could.' But she has the *Imitation,* the *Spiritual Works* of Bossuet and Fénelon, the *Lives of the Saints,* Corneille, Racine, André Chénier,

and Lamartine; Madame de Staël's book on Germany, and French translations of Shakspeare's plays, Ossian, the *Vicar of Wakefield,* Scott's *Old
Mortality* and *Redgauntlet,* and the *Promessi Sposi* of Manzoni. Above all,
she has her own mind; her meditations in the lonely fields, on the oak-
grown hill-side of 'The Seven Springs;' her meditations and writings in her
own room, her *chambrette,* her *délicieux chez moi,* where every night,
before she goes to bed, she opens the window to look out upon the sky,—
the balmy moonlit sky of Languedoc. This life of reading, thinking, and
writing was the life she liked best, the life that most truly suited her. 'I find   340
writing has become almost a necessity to me. Whence does it arise, this
impulse to give utterance to the voice of one's spirit, to pour out my
thoughts before God and one human being? I say one human being,
because I always imagine that you are present, that you see what I write.
In the stillness of a life like this my spirit is happy, and, as it were, dead to
all that goes on upstairs or downstairs, in the house or out of the house.
But this does not last long. "Come, my poor spirit," I then say to myself,
"we must go back to the things of this world." And I take my spinning,
or a book, or a saucepan, or I play with Wolf or Trilby. Such a life as this
I call heaven upon earth.'   350
    Tastes like these, joined with a talent like Mdlle. de Guérin's, naturally
inspire thoughts of literary composition. Such thoughts she had, and perhaps she would have been happier if she had followed them; but she never
could satisfy herself that to follow them was quite consistent with the religious life, and her projects of composition were gradually relinquished:—
    'Would to God that my thoughts, my spirit, had never taken their flight
beyond the narrow round in which it is my lot to live! In spite of all that
people say to the contrary, I feel that I cannot go beyond my needlework
and my spinning without going too far: I feel it, I believe it: well, then, I
will keep in my proper sphere; however much I am tempted, my spirit shall   360
not be allowed to occupy itself with great matters until it occupies itself
with them in Heaven.'
    And again:—
    'My journal has been untouched for a long while. Do you want to know
why? It is because the time seems to me misspent which I spend in writing
it. We owe God an account of every minute; and is it not a wrong use of
our minutes to employ them in writing a history of our transitory days?'
    She overcomes her scruples, and goes on writing the journal; but again
and again they return to her. Her brother tells her of the pleasure and comfort something she has written gives to a friend of his in affliction. She   370
answers:—

'It is from the Cross that those thoughts come, which your friend finds so soothing, so unspeakably tender. None of them come from me. I feel my own aridity; but I feel, too, that God, when he will, can make an ocean flow upon this bed of sand. It is the same with so many simple souls, from which proceed the most admirable things; because they are in direct relation with God, without false science and without pride. And thus I am gradually losing my taste for books; I say to myself: "What can they teach me which I shall not one day know in Heaven? let God be my master and my study here!" I try to make him so, and I find myself the better for it. I read little; I go out little; I plunge myself in the inward life. How infinite are the sayings, doings, feelings, events of that life! Oh, if you could but see them! But what avails it to make them known? God alone should be admitted to the sanctuary of the soul.'

Beautifully as she says all this, one cannot, I think, read it without a sense of disquietude, without a presentiment that this ardent spirit is forcing itself from its natural bent, that the beatitude of the true mystic will never be its earthly portion. And yet how simple and charming is her picture of the life of religion which she chose as her ark of refuge, and in which she desired to place all her happiness:—

'Cloaks, clogs, umbrellas, all the apparatus of winter, went with us this morning to Andillac, where we have passed the whole day; some of it at the curé's house, the rest in church. How I like this life of a country Sunday, with its activity, its journeys to church, its liveliness! You find all your neighbours on the road; you have a curtsey from every woman you meet, and then, as you go along, such a talk about the poultry, the sheep and cows, the good man and the children! My great delight is to give a kiss to these children, and see them run away and hide their blushing faces in their mother's gown. They are alarmed at *las doumaïsélos,*[1] as at a being of another world. One of these little things said the other day to its grandmother, who was talking of coming to see us: "*Minino,* you mustn't go to that castle; there is a black hole there." What is the reason that in all ages the noble's château has been an object of terror? Is it because of the horrors that were committed there in old times? I suppose so.'

This vague horror of the château, still lingering in the mind of the French peasant fifty years after he has stormed it, is indeed curious, and is one of the thousand indications how unlike aristocracy on the Continent has been to aristocracy in England. But this is one of the great matters with which Mdlle. de Guérin would not have us occupied; let us pass to the subject of Christmas in Languedoc:—

[1] The young lady.

'Christmas is come; the beautiful festival, the one I love most, and which gives me the same joy as it gave the shepherds of Bethlehem. In real truth, one's whole soul sings with joy at this beautiful coming of God upon earth,—a coming which here is announced on all sides of us by music and by our charming *nadalet*.[1] Nothing at Paris can give you a notion of what Christmas is with us. You have not even the midnight-mass. We all of us went to it, papa at our head, on the most perfect night possible. Never was there a finer sky than ours was that midnight;—so fine that papa kept perpetually throwing back the hood of his cloak, that he might look up at the sky. The ground was white with hoar-frost, but we were not cold; besides, the air, as we met it, was warmed by the bundles of blazing torchwood which our servants carried in front of us to light us on our way. It was delightful, I do assure you; and I should like you to have seen us there on our road to church, in those lanes with the bushes along their banks as white as if they were in flower. The hoar-frost makes the most lovely flowers. We saw a long spray so beautiful that we wanted to take it with us as a garland for the communion-table, but it melted in our hands; all flowers fade so soon! I was very sorry about my garland; it was mournful to see it drip away, and get smaller and smaller every minute.'

The religious life is at bottom everywhere alike; but it is curious to note the variousness of its setting and outward circumstance. Catholicism has these so different from Protestantism! and in Catholicism these accessories have, it cannot be denied, a nobleness and amplitude which in Protestantism is often wanting to them. In Catholicism they have, from the antiquity of this form of religion, from its pretensions to universality, from its really wide-spread prevalence, from its sensuousness, something European, august, and imaginative: in Protestantism they often have, from its inferiority in all these respects, something provincial, mean, and prosaic. In revenge, Protestantism has a future before it, a prospect of growth in alliance with the vital movement of modern society; while Catholicism appears to be bent on widening the breach between itself and the modern spirit, to be fatally losing itself in the multiplication of dogmas, Mariolatry, and miracle-mongering. But the style and circumstance of actual Catholicism is grander than its present tendency, and the style and circumstance of Protestantism is meaner than its tendency. While I was reading the journal of Mdlle. de Guérin, there came into my hands the memoir and poems of a young Englishwoman, Miss Emma Tatham; and one could not but be struck with the singular contrast which the two lives,—in their setting rather than in their inherent quality,—present. Miss Tatham had not, cer-

[1] A peculiar peal rung at Christmas-time by the church bells of Languedoc.

tainly, Mdlle. de Guérin's talent, but she had a sincere vein of poetic feeling, a genuine aptitude for composition. Both were fervent Christians, and, so far, the two lives have a real resemblance; but, in the setting of them, what a difference! The Frenchwoman is a Catholic in Languedoc; the Englishwoman is a Protestant at Margate; Margate, that brick-and-mortar image of English Protestantism, representing it in all its prose, all its uncomeliness,—let me add, all its salubrity. Between the external form and fashion of these two lives, between the Catholic Mdlle. de Guérin's *nadalet* at the Languedoc Christmas, her chapel of moss at Eastertime, her daily reading of the life of a saint, carrying her to the most diverse times, places, and peoples,—her quoting, when she wants to fix her mind upon the stanchness which the religious aspirant needs, the words of Saint Macedonius to a hunter whom he met in the mountains, 'I pursue after God, as you pursue after game,'—her quoting, when she wants to break a village girl of disobedience to her mother, the story of the ten disobedient children whom at Hippo Saint Augustine saw palsied;—between all this and the bare, blank, narrowly English setting of Miss Tatham's Protestantism, her 'union in church-fellowship with the worshippers at Hawley-Square Chapel, Margate;' her 'singing with soft, sweet voice, the animating lines—

> "My Jesus to know, and feel his blood flow,
> 'Tis life everlasting, 'tis heaven below;" '

her 'young female teachers belonging to the Sunday-school,' and her 'Mr. Thomas Rowe, a venerable class-leader,'—what a dissimilarity! In the ground of the two lives, a likeness; in all their circumstance, what unlikeness! An unlikeness, it will be said, in that which is non-essential and indifferent. Non-essential,—yes; indifferent,—no. The signal want of grace and charm in English Protestantism's setting of its religious life is not an indifferent matter; it is a real weakness. *This ought ye to have done, and not to have left the other undone.*

I have said that the present tendency of Catholicism,—the Catholicism of the main body of the Catholic clergy and laity,—seems likely to exaggerate rather than to remove all that in this form of religion is most repugnant to reason; but this Catholicism was not that of Mdlle. de Guérin. The insufficiency of her Catholicism comes from a doctrine which Protestantism, too, has adopted, although Protestantism, from its inherent element of freedom, may find it easier to escape from it; a doctrine with a certain attraction for all noble natures, but, in the modern world at any rate, incurably sterile,—the doctrine of the emptiness and nothingness of human life, of the superiority of renouncement to activity, of quietism to energy;

the doctrine which makes effort for things on this side of the grave a folly, and joy in things on this side of the grave a sin. But her Catholicism is remarkably free from the faults which Protestants commonly think inseparable from Catholicism; the relation to the priest, the practice of confession, assume, when she speaks of them, an aspect which is not that under which Exeter Hall knows them, but which,—unless one is of the number of those who prefer regarding that by which men and nations die to regarding that by which they live,—one is glad to study. *'La confession,'* she says twice in her journal, *'n'est qu'une expansion du repentir dans l'amour;'* and her weekly journey to the confessional in the little church of Cahuzac is her *'cher pélerinage;'* the little church is the place where she has *'laissé tant de misères.'*

'This morning,' she writes one 28th of November, 'I was up before daylight, dressed quickly, said my prayers, and started with Marie for Cahuzac. When we got there, the chapel was occupied, which I was not sorry for. I like not to be hurried, and to have time, before I go in, to lay bare my soul before God. This often takes me a long time, because my thoughts are apt to be flying about like these autumn leaves. At ten o'clock I was on my knees, listening to words the most salutary that were ever spoken; and I went away, feeling myself a better being. Every burden thrown off leaves us with a sense of brightness; and when the soul has laid down the load of its sins at God's feet, it feels as if it had wings. What an admirable thing is confession! What comfort, what light, what strength is given me every time after I have said, *I have sinned.'*

This blessing of confession is the greater, she says, 'the more the heart of the priest to whom we confide our repentance is like that divine heart which "has so loved us." This is what attaches me to M. Bories.' M. Bories was the curé of her parish, a man no longer young, and of whose loss, when he was about to leave them, she thus speaks:—

'What a grief for me! how much I lose in losing this faithful guide of my conscience, heart, and mind, of my whole self, which God has appointed to be in his charge, and which let itself be in his charge so gladly! He knew the resolves which God had put in my heart, and I had need of his help to follow them. Our new curé cannot supply his place: he is so young! and then he seems so inexperienced, so undecided! It needs firmness to pluck a soul out of the midst of the world, and to uphold it against the assaults of flesh and blood. It is Saturday, my day for going to Cahuzac; I am just going there, perhaps I shall come back more tranquil. God has always given me some good thing there, in that chapel where I have left behind me so many miseries.'

Such is confession for her when the priest is worthy; and, when he is not worthy, she knows how to separate the man from the office:—

'To-day I am going to do something which I dislike; but I will do it, with God's help. Do not think I am on my way to the stake; it is only that I am going to confess to a priest in whom I have not confidence, but who is the only one here. In this act of religion, the man must always be separated from the priest, and sometimes the man must be annihilated.'

The same clear sense, the same freedom from superstition, shows itself in all her religious life. She tells us, to be sure, how once, when she was a little girl, she stained a new frock, and on praying, in her alarm, to an image of the Virgin which hung in her room, saw the stains vanish: even the austerest Protestant will not judge such Mariolatry as this very harshly. But, in general, the Virgin Mary fills, in the religious parts of her journal, no prominent place; it is Jesus, not Mary. 'Oh, how well has Jesus said: "Come unto me, all ye that labour and are heavy laden." It is only there, only in the bosom of God, that we can rightly weep, rightly rid ourselves of our burden.' And again: 'The mystery of suffering makes one grasp the belief of something to be expiated, something to be won. I see it in Jesus Christ, the Man of Sorrow. *It was necessary that the Son of Man should suffer*. That is all we know in the troubles and calamities of life.'

And who has ever spoken of justification more impressively and piously than Mdlle. de Guérin speaks of it, when, after reckoning the number of minutes she has lived, she exclaims:—

'My God, what have we done with all these minutes of ours, which thou, too, wilt one day reckon? Will there be any of them to count for eternal life? will there be many of them? will there be one of them? "If thou, O Lord, wilt be extreme to mark what is done amiss, O Lord, who may abide it?" This close scrutiny of our time may well make us tremble, all of us who have advanced more than a few steps in life; for God will judge us otherwise than as he judges the lilies of the field. I have never been able to understand the security of those who place their whole reliance, in presenting themselves before God, upon a good conduct in the ordinary relations of human life. As if all our duties were confined within the narrow sphere of this world! To be a good parent, a good child, a good citizen, a good brother or sister, is not enough to procure entrance into the kingdom of heaven. God demands other things besides these kindly social virtues, of him whom he means to crown with an eternity of glory.'

And, with this zeal for the spirit and power of religion, what prudence in her counsels of religious practice; what discernment, what measure! She

has been speaking of the charm of the *Lives of the Saints,* and she goes
on:—

'Notwithstanding this, the *Lives of the Saints* seem to me, for a great
many people, dangerous reading. I would not recommend them to a young
girl, or even to some women who are no longer young. What one reads has
such power over one's feelings; and these, even in seeking God, sometimes
go astray. Alas, we have seen it in poor C.'s case. What care one ought to
take with a young person; with what she reads, what she writes, her society,
her prayers,—all of them matters which demand a mother's tender watch-
fulness! I remember many things I did at fourteen, which my mother, had
she lived, would not have let me do. I would have done anything for God's
sake; I would have cast myself into an oven, and assuredly things like that
are not God's will; he is not pleased by the hurt one does to one's health
through that ardent but ill-regulated piety which, while it impairs the body,
often leaves many a fault flourishing. And, therefore, Saint François de
Sales used to say to the nuns who asked his leave to go bare-foot: "Change
your brains and keep your shoes." '

Meanwhile Maurice, in a five years' absence, and amid the distractions
of Paris, lost, or seemed to his sister to lose, something of his fondness for
his home and its inmates: he certainly lost his early religious habits and
feelings. It is on this latter loss that Mdlle. de Guérin's journal oftenest
touches,—with infinite delicacy, but with infinite anguish:—

'Oh, the agony of being in fear for a soul's salvation, who can describe
it! That which caused our Saviour the keenest suffering, in the agony of his
Passion, was not so much the thought of the torments he was to endure,
as the thought that these torments would be of no avail for a multitude of
sinners; for all those who set themselves against their redemption, or who
do not care for it. The mere anticipation of this obstinacy and this heed-
lessness had power to make sorrowful, even unto death, the divine Son of
Man. And this feeling all Christian souls, according to the measure of
faith and love granted them, more or less share.'

Maurice returned to Le Cayla in the summer of 1837, and passed six
months there. This meeting entirely restored the union between him and
his family. 'These six months with us,' writes his sister, 'he ill, and finding
himself so loved by us all, had entirely reattached him to us. Five years
without seeing us, had perhaps made him a little lose sight of our affection
for him; having found it again, he met it with all the strength of his own.
He had so firmly renewed, before he left us, all family-ties, that nothing
but death could have broken them.' The separation in religious matters
between the brother and sister gradually diminished, and before Maurice

died it had ceased. I have elsewhere spoken of Maurice's religious feeling and his character. It is probable that his divergence from his sister in this sphere of religion was never so wide as she feared, and that his reunion with her was never so complete as she hoped. 'His errors were passed,' she says, 'his illusions were cleared away; by the call of his nature, by original disposition, he had come back to sentiments of order. I knew all, I followed each of his steps; out of the fiery sphere of the passions (which held him but a little moment) I saw him pass into the sphere of the Christian life. It was a beautiful soul, the soul of Maurice.' But the illness which had caused his return to Le Cayla reappeared after he got back to Paris in the winter of 1837–8. Again he seemed to recover; and his marriage with a young Creole lady, Mdlle. Caroline de Gervain, took place in the autumn of 1838. At the end of September in that year Mdlle. de Guérin had joined her brother in Paris; she was present at his marriage, and stayed with him and his wife for some months afterwards. Her journal recommences in April 1839. Zealously as she had promoted her brother's marriage, cordial as were her relations with her sister-in-law, it is evident that a sense of loss, of loneliness, invades her, and sometimes weighs her down. She writes in her journal on the 4th of May:—

'God knows when we shall see one another again! My own Maurice, must it be our lot to live apart, to find that this marriage which I had so much share in bringing about, which I hoped would keep us so much together, leaves us more asunder than ever? For the present and for the future, this troubles me more than I can say. My sympathies, my inclinations, carry me more towards you than towards any other member of our family. I have the misfortune to be fonder of you than of anything else in the world, and my heart had from of old built in you its happiness. Youth gone and life declining, I looked forward to quitting the scene with Maurice. At any time of life a great affection is a great happiness; the spirit comes to take refuge in it entirely. O delight and joy which will never be your sister's portion! Only in the direction of God shall I find an issue for my heart to love as it has the notion of loving, as it has the power of loving.'

From such complainings, in which there is undoubtedly something morbid,—complainings which she herself blamed, to which she seldom gave way, but which, in presenting her character, it is not just to put wholly out of sight,—she was called by the news of an alarming return of her brother's illness. For some days the entries in the journal show her agony of apprehension. 'He coughs, he coughs still! Those words keep echoing for ever in my ears, and pursue me wherever I go; I cannot look at the leaves on the trees without thinking that the winter will come, and then the consumptive die.' She went to him, and brought him back by slow stages to Le Cayla, dying. He died on the 19th of July, 1839.

Thenceforward the energy of life ebbed in her; but the main chords of her being, the chord of affection, the chord of religious longing, the chord of intelligence, the chord of sorrow, gave, so long as they answered to the touch at all, a deeper and finer sound than ever. Always she saw before her, 'that beloved pale face;' 'that beautiful head, with all its different expressions, smiling, speaking, suffering, dying,' regarded her always:—

'I have seen his coffin in the same room, in the same spot where I remember seeing, when I was a very little girl, his cradle, when I was brought home from Gaillac, where I was then staying, for his christening. This christening was a grand one, full of rejoicing, more than that of any of the rest of us; specially marked. I enjoyed myself greatly, and went back to Gaillac next day, charmed with my new little brother. Two years afterwards I came home, and brought with me a frock for him of my own making. I dressed him in the frock, and took him out with me along by the warren at the north of the house, and there he walked a few steps alone,— his first walking alone,—and I ran with delight to tell my mother the news: "Maurice, Maurice has begun to walk by himself!"—Recollections which, coming back to-day, break one's heart.'

The shortness and suffering of her brother's life filled her with an agony of pity. 'Poor beloved soul, you have had hardly any happiness here below; your life has been so short, your repose so rare. O God, uphold me, establish my heart in thy faith! Alas, I have too little of this supporting me! How we have gazed at him and loved him, and kissed him,—his wife, and we, his sisters; he lying lifeless in his bed, his head on the pillow as if he were asleep! Then we followed him to the churchyard, to the grave, to his last resting-place, and prayed over him, and wept over him; and we are here again, and I am writing to him again, as if he were staying away from home, as if he were in Paris. My beloved one, can it be, shall we never see one another again on earth?'

But in heaven?—and here, though love and hope finally prevailed, the very passion of the sister's longing sometimes inspired torturing inquietudes:—

'I am broken down with misery. I want to see him. Every moment I pray to God to grant me this grace. Heaven, the world of spirits, is it so far from us? O depth, O mystery of the other life which separates us! I, who was so eagerly anxious about him, who wanted so to know all that happened to him,—wherever he may be now, it is over! I follow him into the three abodes; I stop wistfully before the place of bliss, I pass on to the place of suffering,—to the gulf of fire. My God, my God, no! Not there let my brother be! not there! And he is not: his soul, the soul of Maurice, among the lost . . . horrible fear, no! But in purgatory, where the soul is cleansed by suffering, where the failings of the heart are expiated, the doubtings of the spirit, the half-yieldings to evil? Perhaps my brother is there and suffers, and calls to us amidst his anguish of repentance, as he used to call to us amidst his bodily suffering: "Help me, you who love me." Yes, beloved one, by prayer. I will go and pray; prayer has been such a power to me, and I will pray to the end. Prayer! Oh! and prayer for the dead; it is the dew of purgatory.'

Often, alas, the gracious dew would not fall; the air of her soul was parched; the arid wind, which was somewhere in the depths of her being, blew. She marks in her journal the 1st of May, 'this return of the loveliest month in the year,' only to keep up the old habit; even the month of May can no longer give her any pleasure: *'Tout est changé*—all is changed.' She is crushed by 'the misery which has nothing good in it, the tearless, dry misery, which bruises the heart like a hammer.'

'I am dying to everything. I am dying of a slow moral agony, a condition of unutterable suffering. Lie there, my poor journal! be forgotten with all this world which is fading away from me. I will write here no more until I come to life again, until God re-awakens me out of this tomb in which my soul lies buried. Maurice, my beloved! it was not thus with me when I had *you*! The thought of Maurice could revive me from the most profound depression: to have him in the world was enough for me. With Maurice, to be buried alive would have not seemed dull to me.'

And, as a burden to this funereal strain, the old *vide et néant* of Bossuet, profound, solemn, sterile:—

'So beautiful in the morning, and in the evening, *that*! how the thought disenchants one, and turns one from the world! I can understand that Spanish grandee who, after lifting up the winding-sheet of a beautiful queen, threw himself into the cloister and became a great saint. I would have all my friends at La Trappe, in the interest of their eternal welfare. Not that in the world one cannot be saved, not that there are not in the world duties to be discharged as sacred and beautiful as there are in the cloister, but . . . .'

And there she stops, and a day or two afterwards her journal comes to an end. A few fragments, a few letters carry us on a little later, but after the 22nd of August, 1845, there is nothing. To make known her brother's genius to the world was the one task she set herself after his death; in 1840 came Madame Sand's noble tribute to him in the *Revue des Deux Mondes;*

then followed projects of raising a yet more enduring monument to his fame, by collecting and publishing his scattered compositions; these projects I have already said, were baffled;—Mdlle. de Guérin's letter of the 730 22nd of August, 1845, relates to this disappointment. In silence, during nearly three years more, she faded away at Le Cayla. She died on the 31st of May, 1848.

M. Trebutien has accomplished the pious task in which Mdlle. de Guérin was baffled, and has established Maurice's fame; by publishing this journal he has established Eugénie's also. She was very different from her brother; but she too, like him, had that in her which preserves a reputation. Her soul had the same characteristic quality as his talent,—*distinction.* Of this quality the world is impatient; it chafes against it, rails at it, insults it, hates it;—it ends by receiving its influence, and by undergoing its law. This qual- 740 ity at last inexorably corrects the world's blunders, and fixes the world's ideals. It procures that the popular poet shall not finally pass for a Pindar, nor the popular historian for a Tacitus, nor the popular preacher for a Bossuet. To the circle of spirits marked by this rare quality, Maurice and Eugénie de Guérin belong; they will take their place in the sky which these inhabit, and shine close to one another, *lucida sidera.*

HEINRICH HEINE

———————⟨◆⟩———————

'I know not if I deserve that a laurel-wreath should one day be laid on my coffin. Poetry, dearly as I have loved it, has always been to me but a divine plaything. I have never attached any great value to poetical fame; and I trouble myself very little whether people praise my verses or blame them. But lay on my coffin a *sword;* for I was a brave soldier in the Liberation-War of humanity.'

Heine had his full share of love of fame, and cared quite as much as his brethren of the *genus irritabile* whether people praised his verses or blamed them. And he was very little of a hero. Posterity will certainly decorate his tomb with the emblem of the laurel rather than with the emblem of the sword. Still, for his contemporaries, for us, for the Europe of the present century, he is significant chiefly for the reason which he himself in the words just quoted assigns. He is significant because he was, if not pre-eminently a brave, yet a brilliant, a most effective soldier in the Liberation-War of humanity.

To ascertain the master-current in the literature of an epoch, and to distinguish this from all minor currents, is one of the critic's highest functions; in discharging it he shows how far he possesses the most indispensable quality of his office,—justness of spirit. The living writer who has done most to make England acquainted with German authors, a man of genius, but to whom precisely this one quality of justness of spirit is perhaps wanting,—I mean Mr. Carlyle,—seems to me in the result of his labours on German literature to afford a proof how very necessary to the critic this quality is. Mr. Carlyle has spoken admirably of Goethe: but then Goethe stands before all men's eyes, the manifest centre of German literature; and from this central source many rivers flow. Which of these rivers is the main stream? which of the courses of spirit which we see active in Goethe is the course which will most influence the future, and attract and be continued by the most powerful of Goethe's successors?—that is the question. Mr. Carlyle attaches, it seems to me, far too much importance to the romantic school of Germany,—Tieck, Novalis, Jean Paul Richter,—and gives to these writers, really gifted as two, at any rate, of them are, an undue prominence. These writers, and others with aims and a general tendency the same as theirs, are not the real inheritors and continuators of Goethe's power; the current of their activity is not the main current of German literature after Goethe. Far more in Heine's works flows this main current; Heine, far more than Tieck or Jean Paul Richter, is the continuator of that which, in Goethe's varied activity, is the most powerful and vital; on Heine, of all German authors who survived Goethe, incomparably the largest portion of Goethe's mantle fell. I do not forget that when Mr. Carlyle was dealing with German literature, Heine, though he was clearly risen above the horizon, had not shone forth with all his strength; I do not forget, too, that after ten or twenty years many things may come out plain before the critic which before were hard to be discerned by him; and assuredly no one would dream of imputing it as a fault to Mr. Carlyle that twenty years ago he mistook the central current in German literature, overlooked the rising Heine, and attached undue importance to that romantic school which Heine was to destroy; one may rather note it as a misfortune, sent perhaps as a delicate chastisement to a critic, who,—man of genius as he is, and no one recognises his genius more admiringly than I do,—has, for the functions of the critic, a little too much of the self-will and eccentricity of a genuine son of Great Britain.

Heine is noteworthy, because he is the most important German successor and continuator of Goethe in Goethe's most important line of activity. And which of Goethe's lines of activity is this?—his line of activity as 'a soldier in the war of liberation of humanity.'

Heine himself would hardly have admitted this affiliation, though he was far too powerful-minded a man to decry, with some of the vulgar German liberals, Goethe's genius. 'The wind of the Paris Revolution,' he writes after the three days of 1830, 'blew about the candles a little in the dark night of Germany, so that the red curtains of a German throne or two caught fire; but the old watchmen, who do the police of the German kingdoms, are already bringing out the fire engines, and will keep the candles closer snuffed for the future. Poor, fast-bound German people, lose not all heart in thy bonds! The fashionable coating of ice melts off from my heart, my soul quivers and my eyes burn, and that is a disadvantageous state of things for a writer, who should control his subject-matter and keep himself beautifully objective, as the artistic school would have us, and as Goethe has done; he has come to be eighty years old doing this, and minister, and in good condition;—poor German people! that is thy greatest man!'

But hear Goethe himself: 'If I were to say what I had really been to the Germans in general, and to the young German poets in particular, I should say I had been their *liberator*.'

Modern times find themselves with an immense system of institutions, established facts, accredited dogmas, customs, rules, which have come to them from times not modern. In this system their life has to be carried forward; yet they have a sense that this system is not of their own creation, that it by no means corresponds exactly with the wants of their actual life, that, for them, it is customary, not rational. The awakening of this sense is the awakening of the modern spirit. The modern spirit is now awake almost everywhere; the sense of want of correspondence between the forms of modern Europe and its spirit, between the new wine of the eighteenth and nineteenth centuries, and the old bottles of the eleventh and twelfth centuries, or even of the sixteenth and seventeenth, almost every one now perceives; it is no longer dangerous to affirm that this want of correspondence exists; people are even beginning to be shy of denying it. To remove this want of correspondence is beginning to be the settled endeavour of most persons of good sense. Dissolvents of the old European system of dominant ideas and facts we must all be, all of us who have any power of working; what we have to study is that we may not be acrid dissolvents of it.

And how did Goethe, that grand dissolvent in an age when there were fewer of them than at present, proceed in his task of dissolution, of liberation of the modern European from the old routine? He shall tell us himself. 'Through me the German poets have become aware that, as man must live from within outwards, so the artist must work from within outwards, seeing that, make what contortions he will, he can only bring to light his own individuality. I can clearly mark where this influence of mine has made itself felt; there arises out of it a kind of poetry of nature, and only in this way is it possible to be original.'

My voice shall never be joined to those which decry Goethe, and if it is said that the foregoing is a lame and impotent conclusion to Goethe's declaration that he had been the liberator of the Germans in general, and of the young German poets in particular, I say it is not. Goethe's profound, imperturbable naturalism is absolutely fatal to all routine thinking; he puts the standard, once for all, inside every man instead of outside him; when he is told, such a thing must be so, there is immense authority and custom in favour of its being so, it has been held to be so for a thousand years, he answers with Olympian politeness, 'But *is* it so? is it so to *me?*' Nothing could be more really subversive of the foundations on which the old European order rested; and it may be remarked that no persons are so radically detached from this order, no persons so thoroughly modern, as those who have felt Goethe's influence most deeply. If it is said that Goethe professes to have in this way deeply influenced but a few persons, and those persons poets, one may answer that he could have taken no better way to secure, in the end, the ear of the world; for poetry is simply the most beautiful, impressive, and widely effective mode of saying things, and hence its importance. Nevertheless the process of liberation, as Goethe worked it, though sure, is undoubtedly slow; he came, as Heine says, to be eighty years old in thus working it, and at the end of that time the old Middle-Age machine was still creaking on, the thirty German courts and their chamberlains subsisted in all their glory; Goethe himself was a minister, and the visible triumph of the modern spirit over prescription and routine seemed as far off as ever. It was the year 1830; the German sovereigns had passed the preceding fifteen years in breaking the promises of freedom they had made to their subjects when they wanted their help in the final struggle with Napoleon. Great events were happening in France; the revolution, defeated in 1815, had arisen from its defeat, and was wresting from its adversaries the power. Heinrich Heine, a young man of genius, born at Hamburg, and with all the culture of Germany, but by race a Jew; with warm sympathies for France, whose revolution had given to his race the rights of citizenship, and whose rule had been, as is well known, popular in the Rhine provinces, where he passed his youth; with a passionate admiration for the great French Emperor, with a passionate contempt for the sovereigns who had overthrown him, for their agents, and for their policy,—Henrich Heine was in 1830 in no humour for any such gradual process of liberation from the old order of things as that which Goethe had followed. His counsel was for open war. Taking that terrible modern weapon, the pen, in his hand, he passed the remainder of his life in one fierce battle. What was that battle? the reader will ask. It was a life and death battle with Philistinism.

Philistinism!—we have not the expression in English. Perhaps we have not the word because we have so much of the thing. At Soli, I imagine, they did not talk of solecisms; and here, at the very head-quarters of Goliath, nobody talks of Philistinism. The French have adopted the term *épicier* (grocer), to designate the sort of being whom the Germans designate by the term Philistine; but the French term,—besides that it casts a slur upon a respectable class, composed of living and susceptible members, while the original Philistines are dead and buried long ago,—is really, I think, in itself much less apt and expressive than the German term. Efforts have been made to obtain in English some term equivalent to *Philister* or *épicier;* Mr. Carlyle has made several such efforts: 'respectability with its thousand gigs,' he says;—well, the occupant of every one of these gigs is, Mr. Carlyle means, a Philistine. However, the word respectable is far too valuable a word to be thus perverted from its proper meaning; if the English are ever to have a word for the thing we are speaking of,—and so prodigious are the changes which the modern spirit is introducing, that even we English shall perhaps one day come to want such a word,—I think we had much better take the term *Philistine* itself.

Philistine must have originally meant, in the mind of those who invented the nickname, a strong, dogged, unenlightened opponent of the chosen people, of the children of the light. The party of change, the would-be remodellers of the old traditional European order, the invokers of reason against custom, the representatives of the modern spirit in every sphere where it is applicable, regarded themselves, with the robust self-confidence natural to reformers as a chosen people, as children of the light. They regarded their adversaries as humdrum people, slaves to routine, enemies to light; stupid and oppressive, but at the same time very strong. This explains the love which Heine, that Paladin of the modern spirit, has for France; it explains the preference which he gives to France over Germany: 'the French,' he says, 'are the chosen people of the new religion, its first gospels and dogmas have been drawn up in their language; Paris is the new Jerusalem, and the Rhine is the Jordan which divides the consecrated land of freedom from the land of the Philistines.' He means that the French, as a people, have shown more accessibility to ideas than any other people;

that prescription and routine have had less hold upon them than upon any other people; that they have shown most readiness to move and to alter at the bidding (real or supposed) of reason. This explains, too, the detestation which Heine had for the English: 'I might settle in England,' he says, in his exile, 'if it were not that I should find there two things, coal-smoke and Englishmen; I cannot abide either.' What he hated in the English was the 'ächtbrittische Beschränktheit,' as he calls it,—the *genuine British narrowness*. In truth, the English, profoundly as they have modified the old Middle-Age order, great as is the liberty which they have secured for themselves, have in all their changes proceeded, to use a familiar expression, by the rule of thumb; what was intolerably inconvenient to them they have suppressed, and as they have suppressed it, not because it was irrational, but because it was practically inconvenient, they have seldom in suppressing it appealed to reason, but always, if possible, to some precedent, or form, or letter, which served as a convenient instrument for their purpose, and which saved them from the necessity of recurring to general principles. They have thus become, in a certain sense, of all people the most inaccessible to ideas and the most impatient of them; inaccessible to them, because of their want of familiarity with them; and impatient of them because they have got on so well without them, that they despise those who, not having got on as well as themselves, still make a fuss for what they themselves have done so well without. But there has certainly followed from hence, in this country, somewhat of a general depression of pure intelligence: Philistia has come to be thought by us the true Land of Promise, and it is anything but that; the born lover of ideas, the born hater of commonplaces, must feel in this country, that the sky over his head is of brass and iron. The enthusiast for the idea, for reason, values reason, the idea, in and for themselves; he values them, irrespectively of the practical conveniences which their triumph may obtain for him; and the man who regards the possession of these practical conveniences as something sufficient in itself, something which compensates for the absence or surrender of the idea, of reason, is, in his eyes, a Philistine. This is why Heine so often and so mercilessly attacks the liberals; much as he hates conservatism he hates Philistinism even more, and whoever attacks conservatism itself ignobly, not as a child of light, not in the name of the idea, is a Philistine. Our Cobbett is thus for him, much as he disliked our clergy and aristocracy whom Cobbett attacked, a Philistine with six fingers on every hand and on every foot six toes, four-and-twenty in number: a Philistine, the staff of whose spear is like a weaver's beam. Thus he speaks of him:—

'While I translate Cobbett's words, the man himself comes bodily before my mind's eye, as I saw him at that uproarious dinner at the Crown and Anchor Tavern, with his scolding red face and his radical laugh, in which venomous hate mingles with a mocking exultation at his enemies' surely approaching downfall. He is a chained cur, who falls with equal fury on every one whom he does not know, often bites the best friend of the house in his calves, barks incessantly, and just because of this incessantness of his barking cannot get listened to, even when he barks at a real thief. Therefore, the distinguished thieves who plunder England do not think it necessary to throw the growling Cobbett a bone to stop his mouth. This makes the dog furiously savage, and he shows all his hungry teeth. Poor old Cobbett! England's dog! I have no love for thee, for every vulgar nature my soul abhors: but thou touchest me to the inmost soul with pity, as I see how thou strainest in vain to break loose and to get at those thieves, who make off with their booty before thy very eyes, and mock at thy fruitless springs and thine impotent howling.'

There is balm in Philistia as well as in Gilead. A chosen circle of children of the modern spirit, perfectly emancipated from prejudice and commonplace, regarding the ideal side of things in all its efforts for change, passionately despising half-measures and condescension to human folly and obstinacy,—with a bewildered, timid, torpid multitude behind,—conducts a country to the government of Herr von Bismarck. A nation regarding the practical side of things in its efforts for change, attacking not what is irrational, but what is pressingly inconvenient, and attacking this as one body, 'moving altogether if it move at all,' and treating children of light like the very harshest of step-mothers, comes to the prosperity and liberty of modern England. For all that, however, Philistia (let me say it again) is not the true promised land, as we English commonly imagine it to be; and our excessive neglect of the idea, and consequent inaptitude for it, threatens us, at a moment when the idea is beginning to exercise a real power in human society, with serious future inconvenience, and, in the meanwhile, cuts us off from the sympathy of other nations, which feel its power more than we do.

But, in 1830, Heine very soon found that the fire-engines of the German governments were too much for his direct efforts at incendiarism. 'What demon drove me,' he cries, 'to write my *Reisebilder,* to edit a newspaper, to plague myself with our time and its interests, to try and shake the poor German Hodge out of his thousand years' sleep in his hole? What good did I get by it? Hodge opened his eyes, only to shut them again immediately; he yawned, only to begin snoring again the next minute louder than ever; he stretched his stiff ungainly limbs, only to sink down again directly afterwards, and lie like a dead man in the old bed of his accustomed habits. I must have rest; but where am I to find a resting-place? In Germany I can no longer stay.'

This is Heine's jesting account of his own efforts to rouse Germany: now for his pathetic account of them; it is because he unites so much wit with so much pathos that he is so effective a writer:—

'The Emperor Charles the Fifth sate in sore straits, in the Tyrol, encompassed by his enemies. All his knights and courtiers had forsaken him; not one came to his help. I know not if he had at that time the cheese face with which Holbein has painted him for us. But I am sure that under-lip of his, with its contempt for mankind, stuck out even more than it does in his portraits. How could he but contemn the tribe which in the sunshine of his prosperity had fawned on him so devotedly, and now, in his dark distress, left him all alone? Then suddenly his door opened, and there came in a man in disguise, and, as he threw back his cloak, the Kaiser recognised in him his faithful Conrad von der Rosen, the court jester. This man brought him comfort and counsel, and he was the court jester!

'O German fatherland! dear German people! I am thy Conrad von der Rosen. The man whose proper business was to amuse thee, and who in good times should have catered only for thy mirth, makes his way into thy prison in time of need; here, under my cloak, I bring thee thy sceptre and crown; dost thou not recognise me, my Kaiser? If I cannot free thee, I will at least comfort thee, and thou shalt at least have one with thee who will prattle with thee about thy sorest affliction, and whisper courage to thee, and love thee, and whose best joke and best blood shall be at thy service. For thou, my people, art the true Kaiser, the true lord of the land; thy will is sovereign, and more legitimate far than that purple *Tel est notre plaisir,* which invokes a divine right with no better warrant than the anointings of shaven and shorn jugglers; thy will, my people, is the sole rightful source of power. Though now thou liest down in thy bonds, yet in the end will thy rightful cause prevail; the day of deliverance is at hand, a new time is beginning. My Kaiser, the night is over, and out there glows the ruddy dawn.

' "Conrad von der Rosen, my fool, thou art mistaken; perhaps thou takest a headsman's gleaming axe for the sun, and the red of dawn is only blood."

' "No, my Kaiser, it is the sun, though it is rising in the west; these six thousand years it has always risen in the east; it is high time there should come a change."

' "Conrad von der Rosen, my fool, thou hast lost the bells out of thy red cap, and it has now such an odd look, that red cap of thine!"

' "Ah, my Kaiser, thy distress has made me shake my head so hard and fierce, that the fool's bells have dropped off my cap; the cap is none the worse for that."

' "Conrad von der Rosen, my fool, what is that noise of breaking and cracking outside there?"

' "Hush! that is the saw and the carpenter's axe, and soon the doors of thy prison will be burst open, and thou wilt be free, my Kaiser!"

' "Am I then really Kaiser? Ah, I forgot, it is the fool who tells me so!"

' "Oh, sigh not, my dear master, the air of thy prison makes thee so desponding! when once thou hast got thy rights again, thou wilt feel once more the bold imperial blood in thy veins, and thou wilt be proud like a Kaiser, and violent, and gracious, and unjust, and smiling, and ungrateful, as princes are."

' "Conrad von der Rosen, my fool, when I am free, what wilt thou do then?"

' "I will then sew new bells on to my cap."

' "And how shall I recompense thy fidelity?"

' "Ah, dear master, by not leaving me to die in a ditch!" '

I wish to mark Heine's place in modern European literature, the scope of his activity, and his value. I cannot attempt to give here a detailed account of his life, or a description of his separate works. In May, 1831, he went over his Jordan, the Rhine, and fixed himself in his new Jerusalem, Paris. There, henceforward, he lived, going in general to some French watering-place in the summer, but making only one or two short visits to Germany during the rest of his life. His works, in verse and prose, succeeded each other without stopping; a collected edition of them, filling seven closely-printed octavo volumes, has been published in America; [1] in the collected editions of few people's works is there so little to skip. Those who wish for a single good specimen of him should read his first important work, the work which made his reputation, the *Reisebilder,* or 'Travelling Sketches:' prose and verse, wit and seriousness, are mingled in it, and the mingling of these is characteristic of Heine, and is nowhere to be seen practised more naturally and happily than in his *Reisebilder.* In 1847 his health, which till then had always been perfectly good, gave way. He had a kind of paralytic stroke. His malady proved to be a softening of the spinal marrow: it was incurable; it made rapid progress. In May, 1848, not a year after his first attack, he went out of doors for the

[1] A complete edition has at last appeared in Germany.

last time; but his disease took more than eight years to kill him. For nearly eight years he lay helpless on a couch, with the use of his limbs gone, wasted almost to the proportions of a child, wasted so that a woman could carry him about; the sight of one eye lost, that of the other greatly dimmed, and requiring, that it might be exercised, to have the palsied eyelid lifted and held up by the finger; all this, and besides this, suffering at short intervals paroxysms of nervous agony. I have said he was not preeminently brave; but in the astonishing force of spirit with which he retained his activity of mind, even his gaiety, amid all his suffering, and went on composing with undiminished fire to the last, he was truly brave. Nothing could clog that aërial lightness. 'Pouvez-vous siffler?' his doctor asked him one day, when he was almost at his last gasp;—'siffler,' as every one knows, has the double meaning of *to whistle* and *to hiss:*—'Hélas! non,' was his whispered answer; 'pas même une comédie de M. Scribe!' M. Scribe is, or was, the favourite dramatist of the French Philistine. 'My nerves,' he said to some one who asked him about them in 1855, the year of the Great Exhibition in Paris, 'my nerves are of that quite singularly remarkable miserableness of nature, that I am convinced they would get at the Exhibition the grand medal for pain and misery.' He read all the medical books which treated of his complaint. 'But,' said he to some one who found him thus engaged, 'what good this reading is to do me I don't know, except that it will qualify me to give lectures in heaven on the ignorance of doctors on earth about diseases of the spinal marrow.' What a matter of grim seriousness are our own ailments to most of us! yet with this gaiety Heine treated his to the end. That end, so long in coming, came at last. Heine died on the 17th of February, 1856, at the age of fifty-eight. By his will he forbade that his remains should be transported to Germany. He lies buried in the cemetery of Montmartre, at Paris.

His direct political action was null, and this is neither to be wondered at nor regretted; direct political action is not the true function of literature, and Heine was a born man of letters. Even in his favourite France the turn taken by public affairs was not at all what he wished, though he read French politics by no means as we in England, most of us, read them. He thought things were tending there to the triumph of communism; and to a champion of the idea like Heine, what there is gross and narrow in communism was very repulsive. 'It is all of no use,' he cried on his death-bed, 'the future belongs to our enemies, the Communists, and Louis Napoleon is their John the Baptist.' 'And yet,'—he added with all his old love for that remarkable entity, so full of attraction for him, so profoundly unknown in England, the French people,—'do not believe that God lets all this go forward merely as a grand comedy. Even though the Communists deny him to-day, he knows better than they do, that a time will come when they will learn to believe in him.' After 1831, his hopes of soon upsetting the German Governments had died away, and his propagandism took another, a more truly literary, character. It took the character of an intrepid application of the modern spirit to literature. To the ideas with which the burning questions of modern life filled him, he made all his subject-matter minister. He touched all the great points in the career of the human race, and here he but followed the tendency of the wide culture of Germany; but he touched them with a wand which brought them all under a light where the modern eye cares most to see them, and here he gave a lesson to the culture of Germany,—so wide, so impartial, that it is apt to become slack and powerless, and to lose itself in its materials for want of a strong central idea round which to group all its other ideas. So the mystic and romantic school of Germany lost itself in the Middle Ages, was overpowered by their influence, came to ruin by its vain dreams of renewing them. Heine, with a far profounder sense of the mystic and romantic charm of the Middle Age than Gœrres, or Brentano, or Arnim, Heine the chief romantic poet of Germany, is yet also much more than a romantic poet; he is a great modern poet, he is not conquered by the Middle Age, he has a talisman by which he can feel,—along with but above the power of the fascinating Middle Age itself,—the power of modern ideas.

A French critic of Heine thinks he has said enough in saying that Heine proclaimed in German countries, with beat of drum, the ideas of 1789, and that at the cheerful noise of his drum the ghosts of the Middle Age took to flight. But this is rather too French an account of the matter. Germany, that vast mine of ideas, had no need to import ideas, as such, from any foreign country; and if Heine had carried ideas, as such, from France into Germany, he would but have been carrying coals to Newcastle. But that for which France, far less meditative than Germany, is eminent, is the prompt, ardent, and practical application of an idea, when she seizes it, in all departments of human activity which admit it. And that in which Germany most fails, and by failing in which she appears so helpless and impotent, is just the practical application of her innumerable ideas. 'When Candide,' says Heine himself, 'came to Eldorado, he saw in the streets a number of boys who were playing with gold-nuggets instead of marbles. This degree of luxury made him imagine that they must be the king's children, and he was not a little astonished when he found that in Eldorado gold-nuggets are of no more value than marbles are with us, and that the schoolboys play with them. A similar thing happened to a friend of mine, a foreigner, when he came to Germany and first read German books. He was perfectly astounded at the wealth of ideas which he found in them; but he soon remarked that ideas in Germany are as plentiful as gold-nuggets in Eldorado, and that those writers whom he had taken for intellectual princes, were in reality only common school-boys.' Heine was, as he calls himself, a 'Child of the French Revolution,' an 'Initiator,' because he vigorously assured the Germans that ideas were not counters or marbles, to be played with for their own sake; because he exhibited in literature modern ideas applied with the utmost freedom, clearness, and originality. And therefore he declared that the great task of his life had been the endeavour to establish a cordial relation between France and Germany. It is because he thus operates a junction between the French spirit, and German ideas and German culture, that he founds something new, opens a fresh period, and deserves the attention of criticism far more than the German poets his contemporaries, who merely continue an old period till it expires. It may be predicted that in the literature of other countries, too, the French spirit is destined to make its influence felt,—as an element, in alliance with the native spirit, of novelty and movement,—as it has made its influence felt in German literature; fifty years hence a critic will be demonstrating to our grandchildren how this phenomenon has come to pass.

We in England, in our great burst of literature during the first thirty years of the present century, had no manifestation of the modern spirit, as this spirit manifests itself in Goethe's works or Heine's. And the reason is not far to seek. We had neither the German wealth of ideas, nor the French enthusiasm for applying ideas. There reigned in the mass of the nation that inveterate inaccessibility to ideas, that Philistinism,—to use the German nickname,—which reacts even on the individual genius that is exempt from it. In our greatest literary epoch, that of the Elizabethan age, English society at large was accessible to ideas, was permeated by them, was vivified by them, to a degree which has never been reached in England since. Hence the unique greatness in English literature of Shakspeare and his contemporaries. They were powerfully upheld by the intellectual life of their nation; they applied freely in literature the then modern ideas,— the ideas of the Renascence and the Reformation. A few years afterwards the great English middle class, the kernel of the nation, the class whose intelligent sympathy had upheld a Shakspeare, entered the prison of Puritanism, and had the key turned on its spirit there for two hundred years. *He enlargeth a nation,* says Job, *and straiteneth it again.*

In the literary movement of the beginning of the nineteenth century the

signal attempt to apply freely the modern spirit was made in England by
two members of the aristocratic class, Byron and Shelley. Aristocracies
are, as such, naturally impenetrable by ideas; but their individual members
have a high courage and a turn for breaking bounds; and a man of genius,
who is the born child of the idea, happening to be born in the aristocratic
ranks, chafes against the obstacles which prevent him from freely devel-
oping it. But Byron and Shelley did not succeed in their attempt freely to
apply the modern spirit in English literature; they could not succeed in it;
the resistance to baffle them, the want of intelligent sympathy to guide and
uphold them, were too great. Their literary creation, compared with the
literary creation of Shakspeare and Spenser, compared with the literary creation of Goethe and Heine, is a failure. The best literary creation of that time in England proceeded from men who did not make the
same bold attempt as Byron and Shelley. What, in fact, was the career of
the chief English men of letters, their contemporaries? The gravest of them,
Wordsworth, retired (in Middle-Age phrase) into a monastery. I mean,
he plunged himself in the inward life, he voluntarily cut himself off from
the modern spirit. Coleridge took to opium. Scott became the historiog-
rapher royal of feudalism. Keats passionately gave himself up to a sensuous
genius, to his faculty for interpreting nature; and he died of consumption
at twenty-five. Wordsworth, Scott, and Keats have left admirable works;
far more solid and complete works than those which Byron and Shelley
have left. But their works have this defect;—they do not belong to that
which is the main current of the literature of modern epochs, they do not
apply modern ideas to life; they constitute, therefore, *minor currents,* and
all other literary work of our day, however popular, which has the same
defect, also constitutes but a minor current. Byron and Shelley will long be
remembered, long after the inadequacy of their actual work is clearly
recognised, for their passionate, their Titanic effort to flow in the main
stream of modern literature; their names will be greater than their writings;
stat magni nominis umbra.

Heine's literary good fortune was superior to that of Byron and Shelley.
His theatre of operations was Germany, whose Philistinism does not consist
in her want of ideas, or in her inaccessibility to ideas, for she teems with
them and loves them, but, as I have said, in her feeble and hesitating application of modern ideas to life. Heine's intense modernism, his absolute
freedom, his utter rejection of stock classicism and stock romanticism, his
bringing all things under the point of view of the nineteenth century, were
understood and laid to heart by Germany, through virtue of her immense,
tolerant intellectualism, much as there was in all Heine said to affront and

wound Germany. The wit and ardent modern spirit of France Heine joined to the culture, the sentiment, the thought of Germany. This is what makes him so remarkable; his wonderful clearness, lightness, and freedom, united with such power of feeling, and width of range. Is there anywhere keener wit than in his story of the French abbé who was his tutor, and who wanted to get from him that *la religion* is French for *der Glaube:* 'Six times did he ask me the question: "Henry, what is *der Glaube* in French?" and six times, and each time with a greater burst of tears, did I answer him—"It is *le crédit.*" And at the seventh time, his face purple with rage, the infuriated questioner screamed out: "It is *la religion;*" and a rain of cuffs descended upon me, and all the other boys burst out laughing. Since that day I have never been able to hear *la religion* mentioned, without feeling a tremor run through my back, and my cheeks grow red with shame.' Or in that comment on the fate of Professor Saalfeld, who had been addicted to writing furious pamphlets against Napoleon, and who was a professor at Göttingen, a great seat, according to Heine, of pedantry and Philistinism: 'It is curious,' says Heine, 'the three greatest adversaries of Napoleon have all of them ended miserably. Castlereagh cut his own throat; Louis the Eighteenth rotted upon his throne; and Professor Saalfeld is still a professor at Göttingen.' It is impossible to go beyond that.

What wit, again, in that saying which every one has heard: 'The Englishman loves liberty like his lawful wife, the Frenchman loves her like his mistress, the German loves her like his old grandmother.' But the turn Heine gives to this incomparable saying is not so well known; and it is by that turn he shows himself the born poet he is,—full of delicacy and tenderness, of inexhaustible resource, infinitely new and striking:—

'And yet, after all, no one can ever tell how things may turn out. The grumpy Englishman, in an ill-temper with his wife, is capable of some day putting a rope round her neck, and taking her to be sold at Smithfield. The inconstant Frenchman may become unfaithful to his adored mistress, and be seen fluttering about the Palais Royal after another. *But the German will never quite abandon his old grandmother;* he will always keep for her a nook by the chimney-corner, where she can tell her fairy stories to the listening children.'

Is it possible to touch more delicately and happily both the weakness and the strength of Germany;—pedantic, simple, enslaved, free, ridiculous, admirable Germany?

And Heine's verse,—his *Lieder?* Oh, the comfort, after dealing with French people of genius, irresistibly impelled to try and express themselves in verse, launching out into a deep which destiny has sown with so many rocks for them,—the comfort of coming to a man of genius, who finds in verse his freest and most perfect expression, whose voyage over the deep of poetry destiny makes smooth! After the rhythm, to us, at any rate, with the German paste in our composition, so deeply unsatisfying, of—

> 'Ah! que me dites-vous, et que vous dit mon âme?
> Que dit le ciel à l'aube et la flamme à la flamme?'

what a blessing to arrive at rhythms like—

> 'Take, oh, take those lips away,
> That so sweetly were forsworn—'

or—

> 'Siehst sehr sterbeblässlich aus,
> Doch getrost! du bist zu Haus—'

in which one's soul can take pleasure! The magic of Heine's poetical form is incomparable; he chiefly uses a form of old German popular poetry, a ballad-form which has more rapidity and grace than any ballad-form of ours; he employs this form with the most exquisite lightness and ease, and yet it has at the same time the inborn fulness, pathos, and old-world charm of all true forms of popular poetry. Thus in Heine's poetry, too, one perpetually blends the impression of French modernism and clearness, with that of German sentiment and fulness; and to give this blended impression is, as I have said, Heine's great characteristic. To feel it, one must read him; he gives it in his form as well as in his contents, and by translation I can only reproduce it so far as his contents give it. But even the contents of many of his poems are capable of giving a certain sense of it. Here, for instance, is a poem in which he makes his profession of faith to an innocent beautiful soul, a sort of Gretchen, the child of some simple mining people having their hut among the pines at the foot of the Hartz Mountains, who reproaches him with not holding the old articles of the Christian creed:—

'Ah, my child, while I was yet a little boy, while I yet sate upon my mother's knee, I believed in God the Father, who rules up there in Heaven, good and great;

'Who created the beautiful earth, and the beautiful men and women thereon; who ordained for sun, moon, and stars their courses.

'When I got bigger, my child, I comprehended yet a great deal more than this, and comprehended, and grew intelligent; and I believe on the Son also;

'On the beloved Son, who loved us, and revealed love to us; and, for his reward, as always happens, was crucified by the people.

'Now, when I am grown up, have read much, have travelled much, my heart swells within me, and with my whole heart I believe on the Holy Ghost.

'The greatest miracles were of his working, and still greater miracles doth he even now work; he burst in sunder the oppressor's stronghold, and he burst in sunder the bondsman's yoke.

'He heals old death-wounds, and renews the old right; all mankind are one race of noble equals before him. 580

'He chases away the evil clouds and the dark cobwebs of the brain, which have spoilt love and joy for us, which day and night have loured on us.

'A thousand knights, well harnessed, has the Holy Ghost chosen out to fulfil his will, and he has put courage into their souls.

'Their good swords flash, their bright banners wave; what, thou wouldst give much, my child, to look upon such gallant knights?

'Well, on me, my child, look! kiss me, and look boldly upon me! one of those knights of the Holy Ghost am I.'

One has only to turn over the pages of his *Romancero,*—a collection of 590 poems written in the first years of his illness, with his whole power and charm still in them, and not, like his latest poems of all, painfully touched by the air of his *Matrazzen-gruft,* his 'mattress-grave,'—to see Heine's width of range; the most varied figures succeed one another,—Rhampsinitus, Edith with the Swan Neck, Charles the First, Marie Antoinette, King David, a heroine of *Mabille,* Melisanda of Tripoli, Richard Coeur de Lion, Pedro the Cruel, Firdusi, Cortes, Dr. Döllinger;—but never does Heine attempt to be *hübsch objectiv,* 'beautifully objective,' to become in spirit an old Egyptian, or an old Hebrew, or a Middle-Age knight, or a Spanish adventurer, or an English royalist; he always remains Heinrich 600 Heine, a son of the nineteenth century. To give a notion of his tone I will quote a few stanzas at the end of the *Spanish Atridæ,* in which he describes, in the character of a visitor at the court of Henry of Transtamare at Segovia, Henry's treatment of the children of his brother, Pedro the Cruel. Don Diego Albuquerque, his neighbour, strolls after dinner through the castle with him:

'In the cloister-passage, which leads to the kennels where are kept the king's hounds, that with their growling and yelping let you know a long way off where they are,

'There I saw, built into the wall, and with a strong iron grating for its 610 outer face, a cell like a cage.

'Two human figures sate therein, two young boys; chained by the leg, they crouched in the dirty straw.

'Hardly twelve years old seemed the one, the other not much older; their faces fair and noble, but pale and wan with sickness.

'They were all in rags, almost naked; and their lean bodies showed wounds, the marks of ill-usage; both of them shivered with fever.

'They looked up at me out of the depth of their misery; "Who," I cried in horror to Don Diego, "are these pictures of wretchedness?"

'Don Diego seemed embarrassed; he looked round to see that no one was listening; then he gave a deep sigh; and at last, putting on the easy tone of a man of the world, he said:

' "These are a pair of king's sons, who were early left orphans; the name of their father was King Pedro, the name of their mother, Maria de Padilla.

' "After the great battle of Navarette, when Henry of Transtamare had relieved his brother, King Pedro, of the troublesome burden of the crown,

' "And likewise of that still more troublesome burden, which is called life, then Don Henry's victorious magnanimity had to deal with his brother's children.

' "He has adopted them, as an uncle should; and he has given them free quarters in his own castle.

' "The room which he has assigned to them is certainly rather small, but then it is cool in summer, and not intolerably cold in winter.

' "Their fare is rye-bread, which tastes as sweet as if the goddess Ceres had baked it express for her beloved Proserpine.

' "Not unfrequently, too, he sends a scullion to them with garbanzos, and then the young gentlemen know that it is Sunday in Spain.

' "But it is not Sunday every day, and garbanzos do not come every day; and the master of the hounds gives them the treat of his whip.

' "For the master of the hounds, who has under his superintendence the kennels and the pack, and the nephews' cage also,

' "Is the unfortunate husband of that lemon-faced woman with the white ruff, whom we remarked to-day at dinner.

' "And she scolds so sharp, that often her husband snatches his whip, and rushes down here, and gives it to the dogs and to the poor little boys.

' "But his majesty has expressed his disapproval of such proceedings, and has given orders that for the future his nephews are to be treated differently from the dogs.

' "He has determined no longer to entrust the disciplining of his nephews to a mercenary stranger, but to carry it out with his own hands."

'Don Diego stopped abruptly; for the seneschal of the castle joined us, and politely expressed his hope that we had dined to our satisfaction.'

Observe how the irony of the whole of that, finishing with the grim innuendo of the last stanza but one, is at once truly masterly and truly modern.

No account of Heine is complete which does not notice the Jewish element in him. His race he treated with the same freedom with which he treated everything else, but he derived a great force from it, and no one knew this better than he himself. He has excellently pointed out how in the sixteenth century there was a double renascence,—a Hellenic renascence   660 and a Hebrew renascence,—and how both have been great powers ever since. He himself had in him both the spirit of Greece and the spirit of Judea; both these spirits reach the infinite, which is the true goal of all poetry and all art,—the Greek spirit by beauty, the Hebrew spirit by sublimity. By his perfection of literary form, by his love of clearness, by his love of beauty, Heine is Greek; by his intensity, by his untameableness, by his 'longing which cannot be uttered,' he is Hebrew. Yet what Hebrew ever treated the things of the Hebrews like this?—

'There lives at Hamburg, in a one-roomed lodging in the Baker's Broad Walk, a man whose name is Moses Lump; all the week he goes about in   670 wind and rain, with his pack on his back, to earn his few shillings; but when on Friday evening he comes home, he finds the candlestick with seven candles lighted, and the table covered with a fair white cloth, and he puts away from him his pack and his cares, and he sits down to table with his squinting wife and yet more squinting daughter, and eats fish with them, fish which has been dressed in beautiful white garlic sauce, sings therewith the grandest psalms of King David, rejoices with his whole heart over the deliverance of the children of Israel out of Egypt, rejoices, too, that all the wicked ones who have done the children of Israel hurt, have ended by taking themselves off; that King Pharaoh, Nebuchadnezzar,   680 Haman, Antiochus, Titus, and all such people, are well dead, while he, Moses Lump, is yet alive, and eating fish with wife and daughter; and I can tell you, Doctor, the fish is delicate and the man is happy, he has no call to torment himself about culture, he sits contented in his religion and in his green bed-gown, like Diogenes in his tub, he contemplates with satisfaction his candles, which he on no account will snuff for himself; and I can tell you, if the candles burn a little dim, and the snuffers-woman, whose business it is to snuff them, is not at hand, and Rothschild the Great were at that moment to come in, with all his brokers, bill discounters, agents, and chief clerks, with whom he conquers the world, and Rothschild were to   690 say: "Moses Lump, ask of me what favour you will, and it shall be granted you;"—Doctor, I am convinced, Moses Lump would quietly answer:

"Snuff me those candles!" and Rothschild the Great would exclaim with admiration: "If I were not Rothschild, I would be Moses Lump." '

There Heine shows us his own people by its comic side; in the poem of the *Princess Sabbath* he shows it to us by a more serious die. The Princess Sabbath, 'the *tranquil Princess,* pearl and flower of all beauty, fair as the Queen of Sheba, Solomon's bosom friend, that blue stocking from Ethiopia, who wanted to shine by her *esprit,* and with her wise riddles made herself in the long run a bore' (with Heine the sarcastic turn is never far off), this princess has for her betrothed a prince whom sorcery has transformed into an animal of lower race, the Prince Israel.

'A dog with the desires of a dog, he wallows all the week long in the filth and refuse of life, amidst the jeers of the boys in the street.

'But every Friday evening, at the twilight hour, suddenly the magic passes off, and the dog becomes once more a human being.

'A man with the feelings of a man, with head and heart raised aloft, in festal garb, in almost clean garb, he enters the halls of his Father.

'Hail, beloved halls of my royal Father! Ye tents of Jacob, I kiss with my lips your holy door-posts!'

Still more he shows us this serious side in his beautiful poem on Jehuda ben Halevy, a poet belonging to 'the great golden age of the Arabian, Old-Spanish, Jewish school of poets,' a contemporary of the troubadours:—

'He, too,—the hero whom we sing,—Jehuda ben Halevy, too, had his lady-love; but she was of a special sort.

'She was no Laura, whose eyes, mortal stars, in the cathedral on Good Friday kindled that world-renowned flame.

'She was no châtelaine, who in the blooming glory of her youth presided at tourneys, and awarded the victor's crown.

'No casuistess in the Gay Science was she, no lady *doctrinaire,* who delivered her oracles in the judgment-chamber of a Court of Love.

'She, whom the Rabbi loved, was a woe-begone poor darling, a mourning picture of desolation . . . and her name was Jerusalem.'

Jehuda ben Halevy, like the Crusaders, makes his pilgrimage to Jerusalem; and there, amid the ruins, sings a song of Sion which has become famous among his people:—

'That lay of pearled tears is the wide-famed Lament, which is sung in all the scattered tents of Jacob throughout the world.

'On the ninth day of the month which is called Ab, on the anniversary of Jerusalem's destruction by Titus Vespasianus.

'Yes, that is the song of Sion, which Jehuda ben Halevy sang with his dying breath amid the holy ruins of Jerusalem.

'Barefoot, and in penitential weeds, he sate there upon the fragment of a fallen column; down to his breast fell,

'Like a grey forest, his hair; and cast a weird shadow on the face which looked out through it,—his troubled pale face, with the spiritual eyes.

'So he sate and sang, like unto a seer out of the foretime to look upon; Jeremiah, the Ancient, seemed to have risen out of his grave.

'But a bold Saracen came riding that way, aloft on his barb, lolling in his saddle, and brandishing a naked javelin;

'Into the breast of the poor singer he plunged his deadly shaft, and shot away like a winged shadow.

'Quietly flowed the Rabbi's life-blood, quietly he sang his song to an end; and his last dying sigh was Jerusalem!'

But, most of all, Heine shows us this side in a strange poem describing a public dispute, before King Pedro and his court, between a Jewish and a Christian champion, on the merits of their respective faiths. In the strain of the Jew all the fierceness of the old Hebrew genius, all its rigid defiant Monotheism, appear:—

'Our God has not died like a poor innocent lamb for mankind; he is no gushing philanthropist, no declaimer.

'Our God is not love, caressing is not his line; but he is a God of thunder, and he is a God of revenge.

'The lightnings of his wrath strike inexorably every sinner, and the sins of the fathers are often visited upon their remote posterity.

'Our God, he is alive, and in his hall of heaven he goes on existing away, throughout all the eternities.

'Our God, too, is a God in robust health, no myth, pale and thin as sacrificial wafers, or as shadows by Cocytus.

'Our God is strong. In his hand he upholds sun, moon, and stars; thrones break, nations reel to and fro, when he knits his forehead.

'Our God loves music, the voice of the harp and the song of feasting; but the sound of church-bells he hates, as he hates the grunting of pigs.'

Nor must Heine's sweetest note be unheard,—his plaintive note, his note of melancholy. Here is a strain which came from him as he lay, in the winter night, on his 'mattress-grave' at Paris, and let his thoughts wander home to Germany, 'the great child, entertaining herself with her Christmas-tree.' 'Thou tookest,'—he cries to the German exile,—

'Thou tookest thy flight towards sunshine and happiness; naked and poor returnest thou back. German truth, German shirts,—one gets them worn to tatters in foreign parts.

'Deadly pale are thy looks, but take comfort, thou art at home! one lies warm in German earth, warm as by the old pleasant fireside.

'Many a one, alas, became crippled, and could get home no more! longingly he stretches out his arms; God have mercy upon him!'

God have mercy upon him! for what remain of the days of the years of his life are few and evil. 'Can it be that I still actually exist? My body is so shrunk that there is hardly anything of me left but my voice, and my bed makes me think of the melodious grave of the enchanter Merlin, which is in the forest of Broceliand in Brittany, under high oaks whose tops shine like green flames to heaven. Ah, I envy thee those trees, brother Merlin, and their fresh waving! for over my mattress-grave here in Paris no green leaves rustle; and early and late I hear nothing but the rattle of carriages, hammering, scolding, and the jingle of the piano. A grave without rest, death without the privileges of the departed, who have no longer any need to spend money, or to write letters, or to compose books. What a melancholy situation!'

He died, and has left a blemished name; with his crying faults,—his intemperate susceptibility, his unscrupulousness in passion, his inconceivable attacks on his enemies, his still more inconceivable attacks on his friends, his want of generosity, his sensuality, his incessant mocking,—how could it be otherwise? Not only was he not one of Mr. Carlyle's 'respectable' people, he was profoundly *dis*respectable; and not even the merit of not being a Philistine can make up for a man's being that. To his intellectual deliverance there was an addition of something else wanting, and that something else was something immense; the old-fashioned, laborious, eternally needful moral deliverance. Goethe says that he was deficient in *love;* to me his weakness seems to be not so much a deficiency in love as a deficiency in self-respect, in true dignity of character. But on this negative side of one's criticism of a man of great genius, I for my part, when I have once clearly marked that this negative side is and must be there, have no pleasure in dwelling. I prefer to say of Heine something positive. He is not an adequate interpreter of the modern world. He is only a brilliant soldier in the Liberation-War of humanity. But, such as he is, he is (and posterity too, I am quite sure, will say this), in the European poetry of that quarter of a century which follows the death of Goethe, incomparably the most important figure.

What a spendthrift, one is tempted to cry, is Nature! With what prodigality, in the march of generations, she employs human power, content to gather almost always little result from it, sometimes none! Look at Byron, that Byron whom the present generation of Englishmen are forgetting; Byron, the greatest natural force, the greatest elementary power, I cannot but think, which has appeared in our literature since Shakspeare. And what became of this wonderful production of nature? He shattered himself, he inevitably shattered himself to pieces, against the huge, black, cloud-topped, interminable precipice of British Philistinism. But Byron, it may be said, was eminent only by his genius, only by his inborn force and fire; he had not the intellectual equipment of a supreme modern poet; except for his genius he was an ordinary nineteenth-century English gentleman, with little culture and with no ideas. Well, then, look at Heine. Heine had all the culture of Germany; in his head fermented all the ideas of modern Europe. And what have we got from Heine? A half-result, for want of moral balance, and of nobleness of soul and character. That is what I say; there is so much power, so many seem able to run well, so many give promise of running well;—so few reach the goal, so few are chosen. *Many are called, few chosen.*

PAGAN AND MEDIAEVAL
RELIGIOUS SENTIMENT

————◄◆►————

I read the other day in the *Dublin Review:*—'We Catholics are apt to be cowed and scared by the lordly oppression of public opinion, and not to bear ourselves as men in the face of the anti-Catholic society of England. It is good to have an habitual consciousness that the public opinion of Catholic Europe looks upon Protestant England with a mixture of impatience and compassion, which more than balances the arrogance of the English people towards the Catholic Church in these countries.'

The Holy Catholic Church, Apostolic and Roman, can take very good care of herself, and I am not going to defend her against the scorns of Exeter Hall. Catholicism is not a great visible force in this country, and the mass of mankind will always treat lightly even things the most venerable, if they do not present themselves as visible forces before its eyes. In Catholic countries, as the *Dublin Review* itself says with triumph, they make very little account of the greatness of Exeter Hall. The majority has eyes only for the things of the majority, and in England the immense majority is Protestant. And yet, in spite of all the shocks which the feeling of a good

118

Catholic, like the writer in the *Dublin Review,* has in this Protestant country inevitably to undergo, in spite of the contemptuous insensibility to the
grandeur of Rome which he finds so general and so hard to bear, how
much has he to console him, how many acts of homage to the greatness of
his religion may he see if he has his eyes open! I will tell him of one of
them. Let him go in London to that delightful spot, that Happy Island in
Bloomsbury, the reading-room of the British Museum. Let him visit its
sacred quarter, the region where its theological books are placed. I am
almost afraid to say what he will find there, for fear Mr. Spurgeon, like a
second Caliph Omar, should give the library to the flames. He will find an
immense Catholic work, the collection of the Abbé Migne, lording it over
that whole region, reducing to insignificance the feeble Protestant forces
which hang upon its skirts. Protestantism is duly represented, indeed: the
librarian knows his business too well to suffer it to be otherwise; all the
varieties of Protestantism are there; there is the Library of Anglo-Catholic
Theology, learned, decorous, exemplary, but a little uninteresting; there are
the works of Calvin, rigid, militant, menacing; there are the works of Dr.
Chalmers, the Scotch thistle valiantly doing duty as the rose of Sharon,
but keeping something very Scotch about it all the time; there are the
works of Dr. Channing, the last word of religious philosophy in a land
where every one has some culture, and where superiorities are discoun-
tenanced,—the flower of moral and intelligent mediocrity. But how are all
these divided against one another, and how, though they were all united,
are they dwarfed by the Catholic Leviathan, their neighbour! Majestic in
its blue and gold unity, this fills shelf after shelf and compartment after
compartment, its right mounting up into heaven among the white folios of
the *Acta Sanctorum,* its left plunging down into hell among the yellow
octavos of the *Law Digest.* Everything is there, in that immense *Patrologiae
Cursus Completus,* in that *Encyclopédie Théologique,* that *Nouvelle
Encyclopédie Théologique,* that *Troisième Encyclopédie Théologique;*
religion, philosophy, history, biography, arts, sciences, bibliography, gos-
sip. The work embraces the whole range of human interests; like one of the
great Middle-Age Cathedrals, it is in itself a study for a life. Like the net
in Scripture, it drags everything to land, bad and good, lay and ecclesiastical, sacred and profane, so that it be but matter of human concern. Wide-
embracing as the power whose product it is! a power, for history at any
rate, eminently *the Church;* not, perhaps, the Church of the future, but
indisputably the Church of the past and, in the past, the Church of the
multitude.

This is why the man of imagination—nay, and the philosopher too, in spite of her propensity to burn him—will always have a weakness for the Catholic Church; because of the rich treasures of human life which have been stored within her pale. The mention of other religious bodies, or of their leaders, at once calls up in our mind the thought of men of a definite type as their adherents; the mention of Catholicism suggests no such special following. Anglicanism suggests the English episcopate; Calvin's name suggests Dr. Candlish; Chalmers's, the Duke of Argyll; Channing's, Boston society; but Catholicism suggests,—what shall I say?—all the pell-mell of the men and women of Shakspeare's plays. This abundance the Abbé Migne's collection faithfully reflects. People talk of this or that work which they would choose, if they were to pass their life with only one; for my part I think I would choose the Abbé Migne's collection. *Quicquid agunt homines,*—everything, as I have said, is there. Do not seek in it splendour of form, perfection of editing; its paper is common, its type ugly, its editing indifferent, its printing careless. The greatest and most baffling crowd of misprints I ever met with in my life occurs in a very important page of the introduction to the *Dictionnaire des Apocryphes.* But this is just what you have in the world,—quantity rather than quality. Do not seek in it impartiality, the critical spirit; in reading it you must do the criticism for yourself; it loves criticism as little as the world loves it. Like the world, it chooses to have things all its own way, to abuse its adversary, to back its own notion through thick and thin, to put forward all the *pros* for its own notion, to suppress all the *contras;* it does just all that the world does, and all that the critical spirit shrinks from. Open the *Dictionnaire des Erreurs Sociales:* 'The religious persecutions of Henry the Eighth's and Edward the Sixth's time abated a little in the reign of Mary, to break out again with new fury in the reign of Elizabeth.' There is a summary of the history of religious persecution under the Tudors! But how unreasonable to reproach the Abbé Migne's work with wanting a criticism, which, by the very nature of things, it cannot have, and not rather to be grateful to it for its abundance, its variety, its infinite suggestiveness, its happy adoption, in many a delicate circumstance, of the urbane tone and temper of the man of the world, instead of the acrid tone and temper of the fanatic!

Still, in spite of their fascinations, the contents of this collection sometimes rouse the critical spirit within one. It happened that lately, after I had been thinking much of Marcus Aurelius and his times, I took down the *Dictionnaire des Origines du Christianisme,* to see what it had to say about paganism and pagans. I found much what I expected. I read the article, *Révélation Evangélique, sa Nécessité.* There I found what a sink of iniquity was the whole pagan world; how one Roman fed his oysters on his slaves, how another put a slave to death that a curious friend might see what dying was like; how Galen's mother tore and bit her waiting-women when she was in a passion with them. I found this account of the religion of paganism: 'Paganism invented a mob of divinities with the most hateful character, and attributed to them the most monstrous and abominable crimes. It personified in them drunkenness, incest, kidnapping, adultery, sensuality, knavery, cruelty, and rage.' And I found that from this religion there followed such practice as was to be expected: 'What must naturally have been the state of morals under the influence of such a religion, which penetrated with its own spirit the public life, the family life, and the individual life of antiquity?'

The colours in this picture are laid on very thick, and I for my part cannot believe that any human societies, with a religion and practice such as those just described, could ever have endured as the societies of Greece and Rome endured, still less have done what the societies of Greece and Rome did. We are not brought far by descriptions of the vices of great cities, or even of individuals driven mad by unbounded means of self-indulgence. Feudal and aristocratic life in Christendom has produced horrors of selfishness and cruelty not surpassed by the grandee of pagan Rome; and then, again, in antiquity there is Marcus Aurelius's mother to set against Galen's. Eminent examples of vice and virtue in individuals prove little as to the state of societies. What, under the first emperors, was the condition of the Roman poor upon the Aventine compared with that of our poor in Spitalfields and Bethnal Green? What, in comfort, morals, and happiness, were the rural population of the Sabine country under Augustus's rule, compared with the rural population of Hertfordshire and Buckinghamshire under the rule of Queen Victoria?

But these great questions are not now for me. Without trying to answer them, I ask myself, when I read such declamation as the foregoing, if I can find anything that will give me a near, distinct sense of the real difference in spirit and sentiment between paganism and Christianity, and of the natural effect of this difference upon people in general. I take a representative religious poem of paganism,—of the paganism which all the world has in its mind when it speaks of paganism. To be a representative poem, it must be one for popular use, one that the multitude listens to. Such a religious poem may be found at the end of one of the best and happiest of Theocritus's idylls, the fifteenth. In order that the reader may the better go along with me in the line of thought I am following, I will translate it; and, that he may see the medium in which religious poetry of this sort is found existing, the society out of which it grows, the people who form it and are formed by it, I will translate the whole, or nearly the whole, of the idyll (it is not long) in which the poem occurs.

The idyll is dramatic. Somewhere about two hundred and eighty years before the Christian era, a couple of Syracusan women, staying at Alexandria, agreed on the occasion of a great religious solemnity,—the feast of Adonis,—to go together to the palace of King Ptolemy Philadelphus, to see the image of Adonis, which the queen Arsinoe, Ptolemy's wife, had had decorated with peculiar magnificence. A hymn, by a celebrated performer, was to be recited over the image. The names of the two women are Gorgo and Praxinoe; their maids, who are mentioned in the poem, are called Eunoe and Eutychis. Gorgo comes by appointment to Praxinoe's house to fetch her, and there the dialogue begins:—

Gorgo. Is Praxinoe at home?

Praxinoe. My dear Gorgo, at last! Yes, here I am. Eunoe, find a chair,—get a cushion for it.

Gorgo. It will do beautifully as it is.

Praxinoe. Do sit down.

Gorgo. Oh, this gad-about spirit! I could hardly get to you, Praxinoe, through all the crowd and all the carriages. Nothing but heavy boots, nothing but men in uniform. And what a journey it is! My dear child, you really live *too* far off.

Praxinoe. It is all that insane husband of mine. He has chosen to come out here to the end of the world, and take a hole of a place,—for a house it is not,—on purpose that you and I might not be neighbours. He is always just the same;—anything to quarrel with one! anything for spite!

Gorgo. My dear, don't talk so of your husband before the little fellow. Just see how astonished he looks at you. Never mind, Zopyrio, my pet, she is not talking about papa.

Praxinoe. Good heavens! the child does really understand.

Gorgo. Pretty papa!

Praxinoe. That pretty papa of his the other day (though I told him beforehand to mind what he was about), when I sent him to a shop to buy soap and rouge, brought me home salt instead;—stupid, great, big, interminable animal!

Gorgo. Mine is just the fellow to him. . . . But never mind now, get on your things and let us be off to the palace to see the Adonis. I hear the Queen's decorations are something splendid.

Praxinoe. In grand people's houses everything is grand. What things you have seen in Alexandria! What a deal you will have to tell to anybody who has never been here!

Gorgo. Come, we ought to be going.

Praxinoe. Every day is holiday to people who have nothing to do. Eunoe, pick up your work; and take care, lazy girl, how you leave it lying about again; the cats find it just the bed they like. Come, stir your- [180] self, fetch me some water, quick! I wanted the water first, and the girl brings me the soap. Never mind; give it me. Not all that, extravagant! Now pour out the water;—stupid! why don't you take care of my dress? That will do. I have got my hands washed as it pleased God. Where is the key of the large wardrobe? Bring it here;—quick!

Gorgo. Praxinoe, you can't think how well that dress, made full, as you have got it, suits you. Tell me, how much did it cost?—the dress by itself, I mean.

Praxinoe. Don't talk of it, Gorgo: more than eight guineas of good hard money. And about the work on it I have almost worn my life out. [190]

Gorgo. Well, you couldn't have done better.

Praxinoe. Thank you. Bring me my shawl, and put my hat properly on my head;—properly. No, child (*to her little boy*), I am not going to take you; there's a bogy on horseback, who bites. Cry as much as you like; I'm not going to have you lamed for life. Now we'll start. Nurse, take the little one and amuse him; call the dog in, and shut the street-door. (*They go out.*) Good heavens! what a crowd of people! How on earth are we ever to get through all this? They are like ants: you can't count them. My dearest Gorgo, what will become of us? here are the royal Horse Guards. My good man, don't ride over me! Look at that bay horse rearing bolt [200] upright; what a vicious one! Eunoe, you mad girl, do take care!—that horse will certainly be the death of the man on his back. How glad I am now, that I left the child safe at home!

Gorgo. All right, Praxinoe, we are safe behind them; and they have gone on to where they are stationed.

Praxinoe. Well, yes, I begin to revive again. From the time I was a little girl I have had more horror of horses and snakes than of anything in the world. Let us get on; here's a great crowd coming this way upon us.

Gorgo (*to an old woman*).—Mother, are you from the palace?

Old Woman. Yes, my dears. [210]

Gorgo. Has one a tolerable chance of getting there?

Old Woman. My pretty young lady, the Greeks got to Troy by dint of trying hard; trying will do anything in this world.

Gorgo. The old creature has delivered herself of an oracle and departed.

Praxinoe. Women can tell you everything about everything, Jupiter's marriage with Juno not excepted.

Gorgo. Look, Praxinoe, what a squeeze at the palace gates!

Praxinoe. Tremendous! Take hold of me, Gorgo; and you, Eunoe, take hold of Eutychis!—tight hold, or you'll be lost. Here we go in all together. Hold tight to us, Eunoe! Oh, dear! oh, dear! Gorgo, there's my scarf torn right in two. For heaven's sake, my good man, as you hope to be saved, take care of my dress!

Stranger. I'll do what I can, but it doesn't depend upon me.

Praxinoe. What heaps of people! They push like a drove of pigs.

Stranger. Don't be frightened, ma'am, we are all right.

Praxinoe. May you be all right, my dear sir, to the last day you live, for the care you have taken of us! What a kind, considerate man! There is Eunoe jammed in a squeeze. Push, you goose, push! Capital! We are all of us the right side of the door, as the bridegroom said when he had locked himself in with the bride.

Gorgo. Praxinoe, come this way. Do but look at that work, how delicate it is!—how exquisite! Why, they might wear it in heaven.

Praxinoe. Heavenly patroness of needlewomen, what hands were hired to do that work? Who designed those beautiful patterns? They seem to stand up and move about, as if they were real;—as if they were living things, and not needlework. Well, man is a wonderful creature! And look, look, how charming he lies there on his silver couch, with just a soft down on his cheeks, that beloved Adonis,—Adonis, whom one loves even though he is dead!

Another Stranger. You wretched women, do stop your incessant chatter! Like turtles, you go on for ever. They are enough to kill one with their broad lingo,—nothing but *a, a, a.*

Gorgo. Lord, where does the man come from? What is it to you if we *are* chatterboxes? Order about your own servants! Do you give orders to Syracusan women? If you want to know, we came originally from Corinth, as Bellerophon did; we speak Peloponnesian. I suppose Dorian women may be allowed to have a Dorian accent.

Praxinoe. Oh, honey-sweet Proserpine, let us have no more masters than the one we've got! We don't the least care for *you;* pray don't trouble yourself for nothing.

Gorgo. Be quiet, Praxinoe! That first-rate singer, the Argive woman's daughter, is going to sing the *Adonis* hymn. She is the same who was chosen to sing the dirge last year. We are sure to have something first-rate from *her.* She is going through her airs and graces ready to begin.—

So far the dialogue; and, as it stands in the original, it can hardly be praised too highly. It is a page torn fresh out of the book of human life.

What freedom! What animation! What gaiety! What naturalness! It is said that Theocritus, in composing this poem, borrowed from a work of Sophron, a poet of an earlier and better time; but, even if this is so, the form is still Theocritus's own, and how excellent is that form, how masterly! And this in a Greek poem of the decadence!—for Theocritus's poetry, after all, is poetry of the decadence. When such is Greek poetry of the decadence, what must be Greek poetry of the prime? 260

Then the singer begins her hymn:—

'Mistress, who loveth the haunts of Golgi, and Idalium, and high-peaked Eryx, Aphrodite that playest with gold! how have the delicate-footed Hours, after twelve months, brought thy Adonis back to thee from the ever-flowing Acheron! Tardiest of the immortals are the boon Hours, but all mankind wait their approach with longing, for they ever bring something with them. O Cypris, Dione's child! thou didst change—so is the 270 story among men—Berenice from mortal to immortal, by dropping ambrosia into her fair bosom; and in gratitude to thee for this, O thou of many names and many temples! Berenice's daughter, Arsinoe, lovely Helen's living counterpart, makes much of Adonis with all manner of braveries.

'All fruits that the tree bears are laid before him, all treasures of the garden in silver baskets, and alabaster boxes, gold-inlaid, of Syrian ointment; and all confectionery that cunning women make on their kneading-tray, kneading up every sort of flowers with white meal, and all that they make of sweet honey and delicate oil, and all winged and creeping things 280 are here set before him. And there are built for him green bowers with wealth of tender anise, and little boy-loves flutter about over them, like young nightingales trying their new wings on the tree, from bough to bough. Oh, the ebony, the gold, the eagle of white ivory that bears aloft his cupbearer to Cronos-born Zeus! And up there, see! a second couch strewn for lovely Adonis, scarlet coverlets softer than sleep itself (so Miletus and the Samian wool-grower will say); Cypris has hers, and the rosy-armed Adonis has his, that eighteen or nineteen-year-old bridegroom. His kisses will not wound, the hair on his lip is yet light.

'Now, Cypris, good-night, we leave thee with thy bridegroom; but 290 to-morrow morning, with the earliest dew, we will one and all bear him forth to where the waves splash upon the sea-strand, and letting loose our locks, and letting fall our robes, with bosoms bare, we will set up this, our melodious strain:

' "Beloved Adonis, alone of the demigods (so men say) thou art permitted to visit both us and Acheron! This lot had neither Agamemnon,

nor the mighty moon-struck hero Ajax, nor Hector the first-born of
Hecuba's twenty children, nor Patroclus, nor Pyrrhus who came home
from Troy, nor those yet earlier Lapithae and the sons of Deucalion, nor
the Pelasgians, the root of Argos and of Pelops' isle. Be gracious to us now,
loved Adonis, and be favourable to us for the year to come! Dear to us hast
thou been at this coming, dear to us shalt thou be when thou comest
again." '

The poem concludes with a characteristic speech from Gorgo:—

'Praxinoe, certainly women are wonderful things. That lucky woman
to know all that! and luckier still to have such a splendid voice! And now
we must see about getting home. My husband has not had his dinner.
That man is all vinegar, and nothing else; and if you keep him waiting for
his dinner, he's dangerous to go near. Adieu, precious Adonis, and may
you find us all well when you come next year!'

So, with the hymn still in her ears, says the incorrigible Gorgo.

But what a hymn that is! Of religious emotion, in our acceptation of the
words, and of the comfort springing from religious emotion, not a particle.
And yet many elements of religious emotion are contained in the beautiful
story of Adonis. Symbolically treated, as the thoughtful man might treat
it, as the Greek mysteries undoubtedly treated it, this story was capable of
a noble and touching application, and could lead the soul to elevating and
consoling thoughts. Adonis was the sun in his summer and in his winter
course, in his time of triumph and his time of defeat; but in his time of
triumph still moving towards his defeat, in his time of defeat still returning towards his triumph. Thus he became an emblem of the power of life
and the bloom of beauty, the power of human life and the bloom of
human beauty, hastening inevitably to diminution and decay, yet in that
very decay finding

'Hope, and a renovation without end.'

But nothing of this appears in the story as prepared for popular religious
use, as presented to the multitude in a popular religious ceremony. Its
treatment is not devoid of a certain grace and beauty, but it has nothing
whatever that is elevating, nothing that is consoling, nothing that is in our
sense of the word religious. The religious ceremonies of Christendom, even
on occasion of the most joyful and mundane matters, present the multitude
with strains of profoundly religious character, such as the *Kyrie eleison*
and the *Te Deum*. But this Greek hymn to Adonis adapts itself exactly to
the tone and temper of a gay and pleasure-loving multitude,—of light-

hearted people, like Gorgo and Praxinoe, whose moral nature is much of the same calibre as that of Phillina in Goethe's *Wilhelm Meister,* people who seem never made to be serious, never made to be sick or sorry. And, if they happen to be sick or sorry, what will they do then? But that we have no right to ask. Phillina, within the enchanted bounds of Goethe's novel, Gorgo and Praxinoe, within the enchanted bounds of Theocritus's poem, never will be sick and sorry, never can be sick and sorry. The ideal, cheerful, sensuous, pagan life is not sick or sorry. No; yet its natural end is in the sort of life which Pompeii and Herculaneum bring so vividly before us,—a life which by no means in itself suggests the thought of horror and misery, which even, in many ways, gratifies the senses and the understanding; but by the very intensity and unremittingness of its appeal to the senses and the understanding, by its stimulating a single side of us too absolutely, ends by fatiguing and revolting us; ends by leaving us with a sense of confinement, of oppression,—with a desire for an utter change, for clouds, storms, effusion and relief.

In the beginning of the thirteenth century, when the clouds and storms had come, when the gay sensuous pagan life was gone, when men were not living by the senses and understanding, when they were looking for the speedy coming of Antichrist, there appeared in Italy, to the north of Rome, in the beautiful Umbrian country at the foot of the Appennines, a figure of the most magical power and charm, St. Francis. His century is, I think, the most interesting in the history of Christianity after its primitive age, more interesting than even the century of the Reformation; and one of the chief figures, perhaps the very chief, to which this interest attaches itself, is St. Francis. And why? Because of the profound popular instinct which enabled him, more than any man since the primitive age, to fit religion for popular use. He brought religion to the people. He founded the most popular body of ministers of religion that has ever existed in the Church. He transformed monachism by uprooting the stationary monk, delivering him from the bondage of property, and sending him, as a mendicant friar, to be a stranger and sojourner, not in the wilderness, but in the most crowded haunts of men, to console them and to do them good. This popular instinct of his is at the bottom of his famous marriage with poverty. Poverty and suffering are the condition of the people, the multitude, the immense majority of mankind; and it was towards this *people* that his soul yearned. 'He listens,' it was said of him, 'to those to whom God himself will not listen.'

So in return, as no other man he was listened to. When an Umbrian town or village heard of his approach, the whole population went out in

340

350

360

370

joyful procession to meet him, with green boughs, flags, music, and songs of gladness. The master, who began with two disciples, could in his own life-time (and he died at forty-four) collect to keep Whitsuntide with him, in presence of an immense multitude, five thousand of his Minorites. And thus he found fulfilment to his prophetic cry: 'I hear in my ears the sound of the tongues of all the nations who shall come unto us; Frenchmen, Spaniards, Germans, Englishmen. The Lord will make of us a great people, even unto the ends of the earth.'

Prose could not satisfy this ardent soul, and he made poetry. Latin was too learned for this simple, popular nature, and he composed in his mother tongue, in Italian. The beginnings of the mundane poetry of the Italians are in Sicily, at the court of kings; the beginnings of their religious poetry are in Umbria, with St. Francis. His are the humble upper waters of a mighty stream: at the beginning of the thirteenth century it is St. Francis, at the end, Dante. Now it happens that St. Francis, too, like the Alexandrian songstress, has his hymn for the sun, for Adonis. *Canticle of the Sun, Canticle of the Creatures,*—the poem goes by both names. Like the Alexandrian hymn, it is designed for popular use, but not for use by King Ptolemy's people; artless in language, irregular in rhythm, it matches with the childlike genius that produced it, and the simple natures that loved and repeated it:—

'O most high, almighty, good Lord God, to thee belong praise, glory, honour, and all blessing!

'Praised be my Lord God with all his creatures; and specially our brother the sun, who brings us the day, and who brings us the light; fair is he, and shining with a very great splendour: O Lord, he signifies to us thee!

'Praised be my Lord for our sister the moon, and for the stars, the which he has set clear and lovely in heaven.

'Praised be my Lord for our brother the wind, and for air and cloud, calms and all weather, by the which thou upholdest in life all creatures.

'Praised be my Lord for our sister water, who is very serviceable unto us, and humble, and precious, and clean.

'Praised be my Lord for our brother fire, through whom thou givest us light in the darkness; and he is bright, and pleasant, and very mighty, and strong.

'Praised be my Lord for our mother the earth, the which doth sustain us and keep us, and bringeth forth divers fruits, and flowers of many colours, and grass.

'Praised be my Lord for all those who pardon one another for his love's sake, and who endure weakness and tribulation; blessed are they who peaceably shall endure, for thou, O most Highest, shalt give them a crown! 'Praised be my Lord for our sister, the death of the body, from whom no man escapeth. Woe to him who dieth in mortal sin! Blessed are they who are found walking by thy most holy will, for the second death shall have no power to do them harm.

'Praise ye, and bless ye the Lord, and give thanks unto him, and serve 420 him with great humility.'

It is natural that man should take pleasure in his senses. But it is natural, also, that he should take refuge in his heart and imagination from his misery. And when one thinks what human life is for the vast majority of mankind, how little of a feast for their senses it can possibly be, one understands the charm for them of a refuge offered in the heart and imagination. Above all, when one thinks what human life was in the Middle Ages, one understands the charm of such a refuge.

Now, the poetry of Theocritus's hymn is poetry treating the world according to the demand of the senses; the poetry of St. Francis's hymn is 430 poetry treating the world according to the demand of the heart and imagination. The first takes the world by its outward, sensible side; the second by its inward symbolical side. The first admits as much of the world as is pleasure-giving; the second admits the whole world, rough and smooth, painful and pleasure-giving, all alike, but all transfigured by the power of a spiritual emotion, all brought under a law of supersensual love, having its seat in the soul. It can thus even say: 'Praised be my Lord for *our sister, the death of the body.*'

But these very words are, perhaps, an indication that we are touching upon an extreme. When we see Pompeii, we can put our finger upon the 440 pagan sentiment in its extreme. And when we read of Monte Alverno and the *stigmata;* when we read of the repulsive, because self-caused, sufferings of the end of St. Francis's life; when we find him even saying, 'I have sinned against my brother the ass,' meaning by these words that he had been too hard upon his own body; when we find him assailed, even himself, by the doubt 'whether he who had destroyed himself by the severity of his penances could find mercy in eternity,' we can put our finger on the mediaeval Christian sentiment in its extreme. Human nature is neither all senses and understanding, nor all heart and imagination. Pompeii was a sign that for humanity at large the measure of sensualism had been over- 450 passed; St. Francis's doubt was a sign that for humanity at large the measure of spiritualism had been over-passed. Humanity, in its violent rebound from one extreme, had swung from Pompeii to Monte Alverno; but it was sure not to stay there.

The Renascence is, in part, a return towards the pagan spirit, in the special sense in which I have been using the word pagan; a return towards the life of the senses and the understanding. The Reformation, on the other hand, is the very opposite to this; in Luther there is nothing Greek or pagan; vehemently as he attacked the adoration of St. Francis, Luther had himself something of St. Francis in him; he was a thousand times more akin to St. Francis than to Theocritus or to Voltaire. The Reformation—I do not mean the inferior piece given under that name, by Henry the Eighth and a second-rate company, in this island, but the real Reformation, the German Reformation, Luther's Reformation—was a reaction of the moral and spiritual sense against the carnal and pagan sense; it was a religious revival like St. Francis's, but this time against the Church of Rome, not within her; for the carnal and pagan sense had now, in the government of the Church of Rome herself, its prime representative. But the grand reaction against the rule of the heart and imagination, the strong return towards the rule of the senses and understanding, is in the eighteenth century. And this reaction has had no more brilliant champion than a man of the nineteenth, of whom I have already spoken; a man who could feel not only the pleasurableness but the poetry of the life of the senses (and the life of the senses has its deep poetry); a man who, in his very last poem, divided the whole world into 'barbarians and Greeks,'—Heinrich Heine. No man has reproached the Monte Alverno extreme in sentiment, the Christian extreme, the heart and imagination subjugating the senses and understanding, more bitterly than Heine; no man has extolled the Pompeii extreme, the pagan extreme, more rapturously.

'All through the Middle Age these sufferings, this fever, this over-tension lasted; and we moderns still feel in all our limbs the pain and weakness from them. Even those of us who are cured have still to live with a hospital-atmosphere all around us, and find ourselves as wretched in it as a strong man among the sick. Some day or other, when humanity shall have got quite well again, when the body and soul shall have made their peace together, the factitious quarrel which Christianity has cooked up between them will appear something hardly comprehensible. The fairer and happier generations, offspring of unfettered unions, that will rise up and bloom in the atmosphere of a religion of pleasure, will smile sadly when they think of their poor ancestors, whose life was passed in melancholy abstinence from the joys of this beautiful earth, and who faded away into spectres, from the mortal compression which they put upon the warm and glowing emotions of sense. Yes, with assurance I say it, our descendants will be fairer and happier than we are; for I am a believer in progress, and I hold God to be a kind being who has intended man to be happy.'

That is Heine's sentiment, in the prime of life, in the glow of activity, amid the brilliant whirl of Paris. I will no more blame it than I blamed the sentiment of the Greek hymn to Adonis. I wish to decide nothing as of my own authority; the great art of criticism is to get oneself out of the way and to let humanity decide. Well, the sentiment of the 'religion of pleasure' has   500
much that is natural in it; humanity will gladly accept it if it can live by it; to live by it one must never be sick or sorry, and the old, ideal, limited, pagan world never, I have said, *was* sick or sorry, never at least shows itself to us sick or sorry:—

'What pipes and timbrels! what wild ecstasy!'

For our imagination, Gorgo and Praxinoe cross the human stage chattering in their blithe Doric,—*like turtles,* as the cross stranger said,—and keep gaily chattering on till they disappear. But in the new, real, immense, post-pagan world,—in the barbarian world,—the shock of accident is unceasing, the serenity of existence is perpetually troubled, not even a   510
Greek like Heine can get across the mortal stage without bitter calamity. How does the sentiment of the 'religion of pleasure' serve then? does it help, does it console? Can a man live by it? Heine again shall answer; Heine just twenty years older, stricken with incurable disease, waiting for death:—

'The great pot stands smoking before me, but I have no spoon to help myself. What does it profit me that my health is drunk at banquets out of gold cups and in the most exquisite wines, if I myself, while these ovations are going on, lonely and cut off from the pleasures of the world, can only just wet my lips with barley-water? What good does it do me that all the   520
roses of Shiraz open their leaves and burn for me with passionate tenderness? Alas! Shiraz is some two thousand leagues from the Rue d'Amsterdam, where in the solitude of my sick chamber all the perfume I smell is that of hot towels. Alas! the mockery of God is heavy upon me! The great author of the universe, the Aristophanes of Heaven, has determined to make the petty earthly author, the so-called Aristophanes of Germany, feel to his heart's core what pitiful needle-pricks his cleverest sarcasms have been, compared with the thunderbolts which his divine humour can launch against feeble mortals! . . .

'In the year 1340, says the Chronicle of Limburg, all over Germany   530
everybody was strumming and humming certain songs more lovely and

delightful than any which had ever yet been known in German countries; and all people, old and young, the women particularly, were perfectly mad about them, so that from morning till night you heard nothing else. Only, the Chronicle adds, the author of these songs happened to be a young clerk, afflicted with leprosy, and living apart from all the world in a desolate place. The excellent reader does not require to be told how horrible a complaint was leprosy in the Middle Ages, and how the poor wretches who had this incurable plague were banished from society, and had to keep at a distance from every human being. Like living corpses, in a grey gown reaching down to the feet, and with the hood brought over their face, they went about, carrying in their hands an enormous rattle, called Saint Lazarus's rattle. With this rattle they gave notice of their approach, that every one might have time to get out of their way. This poor clerk, then, whose poetical gift the Limburg Chronicle extols, was a leper, and he sate moping in the dismal deserts of his misery, whilst all Germany, gay and tuneful, was praising his songs.

'Sometimes, in my sombre visions of the night, I imagine that I see before me the poor leprosy-stricken clerk of the Limburg Chronicle, and then from under his grey hood his distressed eyes look out upon me in a fixed and strange fashion; but the next instant he disappears, and I hear dying away in the distance, like the echo of a dream, the dull creak of Saint Lazarus's rattle.'

We have come a long way from Theocritus there! the expression of that has nothing of the clear, positive, happy, pagan character; it has much more the character of one of the indeterminate grotesques of the suffering Middle Age. Profoundness and power it has, though at the same time it is not truly poetical; it is not natural enough for that, there is too much waywardness in it, too much bravado. But as a condition of sentiment to be popular,—to be a comfort for the mass of mankind, under the pressure of calamity, to live by,—what a manifest failure is this last word of the religion of pleasure! One man in many millions, a Heine, may console himself, and keep himself erect in suffering, by a colossal irony of this sort, by covering himself and the universe with the red fire of this sinister mockery; but the many millions cannot,—cannot if they would. That is where the sentiment of a religion of sorrow has such a vast advantage over the sentiment of a religion of pleasure; in its power to be a general, popular, religious sentiment, a stay for the mass of mankind, whose lives are full of hardship. It really succeeds in conveying far more joy, far more of what the mass of mankind are so much without, than its rival. I do not mean joy in prospect only, but joy in possession, actual enjoyment of the world.

Mediaeval Christianity is reproached with its gloom and austerities; it assigns the material world, says Heine, to the devil. But yet what a fulness of delight does St. Francis manage to draw from this material world itself, and from its commonest and most universally enjoyed elements,—sun, air, earth, water, plants! His hymn expresses a far more cordial sense of happiness, even in the material world, than the hymn of Theocritus. It is this which made the fortune of Christianity,—its gladness, not its sorrow; not its assigning the spiritual world to Christ, and the material world to the devil, but its drawing from the spiritual world a source of joy so abundant   580 that it ran over upon the material world and transfigured it.

I have said a great deal of harm of paganism; and, taking paganism to mean a state of things which it is commonly taken to mean, and which did really exist, no more harm than it well deserved. Yet I must not end without reminding the reader, that before this state of things appeared, there was an epoch in Greek life,—in pagan life,—of the highest possible beauty and value. That epoch by itself goes far towards making Greece the Greece we mean when we speak of Greece,—a country hardly less important to mankind than Judaea. The poetry of later paganism lived by the senses and understanding; the poetry of mediaeval Christianity lived by the heart   590 and imagination. But the main element of the modern spirit's life is neither the senses and understanding, nor the heart and imagination; it is the imaginative reason. And there is a century in Greek life,—the century preceding the Peloponnesian war, from about the year 530 to the year 430 B.C.,—in which poetry made, it seems to me, the noblest, the most successful effort she has ever made as the priestess of the imaginative reason, of the element by which the modern spirit, if it would live right, has chiefly to live. Of this effort, of which the four great names are Simonides, Pindar, Æschylus, Sophocles, I must not now attempt more than the bare mention; but it is right, it is necessary, after all I have said, to indicate it.   600 No doubt that effort was imperfect. Perhaps everything, take it at what point in its existence you will, carries within itself the fatal law of its own ulterior development. Perhaps, even of the life of Pindar's time, Pompeii was the inevitable bourne. Perhaps the life of their beautiful Greece could not afford to its poets all that fulness of varied experience, all that power of emotion, which

'. . . the heavy and the weary weight
Of all this unintelligible world'

affords the poet of after-times. Perhaps in Sophocles the thinking-power a little overbalances the religious sense, as in Dante the religious sense   610 overbalances the thinking-power. The present has to make its own poetry, and not even Sophocles and his compeers, any more than Dante and Shakspeare, are enough for it. That I will not dispute; nor will I set up the Greek poets, from Pindar to Sophocles, as objects of blind worship. But no other poets so well show to the poetry of the present the way it must take; no other poets have lived so much by the imaginative reason; no other poets have made their work so well balanced; no other poets, who have so well satisfied the thinking-power, have so well satisfied the religious sense:—

'Oh! that my lot may lead me in the path of holy innocence of word and deed, the path which august laws ordain, laws that in the highest empyrean had their birth, of which Heaven is the father alone, neither did the race of mortal men beget them, nor shall oblivion ever put them to sleep. The power of God is mighty in them, and groweth not old.'

Let St. Francis,—nay, or Luther either,—beat that!

A PERSIAN PASSION PLAY

Everybody has this last autumn [1] been either seeing the Ammergau Passion Play or hearing about it; and to find any one who has seen it and not
been deeply interested and moved by it, is very rare. The peasants of the
neighbouring country, the great and fashionable world, the ordinary tour-
ist, were all at Ammergau, and were all delighted; but what is said to have
been especially remarkable was the affluence there of ministers of religion
of all kinds. That Catholic peasants, whose religion has accustomed them
to show and spectacle, should be attracted by an admirable scenic representation of the great moments in the history of their religion, was natural;
that tourists and the fashionable world should be attracted by what was at   10
once the fashion and a new sensation of a powerful sort, was natural; that
many of the ecclesiastics present should be attracted there, was natural too.
Roman Catholic priests mustered strong, of course. The Protestantism of
a great number of the Anglican clergy is supposed to be but languid, and
Anglican ministers at Ammergau were sympathisers to be expected. But
[1] 1871.

Protestant ministers of the most unimpeachable sort, Protestant Dissenting ministers, were there, too, and showing favour and sympathy; and this, to any one who remembers the almost universal feeling of Protestant Dissenters in this country, not many years ago, towards Rome and her religion,—the sheer abhorrence of Papists and all their practices,—could not but be striking. It agrees with what is seen also in literature, in the writings of Dissenters of the younger and more progressive sort, who show a disposition for regarding the Church of Rome historically rather than polemically, a wish to do justice to the undoubted grandeur of certain institutions and men produced by that Church, quite novel, and quite alien to the simple belief of earlier times, that between Protestants and Rome there was a measureless gulph fixed. Something of this may, no doubt, be due to that keen eye for Nonconformist business in which our great bodies of Protestant Dissenters, to do them justice, are never wanting; to a perception that the case against the Church of England may be yet further improved by contrasting her with the genuine article in her own ecclesiastical line, by pointing out that she is neither one thing nor the other to much purpose, by dilating on the magnitude, reach, and impressiveness, on the great place in history, of her rival, as compared with anything she can herself pretend to. Something of this there is, no doubt, in some of the modern Protestant sympathy for things Catholic. But in general that sympathy springs, in Churchmen and Dissenters alike, from another and a better cause,—from the spread of larger conceptions of religion, of man, and of history, than were current formerly. We have seen lately in the newspapers, that a clergyman, who in a popular lecture gave an account of the Passion Play at Ammergau, and enlarged on its impressiveness, was admonished by certain remonstrants, who told him it was his business, instead of occupying himself with these sensuous shows, to learn to walk by faith, not by sight, and to teach his fellow-men to do the same. But this severity seems to have excited wonder rather than praise; so far had those wider notions about religion and about the range of our interest in religion, of which I have just spoken, conducted us. To this interest I propose to appeal in what I am going to relate. The Passion Play at Ammergau, with its immense audiences, the seriousness of its actors, the passionate emotion of its spectators, brought to my mind something of which I had read an account lately; something produced, not in Bavaria nor in Christendom at all, but far away in that wonderful East, from which, whatever airs of superiority Europe may justly give itself, all our religion has come, and where religion, of some sort or other, has still an empire over men's feelings such as it has nowhere else. This product of the remote East I wish to exhibit while the remembrance of what has been seen at Ammergau is still fresh; and we will see whether that bringing together of strangers and enemies who once seemed to be as far as the poles asunder, which Ammergau in such a remarkable way effected, does not hold good and find a parallel even in Persia.

Count Gobineau, formerly Minister of France at Teheran and at Athens, published, a few years ago, an interesting book on the present state of religion and philosophy in Central Asia. He is favourably known also by his studies in ethnology. His accomplishments and intelligence deserve all respect, and in his book on religion and philosophy in Central Asia he has the great advantage of writing about things which he has followed with his own observation and inquiry in the countries where they happened. The chief purpose of his book is to give a history of the career of Mirza Ali Mahommed, a Persian religious reformer, the original *Bâb,* and the founder of *Bâbism,* of which most people in England have at least heard the name. Bâb means *gate,* the door or gate of life; and in the ferment which now works in the Mahometan East, Mirza Ali Mahommed,—who seems to have been made acquainted by Protestant missionaries with our Scriptures and by the Jews of Shiraz with Jewish traditions, to have studied, besides, the religion of the Ghebers, the old national religion of Persia, and to have made a sort of amalgam of the whole with Mahometanism,—presented himself, about five-and-twenty years ago, as *the door, the gate* of life; found disciples, sent forth writings, and finally became the cause of disturbances which led to his being executed on the 19th of July, 1849, in the citadel of Tabriz. The Bâb and his doctrines are a theme on which much might be said; but I pass them by, except for one incident in the Bâb's life, which I will notice. Like all religious Mahometans, he made the pilgrimage to Mecca; and his meditations at that centre of his religion first suggested his mission to him. But soon after his return to Bagdad he made another pilgrimage; and it was in this pilgrimage that his mission became clear to him, and that his life was fixed. 'He desired'—I will give an abridgment of Count Gobineau's own words—'to complete his impressions by going to Kufa, that he might visit the ruined mosque where Ali was assassinated, and where the place of his murder is still shown. He passed several days there in meditation. The place appears to have made a great impression on him; he was entering on a course which might and must lead to some such catastrophe as had happened on the very spot where he stood, and where his mind's eye showed him the Imam Ali lying at his feet, with his body pierced and bleeding. His followers say that he then passed through a sort of moral agony which put an end to all the hesitations of the natural man within him. It is certain that when he arrived at

Shiraz, on his return, he was a changed man. No doubts troubled him any more: he was penetrated and persuaded; his part was taken.'

This Ali also, at whose tomb the Bâb went through the spiritual crisis here recorded, is a familiar name to most of us. In general our knowledge of the East goes but a very little way; yet almost every one has at least heard the name of Ali, the Lion of God, Mahomet's young cousin, the first person, after his wife, who believed in him, and who was declared by Mahomet in his gratitude his brother, delegate, and vicar. Ali was one of Mahomet's best and most successful captains. He married Fatima, the daughter of the Prophet; his sons, Hassan and Hussein, were, as children, favourites with Mahomet, who had no son of his own to succeed him, and was expected to name Ali as his successor. He named no successor. At his death (the year 632 of our era) Ali was passed over, and the first caliph, or *vicar* and *lieutenant* of Mahomet in the government of the state, was Abu-Bekr; only the spiritual inheritance of Mahomet, the dignity of Imam, or *Primate,* devolved by right on Ali and his children. Ali, lion of God as in war he was, held aloof from politics and political intrigue, loved retirement and prayer, was the most pious and disinterested of men. At Abu-Bekr's death he was again passed over in favour of Omar. Omar was succeeded by Othman, and still Ali remained tranquil. Othman was assassinated, and then Ali, chiefly to prevent disturbance and bloodshed, accepted (A.D. 655) the caliphate. Meanwhile, the Mahometan armies had conquered Persia, Syria, and Egypt; the Governor of Syria, Moawiyah, an able and ambitious man, set himself up as caliph, his title was recognized by Amrou, the Governor of Egypt, and a bloody and indecisive battle was fought in Mesopotamia between Ali's army and Moawiyah's. Gibbon shall tell the rest;—'In the temple of Mecca three Charegites or enthusiasts discoursed of the disorders of the church and state; they soon agreed that the deaths of Ali, of Moawiyah, and of his friend Amrou, the Viceroy of Egypt, would restore the peace and unity of religion. Each of the assassins chose his victim, poisoned his dagger, devoted his life, and secretly repaired to the scene of action. Their resolution was equally desperate; but the first mistook the person of Amrou, and stabbed the deputy who occupied his seat; the prince of Damascus was dangerously hurt by the second; Ali, the lawful caliph, in the mosque of Kufa, received a mortal wound from the hand of the third.'

The events through which we have thus rapidly run ought to be kept in mind, for they are the elements of Mahometan history: any right understanding of the state of the Mahometan world is impossible without them. For that world is divided into the two great sects of Shiahs and Sunis. The

Shiahs are those who reject the first three caliphs as usurpers, and begin with Ali as the first lawful successor of Mahomet; the Sunis recognise Abu-Bekr, Omar, and Othman, as well as Ali, and regard the Shiahs as impious heretics. The Persians are Shiahs, and the Arabs and Turks are Sunis. Hussein, one of Ali's two sons, married a Persian princess, the [140] daughter of Yezdejerd the last of the Sassanian kings, the king whom the Mahometan conquest of Persia expelled; and Persia, through this marriage, became specially connected with the house of Ali. 'In the fourth age of the Hegira,' says Gibbon, 'a tomb, a temple, a city, arose near the ruins of Kufa. Many thousands of the Shiahs repose in holy ground at the feet of the vicar of God; and the desert is vivified by the numerous and annual visits of the Persians, who esteem their devotion not less meritorious than the pilgrimage of Mecca.'

But, to comprehend what I am going to relate from Count Gobineau, we must push our researches into Mahometan history a little further than the [150] assassination of Ali. Moawiyah died in the year 680 of our era, nearly fifty years after the death of Mahomet. His son Yezid succeeded him on the throne of the caliphs at Damascus. During the reign of Moawiyah Ali's two sons, the Imam's Hassan and Hussein, lived with their families in religious retirement at Medina, where their grandfather Mahomet was buried. In them the character of abstention and renouncement, which we have noticed in Ali himself, was marked yet more strongly; but, when Moawiyah died, the people of Kufa, the city on the lower Euphrates where Ali had been assassinated, sent offers to make Hussein caliph if he would come among them, and to support him against the Syrian troops of Yezid. Hus- [160] sein seems to have thought himself bound to accept the proposal. He left Medina, and, with his family and relations, to the number of about eighty persons, set out on his way to Kufa. Then ensued the tragedy so familiar to every Mahometan, and to us so little known, the tragedy of Kerbela. 'O death,' cries the bandit-minstrel of Persia, Kurroglou, in his last song before his execution, 'O death, whom didst thou spare? Were even Hassan and Hussein, those footstools of the throne of God on the seventh heaven, spared by thee? *No! thou madest them martyrs at Kerbela.*'

We cannot do better than again have recourse to Gibbon's history for an account of this famous tragedy. 'Hussein traversed the desert of Arabia [170] with a timorous retinue of women and children; but, as he approached the confines of Irak, he was alarmed by the solitary or hostile face of the country, and suspected either the defection or the ruin of his party. His fears were just; Obeidallah, the governor of Kufa, had extinguished the first sparks of an insurrection; and Hussein, in the plain of Kerbela, was encompassed by a body of 5,000 horse, who intercepted his communication with the city and the river. In a conference with the chief of the enemy he proposed the option of three conditions:—that he should be allowed to return to Medina, or be stationed in a frontier garrison against the Turks, or safely conducted to the presence of Yezid. But the commands of the caliph or his lieutenant were stern and absolute, and Hussein was informed that he must either submit as a captive and a criminal to the Commander of the Faithful, or expect the consequences of his rebellion. "Do you think," replied he, "to terrify me with death?" And during the short respite of a night he prepared, with calm and solemn resignation, to encounter his fate. He checked the lamentations of his sister Fatima, who deplored the impending ruin of his house. "Our trust," said Hussein, "is in God alone. All things, both in heaven and earth, must perish and return to their Creator. My brother, my father, my mother, were better than I, and every Mussulman has an example in the Prophet." He pressed his friends to consult their safety by a timely flight; they unanimously refused to desert or survive their beloved master, and their courage was fortified by a fervent prayer and the assurance of paradise. On the morning of the fatal day he mounted on horseback, with his sword in one hand and the Koran in the other; the flanks and rear of his party were secured by the tent-ropes and by a deep trench, which they had filled with lighted fagots, according to the practice of the Arabs. The enemy advanced with reluctance; and one of their chiefs deserted, with thirty followers, to claim the partnership of inevitable death. In every close onset or single combat the despair of the Fatimites was invincible; but the surrounding multitudes galled them from a distance with a cloud of arrows, and the horses and men were successively slain. A truce was allowed on both sides for the hour of prayer; and the battle at length expired by the death of the last of the companions of Hussein.'

The details of Hussein's own death will come better presently; suffice it at this moment to say he was slain, and that the women and children of his family were taken in chains to the Caliph Yezid at Damascus. Gibbon concludes the story thus: 'In a distant age and climate, the tragic scene of the death of Hussein will awaken the sympathy of the coldest reader. On the annual festival of his martyrdom, in the devout pilgrimage to his sepulchre, his Persian votaries abandon their souls to the religious phrenzy of sorrow and indignation.'

Thus the tombs of Ali and of his son, the Meshed Ali and the Meshed Hussein, standing some thirty miles apart from one another in the plain of the Euphrates, had, when Gibbon wrote, their yearly pilgrims and their

tribute of enthusiastic mourning. But Count Gobineau relates, in his book
of which I have spoken, a development of these solemnities which was
unknown to Gibbon. Within the present century there has arisen, on the
basis of this story of the martyrs of Kerbela, a drama, a Persian national
drama, which Count Gobineau, who has seen and heard it, is bold enough   220
to rank with the Greek drama as a great and serious affair, engaging the
heart and life of the people who have given birth to it; while the Latin,
English, French, and German drama is, he says, in comparison a mere
pastime or amusement, more or less intellectual and elegant. To me it
seems that the Persian *tazyas*—for so these pieces are called—find a better
parallel in the Ammergau Passion Play than in the Greek drama. They turn
entirely on one subject—the sufferings of the *Family of the Tent,* as the
Imam Hussein and the company of persons gathered around him at Kerbela are called. The subject is sometimes introduced by a prologue, which
may perhaps one day, as the need of variety is more felt, become a piece by   230
itself; but at present the prologue leads invariably to the martyrs. For
instance: the Emperor Tamerlane, in his conquering progress through the
world, arrives at Damascus. The keys of the city are brought to him by the
governor; but the governor is a descendant of one of the murderers of the
Imam Hussein; Tamerlane is informed of it, loads him with reproaches,
and drives him from his presence. The emperor presently sees the governor's daughter splendidly dressed, thinks of the sufferings of the holy
women of the Family of the Tent, and upbraids and drives her away as he
did her father. But after this he is haunted by the great tragedy which has
been thus brought to his mind, and he cannot sleep and cannot be com-   240
forted. He calls his vizier, and his vizier tells him that the only way to
soothe his troubled spirit is to see a *tazya.* And so the *tazya* commences.
Or, again (and this will show how strangely, in the religious world which is
now occupying us, what is most familiar to us is blended with that of which
we know nothing): Joseph and his brethren appear on the stage, and the
old Bible story is transacted. Joseph is thrown into the pit and sold to the
merchants, and his blood-stained coat is carried by his brothers to Jacob;
Jacob is then left alone, weeping and bewailing himself; the angel Gabriel
enters, and reproves him for his want of faith and constancy, telling him
that what he suffers is not a hundredth part of what Ali, Hussein, and the   250
children of Hussein will one day suffer. Jacob seems to doubt it; Gabriel,
to convince him, orders the angels to perform a *tazya* of what will
one day happen at Kerbela. And so the *tazya* commences.

These pieces are given in the first ten days of the month of Moharrem, the anniversary of the martyrdom at Kerbela. They are so popular that they now invade other seasons of the year also; but this is the season when the world is given up to them. King and people, every one is in mourning; and at night and while the *tazyas* are not going on, processions keep passing, the air resounds with the beating of breasts and with litanies of 'O Hassan! Hussein!' while the Seyids,—a kind of popular friars claiming to be descendants of Mahomet, and in whose incessant popularising and amplifying of the legend of Kerbela in their homilies during pilgrimages and at the tombs of the martyrs, the *tazyas,* no doubt, had their origin,—keep up by their sermons and hymns the enthusiasm which the drama of the day has excited. It seems as if no one went to bed; and certainly no one who went to bed could sleep. Confraternities go in procession with a black flag and torches, every man with his shirt torn open, and beating himself with the right hand on the left shoulder in a kind of measured cadence to accompany a canticle in honour of the martyrs. These processions come and take post in the theatres where the Seyids are preaching. Still more noisy are the companies of dancers, striking a kind of wooden castanets together, at one time in front of their breasts, at another time behind their heads, and marking time with music and dance to a dirge set up by the bystanders, in which the names of the Imams perpetually recur as a burden. Noisiest of all are the Berbers, men of a darker skin and another race, their feet and the upper part of their body naked, who carry, some of them tambourines and cymbals, others iron chains and long needles. One of their race is said to have formerly derided the Imams in their affliction, and the Berbers now appear in expiation of that crime. At first their music and their march proceed slowly together, but presently the music quickens, the chain and needle-bearing Berbers move violently round, and begin to beat themselves with their chains and to prick their arms and cheeks with the needles—first gently, then with more vehemence; till suddenly the music ceases, and all stops. So we are carried back, on this old Asiatic soil, where beliefs and usages are heaped layer upon layer and ruin upon ruin, far past the martyred Imams, past Mahometanism, past Christianity, to the priests of Baal gashing themselves with knives and to the worship of Adonis.

The *tekyas,* or theatres for the drama which calls forth these celebrations, are constantly multiplying. The king, the great functionaries, the towns, wealthy citizens like the king's goldsmith, or any private person who has the means and the desire, provide them. Every one sends contributions; it is a religious act to furnish a box or to give decorations for a *tekya;* and as religious offerings, all gifts down to the very smallest are accepted.

There are tekyas for not more than three or four hundred spectators, and there are tekyas for three or four thousand. At Ispahan there are representations which bring together more than twenty thousand people. At Teheran, the Persian capital, each quarter of the town has its tekyas, every square and open place is turned to account for establishing them, and spaces have been expressly cleared, besides, for fresh tekyas. Count Gobineau describes particularly one of these theatres,—a tekya of the best class, to hold an audience of about four thousand,—at Teheran. The arrangements are very simple. The tekya is a walled parallelogram, with a brick platform, *sakou,* in the centre of it; this *sakou* is surrounded with black poles at some distance from each other, the poles are joined at the top by horizontal rods of the same colour, and from these rods hang coloured lamps, which are lighted for the praying and preaching at night when the representation is over. The *sakou,* or central platform, makes the stage; in connection with it, at one of the opposite extremities of the parallelogram length-wise, is a reserved box, *tâgnumâ,* higher than the *sakou.* This box is splendidly decorated, and is used for peculiarly interesting and magnificent tableaux,—the court of the Caliph, for example—which occur in the course of the piece. A passage of a few feet wide is left free between the stage and this box; all the rest of the space is for the spectators, of whom the foremost rows are sitting on their heels close up to this passage, so that they help the actors to mount and descend the high steps of the *tâgnumâ* when they have to pass between that and the *sakou.* On each side of the *tâgnumâ* are boxes, and along one wall of the enclosure are other boxes with fronts of elaborate woodwork, which are left to stand as a permanent part of the construction; facing these, with the floor and stage between, rise tiers of seats as in an amphitheatre. All places are free; the great people have generally provided and furnished the boxes, and take care to fill them; but if a box is not occupied when the performance begins, any ragged street-urchin or beggar may walk in and seat himself there. A row of gigantic masts runs across the middle of the space, one or two of them being fixed in the *sakou* itself; and from these masts is stretched an immense awning which protects the whole audience. Up to a certain height these masts are hung with tiger and panther skins, to indicate the violent character of the scenes to be represented. Shields of steel and of hippopotamus skin, flags and naked swords, are also attached to these masts. A sea of colour and splendour meets the eye all round. Woodwork and brickwork disappear under cushions, rich carpets, silk hangings, India muslin embroidered with silver and gold, shawls from Kerman and from Cashmere. There are lamps, lustres of coloured crystal, mirrors, Bohemian and

Venetian glass, porcelain vases of all degrees of magnitude from China and from Europe, paintings and engravings, displayed in profusion everywhere. The taste may not always be soberly correct, but the whole spectacle has just the effect of prodigality, colour, and sumptuousness which we are accustomed to associate with the splendours of the Arabian Nights.

In marked contrast with this display is the poverty of scenic contrivance and stage illusion. The subject is far too interesting and too solemn to need them. The actors are visible on all sides, and the exits, entrances, and stage-play of our theatres are impossible; the imagination of the spectator fills up all gaps and meets all requirements. On the Ammergau arrangements one feels that the archaeologists and artists of Munich have laid their correct finger; at Teheran there has been no schooling of this sort. A copper basin of water represents the Euphrates; a heap of chopped straw in a corner is the sand of the desert of Kerbela, and the actor goes and takes up a handful of it, when his part requires him to throw, in Oriental fashion, dust upon his head. There is no attempt at proper costume; all that is sought is, to do honour to the personages of chief interest by dresses and jewels which would pass for rich and handsome things to wear in modern Persian life. The power of the actors is in their genuine sense of the seriousness of the business they are engaged in. They are, like the public around them, penetrated with this, and so the actor throws his whole soul into what he is about, the public meets the actor halfway, and effects of extraordinary impressiveness are the result. 'The actor is under a charm,' says Count Gobineau; 'he is under it so strongly and completely that almost always one sees Yezid himself (the usurping caliph), the wretched Ibn-Said (Yezid's general), the infamous Shemer (Ibn-Said's lieutenant), at the moment they vent the cruellest insults against the Imams whom they are going to massacre, or against the women of the Imam's family whom they are ill-using, burst into tears and repeat their part with sobs. The public is neither surprised nor displeased at this; on the contrary, it beats its breast at the sight, throws up its arms towards heaven with invocations of God, and redoubles its groans. So it often happens that the actor identifies himself with the personage he represents to such a degree that, when the situation carries him away, he cannot be said to act, he *is* with such truth, such complete enthusiasm, such utter self-forgetfulness, what he represents, that he reaches a reality at one time sublime, at another terrible, and produces impressions on his audience which it would be simply absurd to look for from our more artificial performances. There is nothing stilted, nothing false, nothing conventional; nature, and the facts represented, themselves speak.'

The actors are men and boys, the parts of angels and women being filled by boys. The children who appear in the piece are often the children of the principal families of Teheran; their appearance in this religious solemnity (for such it is thought) being supposed to bring a blessing upon them and their parents. 'Nothing is more touching,' says Count Gobineau, 'than to see these little things of three or four years old, dressed in black gauze [380] frocks with large sleeves, and having on their heads small round black caps embroidered with silver and gold, kneeling beside the body of the actor who represents the martyr of the day, embracing him, and with their little hands covering themselves with chopped straw for sand in sign of grief. These children evidently,' he continues, 'do not consider themselves to be acting; they are full of the feeling that what they are about is something of deep seriousness and importance; and though they are too young to comprehend fully the story, they know, in general, that it is a matter sad and solemn. They are not distracted by the audience, and they are not shy, but go through their prescribed part with the utmost attention and seriousness, [390] always crossing their arms respectfully to receive the blessing of the Imam Hussein; the public beholds them with emotions of the liveliest satisfaction and sympathy.'

The dramatic pieces themselves are without any author's name. They are in popular language, such as the commonest and most ignorant of the Persian people can understand, free from learned Arabic words,—free, comparatively speaking, from Oriental fantasticality and hyperbole. The Seyids, or popular friars, already spoken of, have probably had a hand in the composition of many of them. The Moollahs, or regular ecclesiastical authorities, condemn the whole thing. It is an innovation which they disap- [400] prove and think dangerous; it is addressed to the eye, and their religion forbids to represent religious things to the eye; it departs from the limits of what is revealed and appointed to be taught as the truth, and brings in novelties and heresies;—for these dramas keep growing under the pressure of the actor's imagination and emotion, and of the imagination and emotion of the public, and receive new developments every day. The learned, again, say that these pieces are a heap of lies, the production of ignorant people, and have no words strong enough to express their contempt for them. Still, so irresistible is the vogue of these sacred dramas that, from the king on the throne to the beggar in the street, every one, except perhaps the Moollahs, [410] attends them, and is carried away by them. The Imams and their family speak always in a kind of lyrical chant, said to have rhythmical effects, often of great pathos and beauty; their persecutors, the villains of the piece, speak always in prose.

The stage is under the direction of a choragus, called *oostad,* or 'master,' who is a sacred personage by reason of the functions which he performs. Sometimes he addresses to the audience a commentary on what is passing before them, and asks their compassion and tears for the martyrs; sometimes, in default of a Seyid, he prays and preaches. He is always listened to with veneration, for it is he who arranges the whole sacred spectacle which so deeply moves everybody. With no attempt at concealment, with the book of the piece in his hand, he remains constantly on the stage, gives the actors their cue, puts the children and any inexperienced actor in their right places, dresses the martyr in his winding-sheet when he is going to his death, holds the stirrup for him to mount his horse, and inserts a supply of chopped straw into the hands of those who are about to want it. Let us now see him at work.

The theatre is filled, and the heat is great; young men of rank, the king's pages, officers of the army, smart functionaries of State, move through the crowd with waterskins slung on their backs, dealing out water all round, in memory of the thirst which on these solemn days the Imams suffered in the sands of Kerbela. Wild chants and litanies, such as we have already described, are from time to time set up by a *dervish,* a soldier, a workman in the crowd. These chants are taken up, more or less, by the audience; sometimes they flag and die away for want of support, sometimes they are continued till they reach a paroxysm, and then abruptly stop. Presently a strange, insignificant figure in a green cotton garment, looking like a petty tradesman of one of the Teheran bazaars, mounts upon the *sakou.* He beckons with his hand to the audience, who are silent directly, and addresses them in a tone of lecture and expostulation, thus:—

'Well, you seem happy enough, Mussulmans, sitting there at your ease under the awning; and you imagine Paradise already wide open to you. Do you know what Paradise is? It is a garden, doubtless, but such a garden as you have no idea of. You will say to me: "Friend, tell us what it is like." I have never been there, certainly; but plenty of prophets have described it, and angels have brought news of it. However, all I will tell you is, that there is room for all good people there, for it is 330,000 cubits long. If you do not believe, inquire. As for getting to be one of the good people, let me tell you it is not enough to read the Koran of the Prophet (the salvation and blessing of God be upon him!); it is not enough to do everything which this divine book enjoins; it is not enough to come and weep at the *tazyas,* as you do every day, you sons of dogs you, who know nothing which is of any use; it behoves, besides, that your good works (if you ever do any, which I greatly doubt) should be done in the name and for the love of Hussein. It is Hussein, Mussulmans, who is the door to Paradise; it is Hussein, Mussulmans, who upholds the world; it is Hussein, Mussulmans, by whom comes salvation! Cry, Hassan, Hussein!' And all the multitude cry: 'O Hassan! O Hussein!'

'That is well; and now cry again.' And again all cry: 'O Hassan! O Hussein!' 'And now,' the strange speaker goes on, 'pray to God to keep you continually in the love of Hussein. Come, make your cry to God.' Then the multitude, as one man, throw up their arms into the air, and with a deep and long-drawn cry exclaim: '*Ya Allah!* O God!'

Fifes, drums, and trumpets break out; the *kernas,* great copper trumpets five or six feet long, give notice that the actors are ready and that the *tazya* is to commence. The preacher descends from the *sakou,* and the actors occupy it.

To give a clear notion of the cycle which these dramas fill, we should begin, as on the first day of the Moharrem the actors begin, with some piece relating to the childhood of the Imams, such as, for instance, the piece called *The Children Digging.* Ali and Fatima are living at Medina with their little sons Hassan and Hussein. The simple home and occupations of the pious family are exhibited; it is morning, Fatima is seated with the little Hussein on her lap, dressing him. She combs his hair, talking caressingly to him all the while. A hair comes out with the comb; the child starts. Fatima is in distress at having given the child even this momentary uneasiness, and stops to gaze upon him tenderly. She falls into an anxious reverie, thinking of her fondness for the child, and of the unknown future in store for him. While she muses, the angel Gabriel stands before her. He reproves her weakness: 'A hair falls from the child's head,' he says, 'and you weep; what would you do if you knew the destiny that awaits him, the countless wounds with which that body shall one day be pierced, the agony that shall rend your own soul!' Fatima, in despair, is comforted by her husband Ali, and they go together into the town to hear Mahomet preach. The boys and some of their little friends begin to play; every one makes a great deal of Hussein; he is at once the most spirited and the most amiable child of them all. The party amuse themselves with digging, with making holes in the ground and building mounds. Ali returns from the sermon and asks what they are about; and Hussein is made to reply in ambiguous and prophetic answers, which convey that by these holes and mounds in the earth are prefigured interments and tombs. Ali departs again; there rush in a number of big and fierce boys, and begin to pelt the little Imams with stones. A companion shields Hussein with his own body, but he is struck down with a stone, and with another stone Hussein, too, is stretched on the ground senseless. Who are those boy-tyrants and persecutors? They are Ibn-Said, and Shemer, and others, the future murderers at Kerbela. The audience perceive it with a shudder; the hateful assailants go off in triumph; Ali re-enters, picks up the stunned and wounded children, brings them round, and takes Hussein back to his mother Fatima.

But let us now come at once to the days of martyrdom and to Kerbela. One of the most famous pieces of the cycle is a piece called the *Marriage of Kassem,* which brings us into the very middle of these crowning days. Count Gobineau has given a translation of it, and from this translation we will take a few extracts. Kassem is the son of Hussein's elder brother, the Imam Hassan, who had been poisoned by Yezid's instigation at Medina. Kassem and his mother are with the Imam Hussein at Kerbela; there, too, are the women and children of the holy family, Omm-Leyla, Hussein's wife, the Persian princess, the last child of Yezdejerd the last of the Sassanides; Zeyneb, Hussein's sister, the offspring, like himself, of Ali and Fatima, and the granddaughter of Mahomet; his nephew Abdallah, still a little child; finally, his beautiful daughter Zobeyda. When the piece begins, the Imam's camp in the desert has already been cut off from the Euphrates and besieged several days by the Syrian troops under Ibn-Said and Shemer, and by the treacherous men of Kufa. The Family of the Tent were suffering torments of thirst. One of the children had brought an empty water-bottle, and thrown it, a silent token of distress, before the feet of Abbas, the uncle of Hussein; Abbas had sallied out to cut his way to the river, and had been slain. Afterwards Ali-Akber, Hussein's eldest son, had made the same attempt and met with the same fate. Two younger brothers of Ali-Akber followed his example, and were likewise slain. The Imam Hussein had rushed amidst the enemy, beaten them from the body of Ali-Akber, and brought the body back to his tent; but the river was still inaccessible. At this point the action of the *Marriage of Kassem* begins. Kassem, a youth of sixteen, is burning to go out and avenge his cousin. At one end of the *sakou* is the Imam Hussein seated on his throne; in the middle are grouped all the members of his family; at the other end lies the body of Ali-Akber, with his mother Omm-Leyla, clothed and veiled in black, bending over it. The *kernas* sound, and Kassem, after a solemn appeal from Hussein and his sister Zeyneb to God and to the founders of their house to look upon their great distress, rises and speaks to himself:

Kassem. 'Separate thyself from the women of the harem, Kassem. Consider within thyself for a little; here thou sittest, and presently thou wilt see the body of Hussein, that body like a flower, torn by arrows and lances like thorns, Kassem.

'Thou sawest Ali-Akber's head severed from his body on the field of battle, and yet thou livedst!

'Arise, obey that which is written of thee by thy father; to be slain, that is thy lot, Kassem!

'Go, get leave from the son of Fatima, most honourable among women, and submit thyself to thy fate, Kassem.' ⁵⁴⁰

Hussein sees him approach. 'Alas,' he says, 'it is the orphan nightingale of the garden of Hassan, my brother!' Then Kassem speaks:

Kassem. 'O God, what shall I do beneath this load of affliction? My eyes are wet with tears, my lips are dried up with thirst. To live is worse than to die. What shall I do, seeing what hath befallen Ali-Akber? If Hussein suffereth me not to go forth, oh misery! For then what shall I do, O God, in the day of the resurrection, when I see my father Hassan? When I see my mother in the day of the resurrection, what shall I do, O God, in my sorrow and shame before her? All my kinsmen are gone to appear ⁵⁵⁰ before the Prophet: shall not I also one day stand before the Prophet; and what shall I do, O God, in that day?'

Then he addresses the Imam:—

'Hail, threshold of the honour and majesty on high, threshold of heaven, threshold of God! In the roll of martyrs thou art the chief; in the book of creation thy story will live for ever. An orphan, a fatherless child, downcast and weeping, comes to prefer a request to thee.'

Hussein bids them tell it, and he answers:—

'O light of the eyes of Mahomet the mighty, O lieutenant of Ali the lion! Abbas has perished, Ali-Akber has suffered martyrdom. O my uncle, thou hast no warriors left, and no standard-bearer! The roses are gone and gone ⁵⁶⁰ are their buds; the jessamine is gone, the poppies are gone. I alone, I am still left in the garden of the Faith, a thorn, and miserable. If thou hast any kindness for the orphan, suffer me to go forth and fight.'

Hussein refuses. 'My child,' he says, 'thou wast the light of the eyes of the Imam Hassan, thou art my beloved remembrance of him; ask me not this; urge me not, entreat me not; to have lost Ali-Akber is enough.'

Kassem answers:—'That Kassem should live and Ali-Akber be martyred—sooner let the earth cover me! O king, be generous to the beggar at thy gate. See how my eyes run over with tears and my lips are dried up with thirst. Cast thine eyes toward the waters of the heavenly Euphrates! ⁵⁷⁰ I die of thirst; grant me, O thou marked of God, a full pitcher of the water of life! it flows in the Paradise which awaits me.'

Hussein still refuses; Kassem breaks forth in complaints and lamentations, his mother comes to him and learns the reason. She then says:—

'Complain not against the Imam, light of my eyes; only by his order can the commission of martyrdom be given. In that commission are sealed two-and-seventy witnesses, all righteous, and among the two-and-seventy is thy name. Know that thy destiny of death is commanded in the writing which thou wearest on thine arm.'

This writing is the testament of his father Hassan. He bears it in triumph to the Imam Hussein, who finds written there that he should, on the death-plain of Kerbela, suffer Kassem to have his will, but that he should marry him first to his daughter Zobeyda. Kassem consents, though in astonishment. 'Consider,' he says, 'there lies Ali-Akber, mangled by the enemies' hands! Under this sky of ebon blackness, how can joy show her face? Nevertheless if thou commandest it, what have I to do but obey? Thy commandment is that of the Prophet, and his voice is that of God.' But Hussein has also to overcome the reluctance of the intended bride and of all the women of his family.

'Heir of the vicar of God,' says Kassem's mother to the Imam, 'bid me die, but speak not to me of a bridal. If Zobeyda is to be a bride and Kassem a bridegroom, where is the henna to tinge their hands, where is the bridal chamber?' 'Mother of Kassem,' answers the Imam solemnly, 'yet a few moments, and in this field of anguish the tomb shall be for marriage-bed, and the winding-sheet for bridal garment!' All give way to the will of their sacred Head. The women and children surround Kassem, sprinkle him with rose-water, hang bracelets and necklaces on him, and scatter bon-bons around; and then the marriage procession is formed. Suddenly drums and trumpets are heard, and the Syrian troops appear. Ibn-Said and Shemer are at their head. 'The Prince of the Faith celebrates a marriage in the desert,' they exclaim tauntingly; 'we will soon change his festivity into mourning.' They pass by, and Kassem takes leave of his bride. 'God keep thee, my bride,' he says, embracing her, 'for I must forsake thee!' 'One moment,' she says, 'remain in thy place one moment! thy countenance is as the lamp which giveth us light; suffer me to turn around thee as the butterfly turneth, gently, gently!' And making a turn around him, she performs the ancient Eastern rite of respect from a new-married wife to her husband. Troubled, he rises to go: 'The reins of my will are slipping away from me!' he murmurs. She lays hold of his robe: 'Take off thy hand,' he cries, 'we belong not to ourselves!'

Then he asks the Imam to array him in his winding-sheet. 'O nightingale of the divine orchard of martyrdom,' says Hussein, as he complies with his wish, 'I clothe thee with thy winding-sheet, I kiss thy face; there is no fear, and no hope, but of God!' Kassem commits his little brother Abdallah to the Imam's care. Omm-Leyla looks up from her son's corpse, and says to Kassem: 'When thou enterest the garden of Paradise, kiss for me the head of Ali-Akber!'

The Syrian troops again appear. Kassem rushes upon them and they all go off fighting. The Family of the Tent, at Hussein's command, put the Koran on their heads and pray, covering themselves with sand. Kassem re-appears victorious. He has slain Azrek, a chief captain of the Syrians, but his thirst is intolerable. 'Uncle,' he says to the Imam, who asks him what reward he wishes for his valour, 'my tongue cleaves to the roof of my mouth; the reward I wish is *water*.' 'Thou coverest me with shame, Kassem,' his uncle answers; 'what can I do? Thou askest water; there is no water!'

Kassem. 'If I might but wet my mouth, I could presently make an end of the men of Kufa.'

Hussein. 'As I live, I have not one drop of water!'

Kassem. 'Were it but lawful, I would wet my mouth with my own blood.'

Hussein. 'Beloved child, what the Prophet forbids, that cannot I make lawful.'

Kassem. 'I beseech thee, let my lips be but once moistened, and I will vanquish thine enemies!'

Hussein presses his own lips to those of Kassem, who, refreshed, again rushes forth, and returns bleeding and stuck with darts, to die at the Imam's feet in the tent. So ends the marriage of Kassem.

But the great day is the tenth day of the Moharrem, when comes the death of the Imam himself. The narrative of Gibbon well sums up the events of this great tenth day. 'The battle at length expired by the death of the last of the companions of Hussein. Alone, weary, and wounded, he seated himself at the door of his tent. He was pierced in the mouth with a dart. He lifted his hands to heaven—they were full of blood—and he uttered a funeral prayer for the living and the dead. In a transport of despair, his sister issued from the tent, and adjured the general of the Kufians that he would not suffer Hussein to be murdered before his eyes. A tear trickled down the soldier's venerable beard; and the boldest of his men fell back on every side as the dying Imam threw himself among them. The remorseless Shemer—a name detested by the faithful—reproached their cowardice; and the grandson of Mahomet was slain with three and thirty strokes of lances and swords. After they had trampled on his body, they carried his head to the castle of Kufa, and the inhuman Obeidallah (the governor) struck him on the mouth with a cane. "Alas!" exclaimed an aged Mussulman, "on those lips have I seen the lips of the Apostle of God!" '

For this catastrophe no one *tazya* suffices; all the companies of actors unite in a vast open space; booths and tents are pitched round the outside circle for the spectators; in the centre is the Imam's camp, and the day ends with its conflagration.

Nor are there wanting pieces which carry on the story beyond the death of Hussein. One which produces an extraordinary effect is *The Christian Damsel.* The carnage is over, the enemy are gone. To the awe-struck beholders, the scene shows the silent plain of Kerbela and the tombs of the martyrs. Their bodies, full of wounds, and with weapons sticking in them still, are exposed to view; but around them all are crowns of burning candles, circles of light, to show that they have entered into glory. At one end of the *sakou* is a high tomb by itself; it is the tomb of the Imam Hussein, and his pierced body is seen stretched out upon it. A brilliant caravan enters, with camels, soldiers, servants, and a young lady on horseback, in European costume, or what passes in Persia for European costume. She halts near the tombs and proposes to encamp. Her servants try to pitch a tent; but wherever they drive a pole into the ground, blood springs up, and a groan of horror bursts from the audience. Then the fair traveller, instead of encamping, mounts into the *tâgnumâ,* lies down to rest there, and falls asleep. Jesus Christ appears to her, and makes known that this is Kerbela, and what has happened here. Meanwhile, an Arab of the desert, a Bedouin who had formerly received Hussein's bounty, comes stealthily, intent on plunder, upon the *sakou.* He finds nothing, and in a paroxysm of brutal fury he begins to ill-treat the corpses. Blood flows. The feeling of Asiatics about their dead is well known, and the horror of the audience rises to its height. Presently the ruffian assails and wounds the corpse of the Imam himself, over whom white doves are hovering; the voice of Hussein, deep and mournful, calls from his tomb: *'There is no God but God!'* The robber flies in terror; the angels, the prophets, Mahomet, Jesus Christ, Moses, the Imams, the holy women, all come upon the *sakou,* press round Hussein, load him with honours. The Christian damsel wakes, and embraces Islam, the Islam of the sect of the Shiahs.

Another piece closes the whole story, by bringing the captive women and children of the Imam's family to Damascus, to the presence of the Caliph Yezid. It is in this piece that there comes the magnificent tableau, already mentioned, of the court of the caliph. The crown jewels are lent for it, and the dresses of the ladies of Yezid's court, represented by boys chosen for their good looks, are said to be worth thousands and thousands of pounds; but the audience see them without favour, for this brilliant court of Yezid is cruel to the captives of Kerbela. The captives are thrust into a wretched dungeon under the palace walls; but the Caliph's wife had formerly been a slave of Mahomet's daughter Fatima, the mother of Hussein and Zeyneb. She goes to see Zeyneb in prison, her heart is touched, she passes into an agony of repentance, returns to her husband, upbraids him with his crimes, and intercedes for the women of the holy family, and for the children, who keep calling for the Imam Hussein. Yezid orders his wife to be put to death, and sends the head of Hussein to the children. Sekyna, the Imam's youngest daughter, a child of four years old, takes the beloved head in her arms, kisses it, and lies down beside it. Then Hussein appears to her as in life: 'Oh! my father,' she cries, 'where wast thou? I was hungry, I was cold, I was beaten—where wast thou?' But now she sees him again, and is happy. In the vision of her happiness she passes away out of this troublesome life, she enters into rest, and the piece ends with her mother and her aunts burying her.

These are the martyrs of Kerbela; and these are the sufferings which awaken in an Asiatic audience sympathy so deep and serious, transports so genuine of pity, love, and gratitude, that to match them at all one must take the feelings raised at Ammergau. And now, where are we to look, in the subject-matter of the Persian passion-play, for the source of all this emotion?

Count Gobineau suggests that it is to be found in the feeling of patriotism; and that our Indo-European kinsmen, the Persians, conquered by the Semitic Arabians, find in the sufferings of Hussein a portrait of their own martyrdom. 'Hussein,' says Count Gobineau, 'is not only the son of Ali, he is the husband of a princess of the blood of the Persian kings; he, his father Ali, the whole body of Imams taken together, represent the nation, represent Persia, invaded, ill-treated, despoiled, stripped of its inhabitants, by the Arabians. The right which is insulted and violated in Hussein, is identified with the right of Persia. The Arabians, the Turks, the Afghans,—Persia's implacable and hereditary enemies,—recognize Yezid as legitimate caliph; Persia finds therein an excuse for hating them the more, and identifies herself the more with the usurper's victims. It is *patriotism,* therefore, which has taken the form, here, of the drama to express itself.' No doubt there is much truth in what Count Gobineau thus says; and it is certain that the division of Shiahs and Sunis has its true cause in a division of races, rather than in a difference of religious belief.

But I confess that if the interest of the Persian passion-plays had seemed to me to lie solely in the curious evidence they afford of the workings of patriotic feeling in a conquered people, I should hardly have occupied myself with them at all this length. I believe that they point to something much more interesting. What this is, I cannot do more than simply indicate; but indicate it I will, in conclusion, and then leave the student of human nature to follow it out for himself.

When Mahomet's cousin Jaffer, and others of his first converts, persecuted by the idolaters of Mecca, fled in the year of our era 615, seven years before the Hegira, into Abyssinia, and took refuge with the King of that country, the people of Mecca sent after the fugitives to demand that they should be given up to them. Abyssinia was then already Christian. The King asked Jaffer and his companions what was this new religion for which they had left their country. Jaffer answered: 'We were plunged in the darkness of ignorance, we were worshippers of idols. Given over to all our passions, we knew no law but that of the strongest, when God raised up among us a man of our own race, of noble descent, and long held in esteem by us for his virtues. This apostle called us to believe in one God, to worship God only, to reject the superstitions of our fathers, to despise divinities of wood and stone. He commanded us to eschew wickedness, to be truthful in speech, faithful to our engagements, kind and helpful to our relations and neighbours. He bade us respect the chastity of women, and not to rob the orphan. He exhorted us to prayer, alms-giving, and fasting. We believed in his mission, and we accepted the doctrines and the rule of life which he brought to us from God. For this our countrymen have persecuted us; and now they want to make us return to their idolatry.' The king of Abyssinia refused to surrender the fugitives, and then, turning again to Jaffer, after a few more explanations, he picked up a straw from the ground, and said to him: 'Between your religion and ours there is not the thickness of this straw difference.'

That is not quite so; yet thus much we may affirm, that Jaffer's account of the religion of Mahomet is a great deal truer than the accounts of it which are commonly current amongst us. Indeed, for the credit of humanity, as more than a hundred millions of men are said to profess the Mahometan religion, one is glad to think so. To popular opinion everywhere, religion is proved by miracles. All religions but a man's own are utterly false and vain; the authors of them are mere impostors; and the miracles which are said to attest them, fictitious. We forget that this is a game which two can play at; although the believer of each religion always imagines the prodigies which attest his own religion to be fenced by a guard granted to them alone. Yet how much more safe is it, as well as more fruitful, to look for the main confirmation of a religion in its intrinsic correspondence with urgent wants of human nature, in its profound necessity! Differing religions will then be found to have much in common, but this will be an additional proof of the value of that religion which does most for that which is thus commonly recognized as salutary and necessary. In Christendom one need not go about to establish that the religion of the Hebrews is a better religion than the religion of the Arabs, or that the Bible is a greater book than the Koran. The Bible *grew,* the Koran *was made;* there lies the immense difference in depth and truth between them! This 780 very inferiority may make the Koran, for certain purposes and for people at a low stage of mental growth, a more powerful instrument than the Bible. From the circumstances of its origin, the Koran has the intensely dogmatic character, it has the perpetual insistence on the motive of future rewards and punishments, the palpable exhibition of paradise and hell, which the Bible has not. Among the little known and little advanced races of the great African continent, the Mahometan missionaries, by reason of the sort of power which this character of the Koran gives, are said to be more successful than ours. Nevertheless even in Africa it will assuredly one day be manifest, that whereas the Bible-people trace themselves to Abra- 790 ham through Isaac, and the Koran-people trace themselves to Abraham through Ishmael, the difference between the religion of the Bible and the religion of the Koran is almost as the difference between Isaac and Ishmael. I mean that the seriousness about righteousness, which is what the hatred of idolatry really means, and the profound and inexhaustible doctrines that the righteous Eternal loveth righteousness, that there is no peace for the wicked, that the righteous is an everlasting foundation, are exhibited and inculcated in the Old Testament with an authority, majesty, and truth which leave the Koran immeasurably behind, and which, the more man- kind grows and gains light, the more will be felt to have no fellows. 800 Mahomet was no doubt acquainted with the Jews and their documents, and gained something from this source for his religion. But his religion is not a mere plagiarism from Judea, any more than it is a mere mass of falsehood. No; in the seriousness, elevation, and moral energy of himself and of that Semitic race from which he sprang and to which he spoke, Mahomet mainly found that scorn and hatred of idolatry, that sense of the worth and truth of righteousness, judgment, and justice, which make the real great- ness of him and his Koran, and which are thus rather an independent testi- mony to the essential doctrines of the Old Testament, than a plagiarism from them. The world needs righteousness and the Bible is the grand 810 teacher of it, but for certain times and certain men Mahomet too, in his way, was a teacher of righteousness.

But we know how the Old Testament conception of righteousness ceased with time to have the freshness and force of an intuition, became something petrified, narrow, and formal, needed renewing. We know how Christianity renewed it, carrying into these hard waters of Judaism a sort of warm gulf-stream of tender emotion, due chiefly to qualities which may be summed up as those of inwardness, mildness, and self-renouncement. Mahometanism had no such renewing. It began with a conception of righteousness, lofty indeed, but narrow, and which we may call old Jewish; and there it remained. It is not a *feeling* religion. No one would say that the virtues of gentleness, mildness, and self-sacrifice were its virtues; and the more it went on, the more the faults of its original narrow basis became visible, more and more it became fierce and militant, less and less was it amiable. Now, what are Ali, and Hassan, and Hussein and the Imams, but an insurrection of noble and pious natures against this hardness and aridity of the religion round them? an insurrection making its authors seem weak, helpless, and unsuccessful to the world and amidst the struggles of the world, but enabling them to know the joy and peace for which the world thirsts in vain, and inspiring in the heart of mankind an irresistible sympathy. 'The twelve Imams,' says Gibbon, 'Ali, Hassan, Hussein, and the lineal descendants of Hussein, to the ninth generation, without arms, or treasures, or subjects, successively enjoyed the veneration of the people. Their names were often the pretence of sedition and civil war; but these royal saints despised the pomp of the world, submitted to the will of God and the injustice of man, and devoted their innocent lives to the study and practice of religion.'

Abnegation and mildness, based on the depth of the inner life, and visited by unmerited misfortune, made the power of the first and famous Imams, Ali, Hassan, and Hussein, over the popular imagination. 'O brother,' said Hassan, as he was dying of poison, to Hussein who sought to find out and punish his murderer, 'O brother, let him alone till he and I meet together before God!' So his father Ali had stood back from his rights instead of snatching at them. So of Hussein himself it was said by his successful rival, the usurping Caliph Yezid: 'God loved Hussein, *but he would not suffer him to attain to anything.*' They might attain to nothing, they were too pure, these great ones of the world as by birth they were; but the people, which itself also can attain to so little, loved them all the better on that account, loved them for their abnegation and mildness, felt that they were dear to God, that God loved them, and that they and their lives filled a void in the severe religion of Mahomet. These saintly self-deniers, these resigned sufferers, who would not strive nor cry, supplied a tender and pathetic side in Islam. The conquered Persians, a more mobile, more impressionable, and gentler race than their concentrated, narrow, and austere Semitic conquerors felt the need of it most, and gave most prominence to the ideals which satisfied the need; but in Arabs and Turks also, and in all the Mahometan world, Ali and his sons excite enthusiasm and affection. Round the central sufferer, Hussein, has come to group itself everything which is most tender and touching. His person brings to the Mussulman's mind the most human side of Mahomet himself, his [860] fondness for children,—for Mahomet had loved to nurse the little Hussein on his knee, and to show him from the pulpit to his people. The Family of the Tent is full of women and children, and their devotion and sufferings,— blameless and saintly women, lovely and innocent children. There, too, are lovers with their story, the beauty and the love of youth; and all follow the attraction of the pure and resigned Imam, all die for him. The tender pathos from all these flows into the pathos from him and enhances it, until finally there arises for the popular imagination an immense ideal of mildness and self-sacrifice, melting and overpowering the soul.

Even for us, to whom almost all the names are strange, whose interest [870] in the places and persons is faint, who have them before us for a moment to-day, to see them again, probably, no more for ever,—even for us, unless I err greatly, the power and pathos of this ideal are recognisable. What must they be for those to whom every name is familiar, and calls up the most solemn and cherished associations; who have had their adoring gaze fixed all their lives upon this exemplar of self-denial and gentleness, and who have no other? If it was superfluous to say to English people that the religion of the Koran has not the value of the religion of the Old Testament, still more is it superfluous to say that the religion of the Imams has not the value of Christianity. The character and discourse of Jesus Christ [880] possess, I have elsewhere often said, two signal powers: mildness and sweet reasonableness. The latter, the power which so puts before our view duty of every kind as to give it the force of an intuition, as to make it seem,—to make the total sacrifice of our ordinary self seem,—the most simple, natural, winning, necessary thing in the world, has been hitherto applied with but a very limited range, it is destined to an infinitely wider application, and has a fruitfulness which will yet transform the world. Of this the Imams have nothing, except so far as all mildness and self-sacrifice have in them something of sweet reasonableness and are its indispensable preliminary. This they have, *mildness and self-sacrifice;* and we have seen what an attraction [890] it exercises. Could we ask for a stronger testimony to Christianity? Could we wish for any sign more convincing, that Jesus Christ was indeed, what Christians call him, *the desire of all nations?* So salutary, so necessary is what Christianity contains, that a religion,—a great, powerful, successful religion,—arises without it, and the missing virtue forces its way in! Christianity may say to these Persian Mahometans, with their gaze fondly turned towards the martyred Imams, what in our Bible God says by Isaiah to Cyrus, their great ancestor:—'*I girded thee, though thou hast not known me.*' It is a long way from Kerbela to Calvary; but the sufferers of Kerbela hold aloft to the eyes of millions of our race the lesson so loved by the sufferer of Calvary. For he said: 'Learn of me, that I am *mild,* and *lowly of heart;* and ye shall find *rest unto your souls.*'

JOUBERT

———————◆▶———————

Why should we ever treat of any dead authors but the famous ones?
Mainly for this reason: because, from these famous personages, home or
foreign, whom we all know so well, and of whom so much has been said,
the amount of stimulus which they contain for us has been in a great
measure disengaged; people have formed their opinion about them, and do
not readily change it. One may write of them afresh, combat received
opinions about them, even interest one's readers in so doing; but the interest one's readers receive has to do, in general, rather with the treatment
than with the subject; they are susceptible of a lively impression rather of
the course of the discussion itself,—its turns, vivacity, and novelty,—than   10
of the genius of the author who is the occasion of it. And yet what is really
precious and inspiring, in all that we get from literature, except this sense
of an immediate contact with genius itself, and the stimulus towards what
is true and excellent which we derive from it? Now in literature, besides the
eminent men of genius who have had their deserts in the way of fame,
besides the eminent men of ability who have often had far more than their

deserts in the way of fame, there are a certain number of personages who have been real men of genius,—by which I mean, that they have had a genuine gift for what is true and excellent, and are therefore capable of emitting a life-giving stimulus,—but who, for some reason or other, in most cases for very valid reasons, have remained obscure, nay, beyond a narrow circle in their own country, unknown. It is salutary from time to time to come across a genius of this kind, and to extract his honey. Often he has more of it for us, as I have already said, than greater men; for, though it is by no means true that from what is new to us there is most to be learnt, it is yet indisputably true that from what is new to us we in general learn most.

Of a genius of this kind, Joseph Joubert, I am now going to speak. His name is, I believe, almost unknown in England; and even in France, his native country, it is not famous. M. Sainte-Beuve has given of him one of his incomparable portraits; but,—besides that even M. Sainte-Beuve's writings are far less known amongst us than they deserve to be,—every country has its own point of view from which a remarkable author may most profitably be seen and studied.

Joseph Joubert was born (and his date should be remarked) in 1754, at Montignac, a little town in Périgord. His father was a doctor with small means and a large family; and Joseph, the eldest, had his own way to make in the world. He was for eight years, as pupil first, and afterwards as an assistant-master, in the public school of Toulouse, then managed by the Jesuits, who seem to have left in him a most favourable opinion, not only of their tact and address, but of their really good qualities as teachers and directors. Compelled by the weakness of his health to give up, at twenty-two, the profession of teaching, he passed two important years of his life in hard study, at home at Montignac; and came in 1778 to try his fortune in the literary world of Paris, then perhaps the most tempting field which has ever yet presented itself to a young man of letters. He knew Diderot, D'Alembert, Marmontel, Laharpe; he became intimate with one of the celebrities of the next literary generation, then, like himself, a young man,—Châteaubriand's friend, the future Grand Master of the University, Fontanes. But, even then, it began to be remarked of him, that M. Joubert *'s'inquiétait de perfection bien plus que de gloire*—cared far more about perfecting himself than about making himself a reputation.' His severity of morals may perhaps have been rendered easier to him by the delicacy of his health; but the delicacy of his health will not by itself account for his changeless preference of being to seeming, knowing to showing, studying to publishing; for what terrible public performers have some invalids been! This preference he retained all through his life, and it is by this that he is characterised. 'He has chosen,' Châteaubriand (adopting Epicurus's famous words) said of him, *'to hide his life.'* Of a life which its owner was bent on hiding there can be but little to tell. Yet the only two public inci- 60 dents of Joubert's life, slight as they are, do all concerned in them so much credit that they deserve mention. In 1790 the Constituent Assembly made the office of justice of the peace elective throughout France. The people of Montignac retained such an impression of the character of their young townsman,—one of Plutarch's men of virtue, as he had lived amongst them, simple, studious, severe,—that, though he had left them for years, they elected him in his absence without his knowing anything about it. The appointment little suited Joubert's wishes or tastes; but at such a moment he thought it wrong to decline it. He held it for two years, the legal term, discharging its duties with a firmness and integrity which were long remem- 70 bered; and then, when he went out of office, his fellow-townsmen re-elected him. But Joubert thought that he had now accomplished his duty towards them, and he went back to the retirement which he loved. That seems to me a little episode of the great French Revolution worth remembering. The sage who was asked by the king, why sages were seen at the doors of kings, but not kings at the doors of sages, replied, that it was because sages knew what was good for them, and kings did not. But at Montignac the king—for in 1790 the people in France was king with a vengeance—knew what was good for him, and came to the door of the sage.

The other incident was this. When Napoleon, in 1809, reorganised the 80 public instruction of France, founded the University, and made M. de Fontanes its Grand Master, Fontanes had to submit to the Emperor a list of persons to form the council or governing body of the new University. Third on his list, after two distinguished names, Fontanes placed the unknown name of Joubert. 'This name,' he said in his accompanying memorandum to the Emperor, 'is not known as the two first are; and yet this is the nomination to which I attach most importance. I have known M. Joubert all my life. His character and intelligence are of the very highest order. I shall rejoice if your Majesty will accept my guarantee for him.' Napoleon trusted his Grand Master, and Joubert became a councillor of 90 the University. It is something that a man, elevated to the highest posts of State, should not forget his obscure friends; or that, if he remembers and places them, he should regard in placing them their merit rather than their obscurity. It is more, in the eyes of those whom the necessities, real or supposed, of a political system have long familiarised with such cynical disregard of fitness in the distribution of office, to see a minister and his master alike zealous, in giving away places, to give them to the best men to be found.

Between 1792 and 1809 Joubert had married. His life was passed between Villeneuve-sur-Yonne, where his wife's family lived,—a pretty little Burgundian town, by which the Lyons railroad now passes,—and Paris. Here, in a house in the Rue St.-Honoré, in a room very high up, and admitting plenty of the light which he so loved,—a room from which he saw, in his own words, 'a great deal of sky and very little earth,'—among the treasures of a library collected with infinite pains, taste, and skill, from which every book he thought ill of was rigidly excluded,—he never would possess either a complete Voltaire or a complete Rousseau,—the happiest hours of his life were passed. In the circle of one of those women who leave a sort of perfume in literary history, and who have the gift of inspiring successive generations of readers with an indescribable regret not to have known them,—Pauline de Montmorin, Madame de Beaumont,—he had become intimate with nearly all which at that time, in the Paris world of letters or of society, was most attractive and promising. Amongst his acquaintances one only misses the names of Madame de Staël and Benjamin Constant. Neither of them was to his taste, and with Madame de Staël he always refused to become acquainted; he thought she had more vehemence than truth, and more heat than light.

Years went on, and his friends became conspicuous authors or statesmen; but Joubert remained in the shade. His constitution was of such fragility that how he lived so long, or accomplished so much as he did, is a wonder: his soul had, for its basis of operations, hardly any body at all: both from his stomach and from his chest he seems to have had constant suffering, though he lived by rule, and was as abstemious as a Hindoo. Often, after overwork in thinking, reading, or talking, he remained for days together in a state of utter prostration,—condemned to absolute silence and inaction; too happy if the agitation of his mind would become quiet also, and let him have the repose of which he stood in so much need. With this weakness of health, these repeated suspensions of energy, he was incapable of the prolonged contention of spirit necessary for the creation of great works. But he read and thought immensely; he was an unwearied note-taker, a charming letter-writer; above all, an excellent and delightful talker. The gaiety and amenity of his natural disposition were inexhaustible; and his spirit, too, was of astonishing elasticity; he seemed to hold on to life by a single thread only, but that single thread was very tenacious. More and more, as his soul and knowledge ripened more and more, his friends pressed to his room in the Rue St.-Honoré; often he received them in bed, for he seldom rose before three o'clock in the afternoon; and at his bedroom-door, on his bad days, Madame Joubert stood sentry, trying, not always with success, to keep back the thirsty comers from the fountain which was forbidden to flow. Fontanes did nothing in the University without consulting him, and Joubert's ideas and pen were always at his friend's service.

When he was in the country, at Villeneuve, the young priests of his neighbourhood used to resort to him, in order to profit by his library and by his conversation. He, like our Coleridge, was particularly qualified to attract men of this kind and to benefit them: retaining perfect independence of mind, he was a religious philosopher. As age came on, his infirmities became more and more overwhelming; some of his friends, too, died; others became so immersed in politics, that Joubert, who hated politics, saw them seldomer than of old; but the moroseness of age and infirmity never touched him, and he never quarrelled with a friend or lost one. From these miseries he was preserved by that quality in him of which I have already spoken; a quality which is best expressed by a word, not of common use in English,—alas, we have too little in our national character of the quality which this word expresses,—his inborn, his constant amenity. He lived till the year 1824. On the 4th of May in that year he died, at the age of seventy. A day or two after his death M. de Châteaubriand inserted in the *Journal des Débats* a short notice of him, perfect for its feeling, grace, and propriety. *On ne vit dans la mémoire du monde,* he says and says truly, *que par des travaux pour le monde*—'a man can live in the world's memory only by what he has done for the world.' But Châteaubriand used the privilege which his great name gave him to assert, delicately but firmly, Joubert's real and rare merits, and to tell the world what manner of man had just left it.

Joubert's papers were accumulated in boxes and drawers. He had not meant them for publication; it was very difficult to sort them and to prepare them for it. Madame Joubert, his widow, had a scruple about giving them a publicity which her husband, she felt, would never have permitted. But, as her own end approached, the natural desire to leave of so remarkable a spirit some enduring memorial, some memorial to outlast the admiring recollection of the living who were so fast passing away, made her yield to the entreaties of his friends, and allow the printing, but for private circulation only, of a volume of his fragments. Châteaubriand edited it; it appeared in 1838, fourteen years after Joubert's death. The volume attracted the attention of those who were best fitted to appreciate it, and profoundly impressed them. M. Sainte-Beuve gave of it, in the *Revue des Deux Mondes,* the admirable notice of which I have already spoken; and so much curiosity was excited about Joubert, that the collection of his fragments, enlarged by many additions, was at last published for the benefit of the world in general. It has since been twice reprinted. The first or preliminary chapter has some fancifulness and affectation in it; the reader should begin with the second.

I have likened Joubert to Coleridge; and indeed the points of resemblance between the two men are numerous. Both of them great and celebrated talkers, Joubert attracting pilgrims to his upper chamber in the Rue St.-Honoré, as Coleridge attracted pilgrims to Mr. Gilman's at Highgate; both of them desultory and incomplete writers,—here they had an outward likeness with one another. Both of them passionately devoted to reading in a class of books, and to thinking on a class of subjects, out of the beaten line of the reading and thought of their day; both of them ardent students and critics of old literature, poetry, and the metaphysics of religion; both of them curious explorers of words, and of the latent significance hidden under the popular use of them; both of them, in a certain sense, conservative in religion and politics, by antipathy to the narrow and shallow foolishness of vulgar modern liberalism;—here they had their inward and real likeness. But that in which the essence of their likeness consisted is this,—that they both had from nature an ardent impulse for seeking the genuine truth on all matters they thought about, and a gift for finding it and recognising it when it was found. To have the impulse for seeking this truth is much rarer than most people think; to have the gift for finding it is, I need not say, very rare indeed. By this they have a spiritual relationship of the closest kind with one another, and they become, each of them, a source of stimulus and progress for all of us.

Coleridge had less delicacy and penetration than Joubert, but more richness and power; his production, though far inferior to what his nature at first seemed to promise, was abundant and varied. Yet in all his production how much is there to dissatisfy us! How many reserves must be made in praising either his poetry, or his criticism, or his philosophy! How little either of his poetry, or of his criticism, or of his philosophy, can we expect permanently to stand! But that which will stand of Coleridge is this: the stimulus of his continual effort,—not a moral effort, for he had no morals,—but of his continual instinctive effort, crowned often with rich success, to get at and to lay bare the real truth of his matter in hand, whether that matter were literary, or philosophical, or political, or religious; and this in a country where at that moment such an effort was almost unknown; where the most powerful minds threw themselves upon poetry, which conveys truth, indeed, but conveys it indirectly; and where ordinary minds were so habituated to do without thinking altogether, to regard considerations of established routine and practical convenience as paramount, that any attempt to introduce within the domain of these the disturbing element of thought, they were prompt to resent as an outrage. [220] Coleridge's great usefulness lay in his supplying in England, for many years and under critical circumstances, by the spectacle of this effort of his, a stimulus to all minds capable of profiting by it, in the generation which grew up around him. His action will still be felt as long as the need for it continues. When, with the cessation of the need, the action too has ceased, Coleridge's memory, in spite of the disesteem—nay, repugnance—which his character may and must inspire, will yet for ever remain invested with that interest and gratitude which invests the memory of founders.

M. de Rémusat, indeed, reproaches Coleridge with his *jugements saugrenus;* the criticism of a gifted truth-finder ought not to be *saugrenu,* [230] so on this reproach we must pause for a moment. *Saugrenu* is rather a vulgar French word, but like many other vulgar words, very expressive; used as an epithet for a judgment, it means something like *impudently absurd.* The literary judgments of one nation about another are very apt to be *saugrenus.* It is certainly true, as M. Sainte-Beuve remarks in answer to Goethe's complaint against the French that they have undervalued Du Bartas, that as to the estimate of its own authors every nation is the best judge; the *positive* estimate of them, be it understood, not, of course, the estimate of them in comparison with the authors of other nations. Therefore a foreigner's judgments about the intrinsic merit of a nation's authors [240] will generally, when at complete variance with that nation's own, be wrong; but there is a permissible wrongness in these matters; and to that permissible wrongness there is a limit. When that limit is exceeded, the wrong judgment becomes more than wrong, it becomes *saugrenu,* or impudently absurd. For instance, the high estimate which the French have of Racine is probably in great measure deserved; or, to take a yet stronger case, even the high estimate which Joubert had of the Abbé Delille is probably in great measure deserved; but the common disparaging judgment passed on Racine by English readers is not *saugrenu,* still less is that passed by them on the Abbé Delille *saugrenu,* because the beauty of Racine, and of [250] Delille too, so far as Delille's beauty goes, is eminently in their language, and this is a beauty which a foreigner cannot perfectly seize;—this beauty of diction, *apicibus verborum ligata,* as M. Sainte-Beuve, quoting Quintilian, says of Châteaubriand's. As to Châteaubriand himself, again, the common English judgment, which stamps him as a mere shallow rhetorician, all froth and vanity, is certainly wrong; one may even wonder that we English should judge Châteaubriand so wrongly, for his power goes far beyond beauty of diction; it is a power, as well, of passion and sentiment, and this sort of power the English can perfectly well appreciate. One production of Châteaubriand's, *René,* is akin to the most popular productions of Byron,—to the *Childe Harold* or *Manfred,*—in spirit, equal to them in power, superior to them in form. But this work, I hardly know why, is almost unread in England. And only consider this criticism of Châteaubriand's on the true pathetic! 'It is a dangerous mistake, sanctioned, like so many other dangerous mistakes, by Voltaire, to suppose that the best works of imagination are those which draw most tears. One could name this or that melodrama, which no one would like to own having written, and which yet harrows the feelings far more than the Aeneid. The true tears are those which are called forth by the *beauty* of poetry; there must be as much admiration in them as sorrow. They are the tears which come to our eyes when Priam says to Achilles, ἔτλην δ', οἳ οὔπω . . . —"And I have endured,—the like whereof no soul upon the earth hath yet endured,—to carry to my lips the hand of him who slew my child;" or when Joseph cries out: "I am Joseph your brother, whom ye sold into Egypt." ' Who does not feel that the man who wrote that was no shallow rhetorician, but a born man of genius, with the true instinct of genius for what is really admirable? Nay, take these words of Châteaubriand, an old man of eighty, dying, amidst the noise and bustle of the ignoble revolution of February 1848: 'Mon Dieu, mon Dieu, quand donc, quand donc serai-je délivré de tout ce monde, ce bruit; quand donc, quand donc cela finira-t-il?' Who, with any ear, does not feel that those are not the accents of a trumpery rhetorician, but of a rich and puissant nature,—the cry of the dying lion? I repeat it, Châteaubriand is most ignorantly underrated in England; and we English are capable of rating him far more correctly if we knew him better. Still Châteaubriand has such real and great faults, he falls so decidedly beneath the rank of the truly greatest authors, that the depreciatory judgment passed on him in England, though ignorant and wrong, can hardly be said to transgress the limits of permissible ignorance; it is not a *jugement saugrenu.* But when a critic denies genius to a literature which has produced Bossuet and Molière, he passes the bounds; and Coleridge's judgments on French literature and the French genius are undoubtedly, as M. de Rémusat calls them, *saugrenus.*

And yet, such is the impetuosity of our poor human nature, such its proneness to rush to a decision with imperfect knowledge, that his having delivered a *saugrenu* judgment or two in his life by no means proves a man not to have had, in comparison with his fellowmen in general, a remarkable gift for truth, or disqualifies him for being, by virtue of that gift, a source of vital stimulus for us. Joubert had far less smoke and turbid vehemence in him than Coleridge; he had also a far keener sense of what was absurd. But Joubert can write to M. Molé (the M. Molé who was afterwards Louis Philippe's well-known minister): 'As to your Milton, whom the merit of the Abbé Delille' (the Abbé Delille translated *Paradise Lost*) 'makes me admire, and with whom I have nevertheless still plenty of fault to find, why, I should like to know, are you scandalised that I have not enabled myself to read him? I don't understand the language in which he writes, and I don't much care to. If he is a poet one cannot put up with, even in the prose of the younger Racine, am I to blame for that? If by force you mean beauty manifesting itself with power, I maintain that the Abbé Delille has more force than Milton.' That, to be sure, is a petulant outburst in a private letter; it is not, like Coleridge's, a deliberate proposition in a printed philosophical essay. But is it possible to imagine a more perfect specimen of a *saugrenu* judgment? It is even worse than Coleridge's, because it is *saugrenu* with reasons. That, however, does not prevent Joubert from having been really a man of extraordinary ardour in the search for truth, and of extraordinary fineness in the perception of it; and so was Coleridge.

Joubert had around him in France an atmosphere of literary, philosophical, and religious opinion as alien to him as that in England was to Coleridge. This is what makes Joubert, too, so remarkable, and it is on this account that I begged the reader to remark his date. He was born in 1754; he died in 1824. He was thus in the fulness of his powers at the beginning of the present century, at the epoch of Napoleon's consulate. The French criticism of that day—the criticism of Laharpe's successors, of Geoffroy and his colleagues in the *Journal des Débats*—had a dryness very unlike the telling vivacity of the early Edinburgh reviewers, their contemporaries, but a fundamental narrowness, a want of genuine insight, much on a par with theirs. Joubert, like Coleridge, has no respect for the dominant oracle; he treats his Geoffroy with about as little deference as Coleridge treats his Jeffrey. 'Geoffroy,' he says of an article in the *Journal des Débats* criticising Châteaubriand's *Génie du Christianisme*—'Geoffroy in this article begins by holding out his paw prettily enough; but he ends by a volley of kicks, which lets the whole world see but too clearly the four iron shoes of the four-footed animal.' There is, however, in France a sympathy with intellectual activity for its own sake, and for the sake of its inherent pleasurableness and beauty, keener than any which exists in England; and Joubert had more effect in Paris,—though his conversation was his only weapon, and Coleridge wielded besides his conversation his pen,—than

Coleridge had or could have in London. I mean, a more immediate, appreciable effect; an effect not only upon the young and enthusiastic, to whom the future belongs, but upon formed and important personages to whom the present belongs, and who are actually moving society. He owed this partly to his real advantages over Coleridge. If he had, as I have already said, less power and richness than his English parallel, he had more tact and penetration. He was more *possible* than Coleridge; his doctrine was more intelligible than Coleridge's, more receivable. And yet with Joubert, the striving after a consummate and attractive clearness of expression came from no mere frivolous dislike of labour and inability for going deep, but was a part of his native love of truth and perfection. The delight of his life he found in truth, and in the satisfaction which the enjoying of truth gives to the spirit; and he thought the truth was never really and worthily said, so long as the least cloud, clumsiness, and repulsiveness hung about the expression of it.

Some of his best passages are those in which he upholds this doctrine. Even metaphysics he would not allow to remain difficult and abstract: so long as they spoke a professional jargon, the language of the schools, he maintained,—and who shall gainsay him?—that metaphysics were imperfect; or, at any rate, had not yet reached their ideal perfection.

'The true science of metaphysics,' he says, 'consists not in rendering abstract that which is sensible, but in rendering sensible that which is abstract; apparent that which is hidden; imaginable, if so it may be, that which is only intelligible; and intelligible, finally, that which an ordinary attention fails to seize.' And therefore:—

'Distrust, in books on metaphysics, words which have not been able to get currency in the world, and are only calculated to form a special language.'

Nor would he suffer common words to be employed in a special sense by the schools:—

'Which is the best, if one wants to be useful and to be really understood, to get one's words in the world, or to get them in the schools? I maintain that the good plan is to employ words in their popular sense rather than in their philosophical sense; and the better plan still, to employ them in their natural sense rather than in their popular sense. By their natural sense, I mean the popular and universal acceptation of them brought to that which in this is essential and invariable. To prove a thing by definition proves nothing, if the definition is purely philosophical; for such definitions only bind him who makes them. To prove a thing by definition, when the definition expresses the necessary, inevitable, and clear idea which the world at large attaches to the object, is, on the contrary, all in all; because then what one does is simply to show people what they do really think, in spite of themselves and without knowing it. The rule that one is free to give to words what sense one will, and that the only thing needful is to be agreed upon the sense one gives them, is very well for the mere purposes of argumentation, and may be allowed in the schools where this sort of fencing is to be practised; but in the sphere of the true-born and noble science of metaphysics, and in the genuine world of literature, it is good for nothing. One must never quit sight of realities, and one must employ one's expressions simply as media,—as glasses, through which one's thoughts can be best made evident. I know, by my own experience, how hard this rule is to follow; but I judge of its importance by the failure of every system of metaphysics. Not one of them has succeeded; for the simple reason, that in every one ciphers have been constantly used instead of values, artificial ideas instead of native ideas, jargon instead of idiom.'

I do not know whether the metaphysician will ever adopt Joubert's rules; but I am sure that the man of letters, whenever he has to speak of metaphysics, will do well to adopt them. He, at any rate, must remember:—

'It is by means of familiar words that style takes hold of the reader and gets possession of him. It is by means of these that great thoughts get currency and pass for true metal, like gold and silver which have had a recognised stamp put upon them. They beget confidence in the man who, in order to make his thoughts more clearly perceived, uses them; for people feel that such an employment of the language of common human life betokens a man who knows that life and its concerns, and who keeps himself in contact with them. Besides, these words make a style frank and easy. They show that an author has long made the thought or the feeling expressed his mental food; that he has so assimilated them and familiarised them, that the most common expressions suffice him in order to express ideas which have become every-day ideas to him by the length of time they have been in his mind. And lastly, what one says in such words looks more true; for, of all the words in use, none are so clear as those which we call common words; and clearness is so eminently one of the characteristics of truth, that often it even passes for truth itself.'

These are not, in Joubert, mere counsels of rhetoric; they come from his accurate sense of perfection, from his having clearly seized the fine and just idea that beauty and light are properties of truth, and that truth is incompletely exhibited if it is exhibited without beauty and light:—

'Be profound with clear terms and not with obscure terms. What is difficult will at last become easy; but as one goes deep into things, one must still keep a charm, and one must carry into these dark depths of thought, into which speculation has only recently penetrated, the pure and antique clearness of centuries less learned than ours, but with more light in them.'

And elsewhere he speaks of those 'spirits, lovers of light, who, when they have an idea to put forth, brood long over it first, and wait patiently till it *shines,* as Buffon enjoined, when he defined genius to be the aptitude for patience; spirits who know by experience that the driest matter and the dullest words hide within them the germ and spark of some brightness, like those fairy nuts in which were found diamonds if one broke the shell and was the right person; spirits who maintain that, to see and exhibit things in beauty, is to see and show things as in their essence they really are, and not as they exist for the eye of the careless, who do not look beyond the outside; spirits hard to satisfy, because of a keen-sightedness in them, which makes them discern but too clearly both the models to be followed and those to be shunned; spirits active though meditative, who cannot rest except in solid truths, and whom only beauty can make happy; spirits far less concerned for glory than for perfection, who, because their art is long and life is short, often die without leaving a monument, having had their own inward sense of life and fruitfulness for their best reward.'

No doubt there is something a little too ethereal in all this, something which reminds one of Joubert's physical want of body and substance; no doubt, if a man wishes to be a great author, it is to consider too curiously, to consider as Joubert did; it is a mistake to spend so much of one's time in setting up one's ideal standard of perfection, and in contemplating it. Joubert himself knew this very well: 'I cannot build a house for my ideas,' said he; 'I have tried to do without words, and words take their revenge on me by their difficulty.' 'If there is a man upon earth tormented by the cursed desire to get a whole book into a page, a whole page into a phrase, and this phrase into one word,—that man is myself.' 'I can sow, but I cannot build.' Joubert, however, makes no claim to be a great author; by renouncing all ambition to be this, by not trying to fit his ideas into a house, by making no compromise with words in spite of their difficulty, by being quite single-minded in his pursuit of perfection, perhaps he is enabled to get closer to the truth of the objects of his study, and to be of more service to us by setting before us ideals, than if he had composed a celebrated work. I doubt whether, in an elaborate work on the philosophy of religion, he would have got his ideas about religion to *shine,* to use his own expression, as they shine when he utters them in perfect freedom. Penetration in these matters is valueless without soul, and soul is valueless without penetration; both of these are delicate qualities, and, even in those who have them, easily lost; the charm of Joubert is, that he has and keeps both. Let us try and show that he does.

'One should be fearful of being wrong in poetry when one thinks differently from the poets, and in religion when one thinks differently from the saints.   460

'There is a great difference between taking for idols Mahomet and Luther, and bowing down before Rousseau and Voltaire. People at any rate imagined they were obeying God when they followed Mahomet, and the Scriptures when they hearkened to Luther. And perhaps one ought not too much to disparage that inclination which leads mankind to put into the hands of those whom it thinks the friends of God the direction and government of its heart and mind. It is the subjection to irreligious spirits which alone is fatal, and, in the fullest sense of the word, depraving.

'May I say it? It is not hard to know God, provided one will not force   470
oneself to define him.

'Do not bring into the domain of reasoning that which belongs to our innermost feeling. State truths of sentiment, and do not try to prove them. There is a danger in such proofs; for in arguing it is necessary to treat that which is in question as something problematic: now that which we accustom ourselves to treat as problematic ends by appearing to us as really doubtful. In things that are visible and palpable, never prove what is believed already; in things that are certain and mysterious,—mysterious by their greatness and by their nature,—make people believe them, and do not prove them; in things that are matters of practice and duty, command,   480
and do not explain. "Fear God," has made many men pious; the proofs of the existence of God have made many men atheists. From the defence springs the attack; the advocate begets in his hearer a wish to pick holes; and men are almost always led on, from the desire to contradict the doctor, to the desire to contradict the doctrine. Make truth lovely, and do not try to arm her; mankind will then be far less inclined to contend with her.

'Why is even a bad preacher almost always heard by the pious with pleasure? *Because he talks to them about what they love.* But you who have to expound religion to the children of this world, you who have to speak to them of that which they once loved perhaps, or which they would   490
be glad to love,—remember that they do not love it yet, and, to make them love it take heed to speak with power.

'You may do what you like, mankind will believe no one but God; and he only can persuade mankind who believes that God has spoken to him. No one can give faith unless he has faith; the persuaded persuade, as the indulgent disarm.

'The only happy people in the world are the good man, the sage, and the saint; but the saint is happier than either of the others, so much is man by his nature formed for sanctity.'

The same delicacy and penetration which he here shows in speaking of the inward essence of religion, Joubert shows also in speaking of its outward form, and of its manifestation in the world:—

'Piety is not a religion, though it is the soul of all religions. A man has not a religion simply by having pious inclinations, any more than he has a country simply by having philanthropy. A man has not a country until he is a citizen in a state, until he undertakes to follow and uphold certain laws, to obey certain magistrates, and to adopt certain ways of living and acting.

'Religion is neither a theology nor a theosophy; it is more than all this; it is a discipline, a law, a yoke, an indissoluble engagement.'

Who, again, has ever shown with more truth and beauty the good and imposing side of the wealth and splendour of the Catholic Church, than Joubert in the following passage:—

'The pomp and magnificence with which the Church is reproached are in truth the result and the proof of her incomparable excellence. From whence, let me ask, have come this power of hers and these excessive riches, except from the enchantment into which she threw all the world? Ravished with her beauty, millions of men from age to age kept loading her with gifts, bequests, cessions. She had the talent of making herself loved, and the talent of making men happy. It is that which wrought prodigies for her; it is from thence that she drew her power.'

'She had the talent of making herself *feared*,'—one should add that too, in order to be perfectly just; but Joubert, because he is a true child of light, can see that the wonderful success of the Catholic Church must have been due really to her good rather than to her bad qualities; to her making herself loved rather than to her making herself feared.

How striking and suggestive, again, is this remark on the Old and New Testaments:—

'The Old Testament teaches the knowledge of good and evil; the Gospel, on the other hand, seems written for the predestinated; it is the book of innocence. The one is made for earth, the other seems made for heaven. According as the one or the other of these books takes hold of a nation, what may be called the *religious humours* of nations differ.'

So the British and North-American Puritans are the children of the Old Testament, as Joachim of Flora and St. Francis are the children of the New. And does not the following maxim exactly fit the Church of England, of which Joubert certainly never thought when he was writing it? 'The austere sects excite the most enthusiasm at first; but the temperate sects have always been the most durable.'

And these remarks on the Jansenists and Jesuits, interesting in themselves, are still more interesting because they touch matters we cannot well know at first-hand, and which Joubert, an impartial observer, had had the means of studying closely. We are apt to think of the Jansenists as having failed by reason of their merits; Joubert shows us how far their failure was due to their defects:—

'We ought to lay stress upon what is clear in Scripture, and to pass quickly over what is obscure; to light up what in Scripture is troubled, by what is serene in it; what puzzles and checks the reason, by what satisfies the reason. The Jansenists have done just the reverse. They lay stress upon what is uncertain, obscure, afflicting, and they pass lightly over all the rest; they eclipse the luminous and consoling truths of Scripture, by putting between us and them its opaque and dismal truths. For example, "Many are called;" there is a clear truth: "Few are chosen;" there is an obscure truth. "We are children of wrath;" there is a sombre, cloudy, terrifying truth: "We are all the children of God;" "I came not to call the righteous, but sinners to repentance;" there are truths which are full of clearness, mildness, serenity, light. The Jansenists trouble our cheerfulness, and shed no cheering ray on our trouble. They are not, however, to be condemned for what they say, because what they say is true; but they are to be condemned for what they fail to say, for that is true too,—truer, even, than the other; that is, its truth is easier for us to seize, fuller, rounder, and more complete. Theology, as the Jansenists exhibit her, has but the half of her disk.' Again:—

'The Jansenists erect "grace" into a kind of fourth person of the Trinity. They are, without thinking or intending it, Quaternitarians. St. Paul and St. Augustine, too exclusively studied, have done all the mischief. Instead of "grace," say help, succour, a divine influence, a dew of heaven; then one can come to a right understanding. The word "grace" is a sort of talisman, all the baneful spell of which can be broken by translating it. The trick of personifying words is a fatal source of mischief in theology.' Once more:—

'The Jansenists tell men to love God; the Jesuits make men love him. The doctrine of these last is full of loosenesses, or, if you will, of errors; still,—singular as it may seem, it is undeniable,—they are the better directors of souls.'

'The Jansenists have carried into religion more thought than the Jesuits, and they go deeper; they are faster bound with its sacred bonds. They have in their way of thinking an austerity which incessantly constrains the will to keep the path of duty; all the habits of their understanding, in short, are more Christian. But they seem to love God without affection, and solely from reason, from duty, from justice. The Jesuits, on the other hand, seem to love him from pure inclination; out of admiration, gratitude, tenderness; for the pleasure of loving him, in short. In their books of devotion you find joy, because with the Jesuits nature and religion go hand in hand. In the books of the Jansenists there is a sadness and a moral constraint, because with the Jansenists religion is for ever trying to put nature in bonds.'

The Jesuits have suffered, and deservedly suffered, plenty of discredit from what Joubert gently calls their 'loosenesses;' let them have the merit of their amiability.

The most characteristic thoughts one can quote from any writer are always his thoughts on matters like these; but the maxims of Joubert on purely literary subjects also, have the same purged and subtle delicacy; they show the same sedulousness in him to preserve perfectly true the balance of his soul. Let me begin with this, which contains a truth too many people fail to perceive:—

'Ignorance, which in matters of morals extenuates the crime, is itself, in matters of literature, a crime of the first order.'

And here is another sentence, worthy of Goethe, to clear the air at one's entrance into the region of literature:—

'With the fever of the senses, the delirium of the passions, the weakness of the spirit; with the storms of the passing time and with the great scourges of human life,—hunger, thirst, dishonour, diseases, and death,— authors may as long as they like go on making novels which shall harrow our hearts; but the soul says all the while, "You hurt me." '

And again:—

'Fiction has no business to exist unless it is more beautiful than reality. Certainly the monstrosities of fiction may be found in the booksellers' shops; you buy them there for a certain number of francs, and you talk of them for a certain number of days; but they have no place in literature, because in literature the one aim of art is the beautiful. Once lose sight of that, and you have the mere frightful reality.'

That is just the right criticism to pass on these 'monstrosities:' *they have no place in literature,* and those who produce them are not really men of letters. One would think that this was enough to deter from such produc-tion any man of genuine ambition. But most of us, alas! are what we must be, not what we ought to be,—not even what we know we ought to be.

The following, of which the first part reminds one of Wordsworth's sonnet, 'If thou indeed derive thy light from heaven,' excellently defines the true salutary function of literature, and the limits of this function:—

'Whether one is an eagle or an ant, in the intellectual world, seems to me not to matter much; the essential thing is to have one's place marked there, one's station assigned, and to belong decidedly to a regular and wholesome order. A small talent, if it keeps within its limits and rightly fulfils its task, may reach the goal just as well as a greater one. To accustom mankind to pleasures which depend neither upon the bodily appetites nor upon money, by giving them a taste for the things of the mind, seems to me, in fact, the one proper fruit which nature has meant our literary productions to have. When they have other fruits, it is by accident, and, in general, not for good. Books which absorb our attention to such a degree that they rob us of all fancy for other books, are absolutely pernicious. In this way they only bring fresh crotchets and sects into the world; they multiply the great variety of weights, rules, and measures already existing; they are morally and politically a nuisance.'

Who can read these words and not think of the limiting effect exercised by certain works in certain spheres and for certain periods; exercised even by the works of men of genius or virtue,—by the works of Rousseau, the works of Wesley, the works of Swedenborg? And what is it which makes the Bible so admirable a book, to be the one book of those who can have only one, but the miscellaneous character of the contents of the Bible?

Joubert was all his life a passionate lover of Plato; I hope other lovers of Plato will forgive me for saying that their adored object has never been more truly described than he is here:—

'Plato shows us nothing, but he brings brightness with him; he puts light into our eyes, and fills us with a clearness by which all objects afterwards become illuminated. He teaches us nothing; but he prepares us, fashions us, and makes us ready to know all. Somehow or other, the habit of reading him augments in us the capacity for discerning and entertaining whatever fine truths may afterwards present themselves. Like mountain-air, it sharpens our organs, and gives us an appetite for wholesome food.'

'Plato loses himself in the void' (he says again); 'but one sees the play of his wings, one hears their rustle.' And the conclusion is: 'It is good to breathe his air, but not to live upon him.'

As a pendant to the criticism on Plato, this on the French moralist Nicole is excellent:—

'Nicole is a Pascal without style. It is not what he says which is sublime, but what he thinks; he rises, not by the natural elevation of his own spirit, but by that of his doctrines. One must not look to the form in him, but to the matter, which is exquisite. He ought to be read with a direct view of practice.'

English people have hardly ears to hear the praises of Bossuet, and the Bossuet of Joubert is Bossuet at his very best; but this is a far truer Bossuet than the 'declaimer' Bossuet of Lord Macaulay, himself a born rhetorician, if ever there was one:—

'Bossuet employs all our idioms, as Homer employed all the dialects. The language of kings, of statesmen, and of warriors; the language of the people and of the student, of the country and of the schools, of the sanctuary and of the courts of law; the old and the new, the trivial and the stately, the quiet and the resounding,—he turns all to his use; and out of all this he makes a style, simple, grave, majestic. His ideas are, like his words, varied,—common and sublime together. Times and doctrines in all their multitude were ever before his spirit, as things and words in all their multitude were ever before it. He is not so much a man as a human nature, with the temperance of a saint, the justice of a bishop, the prudence of a doctor, and the might of a great spirit.'

After this on Bossuet, I must quote a criticism on Racine, to show that Joubert did not indiscriminately worship all the French gods of the grand century:—

'Those who find Racine enough for them are poor souls and poor wits; they are souls and wits which have never got beyond the callow and boarding-school stage. Admirable, as no doubt he is, for his skill in having made poetical the most humdrum sentiments and the most middling sort of passions, he can yet stand us in stead of nobody but himself. He is a superior writer; and, in literature, that at once puts a man on a pinnacle. But he is not an inimitable writer.'

And again: 'The talent of Racine is in his works, but Racine himself is not there. That is why he himself became disgusted with them.' 'Of Racine, as of his ancients, the genius lay in taste. His elegance is perfect, but it is not supreme, like that of Virgil.' And, indeed, there is something *supreme* in an elegance which exercises such a fascination as Virgil's does; which makes one return to his poems again and again, long after one thinks one has done with them; which makes them one of those books that, to use Joubert's words, 'lure the reader back to them, as the proverb says good wine lures back the wine-bibber.' And the highest praise Joubert can at last find for Racine is this, that he is the Virgil of the ignorant;—'*Racine est le Virgile des ignorants.*'

Of Boileau, too, Joubert says: 'Boileau is a powerful poet, but only in the world of half poetry.' How true is that of Pope also! And he adds:

'Neither Boileau's poetry nor Racine's flows from the fountain-head.' No Englishman, controverting the exaggerated French estimate of these poets, could desire to use fitter words.

I will end with some remarks on Voltaire and Rousseau, remarks in which Joubert eminently shows his prime merit as a critic,—the soundness and completeness of his judgments. I mean that he has the faculty of judging with all the powers of his mind and soul at work together in due combination; and how rare is this faculty! how seldom is it exercised towards writers who so powerfully as Voltaire and Rousseau stimulate and call into activity a single side in us!

'Voltaire's wits came to their maturity twenty years sooner than the wits of other men, and remained in full vigour thirty years longer. The charm which our style in general gets from our ideas, his ideas get from his style. Voltaire is sometimes afflicted, sometimes strongly moved; but serious he never is. His very graces have an effrontery about them. He had correctness of judgment, liveliness of imagination, nimble wits, quick taste, and a moral sense in ruins. He is the most debauched of spirits, and the worst of him is that one gets debauched along with him. If he had been a wise man, and had had the self-discipline of wisdom, beyond a doubt half his wit would have been gone; it needed an atmosphere of *licence* in order to play freely. Those people who read him every day, create for themselves, by an invincible law, the necessity of liking him. But those people who, having given up reading him, gaze steadily down upon the influences which his spirit has shed abroad, find themselves in simple justice and duty compelled to detest him. It is impossible to be satisfied with him, and impossible not to be fascinated by him.'

The literary sense in us is apt to rebel against so severe a judgment on such a charmer of the literary sense as Voltaire, and perhaps we English are not very liable to catch Voltaire's vices, while of some of his merits we have signal need; still, as the real definitive judgment on Voltaire, Joubert's is undoubtedly the true one. It is nearly identical with that of Goethe. Joubert's sentence on Rousseau is in some respects more favourable:—

'That weight in the speaker (*auctoritas*) which the ancients talk of, is to be found in Bossuet more than in any other French author; Pascal, too, has it, and La Bruyère; even Rousseau has something of it, but Voltaire not a particle. I can understand how a Rousseau—I mean a Rousseau cured of his faults—might at the present day do much good, and may even come to be greatly wanted; but under no circumstances can a Voltaire be of any use.'

The peculiar power of Rousseau's style has never been better hit off than in the following passage:—

'Rousseau imparted, if I may so speak, *bowels of feeling* to the words he used (*donna des entrailles à tous les mots*), and poured into them such a charm, sweetness so penetrating, energy so puissant, that his writings have an effect upon the soul something like that of those illicit pleasures which steal away our taste and intoxicate our reason.'

The final judgment, however, is severe, and justly severe:—

'Life without actions; life entirely resolved into affections and half-sensual thoughts; do-nothingness setting up for a virtue; cowardliness with voluptuousness; fierce pride with nullity underneath it; the strutting phrase of the most sensual of vagabonds, who has made his system of philosophy and can give it eloquently forth: there is Rousseau! A piety in which there is no religion; a severity which brings corruption with it; a dogmatism which serves to ruin all authority: there is Rousseau's philosophy! To all tender, ardent, and elevated natures, I say: Only Rousseau can detach you from religion, and only true religion can cure you of Rousseau.'

I must yet find room, before I end, for one at least of Joubert's sayings on political matters; here, too, the whole man shows himself; and here, too, the affinity with Coleridge is very remarkable. How true, how true in France especially, is this remark on the contrasting direction taken by the aspirations of the community in ancient and in modern states:—

'The ancients were attached to their country by three things,—their temples, their tombs, and their forefathers. The two great bonds which united them to their government were the bonds of habit and antiquity. With the moderns, hope and the love of novelty have produced a total change. The ancients said *our forefathers,* we say *posterity:* we do not, like them, love our *patria,* that is to say, the country and the laws of our fathers, rather we love the laws and the country of our children; the charm we are most sensible to is the charm of the future, and not the charm of the past.'

And how keen and true is this criticism on the changed sense of the word 'liberty';—

'A great many words have changed their meaning. The word *liberty,* for example, had at bottom among the ancients the same meaning as the word *dominion. I would be free* meant, in the mouth of the ancient, *I would take part in governing or administering the State;* in the mouth of a modern it means, *I would be independent.* The word *liberty* has with us a moral sense; with them its sense was purely political.'

Joubert had lived through the French Revolution, and to the modern cry for liberty he was prone to answer:—

'Let your cry be for free souls rather even than for free men. Moral liberty is the one vitally important liberty, the one liberty which is indispensable; the other liberty is good and salutary only so far as it favours this. Subordination is in itself a better thing than independence. The one implies order and arrangement; the other implies only self-sufficiency with isolation. The one means harmony, the other a single tone; the one is the whole, the other is but the part.'

'Liberty! liberty!' he cries again; 'in all things let us have *justice,* and then we shall have enough liberty.'

Let us have justice, and then we shall have enough liberty! The wise man will never refuse to echo those words; but then, such is the imperfection of human governments, that almost always, in order to get justice, one has first to secure liberty.

I do not hold up Joubert as a very astonishing and powerful genius, but rather as a delightful and edifying genius. I have not cared to exhibit him as a sayer of brilliant epigrammatic things, such things as, 'Notre vie est du vent tissu . . . . les dettes abrégent la vie . . . . celui qui a de l'imagination sans érudition a des ailes et n'a pas de pieds (*Our life is woven wind . . . debts take from life . . . the man of imagination without learning has wings and no feet),*' though for such sayings he is famous. In the first place, the French language is in itself so favourable a vehicle for such sayings, that the making them in it has the less merit; at least half the merit ought to go, not to the maker of the saying, but to the French language. In the second place, the peculiar beauty of Joubert is not there; it is not in what is exclusively intellectual,—it is in the union of *soul* with intellect, and in the delightful, satisfying result which this union produces. 'Vivre, c'est penser et sentir son âme . . . le bonheur est de sentir son âme bonne . . . toute vérité nue et crue n'a pas assez passé par l'âme . . . les hommes ne sont justes qu'envers ceux qu'ils aiment (*The essence of life lies in thinking and being conscious of one's soul . . . happiness is the sense of one's soul being good . . . if a truth is nude and crude, that is a proof it has not been steeped long enough in the soul; . . . man cannot even be just to his neighbour, unless he loves him);*' it is much rather in sayings like these that Joubert's best and innermost nature manifests itself. He is the most prepossessing and convincing of witnesses to the good of loving light. Because he sincerely loved light, and did not prefer to it any little private darkness of his own, he found light; his eye was single, and therefore his whole body was full of light. And because he was full of light, he was also full of happiness. In spite of his infirmities, in spite of his sufferings, in spite of his obscurity, he was the happiest man alive; his life was as charming as his thoughts. For certainly it is natural that the love of light, which is already, in some measure, the possession of light, should irradiate and beatify the whole life of him who has it. There is something unnatural and shocking where, as in the case of Coleridge, it does not. Joubert pains us by no such contradiction; 'the same penetration of spirit which made him such delightful company to his friends, served also to make him perfect in his own personal life, by enabling him always to perceive and do what was right;' he loved and sought light till he became so habituated to it, so accustomed to the joyful testimony of a good conscience, that, to use his own words, 'he could no longer exist without this, and was obliged to live without reproach if he would live without misery.'

Joubert was not famous while he lived, and he will not be famous now that he is dead. But, before we pity him for this, let us be sure what we mean, in literature, by *famous*. There are the famous men of genius in literature,—the Homers, Dantes, Shakspeares: of them we need not speak; their praise is for ever and ever. Then there are the famous men of ability in literature: their praise is in their own generation. And what makes this difference? The work of the two orders of men is at the bottom the same,—*a criticism of life*. The end and aim of all literature, if one considers it attentively, is, in truth, nothing but that. But the criticism which the men of genius pass upon human life is permanently acceptable to mankind; the criticism which the men of ability pass upon human life is transitorily acceptable. Between Shakspeare's criticism of human life and Scribe's the difference is there;—the one is permanently acceptable, the other transitorily. Whence then, I repeat, this difference? It is that the acceptableness of Shakspeare's criticism depends upon its inherent truth: the acceptableness of Scribe's upon its suiting itself, by its subject-matter, ideas, mode of treatment, to the taste of the generation that hears it. But the taste and ideas of one generation are not those of the next. This next generation in its turn arrives;—first its sharpshooters, its quick-witted, audacious light troops; then the elephantine main body. The imposing array of its predecessor it confidently assails, riddles it with bullets, passes over its body. It goes hard then with many once popular reputations, with many authorities once oracular. Only two kinds of authors are safe in the general havoc. The first kind are the great abounding fountains of truth, whose criticism of life is a source of illumination and joy to the whole human race for ever,—the Homers, the Shakspeares. These are the sacred personages, whom all civilised warfare respects. The second are those whom the out-skirmishers of the new generation, its forerunners,—quick-witted soldiers, as I have said, the select of the army,—recognise, though the bulk of their comrades behind might not, as of the same family and character with the sacred personages, exercising like them an immortal function, and like them inspiring a permanent interest. They snatch them up, and set them in a place of shelter, where the on-coming multitude may not overwhelm them. These are the Jouberts. They will never, like the Shakspeares, command the homage of the multitude; but they are safe; the multitude will not trample them down. Except these two kinds, no author is safe. Let us consider, for example, Joubert's famous contemporary, Lord Jeffrey. All his vivacity and accomplishment avail him nothing; of the true critic he had in an eminent degree no quality, except one,—curiosity. Curiosity he had, but he had no gift for truth; he cannot illuminate and rejoice us; no intelligent out-skirmisher of the new generation cares about him, cares to put him in safety; at this moment we are all passing over his body. Let us consider a greater than Jeffrey, a critic whose reputation still stands firm,—will stand, many people think, for ever,—the great apostle of the Philistines, Lord Macaulay. Lord Macaulay was, as I have already said, a born rhetorician; a splendid rhetorician doubtless, and, beyond that, an *English* rhetorician also, an *honest* rhetorician; still, beyond the apparent rhetorical truth of things he never could penetrate; for their vital truth, for what the French call the *vraie vérité,* he had absolutely no organ; there-fore his reputation, brilliant as it is, is not secure. Rhetoric so good as his excites and gives pleasure, but by pleasure alone you cannot permanently bind men's spirits to you. Truth illuminates and gives joy, and it is by the bond of joy, not of pleasure, that men's spirits are indissolubly held. As Lord Macaulay's own generation dies out, as a new generation arrives, without those ideas and tendencies of its predecessor which Lord Macaulay so deeply shared and so happily satisfied, will he give the same pleasure? and, if he ceases to give this, has he enough of light in him to make him last? Pleasure the new generation will get from its own novel ideas and tendencies; but light is another and a rarer thing, and must be treasured wherever it can be found. Will Macaulay be saved, in the sweep and pres-sure of time, for his light's sake, as Johnson has already been saved by two generations, Joubert by one? I think it very doubtful. But for a spirit of any delicacy and dignity, what a fate, if he could foresee it! to be an oracle for one generation, and then of little or no account for ever. How far better, to pass with scant notice through one's own generation, but to be singled out and preserved by the very iconoclasts of the next, then in their turn by those of the next, and so, like the lamp of life itself, to be handed on from one generation to another in safety! This is Joubert's lot, and it is a very enviable one. The new men of the new generations, while they let the dust deepen on a thousand Laharpes, will say of him: 'He lived in the Philistine's day, in a place and time when almost every idea current in literature had the mark of Dagon upon it, and not the mark of the children of light. Nay, the children of light were as yet hardly so much as heard of: the Canaanite was then in the land. Still, there were even then a few, who, nourished on some secret tradition, or illumined, perhaps, by a divine inspiration, kept aloof from the reigning superstitions, never bowed the knee to the gods of Canaan; and one of these few was called *Joubert*.'

SPINOZA AND THE BIBLE

———◄◆►———

'By the sentence of the angels, by the decree of the saints, we anathematise, cut off, curse, and execrate Baruch Spinoza, in the presence of these sacred books with the six hundred and thirteen precepts which are written therein, with the anathema wherewith Joshua anathematised Jericho; with the cursing wherewith Elisha cursed the children; and with all the cursings which are written in the Book of the Law: cursed be he by day, and cursed by night; cursed when he lieth down, and cursed when he riseth up; cursed when he goeth out, and cursed when he cometh in; the Lord pardon him never; the wrath and fury of the Lord burn upon this man, and bring upon him all the curses which are written in the Book of the Law. The Lord blot out his name under heaven. The Lord set him apart for destruction from all the tribes of Israel, with all the curses of the firmament which are written in the Book of this Law. . . . There shall no man speak to him, no man write to him, no man show him any kindness, no man stay under the same roof with him, no man come nigh him.'

With these amenities, the current compliments of theological parting, the

10

183

Jews of the Portuguese synagogue at Amsterdam took in 1656 (and not in 1660, as has till now been commonly supposed) their leave of their erring brother, Baruch or Benedict Spinoza. They remained children of Israel, and he became a child of modern Europe.

That was in 1656, and Spinoza died in 1677, at the early age of forty-four. Glory had not found him out. His short life—a life of unbroken diligence, kindliness, and purity—was passed in seclusion. But in spite of that seclusion, in spite of the shortness of his career, in spite of the hostility of the dispensers of renown in the 18th century,—of Voltaire's disparagement and Bayle's detraction,—in spite of the repellent form which he has given to his principal work, in spite of the exterior semblance of a rigid dogmatism alien to the most essential tendencies of modern philosophy, in spite, finally, of the immense weight of disfavour cast upon him by the long-repeated charge of atheism, Spinoza's name has silently risen in importance, the man and his work have attracted a steadily increasing notice, and bid fair to become soon what they deserve to become,—in the history of modern philosophy the central point of interest. An avowed translation of one of his works,—his *Tractatus Theologico-Politicus,*—has at last made its appearance in English. It is the principal work which Spinoza published in his lifetime; his book on ethics, the work on which his fame rests, is posthumous.

The English translator has not done his task well. Of the character of his version there can, I am afraid, be no doubt; one such passage as the following is decisive:—

'I confess that, *while with them* (the theologians) *I have never been able sufficiently to admire the unfathomed mysteries of Scripture, I have still found them giving utterance to nothing but Aristotelian and Platonic speculations,* artfully dressed up and cunningly accommodated to Holy Writ, lest the speakers should show themselves too plainly to belong to the sect of the Grecian heathens. *Nor was it enough for these men to discourse with the Greeks; they have further taken to raving with the Hebrew prophets.'*

This professes to be a translation of these words of Spinoza: 'Fateor, eos nunquam satis mirari potuisse Scripturae profundissima mysteria; attamen praeter Aristotelicorum vel Platonicorum speculationes nihil docuisse video, atque his, ne gentiles sectari viderentur, Scripturam accommodaverunt. Non satis his fuit cum Graecis insanire, sed prophetas, cum iisdem deliravisse voluerunt.' After one such specimen of a translator's force, the experienced reader has a sort of instinct that he may as well close the book at once, with a smile or a sigh, according as he happens to be a follower of the weeping or of the laughing philosopher. If, in spite of this instinct, he persists in going on with the English version of the *Tractatus Theologico-Politicus,* he will find many more such specimens. It is not, however, my intention to fill my space with these, or with strictures upon their author. I prefer to remark, that he renders a service to literary history by pointing out, in his preface, how 'to Bayle may be traced the disfavour in which the name of Spinoza was so long held;' that, in his observations on the system of the Church of England, he shows a laudable freedom from the prejudices of ordinary English Liberals of that advanced school to which he clearly belongs; and lastly, that, though he manifests little familiarity with Latin, he seems to have considerable familiarity with philosophy, and to be well able to follow and comprehend speculative reasoning. Let me advise him to unite his forces with those of some one who has that accurate knowledge of Latin which he himself has not, and then, perhaps, of that union a really good translation of Spinoza will be the result. And, having given him this advice, let me again turn, for a little, to the *Tractatus Theologico-Politicus* itself.

This work, as I have already said, is a work on the interpretation of Scripture,—it treats of the Bible. What was it exactly which Spinoza thought about the Bible and its inspiration? That will be, at the present moment, the central point of interest for the English readers of his Treatise. Now, it is to be observed, that just on this very point the Treatise, interesting and remarkable as it is, will fail to satisfy the reader. It is important to seize this notion quite firmly, and not to quit hold of it while one is reading Spinoza's work. The scope of that work is this. Spinoza sees that the life and practice of Christian nations professing the religion of the Bible, are not the due fruits of the religion of the Bible; he sees only hatred, bitterness, and strife, where he might have expected to see love, joy, and peace in believing; and he asks himself the reason of this. The reason is, he says, that these people misunderstand their Bible. Well, then, is his conclusion, I will write a *Tractatus Theologico-Politicus.* I will show these people, that, taking the Bible for granted, taking it to be all which it asserts itself to be, taking it to have all the authority which it claims, it is not what they imagine it to be, it does not say what they imagine it to say. I will show them what it really does say, and I will show them that they will do well to accept this real teaching of the Bible, instead of the phantom with which they have so long been cheated. I will show their governments that they will do well to remodel the national churches, to make of them institutions informed with the spirit of the true Bible, instead of institutions informed with the spirit of this false phantom.

The comments of men, Spinoza said, had been foisted into the Christian religion; the pure teaching of God had been lost sight of. He determined, therefore, to go again to the Bible, to read it over and over with a perfectly unprejudiced mind, and to accept nothing as its teaching which it did not clearly teach. He began by constructing a method, or set of conditions indispensable for the adequate interpretation of Scripture. These conditions are such, he points out, that a perfectly adequate interpretation of Scripture is now impossible. For example, to understand any prophet thoroughly, we ought to know the life, character, and pursuits of that prophet, under what circumstances his book was composed, and in what state and through what hands it has come down to us; and, in general, most of this we cannot now know. Still, the main sense of the Books of Scripture may be clearly seized by us. Himself a Jew with all the learning of his nation, and a man of the highest natural powers, Spinoza had in the difficult task of seizing this sense every aid which special knowledge or pre-eminent faculties could supply.

In what then, he asks, does Scripture, interpreted by its own aid, and not by the aid of Rabbinical traditions or Greek philosophy, allege its own divinity to consist? In a revelation given by God to the prophets. Now all knowledge is a divine revelation; but prophecy, as represented in Scripture, is one of which the laws of human nature, considered in themselves alone, cannot be the cause. Therefore nothing must be asserted about it, except what is clearly declared by the prophets themselves; for they are our only source of knowledge on a matter which does not fall within the scope of our ordinary knowing faculties. But ignorant people, not knowing the Hebrew genius and phraseology, and not attending to the circumstances of the speaker, often imagine the prophets to assert things which they do not.

The prophets clearly declare themselves to have received the revelation of God through the means of words and images;—not, as Christ, through immediate communication of the mind with the mind of God. Therefore the prophets excelled other men by the power and vividness of their representing and imagining faculty, not by the perfection of their mind. This is why they perceived almost everything through figures, and express themselves so variously, and so improperly, concerning the nature of God. Moses imagined that God could be seen, and attributed to him the passions of anger and jealousy; Micaiah imagined him sitting on a throne, with the host of heaven on his right and left hand; Daniel as an old man, with a white garment and white hair; Ezekiel as a fire; the disciples of Christ thought they saw the Spirit of God in the form of a dove; the apostles in the form of fiery tongues.

Whence, then, could the prophets be certain of the truth of a revelation

which they received through the imagination, and not by a mental process? —for only an idea can carry the sense of its own certainty along with it, not an imagination. To make them certain of the truth of what was revealed to them, a reasoning process came in; they had to rely on the testimony of   140
a sign; and (above all) on the testimony of their own conscience, that they were good men, and spoke for God's sake. Either testimony was incomplete without the other. Even the good prophet needed for his message the confirmation of a sign; but the bad prophet, the utterer of an immoral doctrine, had no certainty for his doctrine, no truth in it, even though he confirmed it by a sign. The testimony of a good conscience was, therefore, the prophet's grand source of certitude. Even this, however, was only a moral certitude, not a mathematical; for no man can be perfectly sure of his own goodness.

The power of imagining, the power of feeling what goodness is, and the   150
habit of practising goodness, were therefore the sole essential qualifications of a true prophet. But for the purpose of the message, the revelation, which God designed him to convey, these qualifications were enough. The sum and substance of this revelation was simply: *Believe in God, and lead a good life.* To be the organ of this revelation, did not make a man more learned; it left his scientific knowledge as it found it. This explains the contradictory and speculatively false opinions about God, and the laws of nature, which the patriarchs, the prophets, the apostles entertained. Abraham and the patriarchs knew God only as *El Sadai,* the power which gives to every man that which suffices him; Moses knew him as *Jehovah,* a self-   160
existent being, but imagined him with the passions of a man. Samuel imagined that God could not repent of his sentences; Jeremiah, that he could. Joshua, on a day of great victory, the ground being white with hail, seeing the daylight last longer than usual, and imaginatively seizing this as a special sign of the help divinely promised to him, declared that the sun was standing still. To be obeyers of God themselves, and inspired leaders of others to obedience and good life, did not make Abraham and Moses metaphysicians, or Joshua a natural philosopher. His revelation no more changed the speculative opinions of each prophet, than it changed his temperament or style. The wrathful Elisha required the natural sedative of   170
music, before he could be the messenger of good fortune to Jehoram. The high-bred Isaiah and Nahum have the style proper to their condition, and the rustic Ezekiel and Amos the style proper to theirs. We are not therefore bound to pay heed to the speculative opinions of this or that prophet, for in uttering these he spoke as a mere man: only in exhorting his hearers to obey God and lead a good life was he the organ of a divine revelation.

To know and love God is the highest blessedness of man, and of all men alike; to this all mankind are called, and not any one nation in particular. The divine law, properly so named, is the method of life for attaining this height of human blessedness: this law is universal, written in the heart, and one for all mankind. Human law is the method of life for attaining and preserving temporal security and prosperity: this law is dictated by a lawgiver, and every nation has its own. In the case of the Jews, this law was dictated, by revelation, through the prophets; its fundamental precept was to obey God and to keep his commandments, and it is therefore, in a secondary sense, called divine; but it was, nevertheless, framed in respect of temporal things only. Even the truly moral and divine precept of this law, to practise for God's sake justice and mercy towards one's neighbour, meant for the Hebrew of the Old Testament his Hebrew neighbour only, and had respect to the concord and stability of the Hebrew commonwealth. The Jews were to obey God and to keep his commandments, that they might continue long in the land given to them, and that it might be well with them there. Their election was a temporal one, and lasted only so long as their State. It is now over; and the only election the Jews now have is that of the *pious,* the *remnant,* which takes place, and has always taken place, in every other nation also. Scripture itself teaches that there is a universal divine law, that this is common to all nations alike, and is the law which truly confers eternal blessedness. Solomon, the wisest of the Jews, knew this law, as the few wisest men in all nations have ever known it; but for the mass of the Jews, as for the mass of mankind everywhere, this law was hidden, and they had no notion of its moral action, its *vera vita* which conducts to eternal blessedness, except so far as this action was enjoined upon them by the prescriptions of their temporal law. When the ruin of their State brought with it the ruin of their temporal law, they would have lost altogether their only clue to eternal blessedness.

Christ came when that fabric of the Jewish State, for the sake of which the Jewish law existed, was about to fall; and he proclaimed the universal divine law. A certain moral action is prescribed by this law, as a certain moral action was prescribed by the Jewish law: but he who truly conceives the universal divine law conceives God's decrees adequately as eternal truths, and for him moral action has liberty and self-knowledge; while the prophets of the Jewish law inadequately conceived God's decrees as mere rules and commands, and for them moral action had no liberty and no self-knowledge. Christ, who beheld the decrees of God as God himself beholds them,—as eternal truths,—proclaimed the love of God and the love of our neighbour as *commands,* only because of the ignorance of the multitude: to those to whom it was 'given to know the mysteries of the kingdom of God,' he announced them, as he himself perceived them, as eternal truths. And the apostles, like Christ, spoke to many of their hearers 'as unto carnal not spiritual;' presented to them, that is, the love of God and their neighbour as a divine command authenticated by the life and death of Christ, not as an eternal idea of reason carrying its own warrant along with it. The presentation of it as this latter their hearers 'were not able to bear.' The apostles, moreover, though they preached and confirmed their doctrine by signs as prophets, wrote their Epistles, not as prophets, but as doctors and reasoners. The essentials of their doctrine, indeed, they took not from reason, but, like the prophets, from fact and revelation; they preached belief in God and goodness of life as a catholic religion existing by virtue of the passion of Christ, as the prophets had preached belief in God and goodness of life as a national religion existing by virtue of the Mosaic covenant: but while the prophets announced their message in a form purely dogmatical, the apostles developed theirs with the forms of reasoning and argumentation, according to each apostle's ability and way of thinking, and as they might best commend their message to their hearers; and for their reasonings they themselves claim no divine authority, submitting them to the judgment of their hearers. Thus each apostle built essential religion on a non-essential foundation of his own, and, as St. Paul says, avoided building on the foundations of another apostle, which might be quite different from his own. Hence the discrepancies between the doctrine of one apostle and another,—between that of St. Paul, for example, and that of St. James; but these discrepancies are in the non-essentials not given to them by revelation, and not in essentials. Human churches, seizing these discrepant non-essentials as essentials, one maintaining one of them, another another, have filled the world with unprofitable disputes, have 'turned the Church into an academy, and religion into a science, or rather a wrangling,' and have fallen into endless schism.

What, then, are the essentials of religion according both to the Old and to the New Testament? Very few and very simple. The precept to love God and our neighbour. The precepts of the first chapter of Isaiah: 'Wash you, make you clean; put away the evil of your doings from before mine eyes; cease to do evil; learn to do well; seek judgment; relieve the oppressed; judge the fatherless; plead for the widow.' The precepts of the Sermon on the Mount, which add to the foregoing the injunction that we should cease to do evil and learn to do well, not to our brethren and fellow-citizens only, but to all mankind. It is by following these precepts that belief in God is to be shown: if we believe in him, we shall keep his commandment; and this is his commandment, that we love one another. It is because it contains these precepts that the Bible is properly called the Word of God, in spite of its containing much that is mere history, and, like all history, sometimes true, sometimes false; in spite of its containing much that is mere reasoning, and, like all reasoning, sometimes sound, sometimes hollow. These precepts are also the precepts of the universal divine law written in our hearts; and it is only by this that the divinity of Scripture is established;—by its containing, namely, precepts identical with those of this inly-written and self-proven law. This law was in the world, as St. John says, before the doctrine of Moses or the doctrine of Christ. And what need was there, then, for these doctrines? Because the world at large 'knew not' this original divine law, in which precepts are ideas, and the belief in God the knowledge and contemplation of him. Reason gives us this law, reason tells us that it leads to eternal blessedness, and that those who follow it have no need of any other. But reason could not have told us that the moral action of the universal divine law,—followed not from a sense of its intrinsic goodness, truth, and necessity, but simply in proof of obedience (for both the Old and New Testament are but one long discipline of obedience), simply because it is so commanded by Moses in virtue of the covenant, simply because it is so commanded by Christ in virtue of his life and passion,—can lead to eternal blessedness, which means, for reason, eternal knowledge. Reason could not have told us this, and this is what the Bible tells us. This is that 'thing which had been kept secret since the foundation of the world.' It is thus that by means of the foolishness of the world God confounds the wise, and with things that are not brings to nought things that are. Of the truth of the promise thus made to obedience without knowledge, we can have no mathematical certainty; for we can have a mathematical certainty only of things deduced by reason from elements which she in herself possesses. But we can have a moral certainty of it; a certainty such as the prophets had themselves, arising out of the goodness and pureness of those to whom this revelation has been made, and rendered possible for us by its contradicting no principles of reason. It is a great comfort to believe it; because 'as it is only the very small minority who can pursue a virtuous life by the sole guidance of reason, we should, unless we had this testimony of Scripture, be in doubt respecting the salvation of nearly the whole human race.'

It follows from this that philosophy has her own independent sphere, and theology hers, and that neither has the right to invade and try to subdue the other. Theology demands perfect obedience, philosophy perfect knowledge: the obedience demanded by theology and the knowledge demanded by philosophy are alike saving. As speculative opinions about God, theology requires only such as are indispensable to the reality of this obedience; the belief that God is, that he is a rewarder of them that seek him, and that the proof of seeking him is a good life. These are the funda- 300 mentals of faith, and they are so clear and simple that none of the inaccuracies provable in the Bible narrative the least affect them, and they have indubitably come to us uncorrupted. He who holds them may make, as the patriarchs and prophets did, other speculations about God most erroneous, and yet their faith is complete and saving. Nay, beyond these fundamentals, speculative opinions are pious or impious, not as they are true or false, but as they confirm or shake the believer in the practice of obedience. The truest speculative opinion about the nature of God is impious if it makes its holder rebellious; the falsest speculative opinion is pious if it makes him obedient. Governments should never render themselves the tools of ecclesi- 310 astical ambition by promulgating as fundamentals of the national Church's faith more than these, and should concede the fullest liberty of speculation.

But the multitude, which respects only what astonishes, terrifies, and overwhelms it, by no means takes this simple view of its own religion. To the multitude, religion seems imposing only when it is subversive of reason, confirmed by miracles, conveyed in documents materially sacred and infallible, and dooming to damnation all without its pale. But this religion of the multitude is not the religion which a true interpretation of Scripture finds in Scripture. Reason tells us that a miracle,—understanding by a miracle a breach of the laws of nature,—is impossible, and that to think it possible 320 is to dishonour God; for the laws of nature are the laws of God, and to say that God violates the laws of nature is to say that he violates his own nature. Reason sees, too, that miracles can never attain their professed object,—that of bringing us to a higher knowledge of God; since our knowledge of God is raised only by perfecting and clearing our conceptions, and the alleged design of miracles is to baffle them. But neither does Scripture anywhere assert, as a general truth, that miracles are possible. Indeed, it asserts the contrary; for Jeremiah declares that Nature follows an invariable order. Scripture, however, like Nature herself, does not lay down speculative propositions (*Scriptura definitiones non tradit, ut nec* 330 *etiam natura*). It relates matters in such an order and with such phraseology as a speaker (often not perfectly instructed himself) who wanted to impress his hearers with a lively sense of God's greatness and goodness would naturally employ; as Moses, for instance, relates to the Israelites the passage of the Red Sea without any mention of the east wind which attended it, and which is brought accidentally to our knowledge in another place. So that to know exactly what Scripture means in the relation of each seeming miracle, we ought to know (besides the tropes and phrases of the Hebrew language) the circumstances, and also,—since every one is swayed in his manner of presenting facts by his own preconceived opinions, and we have seen what those of the prophets were,—the preconceived opinions of each speaker. But this mode of interpreting Scripture is fatal to the vulgar notion of its verbal inspiration, of a sanctity and absolute truth in all the words and sentences of which it is composed. This vulgar notion is, indeed, a palpable error. It is demonstrable from the internal testimony of the Scriptures themselves, that the books from the first of the Pentateuch to the last of Kings were put together, after the first destruction of Jerusalem, by a compiler (probably Ezra) who designed to relate the history of the Jewish people from its origin to that destruction; it is demonstrable, moreover, that the compiler did not put his last hand to the work, but left it with its extracts from various and conflicting sources sometimes unreconciled, left it with errors of text and unsettled readings. The prophetic books are mere fragments of the prophets, collected by the Rabbins where they could find them, and inserted in the Canon according to their discretion. They, at first, proposed to admit neither the Book of Proverbs nor the Book of Ecclesiastes into the Canon, and only admitted them because there were found in them passages which commended the law of Moses. Ezekiel also they had determined to exclude; but one of their number remodelled him, so as to procure his admission. The Books of Ezra, Nehemiah, Esther, and Daniel are the work of a single author, and were not written till after Judas Maccabeus had restored the worship of the Temple. The Book of Psalms was collected and arranged at the same time. Before this time, there was no Canon of the sacred writings, and the great synagogue, by which the Canon was fixed, was first convened after the Macedonian conquest of Asia. Of that synagogue none of the prophets were members; the learned men who composed it were guided by their own fallible judgment. In like manner the uninspired judgment of human councils determined the Canon of the New Testament.

Such, reduced to the briefest and plainest terms possible, stripped of the developments and proofs with which he delivers it, and divested of the metaphysical language in which much of it is clothed by him, is the doctrine of Spinoza's treatise on the interpretation of Scripture. By the whole scope and drift of its argument, by the spirit in which the subject is throughout treated, his work undeniably is most interesting and stimulating to the general culture of Europe. There are errors and contradictions in Scripture; and the question which the general culture of Europe, well aware of this, asks with real interest is: What then? What follows from all this? What change is it, if true, to produce in the relations of mankind to the Christian religion? If the old theory of Scripture inspiration is to be abandoned, what place is the Bible henceforth to hold among books? What 380 is the new Christianity to be like? How are governments to deal with National Churches founded to maintain a very different conception of Christianity? Spinoza addresses himself to these questions. All secondary points of criticism he touches with the utmost possible brevity. He points out that Moses could never have written: 'And the Canaanite was then in the land,' because the Canaanite was in the land still at the death of Moses. He points out that Moses could never have written: 'There arose not a prophet since in Israel like unto Moses.' He points out how such a passage as, 'These are the kings that reigned in Edom *before there reigned any king over the children of Israel,*' clearly indicates an author writing not before 390 the times of the Kings. He points out how the account of Og's iron bedstead: 'Only Og the king of Bashan remained of the remnant of giants; behold, his bedstead was a bedstead of iron; is it not in Rabbath of the children of Ammon?'—probably indicates an author writing after David had taken Rabbath, and found there 'abundance of spoil,' amongst it this iron bedstead, the gigantic relic of another age. He points out how the language of this passage, and of such a passage as that in the Book of Samuel: 'Beforetime in Israel, when a man went to inquire of God, thus he spake: Come and let us go to the seer; for he that is now called prophet was aforetime called seer'—is certainly the language of a writer describing the 400 events of a long-past age, and not the language of a contemporary. But he devotes to all this no more space than is absolutely necessary. He apologises for delaying over such matters so long: *non est cur circa haec diu detinear—nolo taediosâ lectione lectorem detinere.* For him the interesting question is, not whether the fanatical devotee of the letter is to continue, for a longer or for a shorter time, to believe that Moses sate in the land of Moab writing the description of his own death, but what he is to believe when he does not believe this. Is he to take for the guidance of his life a great gloss put upon the Bible by theologians, who, 'not content with going mad themselves with Plato and Aristotle, want to make Christ and 410 the prophets go mad with them too,'—or the Bible itself? Is he to be presented by his national church with metaphysical formularies for his creed, or with the real fundamentals of Christianity? If with the former, religion will never produce its due fruits. A few elect will still be saved; but the vast majority of mankind will remain without grace and without good works, hateful and hating one another. Therefore he calls urgently upon governments to make the national church what it should be. This is the conclusion of the whole matter for him; a fervent appeal to the State, to save us from the untoward generation of metaphysical Article-makers. And therefore, anticipating Mr. Gladstone, he called his book 'The Church in its Relations with the State.'

Such is really the scope of Spinoza's work. He pursues a great object, and pursues it with signal ability. But it is important to observe that he nowhere distinctly gives his own opinion about the Bible's fundamental character. He takes the Bible as it stands, as he might take the phenomena of nature, and he discusses it as he finds it. Revelation differs from natural knowledge, he says, not by being more divine or more certain than natural knowledge, but by being conveyed in a different way; it differs from it because it is a knowledge 'of which the laws of human nature considered in themselves alone cannot be the cause.' What is really its cause, he says, we need not here inquire (*verum nec nobis jam opus est propheticae cognitionis causam scire*), for we take Scripture, which contains this revelation, as it stands, and do not ask how it arose (*documentorum causas nihil curamus*).

Proceeding on this principle, Spinoza leaves the attentive reader somewhat baffled and disappointed, clear as is his way of treating his subject, and remarkable as are the conclusions with which he presents us. He starts, we feel, from what is to him a hypothesis, and we want to know what he really thinks about this hypothesis. His greatest novelties are all within limits fixed for him by this hypothesis. He says that the voice which called Samuel was an imaginary voice; he says that the waters of the Red Sea retreated before a strong wind; he says that the Shunammite's son was revived by the natural heat of Elisha's body; he says that the rainbow which was made a sign to Noah appeared in the ordinary course of nature. Scripture itself, rightly interpreted, says, he affirms, all this. But he asserts that the divine voice which uttered the commandments on Mount Sinai was a real voice, a *vera vox*. He says, indeed, that this voice could not really give to the Israelites that proof which they imagined it gave to them of the existence of God, and that God on Sinai was dealing with the Israelites only according to their imperfect knowledge. Still he asserts the divine voice to have been a real one; and for this reason, that we do violence to Scripture if we do not admit it to have been a real one (*nisi Scripturae vim inferre velimus, omnino concedendum est, Israëlitas veram vocem audivisse*). The attentive reader wants to know what Spinoza himself thought about this *vera vox* and its possibility; he is much more interested in knowing this, than in knowing what Spinoza considered Scripture to affirm about the matter.

The feeling of perplexity thus caused is not diminished by the language of the chapter on miracles. In this chapter Spinoza broadly affirms a miracle to be an impossibility. But he himself contrasts the method of demonstration *à priori,* by which he claims to have established this proposition, with the method which he has pursued in treating of prophetic revelation. 'This revelation,' he says, 'is a matter out of human reach, and therefore I was bound to take it as I found it.' *Monere volo, me aliâ prorsus methodo circa miracula processisse, quam circa prophetiam . . . quod etiam consulto feci, quia de prophetia, quandoquidem ipsa captum humanum superat et quaestio mere theologica est, nihil affirmare, neque etiam scire poteram in quo ipsa potissimum constiterit, nisi ex fundamentis revelatis.* The reader feels that Spinoza, proceeding on a hypothesis, has presented him with the assertion of a miracle, and afterwards, proceeding *à priori,* has presented him with the assertion that a miracle is impossible. He feels that Spinoza does not adequately reconcile these two assertions by declaring that any event really miraculous, if found recorded in Scripture must be 'a spurious addition made to Scripture by sacrilegious men.' Is, then, he asks, the *vera vox* of Mount Sinai in Spinoza's opinion a spurious addition made to Scripture by sacrilegious men; or, if not, how is it not miraculous?

Spinoza, in his own mind, regarded the Bible as a vast collection of miscellaneous documents, many of them quite disparate and not at all to be harmonised with others; documents of unequal value and of varying applicability, some of them conveying ideas salutary for one time, others for another. But in the *Tractatus Theologico-Politicus* he by no means always deals in this free spirit with the Bible. Sometimes he chooses to deal with it in the spirit of the veriest worshipper of the letter; sometimes he chooses to treat the Bible as if all its parts were (so to speak) equipollent; to snatch an isolated text which suits his purpose, without caring whether it is annulled by the context, by the general drift of Scripture, or by other passages of more weight and authority. The great critic thus becomes voluntarily as uncritical as Exeter Hall. The epicurean Solomon, whose *Ecclesiastes* the Hebrew doctors, even after they had received it into the canon, forbade the young and weak-minded among their community to read, Spinoza quotes as of the same authority with the severe Moses; he uses promiscuously, as documents of identical force, without discriminating between their essentially different character, the softened cosmopolitan teaching of the prophets of the captivity and the rigid national teaching of the instructors of Israel's youth. He is capable of extracting, from a chance expression of Jeremiah, the assertion of a speculative idea which Jeremiah certainly never entertained, and from which he would have recoiled in dismay,—the idea, namely, that miracles are impossible; just as the ordinary Englishman can extract from God's words to Noah, *Be fruitful and multiply*, an exhortation to himself to have a large family. Spinoza, I repeat, knew perfectly well what this verbal mode of dealing with the Bible was worth: but he sometimes uses it because of the hypothesis from which he set out; because of his having agreed 'to take Scripture as it stands, and not to ask how it arose.'

No doubt the sagacity of Spinoza's rules for Biblical interpretation, the power of his analysis of the contents of the Bible, the interest of his reflections on Jewish history, are, in spite of this, very great, and have an absolute worth of their own, independent of the silence or ambiguity of their author upon a point of cardinal importance. Few candid people will read his rules of interpretation without exclaiming that they are the very dictates of good sense, that they have always believed in them; and without adding, after a moment's reflection, that they have passed their lives in violating them. And what can be more interesting, than to find that perhaps the main cause of the decay of the Jewish polity was one of which from our English Bible, which entirely mistranslates the 26th verse of the 20th chapter of Ezekiel, we hear nothing,—the perpetual reproach of impurity and rejection cast upon the mass of the Hebrew nation by the exclusive priesthood of the tribe of Levi? What can be more suggestive, after Mr. Mill and Dr. Stanley have been telling us how great an element of strength to the Hebrew nation was the institution of prophets, than to hear from the ablest of Hebrews how this institution seems to him to have been to his nation one of her main elements of weakness? No intelligent man can read the *Tractatus Theologico-Politicus* without being profoundly instructed by it: but neither can he read it without feeling that, as a speculative work, it is, to use a French military expression, *in the air;* that, in a certain sense, it is in want of a base and in want of supports; that this base and these supports are, at any rate, not to be found in the work itself, and, if they exist, must be sought for in other works of the author.

The genuine speculative opinions of Spinoza, which the *Tractatus Theologico-Politicus* but imperfectly reveals, may in his Ethics and in his Letters be found set forth clearly. It is, however, the business of criticism to deal with every independent work as with an independent whole, and instead of establishing between the *Tractatus Theologico-Politicus* and the Ethics of Spinoza a relation which Spinoza himself has not established,—to seize, in dealing with the *Tractatus Theologico-Politicus,* the important fact that this work has its source, not in the axioms and definition of the Ethics, but in a hypothesis. The Ethics are not yet translated into English, and I have not here to speak of them. Then will be the right time for criticism to try and seize the special character and tendencies of that remarkable work, when it is dealing with it directly. The criticism of the Ethics is far too serious a task to be undertaken incidentally, and merely as a supplement to the criticism of the *Tractatus Theologico-Politicus.* Nevertheless, on certain governing ideas of Spinoza, which receive their systematic expression, indeed, in the Ethics, and on which the *Tractatus Theologico-Politicus* is not formally based, but which are yet never absent from Spinoza's mind in the composition of any work, which breathe through all his works, and fill them with a peculiar effect and power, I have a word or two to say.

A philosopher's real power over mankind resides not in his metaphysical formulas, but in the spirit and tendencies which have led him to adopt those formulas. Spinoza's critic, therefore, has rather to bring to light that spirit and those tendencies of his author, than to exhibit his metaphysical formulas. Propositions about substance pass by mankind at large like the idle wind, which mankind at large regards not; it will not even listen to a word about these propositions, unless it first learns what their author was driving at with them, and finds that this object of his is one with which it sympathises, one, at any rate, which commands its attention. And mankind is so far right that this object of the author is really, as has been said, that which is most important, that which sets all his work in motion, that which is the secret of his attraction for other minds, which, by different ways, pursue the same object.

Mr. Maurice, seeking for the cause of Goethe's great admiration for Spinoza, thinks that he finds it in Spinoza's Hebrew genius. 'He spoke of God,' says Mr. Maurice, 'as an actual being, to those who had fancied him a name in a book. The child of the circumcision had a message for Lessing and Goethe which the pagan schools of philosophy could not bring.' This seems to me, I confess, fanciful. An intensity and impressiveness, which came to him from his Hebrew nature, Spinoza no doubt has; but the two things which are most remarkable about him, and by which, as I think, he chiefly impressed Goethe, seem to me not to come to him from his Hebrew nature at all,—I mean his denial of final causes, and his stoicism, a stoicism not passive, but active. For a mind like Goethe's,—a mind profoundly impartial and passionately aspiring after the science, not of men only, but of universal nature,—the popular philosophy which explains all things by reference to man, and regards universal nature as existing for the sake of man, and even of certain classes of men, was utterly repulsive. Unchecked, this philosophy would gladly maintain that the donkey exists in order that the invalid Christian may have donkey's milk before breakfast; and such views of nature as this were exactly what Goethe's whole soul abhorred. Creation, he thought, should be made of sterner stuff; he desired to rest the donkey's existence on larger grounds. More than any philosopher who has ever lived, Spinoza satisfied him here. The full exposition of the counter-doctrine to the popular doctrine of final causes is to be found in the Ethics; but this denial of final causes was so essential an element of all Spinoza's thinking that we shall, as has been said already, find it in the work with which we are here concerned, the *Tractatus Theologico-Politicus,* and, indeed, permeating that work and all his works. From the *Tractatus Theologico-Politicus* one may take as good a general statement of this denial as any which is to be found in the Ethics:—

'Deus naturam dirigit, prout ejus leges universales, non autem prout humanae naturae particulares leges exigunt, adeoque Deus non solius humani generis, sed totius naturae rationem habet. (*God directs nature, according as the universal laws of nature, but not according as the particular laws of human nature require; and so God has regard, not of the human race only, but of entire nature.*)'

And, as a pendant to this denial by Spinoza of final causes, comes his stoicism:—

'Non studemus, ut natura nobis, sed contra ut nos naturae paremus. (*Our desire is not that nature may obey us, but, on the contrary, that we may obey nature.*)'

Here is the second source of his attractiveness for Goethe; and Goethe is but the eminent representative of a whole order of minds whose admiration has made Spinoza's fame. Spinoza first impresses Goethe and any man like Goethe, and then he composes him; first he fills and satisfies his imagination by the width and grandeur of his view of nature, and then he fortifies and stills his mobile, straining, passionate, poetic temperament by the moral lesson he draws from his view of nature. And a moral lesson not of mere resigned acquiescence, not of melancholy quietism, but of joyful activity within the limits of man's true sphere:—

'Ipsa hominis essentia est conatus quo unusquisque suum esse conservare conatur. . . . Virtus hominis est ipsa hominis essentia, quatenus a solo conatu suum esse conservandi definitur. . . . Felicitas in eo consistit quod homo suum esse conservare potest. . . . Laetitia est hominis transitio ad majorem perfectionem. . . . Tristitia est hominis transitio ad minorem perfectionem. (*Man's very essence is the effort wherewith each man strives to maintain his own being. . . . Man's virtue is this very essence, so far as it is defined by this single effort to maintain his own being. . . . Happiness consists in a man's being able to maintain his own being. . . . Joy is man's passage to a greater perfection. . . . Sorrow is man's passage to a lesser perfection.*)'

It seems to me that by neither of these, his grand characteristic doctrines, is Spinoza truly Hebrew or truly Christian. His denial of final causes is essentially alien to the spirit of the Old Testament, and his cheerful and self-sufficing stoicism is essentially alien to the spirit of the New. The doctrine that 'God directs nature, not according as the particular laws of human nature, but according as the universal laws of nature require,' is at utter variance with that Hebrew mode of representing God's dealings, which makes the locusts visit Egypt to punish Pharaoh's hardness of heart, and the falling dew avert itself from the fleece of Gideon. The doctrine that 'all sorrow is a passage to a lesser perfection' is at utter variance with the Christian recognition of the blessedness of sorrow, working 'repentance to salvation not to be repented of;' of sorrow, which, in Dante's words, 'remarries us to God.'

Spinoza's repeated and earnest assertions that the love of God is man's *summum bonum* do not remove the fundamental diversity between his doctrine and the Hebrew and Christian doctrines. By the love of God he does not mean the same thing which the Hebrew and Christian religions mean by the love of God. He makes the love of God to consist in the knowledge of God; and, as we know God only through his manifestation of himself in the laws of all nature, it is by knowing these laws that we love God, and the more we know them the more we love him. This may be true, but this is not what the Christian means by the love of God. Spinoza's ideal is the intellectual life; the Christian's ideal is the religious life. Between the two conditions there is all the difference which there is between the being in love, and the following, with delighted comprehension, a reasoning of Plato. For Spinoza, undoubtedly, the crown of the intellectual life is a transport, as for the saint the crown of the religious life is a transport; but the two transports are not the same.

This is true; yet it is true, also, that by thus crowning the intellectual life with a sacred transport, by thus retaining in philosophy, amid the discontented murmurs of all the army of atheism, the name of God, Spinoza maintains a profound affinity with that which is truest in religion, and inspires an indestructible interest. One of his admirers, M. Van Vloten, has recently published at Amsterdam a supplementary volume to Spinoza's works, containing the interesting document of Spinoza's sentence of excommunication, from which I have already quoted, and containing, besides, several lately found works alleged to be Spinoza's, which seem to me to be of doubtful authenticity, and, even if authentic, of no great importance. M. Van Vloten (who, let me be permitted to say in passing, writes a Latin which would make one think that the art of writing Latin must be now a lost art in the country of Lipsius) is very anxious that Spinoza's unscientific retention of the name of God should not afflict his readers with any doubts as to his perfect scientific orthodoxy:—

'It is a great mistake,' he cries, 'to disparage Spinoza as merely one of the dogmatists before Kant. By keeping the name of God, while he did away with his person and character, he has done himself an injustice. Those who look to the bottom of things will see, that, long ago as he lived, he had even then reached the point to which post-Hegelian philosophy and the study of natural science has only just brought our own times. Leibnitz expressed his apprehension lest those who did away with final causes should do away with God at the same time. But it is in his having done away with final causes, *and with God along with them,* that Spinoza's true merit consists.'

Now it must be remarked that to use Spinoza's denial of final causes in order to identify him with the Coryphaei of atheism, is to make a false use of Spinoza's denial of final causes, just as to use his assertion of the all-importance of loving God to identify him with the saints would be to make a false use of his assertion of the all-importance of loving God. He is no more to be identified with the post-Hegelian philosophers than he is to be identified with St. Augustine. Unction, indeed, Spinoza's writings have not; that name does not precisely fit any quality which they exhibit. And yet, so all-important in the sphere of religious thought is the power of edification, that in this sphere a great fame like Spinoza's can never be founded without it. A court of literature can never be very severe to Voltaire: with that inimitable wit and clear sense of his, he cannot write a page in which the fullest head may not find something suggestive: still, because, handling religious ideas, he yet, with all his wit and clear sense, handles them wholly without the power of edification, his fame as a great man is equivocal. Strauss has treated the question of Scripture miracles with an acuteness and fulness which even to the most informed minds is instructive; but because he treats it almost wholly without the power of edification, his fame as a serious thinker is equivocal. But in Spinoza there is not a trace either of Voltaire's passion for mockery or of Strauss's passion for demolition. His whole soul was filled with desire of the love and knowledge of God, and of that only. Philosophy always proclaims herself on the way to the *summum bonum;* but too often on the road she seems to forget her destination, and suffers her hearers to forget it also. Spinoza never forgets his destination: 'The love of God is man's highest happiness and blessedness, and the final end and aim of all human actions;'—'The supreme reward for keeping God's Word is that Word itself—namely, to know him and with free will and pure and constant heart love him:' these sentences are the 700 keynote to all he produced, and were the inspiration of all his labours. This is why he turns so sternly upon the worshippers of the letter,—the editors of the *Masora,* the editor of the *Record,*—because their doctrine imperils our love and knowledge of God. 'What!' he cries, 'our knowledge of God to depend upon these perishable things, which Moses can dash to the ground and break to pieces like the first tables of stone, or of which the originals can be lost like the original book of the Covenant, like the original book of the Law of God, like the book of the Wars of God! . . . which can come to us confused, imperfect, miswritten by copyists, tampered with by doctors! And you accuse others of impiety! It is you who are impious, 710 to believe that God would commit the treasure of the true record of himself to any substance less enduring than the heart!'

And Spinoza's life was not unworthy of this elevated strain. A philosopher who professed that knowledge was its own reward, a devotee who professed that the love of God was its own reward, this philosopher and this devotee believed in what he said. Spinoza led a life the most spotless, perhaps, to be found among the lives of philosophers; he lived simple, studious, even-tempered, kind; declining honours, declining riches, declining notoriety. He was poor, and his admirer Simon de Vries sent him two thousand florins;—he refused them. The same friend left him his fortune; 720 —he returned it to the heir. He was asked to dedicate one of his works to the magnificent patron of letters in his century, Louis the Fourteenth;— he declined. His great work, his Ethics, published after his death, he gave injunctions to his friends to publish anonymously, for fear he should give his name to a school. Truth, he thought, should bear no man's name. And finally,—'Unless,' he said, 'I had known that my writings would in the end advance the cause of true religion, I would have suppressed them,— *tacuissem.*' It was in this spirit that he lived; and this spirit gives to all he writes not exactly unction,—I have already said so,—but a kind of sacred solemnity. Not of the same order as the saints, he yet follows the same 730 service: *Doubtless thou art our Father, though Abraham be ignorant of us, and Israel acknowledge us not.*

Therefore he has been, in a certain sphere, edifying, and has inspired in many powerful minds an interest and an admiration such as no other philosopher has inspired since Plato. The lonely precursor of German philosophy, he still shines when the light of his successors is fading away; they had celebrity, Spinoza has fame. Not because his peculiar system of philosophy has had more adherents than theirs; on the contrary, it has had fewer. But schools of philosophy arise and fall; their bands of adherents inevitably dwindle; no master can long persuade a large body of disciples that they give to themselves just the same account of the world as he does; it is only the very young and the very enthusiastic who can think themselves sure that they possess the whole mind of Plato, or Spinoza, or Hegel, at all. The very mature and the very sober can even hardly believe that these philosophers possessed it themselves enough to put it all into their works, and to let us know entirely how the world seemed to them. What a remarkable philosopher really does for human thought, is to throw into circulation a certain number of new and striking ideas and expressions, and to stimulate with them the thought and imagination of his century or of after-times. So Spinoza has made his distinction between adequate and inadequate ideas a current notion for educated Europe. So Hegel seized a single pregnant sentence of Heracleitus, and cast it, with a thousand striking applications, into the world of modern thought. But to do this is only enough to make a philosopher noteworthy; it is not enough to make him great. To be great, he must have something in him which can influence character, which is edifying; he must, in short, have a noble and lofty character himself, a character,—to recur to that much-criticised expression of mine,—*in the grand style*. This is what Spinoza had; and because he had it, he stands out from the multitude of philosophers, and has been able to inspire in powerful minds a feeling which the most remarkable philosophers, without this grandiose character, could not inspire. 'There is no possible view of life but Spinoza's,' said Lessing. Goethe has told us how he was calmed and edified by him in his youth, and how he again went to him for support in his maturity. Heine, the man (in spite of his faults) of truest genius that Germany has produced since Goethe,—a man with faults, as I have said, immense faults, the greatest of them being that he could reverence so little,—reverenced Spinoza. Hegel's influence ran off him like water: 'I have seen Hegel,' he cries, 'seated with his doleful air of a hatching hen upon his unhappy eggs, and I have heard his dismal clucking.—How easily one can cheat oneself into thinking that one understands everything, when one has learnt only how to construct dialectical formulas!' But of Spinoza, Heine said: 'His life was a copy of the life of his divine kinsman, Jesus Christ.'

And therefore, when M. Van Vloten violently presses the parallel with the post-Hegelians, one feels that the parallel with St. Augustine is the far truer one. Compared with the soldier of irreligion M. Van Vloten would have him to be, Spinoza is religious. 'It is true,' one may say to the wise and devout Christian, 'Spinoza's conception of beatitude is not yours, and cannot satisfy you; but whose conception of beatitude would you accept as satisfying? Not even that of the devoutest of your fellow-Christians. [780] Fra Angelico, the sweetest and most inspired of devout souls, has given us, in his great picture of the Last Judgment, his conception of beatitude. The elect are going round in a ring on long grass under laden fruit-trees; two of them, more restless than the others, are flying up a battlemented street,—a street blank with all the ennui of the Middle Ages. Across a gulf is visible, for the delectation of the saints, a blazing caldron in which Beelzebub is sousing the damned. This is hardly more your conception of beatitude than Spinoza's is. But "in my Father's house are many mansions;" only, to reach any one of these mansions, there are needed the wings of a genuine sacred transport, of an "immortal longing." ' These [790] wings Spinoza had; and, because he had them, his own language about himself, about his aspirations, and his course, are true: his foot is in the *vera vita,* his eye on the beatific vision.

MARCUS AURELIUS

———————⊰◆⊱———————

Mr. Mill says, in his book on Liberty, that 'Christian morality is in great part merely a protest against paganism; its ideal is negative rather than positive, passive rather than active.' He says, that, in certain most important respects, 'it falls far below the best morality of the ancients.' Now, the object of systems of morality is to take possession of human life, to save it from being abandoned to passion or allowed to drift at hazard, to give it happiness by establishing it in the practice of virtue; and this object they seek to attain by prescribing to human life fixed principles of action, fixed rules of conduct. In its uninspired as well as in its inspired moments, in its days of languor and gloom as well as in its days of sunshine and energy, human life has thus always a clue to follow, and may always be making way towards its goal. Christian morality has not failed to supply to human life aids of this sort. It has supplied them far more abundantly than many of its critics imagine. The most exquisite document, after those of the New Testament, of all the documents the Christian spirit has ever inspired,—the *Imitation,*—by no means contains the whole of Christian morality;

nay, the disparagers of this morality would think themselves sure of triumphing if one agreed to look for it in the *Imitation* only. But even the *Imitation* is full of passages like these: 'Vita sine proposito languida et vaga est;'—'Omni die renovare debemus propositum nostrum, dicentes: nunc hodiè perfectè incipiamus, quia nihil est quod hactenus fecimus;' —'Secundum propositum nostrum est cursus profectûs nostri;'—'Raro etiam unum vitium perfectè vincimus, et ad *quotidianum* profectum non accendimur;'—'Semper aliquid certi proponendum est;'—'Tibi ipsi violentiam frequenter fac:' (*A life without a purpose is a languid, drifting thing;—Every day we ought to renew our purpose, saying to ourselves: This day let us make a sound beginning, for what we have hitherto done is nought;—Our improvement is in proportion to our purpose;—We hardly ever manage to get completely rid even of one fault, and do not set our hearts on* daily *improvement;—Always place a definite purpose before thee;—Get the habit of mastering thine inclination.*) These are moral precepts, and moral precepts of the best kind. As rules to hold possession of our conduct, and to keep us in the right course through outward troubles and inward perplexity, they are equal to the best ever furnished by the great masters of morals,—Epictetus or Marcus Aurelius.

But moral rules, apprehended as ideas first, and then rigorously followed as laws, are, and must be, for the sage only. The mass of mankind have neither force of intellect enough to apprehend them clearly as ideas, nor force of character enough to follow them strictly as laws. The mass of mankind can be carried along a course full of hardship for the natural man, can be borne over the thousand impediments of the narrow way, only by the tide of a joyful and bounding emotion. It is impossible to rise from reading Epictetus or Marcus Aurelius without a sense of constraint and melancholy, without feeling that the burden laid upon man is well-nigh greater than he can bear. Honour to the sages who have felt this, and yet have borne it! Yet, even for the sage, this sense of labour and sorrow in his march towards the goal constitutes a relative inferiority; the noblest souls of whatever creed, the pagan Empedocles as well as the Christian Paul, have insisted on the necessity of an inspiration, a joyful emotion, to make moral action perfect; an obscure indication of this necessity is the one drop of truth in the ocean of verbiage with which the controversy on justification by faith has flooded the world. But, for the ordinary man, this sense of labour and sorrow constitutes an absolute disqualification; it paralyses him; under the weight of it, he cannot make way towards the goal at all. The paramount virtue of religion is, that it has *lighted up* morality; that it has supplied the emotion and inspiration needful for carrying the sage along the narrow way perfectly, for carrying the ordinary man along it at all. Even the religions with most dross in them have had something of this virtue; but the Christian religion manifests it with unexampled splendour. 'Lead me, Zeus and Destiny!' says the prayer of Epictetus, 'whithersoever I am appointed to go; I will follow without wavering; even though I turn coward and shrink, I shall have to follow all the same.' The fortitude of that is for the strong, for the few; even for them the spiritual atmosphere with which it surrounds them is bleak and grey. But, 'Let thy loving spirit lead me forth into the land of righteousness;'—'The Lord shall be unto thee an everlasting light, and thy God thy glory;'—'Unto you that fear my name shall the sun of righteousness arise with healing in his wings,' says the Old Testament; 'Born, not of blood, nor of the will of the flesh, nor of the will of man, but of God;'—'Except a man be born again, he cannot see the kingdom of God;'—'Whatsoever is born of God, overcometh the world,' says the New. The ray of sunshine is there, the glow of a divine warmth;—the austerity of the sage melts away under it, the paralysis of the weak is healed; he who is vivified by it renews his strength; 'all things are possible to him;' 'he is a new creature.'

Epictetus says: 'Every matter has two handles, one of which will bear taking hold of, the other not. If thy brother sin against thee, lay not hold of the matter by this, that he sins against thee; for by this handle the matter will not bear taking hold of. But rather lay hold of it by this, that he is thy brother, thy born mate; and thou wilt take hold of it by what will bear handling.' Jesus, being asked whether a man is bound to forgive his brother as often as seven times, answers: 'I say not unto thee, until seven times, but until seventy times seven.' Epictetus here suggests to the reason grounds for forgiveness of injuries which Jesus does not; but it is vain to say that Epictetus is on that account a better moralist than Jesus, if the warmth, the emotion, of Jesus's answer fires his hearer to the practice of forgiveness of injuries, while the thought in Epictetus's leaves him cold. So with Christian morality in general: its distinction is not that it propounds the maxim, 'Thou shalt love God and thy neighbour,' with more development, closer reasoning, truer sincerity, than other moral systems; it is that it propounds this maxim with an inspiration which wonderfully catches the hearer and makes him act upon it. It is because Mr. Mill has attained to the perception of truths of this nature, that he is,—instead of being, like the school from which he proceeds, doomed to sterility,—a writer of distinguished mark and influence, a writer deserving all attention and respect; it is (I must be pardoned for saying) because he is not sufficiently leavened with them, that he falls just short of being a great writer.

That which gives to the moral writings of the Emperor Marcus Aurelius their peculiar character and charm, is their being suffused and softened by something of this very sentiment whence Christian morality draws its best power. Mr. Long has recently published in a convenient form a translation of these writings, and has thus enabled English readers to judge Marcus Aurelius for themselves; he has rendered his countrymen a real service by so doing. Mr. Long's reputation as a scholar is a sufficient guarantee of the general fidelity and accuracy of his translation; on these matters, besides, I am hardly entitled to speak, and my praise is of no value. But that for which I and the rest of the unlearned may venture to praise Mr. Long is this; that he treats Marcus Aurelius's writings, as he treats all the other remains of Greek and Roman antiquity which he touches, not as a dead and dry matter of learning, but as documents with a side of modern applicability and living interest, and valuable mainly so far as this side in them can be made clear; that as in his notes on Plutarch's Roman Lives he deals with the modern epoch of Caesar and Cicero, not as food for schoolboys, but as food for men, and men engaged in the current of contemporary life and action, so in his remarks and essays on Marcus Aurelius he treats this truly modern striver and thinker not as a Classical Dictionary hero, but as a present source from which to draw 'example of life, and instruction of manners.' Why may not a son of Dr. Arnold say, what might naturally here be said by any other critic, that in this lively and fruitful way of considering the men and affairs of ancient Greece and Rome, Mr. Long resembles Dr. Arnold?

One or two little complaints, however, I have against Mr. Long, and I will get them off my mind at once. In the first place, why could he not have found gentler and juster terms to describe the translation of his predecessor, Jeremy Collier,—the redoubtable enemy of stage plays,—than these: 'a most coarse and vulgar copy of the original'? As a matter of taste, a translator should deal leniently with his predecessor; but putting that out of the question, Mr. Long's language is a great deal too hard. Most English people who knew Marcus Aurelius before Mr. Long appeared as his introducer, knew him through Jeremy Collier. And the acquaintance of a man like Marcus Aurelius is such an imperishable benefit, that one can never lose a peculiar sense of obligation towards the man who confers it. Apart from this claim upon one's tenderness, however, Jeremy Collier's version deserves respect for its genuine spirit and vigour, the spirit and vigour of the age of Dryden. Jeremy Collier too, like Mr. Long, regarded in Marcus Aurelius the living moralist, and not the dead classic; and his warmth of feeling gave to his style an impetuosity and rhythm which from

Mr. Long's style (I do not blame it on that account) are absent. Let us place the two side by side. The impressive opening of Marcus Aurelius's fifth book, Mr. Long translates thus:—

'In the morning when thou risest unwillingly, let this thought be present: I am rising to the work of a human being. Why then am I dissatisfied if I am going to do the things for which I exist and for which I was brought into the world? Or have I been made for this, to lie in the bed-clothes and keep myself warm?—But this is more pleasant.—Dost thou exist then to take thy pleasure, and not at all for action or exertion?'

Jeremy Collier has:—

'When you find an unwillingness to rise early in the morning, make this short speech to yourself: "I am getting up now to do the business of a man; and am I out of humour for going about that which I was made for, and for the sake of which I was sent into the world? Was I then designed for nothing but to doze and batten beneath the counterpane? I thought action had been the end of your being." '

In another striking passage, again, Mr. Long has:—

'No longer wander at hazard; for neither wilt thou read thy own memoirs, nor the acts of the ancient Romans and Hellenes, and the selections from books which thou wast reserving for thy old age. Hasten then to the end which thou hast before thee, and, throwing away idle hopes, come to thine own aid, if thou carest at all for thyself, while it is in thy power.'

Here his despised predecessor has:—

'Don't go too far in your books and overgrasp yourself. Alas, you have no time left to peruse your diary, to read over the Greek and Roman history: come, don't flatter and deceive yourself; look to the main chance, to the end and design of reading, and mind life more than notion: I say, if you have a kindness for your person, drive at the practice and help yourself, for that is in your own power.'

It seems to me that here for style and force Jeremy Collier can (to say the least) perfectly stand comparison with Mr. Long. Jeremy Collier's real defect as a translator is not his coarseness and vulgarity, but his imperfect acquaintance with Greek; this is a serious defect, a fatal one; it rendered a translation like Mr. Long's necessary. Jeremy Collier's work will now be forgotten, and Mr. Long stands master of the field; but he may be content, at any rate, to leave his predecessor's grave unharmed, even if he will not throw upon it, in passing, a handful of kindly earth.

Another complaint I have against Mr. Long is, that he is not quite idiomatic and simple enough. It is a little formal, at least, if not pedantic,

to say *Ethic* and *Dialectic,* instead of *Ethics* and *Dialectics,* and to say
'*Hellenes* and Romans' instead of '*Greeks* and Romans.' And why, too,—
the name of Antoninus being preoccupied by Antoninus Pius,—will Mr.
Long call his author Marcus *Antoninus* instead of Marcus *Aurelius*? Small
as these matters appear, they are important when one has to deal with the
general public, and not with a small circle of scholars; and it is the general
public that the translator of a short masterpiece on morals, such as is the
book of Marcus Aurelius, should have in view; his aim should be to make
Marcus Aurelius's work as popular as the *Imitation,* and Marcus Aurelius's
name as familiar as Socrates's. In rendering or naming him, therefore,
punctilious accuracy of phrase is not so much to be sought as accessibility
and currency; everything which may best enable the Emperor and his precepts *volitare per ora virûm.* It is essential to render him in language perfectly plain and unprofessional, and to call him by the name by which he is
best and most distinctly known. The translators of the Bible talk of *pence*
and not *denarii,* and the admirers of Voltaire do not celebrate him under
the name of Arouet.

But, after these trifling complaints are made, one must end, as one
began, in unfeigned gratitude to Mr. Long for his excellent and substantial
reproduction in English of an invaluable work. In general the substantiality, soundness, and precision of Mr. Long's rendering are (I will venture, after all, to give my opinion about them) as conspicuous as the living
spirit with which he treats antiquity; and these qualities are particularly
desirable in the translator of a work like that of Marcus Aurelius, of which
the language is often corrupt, almost always hard and obscure. Any one
who wants to appreciate Mr. Long's merits as a translator may read, in
the original and in Mr. Long's translation, the seventh chapter of the tenth
book; he will see how, through all the dubiousness and involved manner of
the Greek, Mr. Long has firmly seized upon the clear thought which is
certainly at the bottom of that troubled wording, and, in distinctly rendering this thought, has at the same time thrown round its expression a characteristic shade of painfulness and difficulty which just suits it. And Marcus
Aurelius's book is one which, when it is rendered so accurately as Mr.
Long renders it, even those who know Greek tolerably well may choose to
read rather in the translation than in the original. For not only are the
contents here incomparably more valuable than the external form, but this
form, the Greek of a Roman, is not exactly one of those styles which have
a physiognomy, which are an essential part of their author, which stamp an
indelible impression of him on the reader's mind. An old Lyons commentator finds, indeed, in Marcus Aurelius's Greek, something character-

istic, something specially firm and imperial; but I think an ordinary mortal will hardly find this: he will find crabbed Greek, without any great charm of distinct physiognomy. The Greek of Thucydides and Plato has this charm, and he who reads them in a translation, however accurate, loses it, and loses much in losing it; but the Greek of Marcus Aurelius, like the Greek of the New Testament, and even more than the Greek of the New Testament, is wanting in it. If one could be assured that the English Testament were made perfectly accurate, one might be almost content never to open a Greek Testament again; and, Mr. Long's version of Marcus Aurelius being what it is, an Englishman who reads to live, and does not live to read, may henceforth let the Greek original repose upon its shelf.

The man whose thoughts Mr. Long has thus faithfully reproduced, is perhaps the most beautiful figure in history. He is one of those consoling and hope-inspiring marks, which stand for ever to remind our weak and easily discouraged race how high human goodness and perseverance have once been carried, and may be carried again. The interest of mankind is peculiarly attracted by examples of signal goodness in high places; for that testimony to the worth of goodness is the most striking which is borne by those to whom all the means of pleasure and self-indulgence lay open, by those who had at their command the kingdoms of the world and the glory of them. Marcus Aurelius was the ruler of the grandest of empires; and he was one of the best of men. Besides him, history presents one or two other sovereigns eminent for their goodness, such as Saint Louis or Alfred. But Marcus Aurelius has, for us moderns, this great superiority in interest over Saint Louis or Alfred, that he lived and acted in a state of society modern by its essential characteristics, in an epoch akin to our own, in a brilliant centre of civilisation. Trajan talks of 'our enlightened age' just as glibly as the *Times* talks of it. Marcus Aurelius thus becomes for us a man like ourselves, a man in all things tempted as we are. Saint Louis inhabits an atmosphere of mediaeval Catholicism, which the man of the nineteenth century may admire, indeed, may even passionately wish to inhabit, but which strive as he will, he cannot really inhabit. Alfred belongs to a state of society (I say it with all deference to the *Saturday Review* critic who keeps such jealous watch over the honour of our Saxon ancestors) half barbarous. Neither Alfred nor Saint Louis can be morally and intellectually as near to us as Marcus Aurelius.

The record of the outward life of this admirable man has in it little of striking incident. He was born at Rome on the 26th of April, in the year 121 of the Christian era. He was nephew and son-in-law to his predecessor on the throne, Antoninus Pius. When Antoninus died, he was forty years old, but from the time of his earliest manhood he had assisted in administering public affairs. Then, after his uncle's death in 161, for nineteen years he reigned as emperor. The barbarians were pressing on the Roman frontier, and a great part of Marcus Aurelius's nineteen years of reign was passed in campaigning. His absences from Rome were numerous and long. We hear of him in Asia Minor, Syria, Egypt, Greece; but, above all, in the countries on the Danube, where the war with the barbarians was going on,—in Austria, Moravia, Hungary. In these countries much of his Journal seems to have been written; parts of it are dated from them; and there, a few weeks before his fifty-ninth birthday, he fell sick and died.[1] The record of him on which his fame chiefly rests is the record of his inward life,—his *Journal,* or *Commentaries,* or *Meditations,* or *Thoughts,* for by all these names has the work been called. Perhaps the most interesting of the records of his outward life is that which the first book of this work supplies, where he gives an account of his education, recites the names of those to whom he is indebted for it, and enumerates his obligations to each of them. It is a refreshing and consoling picture, a priceless treasure for those, who, sick of the 'wild and dreamlike trade of blood and guile,' which seems to be nearly the whole of what history has to offer to our view, seek eagerly for that substratum of right thinking and well doing which in all ages must surely have somewhere existed, for without it the continued life of humanity would have been impossible. 'From my mother I learnt piety and beneficence, and abstinence not only from evil deeds but even from evil thoughts; and further, simplicity in my way of living, far removed from the habits of the rich.' Let us remember that, the next time we are reading the sixth satire of Juvenal. 'From my tutor I learnt' (hear it, ye tutors of princes!) 'endurance of labour, and to want little, and to work with my own hands, and not to meddle with other people's affairs, and not to be ready to listen to slander.' The vices and foibles of the Greek sophist or rhetorician—the *Graeculus esuriens*—are in everybody's mind; but he who reads Marcus Aurelius's account of his Greek teachers and masters, will understand how it is that, in spite of the vices and foibles of individual *Graeculi,* the education of the human race owes to Greece a debt which can never be overrated. The vague and colourless praise of history leaves on the mind hardly any impression of Antoninus Pius: it is only from the private memoranda of his nephew that we learn what a disciplined, hard-working, gentle, wise, virtuous man he was; a man who, perhaps, interests mankind less than his immortal nephew

---

[1] He died on the 17th of March, A.D. 180.

only because he has left in writing no record of his inner life,—*caret quia vate sacro.*

Of the outward life and circumstances of Marcus Aurelius, beyond these notices which he has himself supplied, there are few of much interest and importance. There is the fine anecdote of his speech when he heard of the assassination of the revolted Avidius Cassius, against whom he was marching; *he was sorry,* he said, *to be deprived of the pleasure of pardoning him.* And there are one or two more anecdotes of him which show the same spirit. But the great record for the outward life of a man who has left such a record of his lofty inward aspirations as that which Marcus Aurelius has left, is the clear consenting voice of all his contemporaries,—high and low, friend and enemy, pagan and Christian,—in praise of his sincerity, justice, and goodness. The world's charity does not err on the side of excess, and here was a man occupying the most conspicuous station in the world, and professing the highest possible standard of conduct;—yet the world was obliged to declare that he walked worthily of his profession. Long after his death, his bust was to be seen in the houses of private men through the wide Roman empire. It may be the vulgar part of human nature which busies itself with the semblance and doings of living sovereigns, it is its nobler part which busies itself with those of the dead; these busts of Marcus Aurelius, in the homes of Gaul, Britain, and Italy, bear witness, not to the inmates' frivolous curiosity about princes and palaces, but to their reverential memory of the passage of a great man upon the earth.

Two things, however, before one turns from the outward to the inward life of Marcus Aurelius, force themselves upon one's notice, and demand a word of comment; he persecuted the Christians, and he had for his son the vicious and brutal Commodus. The persecution at Lyons, in which Attalus and Pothinus suffered, the persecution at Smyrna, in which Polycarp suffered, took place in his reign. Of his humanity, of his tolerance, of his horror of cruelty and violence, of his wish to refrain from severe measures against the Christians, of his anxiety to temper the severity of these measures when they appeared to him indispensable, there is no doubt: but, on the one hand, it is certain that the letter, attributed to him, directing that no Christian should be punished for being a Christian, is spurious; it is almost certain that his alleged answer to the authorities of Lyons, in which he directs that Christians persisting in their profession shall be dealt with according to law, is genuine. Mr. Long seems inclined to try and throw doubt over the persecution at Lyons, by pointing out that the letter of the Lyons Christians relating it, alleges it to have been attended by miraculous and incredible incidents. 'A man,' he says, 'can only act consistently by accepting all this letter or rejecting it all, and we cannot blame him for either.' But it is contrary to all experience to say that because a fact is related with incorrect additions, and embellishments, therefore it probably never happened at all; or that it is not, in general, easy for an impartial mind to distinguish between the fact and the embellishments. I cannot doubt that the Lyons persecution took place, and that the punishment of Christians for being Christians was sanctioned by Marcus Aurelius. But then I must add that nine modern readers out of ten, when they read this, will, I believe, have a perfectly false notion of what the moral action of Marcus Aurelius, in sanctioning that punishment, really was. They imagine Trajan, or Antoninus Pius, or Marcus Aurelius, fresh from the perusal of the Gospel, fully aware of the spirit and holiness of the Christian saints, ordering their extermination because he loved darkness rather than light. Far from this, the Christianity which these emperors aimed at repressing was, in their conception of it, something philosophically contemptible, politically subversive, and morally abominable. As men, they sincerely regarded it much as well-conditioned people, with us, regard Mormonism; as rulers, they regarded it much as Liberal statesmen, with us, regard the Jesuits. A kind of Mormonism, constituted as a vast secret society, with obscure aims of political and social subversion, was what Antoninus Pius and Marcus Aurelius believed themselves to be repressing when they punished Christians. The early Christian apologists again and again declare to us under what odious imputations the Christians lay, how general was the belief that these imputations were well-grounded, how sincere was the horror which the belief inspired. The multitude, convinced that the Christians were atheists who ate human flesh and thought incest no crime, displayed against them a fury so passionate as to embarrass and alarm their rulers. The severe expressions of Tacitus, *exitiabilis superstitio—odio humani generis convicti,* show how deeply the prejudices of the multitude imbued the educated class also. One asks oneself with astonishment how a doctrine so benign as that of Jesus Christ can have incurred misrepresentation so monstrous. The inner and moving cause of the misrepresentation lay, no doubt, in this,—that Christianity was a new spirit in the Roman world, destined to act in that world as its dissolvent; and it was inevitable that Christianity in the Roman world, like democracy in the modern world, like every new spirit with a similar mission assigned to it, should at its first appearance occasion an instinctive shrinking and repugnance in the world which it was to dissolve. The outer and palpable causes of the misrepresentation were, for the Roman public at large, the confounding of the Christians with the Jews, that isolated, fierce, and stubborn race, whose stubbornness, fierceness, and isolation, real as they were, the fancy of a civilised Roman yet further exaggerated; the atmosphere of mystery and novelty which surrounded the Christian rites; the very simplicity of Christian theism. For the Roman statesman, the cause of mistake lay in that character of secret assemblages which the meetings of the Christian community wore, under a State-system as jealous of unauthorised associations as is the State-system of modern France.

A Roman of Marcus Aurelius's time and position could not well see the Christians except through the mist of these prejudices. Seen through such a mist, the Christians appeared with a thousand faults not their own; but it has not been sufficiently remarked that faults really their own many of them assuredly appeared with besides, faults especially likely to strike such an observer as Marcus Aurelius, and to confirm him in the prejudices of his race, station, and rearing. We look back upon Christianity after it has proved what a future it bore within it, and for us the sole representatives of its early struggles are the pure and devoted spirits through whom it proved this; Marcus Aurelius saw it with its future yet unshown, and with the tares among its professed progeny not less conspicuous than the wheat. Who can doubt that among the professing Christians of the second century, as among the professing Christians of the nineteenth, there was plenty of folly, plenty of rabid nonsense, plenty of gross fanaticism? who will even venture to affirm that, separated in great measure from the intellect and civilisation of the world for one or two centuries, Christianity, wonderful as have been its fruits, had the development perfectly worthy of its inestimable germ? Who will venture to affirm that, by the alliance of Christianity with the virtue and intelligence of men like the Antonines,—of the best product of Greek and Roman civilisation, while Greek and Roman civilisation had yet life and power,—Christianity and the world, as well as the Antonines themselves, would not have been gainers? That alliance was not to be. The Antonines lived and died with an utter misconception of Christianity; Christianity grew up in the Catacombs, not on the Palatine. And Marcus Aurelius incurs no moral reproach by having authorised the punishment of the Christians; he does not thereby become in the least what we mean by a *persecutor*. One may concede that it was impossible for him to see Christianity as it really was;—as impossible as for even the moderate and sensible Fleury to see the Antonines as they really were;—one may concede that the point of view from which Christianity appeared something anti-civil and anti-social, which the State had the faculty to judge and the duty to suppress, was inevitably his. Still, however, it remains true that this sage, who made perfection his aim and reason his law, did

Christianity an immense injustice and rested in an idea of State-attributes which was illusive. And this is, in truth, characteristic of Marcus Aurelius, that he is blameless, yet, in a certain sense, unfortunate; in his character, beautiful as it is, there is something melancholy, circumscribed, and ineffectual.

For of his having such a son as Commodus, too, one must say that he is not to be blamed on that account, but that he is unfortunate. Disposition and temperament are inexplicable things; there are natures on which the best education and example are thrown away; excellent fathers may have, without any fault of theirs, incurably vicious sons. It is to be remembered, also, that Commodus was left, at the perilous age of nineteen, master of the world; while his father, at that age, was but beginning a twenty years' apprenticeship to wisdom, labour, and self-command, under the sheltering teachership of his uncle Antoninus. Commodus was a prince apt to be led by favourites; and if the story is true which says that he left, all through his reign, the Christians untroubled, and ascribes this lenity to the influence of his mistress Marcia, it shows that he could be led to good as well as to evil. But for such a nature to be left at a critical age with absolute power, and wholly without good counsel and direction, was the more fatal. Still one cannot help wishing that the example of Marcus Aurelius could have availed more with his own only son. One cannot but think that with such virtue as his there should go, too, the ardour which removes mountains, and that the ardour which removes mountains might have even won Commodus. The word *ineffectual* again rises to one's mind; Marcus Aurelius saved his own soul by his righteousness, and he could do no more. Happy they who can do this! but still happier, who can do more!

Yet, when one passes from his outward to his inward life, when one turns over the pages of his *Meditations,*—entries jotted down from day to day, amid the business of the city or the fatigues of the camp, for his own guidance and support, meant for no eye but his own, without the slightest attempt at style, with no care, even, for correct writing, not to be surpassed for naturalness and sincerity,—all disposition to carp and cavil dies away, and one is overpowered by the charm of a character of such purity, delicacy, and virtue. He fails neither in small things nor in great; he keeps watch over himself both that the great springs of action may be right in him, and that the minute details of action may be right also. How admirable in a hard-tasked ruler, and a ruler, too, with a passion for thinking and reading, is such a memorandum as the following:—

'Not frequently nor without necessity to say to any one, or to write in a letter, that I have no leisure; nor continually to excuse the neglect of duties

420

430

440

450

required by our relation to those with whom we live, by alleging urgent occupation.'

And, when that ruler is a Roman emperor, what an 'idea' is this to be written down and meditated by him:—

'The idea of a polity in which there is the same law for all, a polity administered with regard to equal rights and equal freedom of speech, and the idea of a kingly government which respects most of all the freedom of the governed.'

And, for all men who 'drive at practice,' what practical rules may not one accumulate out of these *Meditations:*—

'The greatest part of what we say or do being unnecessary, if a man takes this away, he will have more leisure and less uneasiness. Accordingly, on every occasion a man should ask himself: "Is this one of the unnecessary things?" Now a man should take away not only unnecessary acts, but also unnecessary thoughts, for thus superfluous acts will not follow after.'

And again:—

'We ought to check in the series of our thoughts everything that is without a purpose and useless, but most of all the over-curious feeling and the malignant; and a man should use himself to think of those things only about which if one should suddenly ask, "What hast thou now in thy thoughts?" with perfect openness thou mightest immediately answer, "This or That;" so that from thy words it should be plain that everything in thee is simple and benevolent, and such as befits a social animal, and one that cares not for thoughts about sensual enjoyments, or any rivalry or envy and suspicion, or anything else for which thou wouldst blush if thou shouldst say thou hadst it in thy mind.'

So, with a stringent practicalness worthy of Franklin, he discourses on his favourite text, *Let nothing be done without a purpose.* But it is when he enters the region where Franklin cannot follow him, when he utters his thoughts on the ground-motives of human action, that he is most interesting;—that he becomes the unique, the incomparable Marcus Aurelius. Christianity uses language very liable to be misunderstood when it seems to tell men to do good, not, certainly, from the vulgar motives of worldly interest, or vanity, or love of human praise, but that 'their Father which seeth in secret may reward them openly.' The motives of reward and punishment have come, from the misconception of language of this kind, to be strangely overpressed by many Christian moralists, to the deterioration and disfigurement of Christianity. Marcus Aurelius says, truly and nobly:—

'One man, when he has done a service to another, is ready to set it down to his account as a favour conferred. Another is not ready to do this, but still in his own mind he thinks of the man as his debtor, and he knows what he has done. A third in a manner does not even know what he has done, *but he is like a vine which has produced grapes, and seeks for nothing more after it has once produced its proper fruit.* As a horse when he has run, a dog when he has caught the game, a bee when it has made its honey, so a man when he has done a good act, does not call out for others to come 500 and see, but he goes on to another act, as a vine goes on to produce again the grapes in season. Must a man, then, be one of these, who in a manner acts thus without observing it? Yes.'

And again:—

'What more dost thou want when thou hast done a man a service? Art thou not content that thou hast done something conformable to thy nature, and dost thou seek to be paid for it, *just as if the eye demanded a recompense for seeing, or the feet for walking?*'

Christianity, in order to match morality of this strain, has to correct its apparent offers of external reward, and to say: *The kingdom of God is* 510 *within you.*

I have said that it is by its accent of emotion that the morality of Marcus Aurelius acquires a special character, and reminds one of Christian morality. The sentences of Seneca are stimulating to the intellect; the sentences of Epictetus are fortifying to the character; the sentences of Marcus Aurelius find their way to the soul. I have said that religious emotion has the power to *light up* morality: the emotion of Marcus Aurelius does not quite light up his morality, but it suffuses it; it has not power to melt the clouds of effort and austerity quite away, but it shines through them and glorifies them; it is a spirit, not so much of gladness and elation, as of gentleness 520 and sweetness; a delicate and tender sentiment, which is less than joy and more than resignation. He says that in his youth he learned from Maximus, one of his teachers, 'cheerfulness in all circumstances as well as in illness; *and a just admixture in the moral character of sweetness and dignity:*' and it is this very admixture of sweetness with his dignity which makes him so beautiful a moralist. It enables him to carry even into his observation of nature a delicate penetration, a sympathetic tenderness, worthy of Wordsworth; the spirit of such a remark as the following has hardly a parallel, so far as my knowledge goes, in the whole range of Greek and Roman literature:— 530

'Figs, when they are quite ripe, gape open; and in the ripe olives the very circumstance of their being near to rottenness adds a peculiar beauty to the fruit. And the ears of corn bending down, and the lion's eyebrows, and the foam which flows from the mouth of wild boars, and many other things,—

though they are far from being beautiful, in a certain sense,—still, because
they come in the course of nature, have a beauty in them, and they please
the mind; so that if a man should have a feeling and a deeper insight with
respect to the things which are produced in the universe, there is hardly
anything which comes in the course of nature which will not seem to him to
be in a manner disposed so as to give pleasure.'   540

But it is when his strain passes to directly moral subjects that his delicacy
and sweetness lend to it the greatest charm. Let those who can feel the
beauty of spiritual refinement read this, the reflection of an emperor who
prized mental superiority highly:—

'Thou sayest, "Men cannot admire the sharpness of thy wits." Be it so;
but there are many other things of which thou canst not say, "I am not
formed for them by nature." Show those qualities, then, which are altogether in thy power,—sincerity, gravity, endurance of labour, aversion to
pleasure, contentment with thy portion and with few things, benevolence,
frankness, no love of superfluity, freedom from trifling, magnanimity. Dost   550
thou not see how many qualities thou art at once able to exhibit, as to
which there is no excuse of natural incapacity and unfitness, and yet thou
still remainest voluntarily below the mark? Or art thou compelled, through
being defectively furnished by nature, to murmur, and to be mean, and to
flatter, and to find fault with thy poor body, and to try to please men,
and to make great display, and to be so restless in thy mind? No, indeed;
but thou mightest have been delivered from these things long ago. Only,
if in truth thou canst be charged with being rather slow and dull of comprehension, thou must exert thyself about this also, not neglecting nor
yet taking pleasure in thy dulness.'   560

The same sweetness enables him to fix his mind, when he sees the isolation and moral death caused by sin, not on the cheerless thought of the
misery of this condition, but on the inspiriting thought that man is blest
with the power to escape from it:—

'Suppose that thou hast detached thyself from the natural unity,—for
thou wast made by nature a part, but now thou hast cut thyself off,—yet
here is this beautiful provision, that it is in thy power again to unite thyself.
God has allowed this to no other part,—after it has been separated and cut
asunder, to come together again. But consider the goodness with which
he has privileged man; for he has put it in his power, when he has been   570
separated, to return and to be united and to resume his place.'

It enables him to control even the passion for retreat and solitude, so
strong in a soul like his, to which the world could offer no abiding city:—

'Men seek retreat for themselves, houses in the country, sea-shores, and mountains; and thou, too, art wont to desire such things very much. But this is altogether a mark of the most common sort of men, for it is in thy power whenever thou shalt choose to retire into thyself. For nowhere either with more quiet or more freedom from trouble does a man retire than into his own soul, particularly when he has within him such thoughts that by looking into them he is immediately in perfect tranquillity. Constantly, ⁵⁸⁰ then, give to thyself this retreat, and renew thyself; and let thy principles be brief and fundamental, which, as soon as thou shalt recur to them, will be sufficient to cleanse the soul completely, and to send thee back free from all discontent with the things to which thou returnest.'

Against this feeling of discontent and weariness, so natural to the great for whom there seems nothing left to desire or to strive after, but so enfeebling to them, so deteriorating, Marcus Aurelius never ceased to struggle. With resolute thankfulness he kept in remembrance the blessings of his lot; the true blessings of it, not the false:—

'I have to thank Heaven that I was subjected to a ruler and a father ⁵⁹⁰ (Antoninus Pius) who was able to take away all pride from me, and to bring me to the knowledge that it is possible for a man to live in a palace without either guards, or embroidered dresses, or any show of this kind; but that it is in such a man's power to bring himself very near to the fashion of a private person, without being for this reason either meaner in thought or more remiss in action with respect to the things which must be done for public interest. . . . I have to be thankful that my children have not been stupid nor deformed in body; that I did not make more proficiency in rhetoric, poetry, and the other studies, by which I should perhaps have been completely engrossed, if I had seen that I was making great ⁶⁰⁰ progress in them; . . . that I knew Apollonius, Rusticus, Maximus; . . . that I received clear and frequent impressions about living according to nature, and what kind of a life that is, so that, so far as depended on Heaven, and its gifts, help, and inspiration, nothing hindered me from forthwith living according to nature, though I still fall short of it through my own fault, and through not observing the admonitions of Heaven, and, I may almost say, its direct instructions; that my body has held out so long in such a kind of life as mine; that though it was my mother's lot to die young, she spent the last years of her life with me; that whenever I wished to help any man in his need, I was never told that I had not the means of ⁶¹⁰ doing it; that, when I had an inclination to philosophy, I did not fall into the hands of a sophist.'

And, as he dwelt with gratitude on these helps and blessings vouchsafed to him, his mind (so, at least, it seems to me) would sometimes revert with awe to the perils and temptations of the lonely height where he stood, to and ruin; and then he wrote down for himself such a warning entry as this, the lives of Tiberius, Caligula, Nero, Domitian, in their hideous blackness significant and terrible in its abruptness:—

'A black character, a womanish character, a stubborn character, bestial, childish, animal, stupid, counterfeit, scurrilous, fraudulent, tyrannical!'

Or this:—

'About what am I now employing my soul? On every occasion I must ask myself this question, and enquire, What have I now in this part of me which they call the ruling principle, and whose soul have I now?—that of a child, or of a young man, or of a weak woman, or of a tyrant, or of one of the lower animals in the service of man, or of a wild beast?'

The character he wished to attain he knew well, and beautifully he has marked it, and marked, too, his sense of shortcoming:—

'When thou hast assumed these names,—good, modest, true, rational, equal-minded, magnanimous,—take care that thou dost not change these names; and, if thou shouldst lose them, quickly return to them. If thou maintainest thyself in possession of these names without desiring that others should call thee by them, thou wilt be another being, and wilt enter on another life. For to continue to be such as thou hast hitherto been, and to be torn in pieces and defiled in such a life, is the character of a very stupid man, and one overfond of his life, and like those half-devoured fighters with wild beasts, who though covered with wounds and gore still entreat to be kept to the following day, though they will be exposed in the same state to the same claws and bites. Therefore fix thyself in the possession of these few names: and if thou art able to abide in them, abide as if thou wast removed to the Happy Islands.'

For all his sweetness and serenity, however, man's point of life 'between two infinities' (of that expression Marcus Aurelius is the real owner) was to him anything but a Happy Island, and the performances on it he saw through no veils of illusion. Nothing is in general more gloomy and monotonous than declamations on the hollowness and transitoriness of human life and grandeur: but here, too, the great charm of Marcus Aurelius, his emotion, comes in to relieve the monotony and to break through the gloom; and even on this eternally used topic he is imaginative, fresh, and striking:—

'Consider, for example, the times of Vespasian. Thou wilt see all these things, people marrying, bringing up children, sick, dying, warring, feasting, trafficking, cultivating the ground, flattering, obstinately arrogant, suspecting, plotting, wishing for somebody to die, grumbling about the present, loving, heaping up treasure, desiring to be consuls or kings. Well then, that life of these people no longer exists at all. Again, go to the times of Trajan. All is again the same. Their life too is gone. But chiefly thou shouldst think of those whom thou hast thyself known distracting themselves about idle things, neglecting to do what was in accordance with their proper constitution, and to hold firmly to this and to be content with it.' 660

Again:—

'The things which are much valued in life are empty, and rotten, and trifling; and people are like little dogs, biting one another, and little children quarrelling, crying, and then straightway laughing. But fidelity, and modesty, and justice, and truth, are fled

"Up to Olympus from the wide-spread earth."

What then is there which still detains thee here?'

And once more:—

'Look down from above on the countless herds of men, and their countless solemnities, and the infinitely varied voyagings in storms and calms, 670 and the differences among those who are born, who live together, and die. And consider too the life lived by others in olden time, and the life now lived among barbarous nations, and how many know not even thy name, and how many will soon forget it, and how they who perhaps now are praising thee will very soon blame thee, and that neither a posthumous name is of any value, nor reputation, nor anything else.'

He recognised, indeed, that (to use his own words) 'the prime principle in man's constitution is the social;' and he laboured sincerely to make not only his acts towards his fellow-men, but his thoughts also, suitable to this conviction:— 680

'When thou wishest to delight thyself, think of the virtues of those who live with thee; for instance, the activity of one, and the modesty of another, and the liberality of a third, and some other good quality of a fourth.'

Still, it is hard for a pure and thoughtful man to live in a state of rapture at the spectacle afforded to him by his fellow-creatures; above all it is hard, when such a man is placed as Marcus Aurelius was placed, and has had the meanness and perversity of his fellow-creatures thrust, in no common measure, upon his notice,—has had, time after time, to experience how 'within ten days thou wilt seem a god to those to whom thou art now a beast and an ape.' His true strain of thought as to his relations with his 690 fellow-men is rather the following. He has been enumerating the higher consolations which may support a man at the approach of death, and he goes on:—

'But if thou requirest also a vulgar kind of comfort which shall reach thy heart, thou wilt be made best reconciled to death by observing the objects from which thou art going to be removed, and the morals of those with whom thy soul will no longer be mingled. For it is no way right to be offended with men, but it is thy duty to care for them and to bear with them gently; and yet to remember that thy departure will not be from men who have the same principles as thyself. For this is the only thing, if there be any, which could draw us the contrary way and attach us to life, to be permitted to live with those who have the same principles as ourselves. But now thou seest how great is the distress caused by the difference of those who live together, so that thou mayest say: "Come quick, O death, lest perchance I too should forget myself." '

O faithless and perverse generation! how long shall I be with you? how long shall I suffer you? Sometimes this strain rises even to passion:—

'Short is the little which remains to thee of life. Live as on a mountain. Let men see, let them know, a real man, who lives as he was meant to live. If they cannot endure him, let them kill him. For that is better than to live as men do.'

It is remarkable how little of a merely local and temporary character, how little of those *scoriae* which a reader has to clear away before he gets to the precious ore, how little that even admits of doubt or question, the morality of Marcus Aurelius exhibits. Perhaps as to one point we must make an exception. Marcus Aurelius is fond of urging as a motive for man's cheerful acquiescence in whatever befalls him, that 'whatever happens to every man *is for the interest of the universal;*' that the whole contains nothing *which is not for its advantage;* that everything which happens to a man is to be accepted, 'even if it seems disagreeable, *because it leads to the health of the universe.*' And the whole course of the universe, he adds, has a providential reference to man's welfare: '*all other things have been made for the sake of rational beings.*' Religion has in all ages freely used this language, and it is not religion which will object to Marcus Aurelius's use of it; but science can hardly accept as severely accurate this employment of the terms *interest* and *advantage.* To a sound nature and a clear reason the proposition that things happen 'for the interest of the universal,' as men conceive of interest, may seem to have no meaning at all, and the proposition that 'all things have been made for the sake of rational beings' may seem to be false. Yet even to this language, not irresistibly cogent when it is thus absolutely used, Marcus Aurelius gives a turn which makes it true and useful, when he says: 'The ruling part of man can make a material for itself out of that which opposes it, as fire lays hold of what falls into it, and rises higher by means of this very material;'—when he says: 'What else are all things except exercises for the reason? Persevere then until thou shalt have made all things thine own, as the stomach which is strengthened makes all things its own, as the blazing fire makes flame and brightness out of everything that is thrown into it;'—when he says: 'Thou wilt not cease to be miserable till thy mind is in such a condition, that, what luxury is to those who enjoy pleasure, such shall be to thee, in every matter which presents itself, the doing of the things which are conformable to man's constitution; for a man ought to consider as an enjoyment everything which it is in his power to do according to his own nature,—and it is in his power everywhere.' In this sense it is, indeed, most true that 'all things have been made for the sake of rational beings;' that 'all things work together for good.'

In general, however, the action Marcus Aurelius prescribes is action which every sound nature must recognise as right, and the motives he assigns are motives which every clear reason must recognise as valid. And so he remains the especial friend and comforter of all clear-headed and scrupulous, yet pure-hearted and upward-striving men, in those ages most especially that walk by sight, not by faith, but yet have no open vision. He cannot give such souls, perhaps, all they yearn for, but he gives them much; and what he gives them, they can receive.

Yet no, it is not for what he thus gives them that such souls love him most! it is rather because of the emotion which lends to his voice so touching an accent, it is because he too yearns as they do for something unattained by him. What an affinity for Christianity had this persecutor of the Christians! The effusion of Christianity, its relieving tears, its happy self-sacrifice, were the very element, one feels, for which his soul longed; they were near him, they brushed him, he touched them, he passed them by. One feels, too, that the Marcus Aurelius one reads must still have remained, even had Christianity been fully known to him, in a great measure himself; he would have been no Justin;—but how would Christianity have affected him? in what measure would it have changed him? Granted that he might have found, like the *Alogi* of modern times, in the most beautiful of the Gospels, the Gospel which has leavened Christendom most powerfully, the Gospel of St. John, too much Greek metaphysics, too much *gnosis;* granted that this Gospel might have looked too like what he knew already to be a total surprise to him: what, then, would he have said to the Sermon on the Mount, to the twenty-sixth chapter of St. Matthew? What would have become of his notions of the *exitiabilis superstitio,* of the 'obstinacy of the Christians'? Vain question! yet the greatest charm of

Marcus Aurelius is that he makes us ask it. We see him wise, just, self-governed, tender, thankful, blameless; yet, with all this, agitated, stretching out his arms for something beyond,—*tendentemque manus ripae ulterioris amore.*

THE END

TEXTUAL NOTES

INTRODUCTION
TO THE TEXTUAL NOTES

The following discussion concerns the development of the text of *Essays in Criticism: First Series,* and in particular the evidence which establishes the text of 1875 as the version which represents Arnold's final intention for the volume. For the choice of the 1875 edition as the authoritative text is not an arbitrary one, but one which rests on strong internal and external evidence. As the textual notes in the present edition clearly demonstrate, Arnold introduced significant alterations into the texts of each of the three editions of *Essays in Criticism: First Series* which appeared during his own lifetime. But whereas he continued to revise the text considerably after the editions of 1865 and 1869 appeared, he ceased to do so after the publication of the third edition in 1875.[1]

[1] This matter of textual revision appears to have aroused little curiosity among Arnold scholars. Prior to this edition, completed in 1958, no thorough study of the text of *Essays in Criticism: First Series* had been made. Since the Miles and Smith edition contains no textual annotation whatever, E. K. Brown's chapter in his *Studies in the Text of Matthew Arnold's Prose Works* (Paris, 1935) represented the sole pre-

A few examples will serve to illustrate the argument from internal evidence. In the 1865 text of "The Function of Criticism at the Present Time," Arnold inserted a passage explaining his original statement about Renan's effort at a "fresh synthesis of the New Testament data." [2] Both the edition of 1865 and that of 1869 read: "the taking them [these data] out from under the old, adoptive, traditional, unspiritual point of view and placing them under a new one." But for the text of 1875 Arnold supplied a more effective reading: "the taking them out from under the old, traditional, conventional point of view and placing them under a new one." Similarly, in the essay on Spinoza, Arnold had asserted in the texts of 1865 and 1869: "He [Spinoza] does not give us his own opinion about the Bible's fundamental character." For the third edition Arnold altered this to: "He nowhere distinctly gives his own opinion about the Bible's fundamental character." Still another significant alteration occurs in the same essay. In a section from "The Bishop and the Philosopher," [3] first inserted in the revised version of the essay which appeared in 1869, Arnold wrote:

> A court of literature can never be very severe to Voltaire: with that inimitable wit and clear sense of his, he cannot write a page in which the fullest head may not find something suggestive: still, because, with all his wit and clear sense, he handles religious ideas wholly without the power of edification, his fame as a great man is equivocal.

In an effort to make his meaning more precise, Arnold reworked this for the edition of 1875 to read:

> A court of literature can never be very severe to Voltaire: with that inimitable wit and clear sense of his, he cannot write a page in which the fullest head may not find something suggestive: still, because, handling religious ideas, he yet, with all his wit and clear sense, handles them wholly without the power of edification, his fame as a great man is equivocal.

The second reading directs the reader's attention much more surely to the point which Arnold is trying to make, namely, that one class of ideas, at

vious attempt to deal with the text of this work. Unfortunately, Brown's study of this particular book is incomplete and inaccurate. In the present discussion of the textual alterations of the essays, Brown's chapter will be considered in some detail in order that his conclusions may be corrected and completed.

   R. H. Super's excellent third volume, *Matthew Arnold: Lectures and Essays in Criticism* (Ann Arbor, 1962), contains the most recent textual criticism of this work. Professor Super's volume is not, however, intended as an edition of the complete *Essays in Criticism: First Series*.

   [2] For the context of this and succeeding passages, see the textual notes.

   [3] For an explanation of the rather complicated textual development of this essay, see pp. 234–36 of this introduction and the textual notes on "Spinoza and the Bible."

least, must be treated with something more than mere "wit and clear sense."

An interesting alteration, made for the sake of clarity, occurs in the text of "Marcus Aurelius":

> The outer and palpable causes of the misrepresentation were . . . for the Roman statesman, the character of secret assemblages which the meetings of the Christian community wore, under a State-system as jealous of unauthorised associations as the State-system of modern France.

In context this construction is extremely awkward; while trying to achieve a certain structural balance, Arnold has confused and obscured his meaning. In the 1875 text an explanatory phrase was added in order to make the assertion about the Roman statesman a separate sentence:

> For the Roman statesman, the cause of mistake lay in that character of secret assemblages which the meetings of the Christian community wore, under a State-system as jealous of unauthorised associations as is the State-system of modern France.

Many more such revisions for the edition of 1875 will be found in the textual notes which follow; the number and character of these changes furnish conclusive evidence that Arnold considered none of the previous texts of *Essays in Criticism: First Series* as a final version.

Arnold's own observations regarding necessary revisions for the 1875 edition can be found in his letters to his publisher, Alexander Macmillan. In a letter of July 13, 1875, Arnold wrote:

> I think you had better send me here [Athenaeum Club] a copy of the Essays —I have not got one. I should like to look through them—there may be one or two personalities to strike out;—as I draw nearer to my bitter end, the desire increases in me to die at peace with all men. I have told the Cornhill people to send me the "Persian Passion Play" and I will look through that too.

A little later, in a letter dated August 9, 1875, Arnold pronounced his work of revision completed:

> By book-post I send the copy of the new edition of the Essays. I have been carefully through the Persian Passion Play—It will come in capitally. I have also improved many things in the original scheme of the Essays.

Finally, toward the end of 1883, the year in which the third edition had first found an American market, Frederick Macmillan proposed the following scheme to Arnold:

> The English Edition of your "Essays in Criticism" is nearly sold out, and we are therefore reprinting it in the same shape as before. I do not suppose you have the time to make any alterations in it just now, besides which it would

hardly be fair to your buyers in the United States to bring out an altered English Edition so soon after the appearance of the new American Edition.

These extracts [4] suffice as external evidence to verify Arnold's claim on the title page of the 1875 volume, "Third Edition / Revised and Enlarged," and to substantiate the assertion that the last text over which he labored was that of 1875.

Some consideration should now be given to subsequent editions of *Essays in Criticism: First Series* in relation to the edition of 1875. Concerning its own later editions, the Macmillan Company of London has supplied this information:

> [Our] first American edition was printed in the United Kingdom in October, 1883; it was, as far as we can tell from our records, set up afresh and stereo plates were then made from it. The fourth English edition was printed from the same plates as the American edition and published in 1884. Further reprints were made from the same plates in subsequent years.[5]

The editions of 1884, 1886, 1888, 1891, and 1894 are, then, in format, page-for-page, word-for-word reprints of the 1883 edition,[6] with no deliberate alterations beyond the correction of a few obvious misprints. One must conclude, therefore, that Arnold considered the text of the third edition as a finished product.

Prior to the appearance of Professor Super's volume in 1962, copies of the essays generally available consisted of the edition of 1883 and its reprints, the Eversley Series volumes, and Volume III of the Macmillan Edition de Luxe of *The Works of Matthew Arnold,* which appeared in 1903.[7] Although these editions supplied the 1875 text, no one of them

---

[4] This information was supplied by Professor William E. Buckler, of New York University. See his *Matthew Arnold's Books: Towards a Publishing Diary* (Geneva, 1958), pp. 72–74. The last excerpt is from a letter dated November 29, 1883.

A volume containing the original collection of essays and also the lectures on Homer had been published in Boston by Ticknor and Fields in 1865.

[5] This is a passage from a letter dated January 9, 1957, which is in the possession of the present editor.

[6] E. K. Brown incorrectly states that the editions of 1883 and following are "page-for-page, word-for-word reprints" of the 1875 edition; see *Studies in Text,* p. 1.

Although the Eversley Series editions, first published in 1895, are identical in format with the 1883 edition, it can be demonstrated that they were not printed from the 1883 stereo plates. See, for example, page 11, line 12, of the 1905 Eversley edition, in which "the natives" should read "the motives" as in the 1883 edition. The Eversley Series appeared in 1895, 1896, 1898, 1900, 1902, 1903, 1905, 1907, 1910, 1911, and again in a "New Eversley" Series in 1935–37.

[7] In the succeeding discussion, the abbreviations used are to be interpreted as follows: *CH: Cornhill Magazine; NR: National Review; VIC: Victoria Magazine; FR: Fraser's Magazine; MACM: Macmillan's Magazine;* 65: first edition, 1865; 69: second edition, 1869; 75: third edition, 1875; 83: first American edition, 1883; *DL:* Volume III of Macmillan's Edition de Luxe, 1903; 05: Eversley Series edition, 1905.

could be styled an authentic edition of the work. A brief examination of certain passages in three editions, those of 1883, 1905 (Eversley Series), and the third volume of the Macmillan Edition de Luxe will reveal a surprising amount of textual corruption.

Perhaps the most interesting error of this sort occurs in the essay "Spinoza and the Bible," in the section where Arnold weighs the strengths of Spinoza's "rules for Biblical interpretation" against the weaknesses of contemporary exegesis; the correct reading, based on the texts of the periodical essay and the first and second editions is as follows:

> the perpetual reproach of impurity and rejection cast
> upon the mass of the Hebrew nation by the exclusive
> priesthood of the tribe of Levi? What can be more . . .

In the edition of 1875, however, the compositor has accidentally omitted the second of the three lines just quoted, and the resulting reading is completely unintelligible. Evidently Arnold never saw to its correction personally, since the attempts to rectify it in later editions are clumsy. At any rate, only a careless search—or no search at all—was made in earlier editions for the original reading; 83, *DL,* and 05, for instance, simply insert "upon the" between "cast" and "priesthood," with this result:

> the perpetual reproach
> of impurity and rejection cast upon the priesthood
> of the tribe of Levi? What can be more . . .

Obviously the entire sense of Arnold's remarks has been distorted, the point about the sacerdotal aristocracy completely lost.

In "The Literary Influence of Academies," another error first introduced in 75 persisted in 83. In speaking of the "conscience in literary matters" peculiar to the French, Arnold remarked on the necessity of a "like deference" to authority in both moral and intellectual questions. In 75, however, the word "difference" was substituted for the original word "deference." The same error occurs in 83, though it has been corrected in *DL* and 05. Likewise, at the conclusion of the essay on Eugénie de Guérin, the erroneous reading "as here are in the cloister" occurs first in 75 and is repeated in 83, being corrected in *DL* and 05. Still another error introduced in 75 occurs in "Heinrich Heine": "And that in which Germany most fails, and by failing in which" (*CH,* 65, 69) becomes "and by falling in which" (75, 83), an error which is rectified in *DL* and 05.

Two misprints occurred on facing pages of "Joubert" in 75. In the paragraph concerning the Jansenist doctrine of grace, Arnold's translation reads "a dew of heaven" in *NR,* 65, 69, 83, *DL,* and 05, but "a due of heaven" in 75. On the next page of the third edition text an error occurs in the reading "the maxims of Joubert on purely literary subjects" (*NR*, 65, 69). In 75 "the maxims of Joubert *are* purely literary subjects" is substituted. This error also appears in 83, *DL*, and 05. Yet another case of this kind can be found at the end of "Marcus Aurelius," where Arnold states that "the motives [Marcus Aurelius] assigns are motives which every clear reason must recognise as valid" (*VIC*, 65, 69). In 75 "motives which *very* clear reason must recognise" appears. This error continues in 83, but it has been corrected in *DL* and 05.

One alteration which begins with the 75 text requires special consideration, since it cannot definitely be dismissed as a mistake. In "The Function of Criticism at the Present Time," Arnold had originally written: "to make one of the party of movement" (*NR*, 65, 69). The second "of" is omitted in 75, 83, *DL*, and 05, so that the present reading is "to make one of the party movement." It is difficult to decide whether this change is a simple error or a deliberate alteration of Arnold's, since both readings are quite intelligible. One is inclined to think, however, that the omission was unintentional, since Arnold's context at this point does not concern the abstract notion of "party movement" or partisanship so much as the particular party which he is describing as intent upon social movement of any kind, at any price.

Other errors intrude for the first time in the text of 83. Early in the essay on Heine, for example, one such instance occurs. The reading "no one recognises his genius more admiringly than I do" (*CH*, 65, 69, 75) becomes "no one recognises his genius more *admirably* than I do." This error persists in *DL*, and 05. In "Pagan and Medieval Religious Sentiment," "the factitious quarrel" (*CH*, 65, 69, 75) was altered to "the fictitious quarrel" (83, *DL*, 05). This reading is sufficiently accurate to render the error rather difficult to detect. A similar mistake appears in the essay on Joubert. "He says of an article" (*NR*, 65, 69, 75) becomes "he says *in* an article" (83, *DL*, 05). This time the error is more serious, since it results in a misrepresentation of the authorship and content of the article in question.

Two last errors invite mention, errors of simple omission. The first occurred as early as 69, in "Pagan and Mediaeval Religious Sentiment." The reading of *CH* and 65 is: "all that the critical spirit shrinks from." But 69, 75, 83, *DL*, and 05 all omit "spirit," with the resulting reading: "all that the critical shrinks from." And in the essay on Marcus Aurelius, Arnold's comment upon the historical interest of the Emperor's goodness of character has been damaged. "History presents one or two other sovereigns eminent for their goodness," Arnold had stated in *VIC*, 65, 69, and

75. But the word "other" disappears from 83, 91, *DL,* and 05, making the entire sentence a bit lame.

These are small details, it is true, but a survey such as this is not without value. For one thing, it indicates to what a remarkable extent inaccuracies can crowd into a fairly recent text. Indeed, no text is safe, but the more complicated the textual history, the greater the risk.

SIGNIFICANCE OF ARNOLD'S REVISIONS OF ESSAYS IN CRITICISM: FIRST SERIES.

Arnold's revisions of the text of *Essays in Criticism: First Series* constitute a useful body of material for the Arnold scholar. The data thus assembled afford excellent opportunities for studying his prose-techniques at first hand. After examining E. K. Brown's *Studies in the Text of Matthew Arnold's Prose Works,* Professor Howard F. Lowry published this analysis of Arnold's methods of revision:

> Arnold revised his work for various reasons: to remove obvious digressions; to make corrections of fact in the light of fresh knowledge; to quench flaming ubiquities; to establish a better temper towards men and ideas; to attain more of that "regularity, precision, uniformity, and balance" which was esteemed by a poet who had discovered, "How hard it is to write prose." [8]

Although Professor Lowry is here generalizing about the whole of Arnold's prose, each of his observations can be applied specifically to the text of *Essays in Criticism: First Series.* For instance, Arnold soon thought better of his witty but unnecessary digressions about Mr. Wright, Mr. Stephen, and Mr. Kinglake, excising nearly all this banter from the second edition. He also saw to the correction of such an error of fact as that on the supposed fate of Guérin's *Bacchante,* this time for the first edition. Then, lest indignation against Bishop Colenso and his inadequate ideas on Scriptural interpretation destroy disinterestedness, Arnold chose to ignore the Bishop altogether while he reorganized his Spinoza material into a suitable essay. And an infinity of scarcely perceptible alterations reveals Arnold's determination to achieve a kind of artistic perfection in the writing of prose.[9]

[8] See his review of Brown's book in *Modern Language Notes,* LII (November, 1937), 536.

[9] Not all these minute alterations are listed in the textual notes to this edition, which rather features the more extensive revisions, especially those which establish the 1875 text as the authoritative one.

All but the last of Professor Lowry's observations concern the negative side of revision: correction, deletion, and the like. In revising *Essays in Criticism: First Series,* however, Arnold nearly always aimed at something more positive.

First of all, a number of alterations were necessary in order to adapt the periodical essays to publication in book form.[10] Actually, the periodical texts themselves furnish important evidence that from the beginning Arnold intended the lectures to serve as so many illustrations of the "new criticism" he was determined to inaugurate. True, most of them were first designed for the lecture hall: "I am convinced that the novelty of one's subjects acts as a great and useful stimulus," Arnold wrote on December 12, 1863, after delivering his paper on Joubert to his students of poetry.[11] But he had also another end, publication, in view: "I am obliged always to think, in composing my lectures, of the public who will read me, not of the dead bones who will hear me, or my spirit would fail."[12]

The Spinoza essay shows the most extensive revision and is the only essay in which Arnold made a radical change in the original structure. The 1865 edition contained the article, "A Word More about Spinoza," almost exactly as it had appeared in *Macmillan's Magazine* for December, 1863, so that it covered only about sixteen and a quarter pages in the volume. In 1869 the revised essay required thirty-five pages, since two long sections from "The Bishop and the Philosopher," an article which had appeared in *Macmillan's Magazine* in January, 1863, were inserted at strategic points.

10 For most of the essays, the periodical texts are not the original versions. All but three of the nine essays collected for the first edition originated as Oxford lectures; those on Eugénie de Guérin, Spinoza, and Marcus Aurelius grew out of other circumstances.

In a letter to his mother, dated March 17, 1864, Arnold mentioned his intent to have "Pagan and Christian Religious Sentiment" appear "with a good deal about Protestantism left out . . . as it could not be stated fully enough quite to explain and secure itself" (*Letters,* I, 265–66). Similarly, Arnold's lecture entitled "The Influence of Academies on National Life and Spirit" underwent considerable revision before it appeared in the *Cornhill Magazine* as "The Literary Influence of Academies." Arnold's letter to George Smith (June 25, 1864) mentions "two or three pages at the beginning about the limits of criticism which might as well be left out" of the article, as well as a censure of Ruskin which he agreed to soften at the publisher's request. Earlier letters, dated July 10 and July 13, 1863, authorize similar alterations in the essay on Heinrich Heine. See William Buckler, *Publishing Diary,* pp. 64–66.

Doubtless Arnold altered each lecture somehow before it appeared for the first time in print, but no original manuscripts are now available. The textual history of *Essays in Criticism: First Series* must begin with the periodical papers.

11 See Arnold's letter to his mother for this date; *Letters,* I, 243.

12 The quotation is from Arnold's letter to his mother, June 16, 1863, written after he had delivered his lecture on Heine to an Oxford audience. See *Letters,* I, 226.

E. K. Brown commends Arnold's restructuring of the essay as "an artistic *tour de force*." [13] But it is only from a distance that critics have begun to concentrate on the clever "scissors-and-paste" accomplishment while regarding the content of the essay with equanimity. A *North British* critic of Arnold's day, for example, saw "Joubert, the French Coleridge" as "the best paper in the book," but contemptuously dismissed Arnold's original version of the Spinoza essay as "plainly the most unsatisfactory and inadequate." [14] Similarly, a writer for the *North American Review* spoke of the essay on Joubert as "next in the order of excellence" to the first two essays, judging "the others, with the exception, perhaps, of that on Spinoza," as of about equal merit. [15] And the *British Quarterly* scorned altogether Arnold's "attempted replies to Bishop Colenso" as "the most unsatisfactory of all." [16]

Whatever the current reaction, Arnold's development of the Spinoza essay from the original periodical papers particularly reveals a growing recognition of the value of consolidation, of assembling facts and arguments in their totality and then letting the reader judge. This "sinuous, easy, unpolemical mode of proceeding," [17] Arnold was to adopt deliberately in an effort to persuade without antagonizing.

One aspect of Arnold's work on the Spinoza essay deserves incidental mention here. Shortly after the appearance of "The Bishop and the Philosopher" in *Macmillan's Magazine,* Arnold spoke of the necessity of defending the position he had adopted in this article. His plans included "something for *Macmillan,* to remove the misrepresentation of my doctrine about edifying the many," and, at a later date, an article for the *Times.*[18] The *Macmillan* article was, of course, "Dr. Stanley's *Lectures on the Jewish Church,*" which appeared in the number for February, 1863. But so far the article in the *Times* has never been discovered, if, indeed, it was ever printed in that paper. Hints of it appear from time to time in Arnold's letters, notebooks, and diaries, but the article itself still eludes all seekers. In his letter of April 17, 1863, Arnold referred to the article as finished, expressing some doubt as to whether the *Times* could spare him a column

---

[13] *Studies in Text,* p. 11.
[14] See the review of *Essays in Criticism: First Series* in the *North British Review,* XLII (March, 1865), 158–82; the judgment quoted appears on p. 170.
[15] See *North American Review,* CI (July, 1865), 206–13; the quotation is from p. 206.
[16] See *British Quarterly Review,* XLI (April, 1865), 544.
[17] See *Letters,* I, 282, 255.
[18] See Arnold's letter to his mother, January 7, 1863; *Letters,* I, 208–9.

from the current Parliamentary session.[19] The *Times* almost certainly did not do so, but in his diary for Saturday, June 6, 1863, Arnold wrote: "Correct Spinoza article." [20] It seems unlikely that this entry refers to proofs for "A Word More about Spinoza," which was to appear in *Macmillan's Magazine* the following December. Besides, entries throughout February and April, 1863, specify a "Spinoza article for the *Times*," which had definitely been completed by mid-April, 1863.

Another clue appears in Arnold's letter of November 19, 1863, when he observes: "I am not quite pleased with my *Times* Spinoza as an article for *Macmillan;* it has too much of the brassiness and smartness of a *Times* article in it. This should be a warning to me not to write for the *Times,* or indeed for any newspaper." [21] This sounds as if the *Times* had accepted the article by that time. On the other hand, Arnold may simply have been using the expression "*Times* Spinoza" to designate a rejected article which he intended to rewrite for periodical publication. In any case, the "*Times* Spinoza" would prove an interesting counterpart to the third *Macmillan* article, which ultimately appeared in the 1865 edition as "Spinoza."

In adapting "The Function of Criticism at the Present Time" to book form, Arnold made one important and lengthy insertion: he expanded the conclusion to include two pages defining his notion of the meaning of "criticism." This definition was intended to be the operative principle from which all the other essays should proceed; the first essay is, therefore, legislative, while the others are illustrative. A special paragraph set down in unmistakable terms the kind of unity Arnold intended for his collection, a unity to be sought in the very definite idea he had of "the critic's business." For Arnold, criticism meant judgment, and "growth in perfection" was a matter of literary conscience. Without such an insertion as this, the volume would have amounted simply to a random collection; with it, Arnold's design for the book becomes perfectly clear.

In other instances where Arnold concerned himself with book form, he merely found it necessary to move away from the particular situation which had originally stimulated the essay. In "Maurice de Guérin," for example, Arnold removed as inappropriate a prediction that Guérin would remain a slender classic. Guérin's reception by English reviewers indicated otherwise. In fact, by 1875, Arnold saw fit to alter the whole sense of this passage about Guérin's reputation. He did it by the omission of a single

[19] See *Letters,* I, 221.
[20] This information has been supplied by Mr. William B. Guthrie, of the University of Richmond, Virginia, who has recently edited Arnold's *Diaries.*
[21] *Letters,* I, 242.

word: "To make my English readers see" became "to make English readers see" since it was no longer a question of the reader's fleeting contact with Arnold's essay alone. On the contrary, Guérin was holding his own quite independently of Arnold by that time.[22] The essays on Eugénie de Guérin and Spinoza likewise required modifications of this kind as various editions of their works appeared.

A second significant feature of Arnold's mode of revision is his careful clarification of certain arguments by removing ambiguities arising from the manner in which these arguments had been expressed earlier. One such instance occurs in "The Function of Criticism at the Present Time," where Arnold compares the period of the French Revolution with that of the English Renaissance. After indicating that both periods were times of "immense stir," Arnold concludes that the resemblance ceases right there. When looking for sheer intellectual vitality, "disinterestedly intellectual and spiritual movements," one must search the earlier half of the eighteenth century, "France under the old *régime,*" a time which "told far more powerfully upon the mind of Europe than the France of the Revolution." In the periodical text, Arnold's emphasis on the ideational basis of the French Revolution really outweighs his regret at "the political, practical character" these ideas quickly took. By pointing up an analogy between the France of the earlier half of the eighteenth century and England at the time of the Renaissance as periods of "great movement of mind," and then contrasting these two periods with that of the French Revolution, which he designates a period of "great movement of feeling," Arnold enables his reader to grasp the point more readily.

A similar case occurs in the Spinoza essay in a section dealing with the "higher criticism." Here content as well as expression is improved by a brief insertion. Arnold had been scoffed at by a number of reviewers for insulting the English intelligence; his question "What, then?" had proved the object of special contempt.[23] In the text of 1869 Arnold had acknowledged that, since verbal inspiration of the Scripture was being contested, "the general culture of Europe" wished to know: "What, then?" Arnold dealt with this problem by inserting a series of five questions demonstrating

[22] See, for example, "French Thought," *Saturday Review,* XV (February 14, 1863), 196–97. Actually Eugénie's fame spread more rapidly than Guérin's own, and he was better known as Eugénie de Guérin's brother. See the reviews of Eugénie de Guérin's works in the *Saturday Review,* XVI (August 15, 1863), 221; and in the *Edinburgh Review,* CXX (July, 1864) 249–67.

[23] See W. R. Greg's "Truth *versus* Edification," *Westminster Review,* NS XXIII (April, 1863), 503–16; and "The Bishop and the Professor," *Examiner,* January 10, 1863, p. 20.

how many practical difficulties could actually arise: the relationship of the Bible to literature, for example, or the antipathy toward conventional Christianity in minds dominated by the "modern spirit." Not only did the new material serve to reinforce his argument by presenting specific problems to be considered, but it also improved the passage rhetorically by the cumulative impact of five questions confronting the reader in rapid succession.

Another confusing passage, this one in the periodical text of "A Persian Passion Play," was improved for the text of the third edition, the only other version in which it appeared. Arnold had originally remarked on the tendency of popular Christianity to abuse the nature of the Bible, identifying its tactics with those of users of the Koran:

> From the circumstances of its origin, the Koran has the intensely dogmatic character . . . which the Bible has not. Therefore, to get the sort of power which all this gives, popular Christianity is apt to treat the Bible as if it was just like the Koran; and because of this sort of power, among the little known and little advanced races of the great African continent, the Mahometan missionaries are said to be much more successful than ours.

This obviously involves a contradiction, since, as the case is presented, there is no reason why either group should eclipse the other. By removing the distracting reference to the excesses of popular Christianity, Arnold rendered the passage more intelligible and, of course, more convincing:

> From the circumstances of its origin, the Koran has the intensely dogmatic character . . . which the Bible has not. Among the little known and little advanced races of the great African continent, the Mahometan missionaries, by reason of the sort of power which this character of the Koran gives, are said to be more successful than ours.

A third feature of Arnold's revisions of the text of *Essays in Criticism: First Series* is what might be termed an attempt at self-defense. Two such instances arise from Arnold's obsession with the importance of "the idea" in and for itself. In "The Function of Criticism at the Present Time," Arnold had originally argued for "a fresh synthesis of the New Testament data" in the manner of Renan. For the text of the first edition Arnold felt it necessary to explain himself further: this was not a question of exploding hypotheses and disillusioning the many, as Bishop Colenso delighted in doing; neither was it a case of dismissing the whole issue as unscientific. What was needed was a delicate balance of these extremes, taking the New Testament data seriously but intelligently, reworking them until they again made adequate sense. Here, of course, one perceives the first stirrings of *Literature and Dogma*.

In his essay on Heine, Arnold restored in the first edition a passage on the surface advantages of Philistinism, immediately following Heine's remarks on Cobbett.[24] One can easily imagine Arnold, the "transcendentalist," defending himself against the charge of being unrealistic. Arnold's esoteric theories have no practical value, the critics clamored.[25] In this passage Arnold again took the opportunity of arguing that no achievement is really valuable unless it can be related to a true idea. Whereas the "prosperity and liberty of modern England" seem preferable to "the government of Herr von Bismarck," the modern Philistine had only proved himself more fortunate, not more intelligent, in these matters.

In at least one case Arnold fought a losing battle. Reviewers had objected so strenuously to Arnold's "dogmatic" assumption that "instruction for the few" constituted a valid norm for a literary work, that Arnold refrained, for the sake of peace, from reviving it. In "The Bishop and the Philosopher" Arnold had originally written:

> Unction Spinoza's work has not; that name does not precisely fit any quality which it exhibits. But he is instructive and suggestive, even to the most instructed thinker; and to give him full right of citizenship in the Republic of Letters this is enough.[26]

When revising this material for insertion into the expanded version of the Spinoza essay, to be included in the 1869 edition, Arnold carefully excised the second sentence, confining his remarks to the necessity of edification in the treatment of religious subjects.

A similar retreat occurs in Arnold's comparison of the poetic talents of Guérin and Keats in the essay on Eugénie de Guérin. The first three texts of the essay have: "[Guérin's] talent, exquisite as that of Keats, with less of sunlight, abundance, and fertility in it than that of Keats, but with more of distinction and power." For the third edition Arnold modified this to read: "[Guérin's] talent, exquisite as that of Keats, with much less of sunlight, abundance, inventiveness, and facility in it than that of Keats, but with more of distinction and power." Arnold is here obviously bowing to necessity, deferring to the demands of readers who resented an alleged preference of Guérin to Keats.

One last type of revision, the stylistic alteration, also deserves consideration, since these alterations often reveal something significant about

---

[24] George Smith had urged several deletions before the publication of this essay in his *Cornhill Magazine* for August, 1863. See W. E. Buckler, *Publishing Diary,* p. 64.

[25] See, for example, Fitzjames Stephen, "Mr. Matthew Arnold and His Countrymen," *Saturday Review,* XVIII (December 3, 1864), 684–85 (pp. 328–32 below).

[26] See *Macmillan's Magazine,* VII (January, 1863), 254.

Arnold's techniques in writing prose. Examination of the textual notes against the final text of *Essays in Criticism: First Series* will give the full effect of Arnold's persistent reworking of his expression. A few instances in which the revision is of special interest will be discussed here.

One of the most striking changes of this type is the change from "Renaissance" to "Renascence." As early as June, 1868, Arnold had introduced this new spelling, in an article which later became Chapter Four of *Culture and Anarchy,* under the title "Hebraism and Hellenism." Here, in a footnote, Arnold explained: "I have ventured to give to the foreign word *Renaissance*—destined to become of more common use amongst us as the movement which it denotes comes, as it will come, increasingly, to interest us,—an English form." [27] Arnold did not introduce this new spelling into the 1869 text of the *Essays,* however; it first appeared in 1875.

Another alteration in "The Function of Criticism at the Present Time" indicates that Arnold was decidedly more intent upon effective writing than upon mere accuracy. One method of keeping up to date was his free use of such casual expressions as "the other day," "a little while back," and the like. For the third edition Arnold changed the reading "soon after reading Mr. Roebuck" to "immediately after reading Mr. Roebuck." Yet Arnold had been "reading Mr. Roebuck" in the *Times* for August 19, 1864, while no report about Wragg could possibly have appeared in any paper before September 10, 1864. One is tempted to conclude that Arnold's expressions indicating time ought not to be taken too literally.

Arnold's sensitivity to vividness as well as to sound in his prose accounts for a great number of stylistic changes, several of which occur in "The Function of Criticism at the Present Time." In his description of the infamous English Divorce Court, "its crowded benches" was replaced by "its crowded trials." "A period of check and suppression" became "a period of blight and suppression," while creative activity was elevated from "the true function of man" to "the highest function of man." Critics progressed from a sphere "perfectly unintelligent" to one "perfectly unvital," and Byron, elsewhere demoted from an "English nobleman" to an "English gentleman," was not simply "one-toned" but totally "empty of matter." Again, in "Pagan and Mediaeval Religious Sentiment," the "Syrian spikenard"

[27] See the edition of *Culture and Anarchy* by J. Dover Wilson (Cambridge, 1955), p. 139. In its original periodical form this passage read: "the great movement which goes by the name of the Renaissance (but why should we not give to this foreign word, destined to become of more common use amongst us, a more English form, and say Renascence?). See "Anarchy and Authority," *Cornhill Magazine,* XVII (June, 1868), 751.

became first "Syrian unguent" (65) and finally "Syrian ointment" (69), while the "law of supernatural love" was eventually designated rather one of "supersensual love." One last instance illustrates how the alteration of a single word improved the sound of a whole paragraph:

> But right . . . [implies] free assent of the will; we are not ready for right . . . until we have attained this sense of seeing it and willing it. The way in which for us it may change and transform force . . . will depend on the way in which we see it and will it.

It was not until Arnold was once again intent on polishing the text of "The Function of Criticism at the Present Time" for the 1875 edition that the use here of "will" in two senses disturbed him. In the last of the sentences just quoted, Arnold altered the reading to "should depend on the way in which we see it and will it," smoothing both sound and sense considerably. The textual notes which follow should thus offer useful insights into the methods of Arnold's literary craftsmanship, and even, occasionally, into his literary aims as well. Their purpose, after all, is to enable the reader to see what Arnold was really about while he was preparing "the central book, so to speak, of his life." [28]

A NOTE ON E. K. BROWN'S STUDIES IN THE TEXT OF
MATTHEW ARNOLD'S PROSE WORKS

Although Professor Brown's diligence and devotion to Arnold's prose are most apparent in his study of Arnold's prose texts, some observations regarding his work on *Essays in Criticism: First Series* are in order. Necessary corrections of his treatment of six of these essays, "The Function of Criticism at the Present Time," "The Literary Influence of Academies," "Maurice de Guérin," "Eugénie de Guérin," "Pagan and Mediaeval Religious Sentiment," and "Joubert," will be briefly noted.

Because "The Function of Criticism at the Present Time" was to serve as Arnold's introduction to the series, this essay underwent its most extensive revision for the first edition. Brown's remarks on Arnold's famous footnotes in the 1865 text of this essay must be amended. Arnold attached five footnotes to this essay in 1865, and not four as Brown states.[29] The first note did refer to critical introductions, and another vindicated Arnold's

---

[28] Herbert W. Paul thus describes the *Essays* in his *Matthew Arnold* (New York, 902), p. 74.
[29] *Studies in Text*, pp. 5–7.

remarks about Bishop Colenso. But a third footnote, also concerned with the Colenso controversy, appeared in the 1865 edition (pp. 28–29); it was not inserted in 1869, as Brown asserts. Finally, two long notes which expostulate with Fitzjames Stephen were inserted in 1865 but deleted for the second edition and for all subsequent editions.

For "The Literary Influence of Academies," the most interesting revisions are, as Brown points out, those begun in 1865 and completed in 1869 in Arnold's portrait of Kinglake. Once again, however, Brown's information regarding Arnold's insertion of footnotes is inaccurate; the note on Palgrave's *Handbook* and that in defense of Arnold's interpretation of Renan were both inserted in 1865. Only the note about the *Times's* spelling of "diocese" was added in 1869.

Arnold's revision of the essays on the de Guérins was, as Brown points out, largely confined to improving his translation of passages quoted from their writings. Contrary to Brown's statement, however, Arnold's introductory sentence in the essay on Maurice de Guérin was never "shorn of its most diverting member, the 'now'." [30] And in a later chapter, "A Note on Matters of Style," Brown again slips in noting revisions in the Guérin essays. Lamennais's "impropriety" does not occur in the essay on Eugénie at all, but rather in that on her brother. The error, furthermore, did not result from a confusion between "l'est" and "l'ouest," but probably from a mistranslation of the idiom "du côté de l'orient" in the original text of Guérin's letter to Eugénie from Paris, April 9, 1834. For the sake of accuracy it should be noted also that no alteration of the word "trunk" occurred in 1865, since the periodical text already had the correct reading.[31]

One other revision in the essay on Maurice de Guérin, though unnoticed by Brown, deserves some consideration. In drawing from Sainte-Beuve's reviews of Guérin's *Reliquiae* and *Journal,* reviews from which M. Trébutien had fashioned a prefatory memoir for his editions, Arnold reproduced an error originated by Sainte-Beuve. In mentioning Guérin's *Bacchante,* Sainte-Beuve assumed that it had been lost. Arnold asserted this also in the first version of his essay. But Trébutien recovered the *Bacchante* after the appearance of the *Reliquiae* in 1860. His one-volume edition of Guérin's journal, letters, and poems, a volume published in 1862, included selections from the *Bacchante.* Arnold's remark on the supposed fate of the

---

[30] *Studies in Text,* p. 9. It is difficult to understand why Brown makes this assertion, since no text of the essay on Maurice de Guérin lacks the "now."

[31] See *Studies in Text,* p. 127, and *Fraser's Magazine,* LXVII (January, 1863), 60 The reference is to the first passage which Arnold quotes from Guérin's poem, *The Centaur.*

poem was accordingly deleted from his essay for the 1865 edition, indicating that Arnold had some acquaintance with this second volume of Trébutien's before 1865.

No major textual alterations occurred in the essay "Pagan and Mediaeval Religious Sentiment" after its publication in the *Cornhill Magazine* for April, 1864. Brown's statement that the essay "underwent no organic modification correlative with the specialization of the title," [32] however, is rather misleading. Arnold's original title, that for the Oxford lecture, "Pagan and Christian Religious Sentiment," was retained when the article appeared in the *Cornhill Magazine*. But Arnold clearly stated that he had altered the text considerably before publishing it at all, recognizing the finality of the printed word and the risk he would otherwise run of being completely misunderstood.[33] For the 1865 edition of the essays Arnold altered the title to "Pagan and Mediaeval Religious Sentiment," but the necessary deletions had long since been made in the text itself.

The alterations which Brown lists for this essay are stated correctly. He does not, though, draw the obvious conclusions from a study of these revisions. Of twenty-five instances in which some change in word or phrase occurs, eighteen show alteration for the text of 1869, with that reading retained for the 1875 edition. It is almost incredible that Arnold should have reworked the expression of his ideas so painstakingly, but in fact he did. And in this case, he exerted himself considerably for the second edition.

Of Arnold's essay on Joubert, Brown remarks that for the 1865 edition the essay "was relieved of its specious title, but not of the specious comparison which is, in a sense, its makeweight." [34] The title was simplified for the collected editions, it is true. But Arnold never intended the comparison with Coleridge as an authoritative literary judgment, much less as a "makeweight" for the essay, and it is hardly fair to censure him for retaining it. The essay itself is an appreciation, and an appreciation rather of Joubert's "delightful and edifying genius" than of his total achievement, literary or otherwise. Above all, the essay does not purport to be a detailed study of either Joubert or Coleridge. Arnold introduced Coleridge into his discussion, not as Joubert's competitor but simply as his "parallel," as one with whom Joubert possessed a few features in common. To regard Arnold's

---

[32] *Studies in Text,* p. 12.

[33] See Arnold's letter to his mother, March 17, 1864; *Letters,* I, 265–66. Since no copy of the lecture is now extant, this very significant part of the textual history of the essay cannot be traced.

[34] *Studies in Text,* p. 11.

comparison as a "specious" literary estimate is an error. Arnold offers no value judgment at all; he simply illuminates the qualities of Joubert's "genius" by contrasting them with certain qualities of Coleridge's.[35]

As for Arnold's textual revisions in the essay on Joubert, there were at least six different alterations for each of the three editions, indicating that Arnold must have gone carefully over the essay each time before reprinting it. "Gift" is substituted for "organ" consistently in the text of the first edition, except for a single instance. The "junctive sentence" [36] to which Brown refers was inserted not in 1869, but rather in 1875. In one instance only, and that for the text of 1865, was the expression "Joubert's English parallel" changed to "Coleridge"; in the other place where it occurred, the original expression has been retained in all editions. The alteration was not, after all, "four years belated," as Brown charges, since Arnold chose to alter it in only one case, and that in 1865.

It would be unkind to end on a negative note such as this. In his discussion of Arnold's "confused and polemical" Preface to the 1865 edition, E. K. Brown insists that "the abridgement of the *Preface* in 1869 was the most important modification to which the volume was ever subjected." [37] Certainly it is also one of the most interesting and significant of Arnold's revisions. The original Preface, which appeared in the 1865 edition only, is here included in its entirety, in the pages which follow, since it is not generally accessible elsewhere.[38] Although Arnold's deliberate and drastic modification of this Preface for subsequent editions does constitute a virtual retraction of the 1865 version, that version is nevertheless a significant part of the text of *Essays in Criticism: First Series*. In the pages which follow, the five large sections which Arnold removed altogether are set in reduced type. Careful comparison of the two versions of Arnold's Preface will reveal a number of minor changes with which Arnold disguised these deletions.

[35] For an analysis of Arnold's use of the "comparative method" and of the unity inherent in the 1865 collection of essays, see Robert A. Donovan, "The Method of Arnold's *Essays in Criticism*," *PMLA*, LXXI (December, 1956), 922–31.

[36] *Studies in Text*, p. 12; the "junctive sentence" is the transitional one: "Let us try and show that he does."

[37] *Studies in Text*, p. 2. In a letter to Alexander Macmillan, dated August 16, 1875, Arnold directed: "I think it would be better to call the Preface to the Essays *Preface to the First Edition* instead of merely *Preface*. Then you may omit the date underneath." See William Buckler, *Publishing Diary*, p. 73. This accounts for an apparent inconsistency in dating the two versions of the Preface.

[38] The original Preface, with excellent annotation, can also be found in Fraser Neiman's publication, *Essays, Letters, and Reviews by Matthew Arnold* (Cambridge, Mass., 1960), pp. 92–101, and in R. H. Super's *Matthew Arnold: Lectures and Essays in Criticism*, pp. 286–90 and 535–39.

THE PREFACE OF 1865

———————◆———————

Several of the Essays which are here collected and reprinted have had the good or the bad fortune to be much criticised at the time of their first appearance. I am not now going to inflict upon the reader a reply to those criticisms; for one or two explanations which are desirable I shall else-where, perhaps, be able some day to find an opportunity; but, indeed, it is not in my nature,—some of my critics would rather say, not in my power, —to dispute on behalf of any opinion, even my own, very obstinately. To try and approach Truth on one side after another, not to strive or cry, not to persist in pressing forward, on any one side, with violence and self-will,—it is only thus, it seems to me, that mortals may hope to gain any 10 vision of the mysterious Goddess, whom we shall never see except in out-line, but only thus even in outline. He who will do nothing but fight impetu-ously towards her on his own, one, favourite, particular line, is inevitably destined to run his head into the folds of the black robe in which she is wrapped.

I am very sensible that this way of thinking leaves me under great disadvantages in addressing a public composed from a people "the most logical," says the *Saturday Review*, "in the whole world." But the truth is, I have never been able to hit it off happily with the logicians, and it would be mere affectation in me to give myself the airs of doing so. They imagine truth something to be proved, I something to be seen; they something to be manufactured, I as something to be found. I have a profound respect for intuitions, and a very lukewarm respect for the elaborate machine-work of my friends the logicians. I have always thought that all which was worth much in this elaborate machine-work of theirs came from an intuition, to which they gave a grand name of their own. How did they come by this intuition? Ah! if they could tell us that. But no; they set their machine in motion, and build up a fine showy edifice, glittering and unsubstantial like a pyramid of eggs; and then they say: "Come and look at our pyramid." And what does one find it? Of all that heap of eggs, the one poor little fresh egg, the original intuition, has got hidden away far out of sight and forgotten. And all the other eggs are addled.

So it is not to build rival pyramids against my logical enemies that I write this preface, but to prevent a misunderstanding, of which certain phrases that some of them use make me apprehensive. Mr. Wright, one of the many translators of Homer, has just published a Letter to the Dean of Canterbury, complaining of some remarks of mine, uttered now a long while ago, on his version of the Iliad. One cannot be always studying one's own works, and I was really under the impression, till I saw Mr. Wright's complaint, that I had spoken of him with all respect. The reader may judge of my astonishment, therefore, at finding, from Mr. Wright's pamphlet, that I had "declared with much solemnity that there is not any proper reason for his existing." That I never said; but, on looking back at my Lectures on translating Homer, I find that I did say, not that Mr. Wright, but that Mr. Wright's version of the Iliad, repeating in the main the merits and defects of Cowper's version, as Mr. Sotheby's repeated those of Pope's version, had, if I might be pardoned for saying so, no proper reason for existing. Elsewhere I expressly spoke of the merit of his version; but I confess that the phrase, qualified as I have shown, about its want of a proper reason for existing, I used. Well, the phrase had, perhaps, too much vivacity; alas! vivacity is one of those faults which advancing years will only too certainly cure; that, however, is no real excuse; we have all of us a right to exist, we and our works; an unpopular author should be the last person to call in question this right. So I gladly withdraw the offending phrase, and I am sorry for having used it;

Mr. Wright, however, will allow me to observe that he has taken an ample revenge. He has held me up before the public as "condemned by my own umpire;" as "rebutted," and "with an extinguisher put upon me" by Mr. Tennyson's remarkable pentameter,

"When did a frog coarser croak upon our Helicon?" 60

(till I read Mr. Wright I had no notion, I protest, that this exquisite stroke of pleasantry was aimed at me); he has exhibited me as "condemned by myself, refuted by myself," and, finally, my hexameters having been rejected by all the world, "somewhat crest-fallen." And he has himself made game of me, in this forlorn condition, by parodying those unlucky hexameters. So that now, I should think, he must be quite happy.

Partly, no doubt, from being crest-fallen, but partly, too, from sincere contrition for that fault of over-vivacity which I have acknowledged, I will not raise a finger in self-defence against Mr. Wright's blows. I will not even ask him,—what it almost irresistibly rises to my lips to ask him when I see 70 he writes from Mapperly,—if he can tell me what has become of that poor girl, Wragg? She has been tried, I suppose: I know how merciful a view judges and juries are apt to take of these cases, so I cannot but hope she has got off. But what I should so like to ask is, whether the impression the poor thing made was, in general, satisfactory: did she come up to the right standard as a member of "the best breed in the whole world?" were her life-experiences an edifying testimony to "our unrivalled happiness?" did she find Mr. Roebuck's speech a comfort to her in her prison? But I must stop; or my kind monitor, the *Guardian,* whose own gravity is so profound that the frivolous are sometimes apt to give it a heavier name, will be putting a 80 harsh construction upon my innocent thirst for knowledge, and again taxing me with the unpardonable crime of being amusing.

Amusing—good heavens! we shall none of us be amusing much longer.

Mr. Wright would perhaps be more indulgent to my vivacity if he considered this. It is but the last sparkle of flame before we are all in the dark; the last glimpse of colour before we all go into drab.

Who that reads the *Examiner* does not know that representative man, that Ajax of liberalism, one of our modern leaders of thought, who signs himself "Presbyter Anglicanus"? For my part, I have good cause to know him; terribly severe he was with me two years ago, when he thought I had spoken 90 with levity of that favourite pontiff of the Philistines, the Bishop of Natal. But his masterpiece was the other day. Mr. Disraeli, in the course of his lively speech at Oxford, talked of "nebulous professors, who, if they could only succeed in obtaining a perpetual study of their writings, would go far to realise that eternity of punishment which they object to." Presbyter Anglicanus says "it would be childish to affect ignorance" that this was aimed at Mr. Maurice. If it was, who can doubt that Mr. Maurice himself, full of culture and urbanity as he is, would be the first to pronounce it a very smart saying, and to laugh at it good-humouredly? But only listen to Mr. Maurice's champion:—"This passage must fill all sober-minded men with astonishment 100 and dismay; they will regard it as one of the most ominous signs of the time. This contemptible joke, which betrays a spirit of ribald profanity not easily surpassed, excited from the Bishop, the clergy, and laity present, not an indignant rebuke, but 'continued laughter.' Such was the assembly of Englishmen and Christians, who could listen in uproarious merriment to a Parliamentary leader while he asserted that the vilest iniquity would be well compensated by a forced perusal of the writings of Frederick Denison Maurice!" And, for fear this trumpet-blast should not be carried far enough by the *Examiner,* its author, if I am not greatly mistaken, blew it also, under a different name, in half a dozen of the daily newspapers. As Wordsworth asks:

> ". . . the happiest mood
> Of that man's mind, what can it be . . ."

was he really born of human parents, or of Hyrcanian tigers? if the former, surely to some of his remote ancestors, at any rate,—in far distant ages, I mean, long before the birth of Puritanism,—some conception of a joke must, at one moment or other of their lives, have been conveyed. But there is the coming east wind! there is the tone of the future!—I hope it is grave enough for even the *Guardian;*

—the earnest, prosaic, practical, austerely literal future! Yes, the world will soon be the Philistines'; and then, with every voice, not of thunder, silenced, and the whole earth filled and ennobled every morning by the magnificent roaring of the young lions of the *Daily Telegraph,* we shall all yawn in one another's faces with the dismallest, the most unimpeachable gravity.

No more vivacity then! my hexameters, and dogmatism, and scoffs at the Divorce Court, will all have been put down; I shall be quite crest-fallen. But does Mr. Wright imagine that there will be any more place, in that world, for his heroic blank verse Homer than for my paradoxes? If he does, he deceives himself, and knows little of the Palatine Library of the future. A plain edifice, like the British College of Health enlarged: inside, a light, bleak room, with a few statues; Dagon in the centre, with our English Caabah, or Palladium of enlightenment, the hare's stomach; around, a few leading friends of humanity or fathers of British philosophy;—Goliath, the great Bentham, Presbyter Anglicanus, our intellectual deliverer Mr. James Clay, and . . . yes! with the embarrassed air of a late convert, the editor of the *Saturday Review.* Many a shrewd nip has he in old days given to the Philistines, this editor; many a bad half-hour has he made them pass; but in his old age he has mended his courses, and declares that his heart has always been in the right place, and that he is at bottom, however appearances may have been against him, staunch for Goliath and "the most logical nation in the whole world." Then, for the book-shelves. There will be found on them a monograph by Mr. Lowe on the literature of the ancient Scythians, to revenge them for the iniquitous neglect with which the Greeks treated them; there will be Demosthenes, because he was like Mr. Spurgeon: but else, from all the lumber of antiquity they will be free. Everything they contain will be modern, intelligible, improving; *Joyce's Scientific Dialogues, Old Humphrey, Bentham's Deontology, Little Dorrit, Mangnall's Questions. The Wide Wide World, D'Iffanger's Speeches, Beecher's Sermons;*—a library, in short, the fruit of a happy marriage between the profound philosophic reflection of Mr. Clay, and the healthy natural taste of Inspector Tanner. 150

But I return to my design in writing this Preface. That design was, after apologizing to Mr. Wright for my vivacity of five years ago, to beg him and others to let me bear my own burdens, without saddling the great and famous University, to which I have the honour to belong, with any portion of them. What I mean to deprecate is such phrases as, "his professional assault," "his assertions issued *ex cathedrâ*," "the sanction of his name as the representative of poetry," and so on. Proud as I am of my connection with the University of Oxford, I can truly say, that, knowing how unpopular a task one is undertaking when one tries to pull out a few more stops 160 in that powerful, but at present somewhat narrow-toned organ, the modern Englishman, I have always sought to stand by myself, and to compromise others as little as possible. Besides this, my native modesty is such, that I have always been shy of assuming the honourable style of Professor, because this is a title I share with so many distinguished men,—Professor Pepper, Professor Anderson, Professor Frickel, and others,—who adorn it, I feel, much more than I do.

These eminent men, however, belonging to a hierarchy of which Urania, the Goddess of Science herself, is the sole head, cannot well by any vivacity or unpopularity of theirs compromise themselves with their superiors; 170 because with their Goddess they are not likely, until they are translated to the stars, to come into contact. I, on the other hand, have my humble place in a hierarchy whose seat is on earth; and I serve under an illustrious Chancellor who translates Homer, and calls his Professor's leaning towards hexameters "a pestilent heresy." Nevertheless, that cannot keep me from admiring the performance of my severe chief; I admire its freshness, its manliness, its simplicity; although, perhaps, if one looks for the charm of Homer, for his play of a divine light . . . . . . Professor Pepper must go on, I cannot.

My position is, therefore, one of great delicacy; but it is not from any selfish motives that I prefer to stand alone, and to concentrate on myself, as 180 a plain citizen of the republic of letters, and not as an office-bearer in a hierarchy, the whole responsibility for all I write; it is much more out of genuine devotion to the University of Oxford, for which I feel, and always must feel, the fondest, the most reverential attachment. In an epoch of dissolution and transformation, such as that on which we are now entered, habits, ties, and associations are inevitably broken up, the action of individuals becomes more distinct, the short-comings, errors, heats, disputes, which necessarily attend individual action, are brought into greater prominence. Who would not gladly keep clear, from all these passing clouds, an august institution which was there before they arose, and which will be there when they have blown over?

It is true, the *Saturday Review* maintains that our epoch of transformation is finished; that we have found our philosophy; that the British nation has searched all anchorages for the spirit, and has finally anchored itself, in the fulness of perfected knowledge, to Benthamism. This idea at first made a great impression on me; not only because it is so consoling in itself, but also because it explained a phenomenon which in the summer of last year, had, I confess, a good deal troubled me. At that time my avocations led me to travel almost daily on one of the Great Eastern lines,—the Woodford Branch. Every one knows that Müller perpetrated his detestable act on the North London Railway, close by. The English middle class, of which I am myself a feeble unit, travel on the Woodford Branch in large numbers. Well, the demoralisation of our class,—which (the newspapers are constantly saying it, so I may repeat it without vanity) has done all the great things which have ever been done in England,—the demoralisation, I say, of our class, caused by the Bow tragedy, was something bewildering. Myself, a transcendentalist (as the *Saturday Review* knows), I escaped the infection; and, day after day, I used to ply my agitated fellow-travellers with all the consolations which my transcendentalism, and my turn for the French, would naturally suggest to me. I reminded them how Caesar refused to take precautions against assassination, because life was not worth having at the price of an ignoble solicitude for it. I reminded them what insignificant atoms we all are in the life of the world. "Suppose the worst to happen," I said, addressing a portly jeweller from Cheapside; "suppose even yourself to be the victim; *il n'y a pas d'homme nécessaire.* We should miss you for a day or two upon the Woodford Branch; but the great mundane movement would still go on; the gravel walks of your villa would still be rolled; dividends would still be paid at the Bank; omnibuses would still run; there would still be the old crush at the corner of Fenchurch Street." All was of no avail. Nothing could moderate, in the bosom of the great English middle class, their passionate, absorbing, almost blood-thirsty clinging to life. At the moment I thought this over-concern a little unworthy; but the *Saturday Review* suggests a touching explanation of it. What I took for the ignoble clinging to life of a comfortable worldling, was, perhaps, only the ardent longing of a faithful Benthamite, traversing an age still dimmed by the last mists of transcendentalism, to be spared long enough to see his religion in the full and final blaze of its triumph. This respectable man,—whom I imagined to be going up to London to buy shares, or to attend an Exeter Hall meeting, or to hear Mr. D'Iffanger speak, or to see Mr. Spurgeon, with his well-known reverence for every authentic *Thus saith the Lord,* turn his other cheek to the amiable Dean of Ripon,—was, perhaps, in real truth, on a pious pilgrimage, to obtain, from Mr. Bentham's executors, a sacred bone of his great dissected Master.

And yet, after all, I cannot but think that the *Saturday Review* has here, for once, fallen a victim to an idea,—a beautiful but deluding idea,—and that the British nation has not yet, so entirely as the reviewer seems to imagine, found the last word of its philosophy. No; we are all seekers still: seekers often make mistakes, and I wish mine to redound to my own discredit only, and not to touch Oxford. Beautiful city! so venerable, so lovely, so unravaged by the fierce intellectual life of our century, so serene!

"There are our young barbarians, all at play."

And yet, steeped in sentiment as she lies, spreading her gardens to the moonlight, and whispering from her towers the last enchantments of the Middle Age, who will deny that Oxford, by her ineffable charm, keeps ever calling us near to the true goal of all of us, to the ideal, to perfection,—to beauty, in a word, which is only truth seen from another side?—nearer, perhaps, than all the science of Tübingen. Adorable dreamer, whose heart has been so romantic! who hast given thyself so prodigally, given thyself to sides and to heroes not mine, only never to the Philistines! home of lost causes, and forsaken beliefs, and unpopular names, and impossible loyalties! what example could ever so inspire us to keep down the Philistine in ourselves, what teacher could ever so save us from that bondage to which we are all prone, that bondage which Goethe, in those incomparable lines on the death of Schiller, make it his friend's highest praise (and nobly did Schiller deserve the praise) to have left miles out of sight behind him;— the bondage of *was uns alle bändigt,* DAS GEMEINE? She will forgive me, even if I have unwittingly drawn upon her a shot or two aimed at her unworthy son; for she is generous, and the cause in which I fight is, after all, hers. Apparitions of a day, what is our puny warfare against the Philistines, compared with the warfare which this Queen of Romance has been waging against them for centuries, and will wage after we are gone?

TEXTUAL NOTES

———————◄►►———————

Title: "The Functions of Criticism at the Present Time" (NR)

8: 14–15   an excellent notice of Wordsworth, published in the *North British Review* (NR, 65, 69)

9: note   Mr. Shairp's notice (it is permitted, I hope, to mention his name) might (65, 69). This footnote was first inserted in 65.

10: 63   is the true function (NR, 65, 69)

13: 176   of the Renaissance (NR, 65, 69). Arnold substituted the new spelling in 75.

13: 181–92   its own activity; the French Revolution took a political, practical character. This Revolution—the object of so much blind love and so much blind hatred—found, indeed, its motive-power in the intelligence of men (NR)

13: 207–8   *to count by tens is the easiest way of counting:* [Arnold's footnote] A writer in the *Saturday Review*, who has offered me some counsels about style for which I am truly grateful, suggests that this should stand as follows:—*To take as your unit an established base of notation, ten being given as the base of notation, is, except for numbers under twenty, the simplest way of counting.* I tried it so, but I assure him, without jealousy, that the more I looked at his improved way of putting the thing, the less I liked it. It seems to me that the maxim, in this shape, would never make the tour of a world, where most of us are plain, easy-spoken people. He forgets that he is a reasoner, a member of a school, a disciple of the great Bentham, and that he naturally talks in the scientific way of his school, with exact accuracy, philosophic propriety; I am a mere solitary wanderer in search of the light, and I talk an artless, unstudied, every-day, familiar language. But, after all, this is the language of the mass of the world.

The mass of Frenchmen who felt the force of that prescription of the reason which my reviewer, in his purified language, states thus:—*to count by tens has the advantage of taking as your unit the base of an established system of notation*—certainly rendered this, for themselves, in some such loose language as mine. My point is that they felt the force of a prescription of the reason so strongly that they legislated in accordance with it. They may have been wrong in so doing; they may have foolishly omitted to take other prescriptions of reason into account;—the non-English world does not seem to think so, but let that pass;—what I say is, that by legislating as they did they showed a keen susceptibility to purely rational, intellectual considerations. On the other hand, does my reviewer say that we keep our monetary system unchanged because our nation has grasped the intellectual proposition which he puts, in his masterly way, thus: *to count by twelves has the advantage of taking as your unit a number in itself far more convenient than ten for that purpose?* Surely not; but because our system is there, and we are too practical a people to trouble ourselves about its intellectual aspect.

To take a second case. The French Revolutionists abolished the sale of offices, because they thought (my reviewer will kindly allow me to put the thing in my imperfect, popular language) the sale of offices a gross anomaly. We still sell commissions in the army. I have no doubt my reviewer, with his scientific powers, can easily invent some beautiful formula to make us appear to be doing this on the purest philosophical principles; the principles of Hobbes, Locke, Bentham, Mr. Mill, Mr. Bain, and himself, their worthy disciple. But surely the plain unscientific account of the matter is, that we have the anomalous practice (he will allow it is, in itself, an anomalous practice?) established, and that (in the words of senatorial wisdom already quoted) "for a thing to be an anomaly we consider to be no objection to it whatever." (65)

15: 252   will depend on the way (*NR*, 65, 69)

18: 371–75   It is of the last importance that English criticism should clearly discern what rules for its course, in order to avail itself of the field now opening to it, and to produce fruit for the future, it ought to take. The rules may be given in one word: by being *disinterested*. And how is it to be disinterested? (*NR*)

18: 375–77   By keeping aloof from practice; . . . touches; by steadily (*NR*, 65, 69)

19: 437   Mr. Adderley (*NR*, 65, 69)

20: 482 soon after reading Mr. Roebuck (*NR*, 65, 69)

22: 542 more than deserves (*NR*, 65, 69)

23: 587–88 party of movement (*NR*, 65, 69). 75 omits the "of," which is restored in the present text. Subsequent editions, following 75, also omit the "of," and there is some doubt as to Arnold's intent here.

23: 593–94 *the celebrated first volume of Bishop Colenso:* [Arnold's footnote; inserted in 65, modified in 69, 75, etc.] So sincere is my dislike to all personal attack and controversy, that I abstain from reprinting, at this distance of time from the occasion which called them forth, the essays in which I criticized the Bishop of Natal's book; I feel bound, however, after all that has passed, to make here a final declaration of my sincere impenitence for having published them. The Bishop of Natal's subsequent volumes are in great measure free from the crying fault of his first; he has at length succeeded in more clearly separating, in his own thoughts, the idea of science from the idea of religion; his mind appears to be opening as he goes along, and he may perhaps end by becoming a useful biblical critic, though never, I think, of the first order.

Still, in here taking leave of him at the moment when he is publishing, for popular use, a cheap edition of his work, I cannot forbear repeating yet once more, for his benefit and that of his readers, this sentence from my original remarks upon him: *There is truth of science and truth of religion; truth of science does not become truth of religion until it is made religious.* And I will add: Let us have all the science there is from the men of science; from the men of religion let us have religion. (65)

23: note [Inserted in 65; same in 69, 75, etc.]

25: 661–66 of the New Testament *data,* is the very essence (*NR*)

25: 661–66 of the New Testament *data,*—not a making war on them in Voltaire's fashion, not a leaving them out of mind, in the world's fashion, but the putting a new construction upon them, the taking them from under the old adoptive, traditional, unspiritual point of view and placing them under a new one,—is the very essence of the religious problem as now presented; (65, 69)

27: 718–19 *an institution which . . . in the ideal sphere is so hideous:* [Arnold's footnote] A critic, already quoted, says that I have no right, on my own principles, to "object to practical measures on theoretical grounds," and that only "when a man has got a theory which will fully explain all the duties of the legislator on the matter of marriage, will he have a right to abuse the Divorce Court." In short, he wants me to produce a plan for a new and improved Divorce Court, before I call the present one hideous. But God forbid that I should thus enter into competition with the Lord Chancellor! It is just this invasion of the practical sphere which is really against my principles; the taking a practical measure into the world of ideas, and seeing how it looks there, is, on the other hand, just what I am recommending. It is because we have not been conversant enough with ideas that our practice now falls so short; it is only by becoming more conversant with them that we shall make it better. Our present Divorce Court is not the result of any legislator's meditations on the subject of marriage; rich people had an anomalous privilege of getting divorced; privileges are odious, and we said everybody should have the same chance. There was no meditation about marriage here; that was just the mischief. If my practical critic will but himself accompany me, for a little while, into the despised world of ideas;—if, renouncing any attempt to patch hastily up, with a noble disdain for transcendentalists, our present Divorce law, he will but allow his mind to dwell a little, first on the Catholic idea of marriage, which exhibits marriage as indissoluble, and then upon that Protestant idea of marriage, which exhibits it as a union terminable by mutual consent,—if he will meditate well on these, and afterwards on the thought of what married life, according to its idea, really is, of what family life really is, of what social life really is, and national life, and public morals,—he will find, after a while, I do assure him, the whole state of his spirit quite changed; the Divorce Court will then seem to him, if he looks at it, strangely hideous; and he will at the same time discover in himself, as the fruit of his inward discipline, lights and resources for making it better, of which now he does not dream.

He must make haste, though, for the condition of his "practical measure" is getting awkward; even the British Philistine begins to have qualms as he looks at his offspring; even his "thrice-battered God of Palestine" is beginning to roll its eyes convulsively. (65)

27: 724   with its crowded benches (*NR*, 65, 69)

28: 767–71   is most likely to go astray. In general its course (*NR*, 65)

28: 767–71   is most likely to go astray. I have wished, above all, to insist on the attitude which criticism should adopt towards everything; on its right tone and temper of mind. Then comes the question as to the subject-matter which literary criticism should most seek. Here, in general, its course (69)

28: 779   The English critic, therefore, (*NR*, 65, 69)

28: 789   that he will generally do (*NR*, 65, 69)

29: 800—30: 844   cannot well give us, like fresh learning, the sense of creative activity. To have this sense is, as I said at the beginning, the great happiness and the great proof of being alive (*NR*). [The two paragraphs beginning "But stop, some one will say" and "There is so much inviting us" were first inserted here in 65.]

THE LITERARY INFLUENCE OF ACADEMIES

37: 234–36   No doubt his verse suffers from the same defects which impair his prose, and he cannot express himself with real success in it; (*CH*, 65, 69).

50; 718–25   Again, the most successful English book of last season was certainly Mr. Kinglake's *Invasion of the Crimea*. Its style was one of the most renowned things about it . . . but, if it were so, on what a height would Mr. Kinglake stand! (*CH*, 65)

50: 733   to damage its adversaries, to be admired, to triumph. "His features put on that glow which, seen in men of his race—race known by the kindling gray eye, and the light, stubborn, crisping hair—discloses the rapture of instant fight." How glittering that is, but how perfectly frosty! "There was a salient point of difference between the boulevards and the hillsides of the Alma. The Russians were armed." How trenchant that is, but how perfectly unscrupulous! This is the Corinthian style; the glitter of the East with the hardness of the West; "the passion for tinsel," some one, himself a Corinthian, said of Mr. Kinglake's style,—"of a sensuous Jew, with the savage spleen of a dyspeptic Englishman." I do not say this of Mr. Kinglake's style,—I am very far from saying it. To say it is to fall into just that cold (*CH*), hard (65), brassy, over-stretched style which Mr. Kinglake himself employs so far too much, and which I, for my part, reprobate. But when a brother Corinthian of Mr. Kinglake's says it, I feel what he means.

A style so bent on effect at the expense of soul (*CH*, 65)

50: 740–41 that criticism should not be dazzled by them, but should try closely this, the form of his work. The matter of the work is a separate thing; and, indeed, this has been, I believe, withdrawn from discussion, Mr. Kinglake declaring that this must and shall stay as it is, and that he is resolved, like Pontius Pilate, to stand by what he has written. And here, I must say, he seems to me to be quite right. On the breast of that huge Mississippi of falsehood called history, a foam-bell more or less is of no consequence. But he may, at any rate, ease and soften his style.

We must not compare a man of Mr. Kinglake's literary talent (*CH*, 65, 69)

MAURICE DE GUÉRIN

53: 1 [In his *Studies in the Text of Matthew Arnold's Prose Works*, E. K. Brown incorrectly states that in Arnold's revision "the playful first sentence beginning 'I will not presume to say that I now know the French language well' is shorn of its most diverting member, the 'now'" (p. 9). *FR*, 65, 69, 75, and subsequent editions all retain the "now."]

55: 88–89 Gray,—does not use that couplet at all (*FR*, 65)

56: 118 in finding expressions to render that sense. Brief notices of him the reader may have seen here and there in English or in foreign periodicals; but it is not likely that the two volumes of his remains will have met the eye of more than a very few of those who read this, or that they will ever be widely circulated in this country. To all who love poetry (*FR*)

59: 232–33 surprised by a wave (*FR*, 65)

59: 233 under a white cloth (*FR*, 65)

67: 550 with his face set to the East (*FR*). "Ce soir il sortira de Paris, du côté de l'orient, un homme" etc. *Journal*, p. 292.

69: 636–37 but the other day unheard of, is henceforth written (*FR*)

72: 744 he composed a *Bacchante,* which is lost, and which was meant (*FR*)

EUGÉNIE DE GUÉRIN

76: 5   pretty bows of ribbon (*CH*, 65, 69)
77: 21-22   with less of sunlight, abundance, and facility (*CH*, 65, 69)
78: 86   out of one forehead (*CH*)
91: 573   has such power upon one's feelings (*CH*)
92: 608-9   of Maurice's religious feeling and its character (*CH*, 65, 69)

HEINRICH HEINE

96: 5-6, 14; 116: 805   war of liberation (*CH*, 65, 69). [The earlier reading is kept at 97: 46 only.]
97: 17   is the critic's highest function (*CH*)
102: 232 ff.; 115: 746-64   The entire paragraph beginning "There is balm in Philistia" and also the "King Pedro" excerpt, both deleted by Arnold from his lecture before it appeared in *CH*, were restored in 65 and subsequent editions. See W. E. Buckler, *Publishing Diary*, p. 64.
102: 237   conducts a country to the ministry of Herr von Bismarck (65, 69)
116: 806   the European literature of that quarter of a century (*CH*, 65)
117: 820-21   nineteenth-century English nobleman (*CH*)

PAGAN AND MEDIAEVAL RELIGIOUS SENTIMENT

Title: "Pagan and Christian Religious Sentiment" (*CH*)
119: 53   not, I think, the Church of the future, but indisputably the Church of the past (*CH*, 65)
127: 348-49   ends by leaving us with a sense of tightness, of oppression,—with a desire (*CH*, 65)
129: 436   law of supernatural love (*CH*)
129: 444-46   that he had been too hard upon his own body; when we find him doubting 'whether he who had destroyed (*CH*, 65)
130: 455   The Renaissance is (*CH*, 65, 69)
130: 460-65   a thousand times more akin to St. Francis than to Theocritus or to Voltaire. The real Reformation, Luther's Reformation, the German Reformation, was a reaction of the moral and spiritual sense (*CH*)
133: 586-87   of the highest possible beauty and value; an epoch which alone goes far towards making (*CH*, 65, 69)
134: 624   Let Theocritus or St. Francis beat that! (*CH*, 65)

A PERSIAN PASSION PLAY

138: 101-2   Mahomet's young cousin, and the first who, after his wife, believed in him (*CH*)

144: 348–49   and the actor goes and takes up a handful of it, when his part is about to require him to throw (*CH*)

155: 786–89   which the Bible has not. Therefore, to get the sort of power which all this gives, popular Christianity is apt to treat the Bible as if it was just like the Koran, and because of this sort of power, among the little known and little advanced races of the great African continent, the Mahometan missionaries are said to be much more successful than ours (*CH*)

157: 864–68   lovely and innocent children; there, too, are the beauty and the love of youth; and all follow the attraction of the pure and resigned Imam, all die for him; their tender pathos flows into his and enhances it, till there arises for the popular imagination (*CH*)

JOUBERT

Title: "Joubert; or: A French Coleridge" (*NR*)

160: 17–19   who have been real men of genius,—by which we mean, that they have had a genuine organ for what is true (*NR*). [This alteration of "we" to "I" and "organ" to "gift" took place consistently in 65.]

163: 145–46   to attract men of this kind and to benefit them: retaining perfect independence of mind, he was religious; he was a religious philosopher (*NR, 65, 69*)

165: 220–21   to resent as an outrage. Coleridge's great action lay in his supplying (*NR, 65, 69*)

170: 450–51   and to be of more service to us by setting ideals, than if he had composed (*NR, 65, 69*)

171: 458   Let us try and show that he does. (Not in *NR, 65, 69*; inserted in 75.)

180: 819–20   There is something unnatural and shocking where, as in the case of Joubert's English parallel, it does not (*NR*)

181: 884–85   if he ceases to give this, has he enough of light in him to make him safe? Pleasure (*NR, 65, 69*)

SPINOZA AND THE BIBLE

[The letters A, B, C, D, and E designate five sections into which the essay in its final form can be divided. A, C, and E represent the material from Arnold's article, "A Word More About Spinoza," which appeared in the 1865 edition as "Spinoza." B and D represent the two lengthy interpolations from "The Bishop and the Philosopher" which Arnold incorporated into the 1865 version of the essay for the second edition, 1869.

A   Pp. 183–85. This is from "Word More"; virtually the same in both *MACM* and 65.

B   First interpolation from "The Bishop and the Philosopher." This covers pp. 186–94 as far as "Such is really the scope" etc.

C   *MACM* and 65 text resumed here, with slight variations from *MACM* to 65. This covers 194: 422 – 200: 679 (to "St. Augustine"). One para-

graph from this section ("It is true" etc.) was moved from C to E in
69; see 203: 777.

D   Second interpolation from "The Bishop and the Philosopher." This
covers 200: 679–202 (end).

E   Last three sentences of *MACM* and 65, with the addition of the section from C moved to the end in 69. This is now p. 203.]

192: 369   Such, reduced to the briefest and plainest terms possible, stripped of
the developments and proofs with which he delivers it, and divested of the
metaphysical language in which much of it is clothed by him, is the doctrine of Spinoza's treatise on the interpretation of Scripture [*MACM*, p.
252, col. 1. The rest of this column and most of the second column are
omitted; the next section begins on p. 252, col. 2, line 14 from the bottom
of the page]. But, by the whole scope and drift of its argument, by the
spirit in which the subject is throughout treated, his work undeniably
becomes interesting and stimulating to the general culture of Europe.
There are alleged contradictions in Scripture; and the question which the
general culture of Europe, informed of this, asks is, as I have said, —*What
then?* To this question Spinoza returns an answer, and the Bishop of Natal
returns none. The Bishop of Natal keeps going round for ever within the
barren sphere of these contradictions themselves; he treats them as if they
were supremely interesting in themselves, as if we had never heard of them
before, and could never hear enough of them now. Spinoza touches these
verbal matters with all possible brevity and presses on to the more important. It is enough for him to give us what is indispensably necessary of
them. He points out that Moses could never have written (*MACM*)

192: 375   There are alleged contradictions in Scripture; and the question which
the general culture of Europe, informed of this, asks with real interest is:
What then? Spinoza addresses himself to this question. All secondary
points (69)

193: 401–2   But he devotes to all this no more space than is absolutely necessary. He, too, like the Bishop of Natal, touches on the family of Judah;
but he devotes one page to this topic and the Bishop of Natal devotes
thirteen. To the sums in Ezra,—with which the Bishop of Natal, "should
God, in His providence call him to continue the work," will assuredly fill
folios—Spinoza devotes barely a page. He is anxious to escape from the
region of these verbal matters, which to the Bishop of Natal are a sort of
intellectual land of Beulah, into a higher region; he apologizes for lingering over them so long; *non est cur circa haec diu detinear: nolo taediosa
lectione lectorem detinere.* [*MACM*, p. 253, col. 1, line 44—col. 2, line 7.]

196: 516–18   the perpetual reproach of impurity and rejection cast
upon the mass of the Hebrew nation by the exclusive
priesthood of the tribe of Levi? What can be more

[In the edition of 1875 the compositor accidentally omitted the second of
these three lines, rendering the resulting reading completely unintelligible.
In editions subsequent to 75, attempts to rectify the error have proved
incorrect. For example, the editions of 1883, 1891, the Edition de Luxe

of 1903, and the 1905 Eversley edition all have: *the perpetual reproach of impurity and rejection cast upon the priesthood of the tribe of Levi?*]

200: 679   Unction Spinoza's work has not; that name does not precisely fit any quality which it exhibits. But he is instructive and suggestive, even to the most instructed thinker; and to give him full right of citizenship in the Republic of Letters this is enough. And yet so all-important (*MACM*)

200: 685–87   find something suggestive: still, because with all his wit and clear sense, he handles religious ideas wholly without the power of edification, his fame as a great man is equivocal (*MACM, 69*)

203: 779–90   " 'It is true,' one may say . . . of an 'immortal longing' ": This section was originally part of the earlier paragraph beginning: "This is true; yet it is true, also, that by thus crowning the intellectual life" etc. (199: 648). The remainder of the present paragraph constituted a separate paragraph in *MACM* and 65. The conclusion for "Word More" and 65 was as follows:

Now it must be remarked that to use Spinoza's denial of final causes in order to identify him with the Coryphaei of atheism is to make a false use of Spinoza's denial of final causes, just as to use his assertion of the all-importance of loving God to identify him with the saints would be to make a false use of his assertion of the all-importance of loving God. He is no more to be identified with the post-Hegelian philosophers than he is to be identified with St. Augustine. Nay, when M. Van Vloten violently presses the parallel with the post-Hegelians, one feels that the parallel with St. Augustine is the far truer one. Compared with the soldier of irreligion M. Van Vloten would have him to be, Spinoza is religious. His own language about himself, about his aspirations and his course, are true; his foot is in the *vera vita*, his eye on the beatific vision. (*MACM, 65*)

MARCUS AURELIUS

[In his book *Representative Essays of Matthew Arnold* (p. 4), E. K. Brown incorrectly states that the reading of "constraint" is altered to "restraint" in 69. *VIC*, 65, 69 and 75 all have "constraint."]

207: 123–24   to describe the translation of his best-known predecessor, Jeremy Collier (*VIC*, 65, 69)

209: 196–200   In general the substantiality, soundness, and precision of his rendering are (I cannot but think) as conspicuous as the living spirit with which he treats antiquity; and these qualities are particularly desirable in the translator of a work like Marcus Aurelius's (*VIC*)

209: 196–200   In general the substantiality, soundness, and precision of his rendering are (I will venture, after all, to give my opinion about them) as conspicuous as the living spirit with which he treats antiquity; and these qualities are particularly desirable in the translator of a work like Marcus Aurelius's (65)

209: 196–200   In general the substantiality, soundness, and precision of Mr.

Long's rendering are (I will venture, after all, to give my opinion about them) as conspicuous as the living spirit with which he treats antiquity; and these qualities are particularly desirable in the translator of a work like Marcus Aurelius's (69)

214: 377–80   the very simplicity of Christian theism: for the Roman statesman, the character of secret assemblages which the meetings of the Christian community wore, under a State-system as jealous of unauthorized associations as the Code Napoleon (*VIC*)

214: 377–80   the very simplicity of Christian theism: for the Roman statesman, the character of secret assemblages which the meetings of the Christian community wore, under a State-system as jealous of unauthorized associations as the State-system of modern France (65, 69)

217: 528–30   such a remark as the following seems to me to have no parallel in the whole range of Greek and Roman literature (*VIC*)

222: 712—223: 749   It is remarkable how little of a merely local and temporary character, how little of those *scoriae* which a reader has to clear away before he gets to the precious ore, how little that even admits of doubt or question, the morality of Marcus Aurelius exhibits. In general, the action he prescribes is action which every sound nature must recognise as right, and the motives he assigns are motives which every clear reason must recognise as valid.* [The intervening section in 69, 75, etc., with slight variations, appeared as a footnote in reduced type in *VIC* and 65.]

223: 749–52   And so he remains the especial friend and comforter of all scrupulous and difficult, yet pure and upward-striving souls, in those ages most especially that walk by sight, not by faith, that have no open vision (*VIC*, 65)

223: 762–66   One feels, too, that the Marcus Aurelius one knows must still have remained, even had they presented themselves to him, in a great measure himself; he would have been no Justin: but how would they have affected him? in what measure would they have changed him? Granted that he might have found (*VIC*, 65)

223: 766   like the *Alogi* in ancient and modern times (*VIC*, 65, 69)

EXPLANATORY NOTES

EXPLANATORY NOTES

———————◆▶——————

The explanatory notes are intended not only to document Arnold's remarks, but also to illuminate them and to assemble source material for those interested in pursuing further some idea which Arnold introduces. Biographical data not demanded by Arnold's text, however, have been generally excluded from the notes.

PREFACE

3: 1–2; 245: 1–2   *Several of the Essays . . . much criticized:* Fitzjames Stephen's reply to "The Functions of Criticism at the Present Time" appeared shortly after Arnold's essay; see "Mr. Matthew Arnold and His Countrymen," *Saturday Review,* XVIII (December 3, 1864), 683–85 (pp. 325–32 below). Subsequent thrusts at the *Saturday Review* in the Preface are directed at Stephen's article. Arnold's later essay, "My Countrymen," *Cornhill Magazine,* XIII (February, 1866), 153–72, reprinted in *Friendship's Garland,* is also a reply to Stephen.

"Provincial Style," *Saturday Review,* XVIII (August 6, 1864), 175–76, was one review of "The Literary Influence of Academies," in which a critic commended Arnold's theory about the beneficial effects of an Academy upon the development of style, but expressed his regret that Arnold "did not think it worth while to devote more of his space to what the central and the provincial are in style, and that he preferred to amuse himself with quoting passages from modern writers which show how great are the audacities that even persons of mark permit themselves, and the abysses of bad style into which they fall" (p. 175).

"The Bishop and the Philosopher," parts of which were later incorporated into the 1865 "Spinoza" essay, suffered most at the hands of reviewers. See: "Mr. Matthew Arnold on the Aristocratic Creed," *Spectator*, XXXV (December 27, 1862), 1438–39; "The Bishop and the Professor," *Examiner*, January 10, 1863, p. 20; a letter and an editorial captioned "The Bishop and the Philosopher," *Examiner*, January 17, 1863, p. 36; "Bishop Colenso and His Critics," *Examiner*, January 24, 1863, p. 52; "The Educated Few," *Saturday Review*, XV (January 17, 1863), 71–72; W. R. Greg's "Truth *Vs*. Edification," *Westminster Review*, XXIII, N.S. (April, 1863), 503–16. This last was later reprinted in W. R. Greg, *Literary and Social Judgments* (Boston, 1873), 309–27.

3: 6; 245: 6   *not in my power:* This is what Fitzjames Stephen had alleged against Arnold in "Mr. Matthew Arnold and His Countrymen": "The truth is that, like his French models, Mr. Arnold has quick sympathies and a great gift of making telling remarks; but, also like them, he has hardly any power of argument. At least, if he has, he rarely shows it" (p. 326 below).

246: 16–17   *"the most logical," says the Saturday Review:* "Mr. Matthew Arnold and His Countrymen," pp. 328–30 below.

4: 2–3; 246: 35–36   *Mr. Wright . . . has just published:* Ichabod Charles Wright, *A Letter to the Dean of Canterbury on the Homeric Lectures of Matthew Arnold* (London, 1864). In a letter to his mother, dated December 7, 1864, Arnold remarked: "Mr. Wright, the translator of Homer, has printed a letter of attack upon my Homer lectures, but it is of no consequence." *The Letters of Matthew Arnold, 1848–1888,* ed. George W. E. Russell (New York, 1900), I, 283.

4: 20; 246: 38   *his version of the Iliad:* The *Iliad of Homer Translated into Blank Verse* by I. C. Wright, M. A., translator of Dante, late fellow of Magdalen College, Oxford. Books I–VI (London, 1861). Wright was still working on his translation in 1865.

4: 27; 246: 44   *I did say:* "For want of duly penetrating themselves with the first-named quality of Homer, his rapidity, Cowper and Mr. Wright have failed in rendering him . . . . (Mr. Wright repeats in the main Cowper's manner, as Mr. Sotheby repeats Pope's manner, and neither Mr. Wright's translation nor Mr. Sotheby's has, I must be forgiven for saying, any proper reason for existing)." "On Translating Homer," Lecture I. See *Matthew Arnold: On the Classical Tradition,* ed. R. H. Super (Ann Arbor, 1960), p. 103.

247: 71–72   *that poor girl, Wragg:* See the note to "The Function of Criticism at the Present Time," at 20: 483–84. Fitzjames Stephen enjoyed Arnold's exemplum about Wragg enough to offer a reply. See "Mr. Matthew Arnold Amongst the Philistines," *Saturday Review,* XIX (February 25, 1865), 235–36 (p. 333 below).

247: 79   *my kind monitor, the Guardian:* Arnold here refers to the High Church weekly, established in 1846. In a letter to his mother, May 19, 1863, Arnold had noted the tendency of this "eminently *decorous* clerical journal" to grow alarmed at his outspokenness, probably regarding Spinoza and Bishop Colenso.

A review of Professor John Conington's translation of the *Odes and Carmen Seculare* of Horace had appeared in the *Guardian* for May 13, 1863, but though it suggests Arnold's Homer lectures had lacked "courteous discretion," it could scarcely be considered an admonition.

247: 87–88   *that Ajax of liberalism . . . "Presbyter Anglicanus":* "Presbyter Anglicanus" was a regular contributor to the editorial columns of the *Examiner,* submitting letters on current theological issues. Some of his letters include: "Fairness in Theological Controversy," October 1, 1864, pp. 628–29; "Fair Play," October 8, 1864, p. 644; "A Question for Dr. Pusey," October 22, 1864, p. 675; "The Established Church," October 29, 1864, p. 692; and "Archbishop Longley on the Decalogue," December 10, 1864, p. 788.

In his reply to Arnold's Preface, "Presbyter Anglicanus" expressly denied having blown his "trumpet-blast" in "half a dozen of the daily newspapers." He made no mention, however, of another accusation in this same paragraph of the Preface, the charge that Presbyter Anglicanus had been "terribly severe" in censuring Arnold's "levity" toward Bishop Colenso a few years earlier. See "The Philistines of the Nineteenth Century," *Examiner,* March 11, 1865, pp. 147–48. Oddly enough, the letters in the *Examiner* on Arnold and Bishop Colenso at this time are all signed "Anti-Esotericus." See "The Bishop and the Professor," *Examiner,* January 10, 1863, p. 20; and "Bishop Colenso and His Critics," *Examiner,* January 24, 1863, p. 52. No letters from Presbyter Anglicanus appeared in the *Examiner* for these dates, but those signed "Anti-Esotericus" may easily have come from his pen.

247: 92   *his masterpiece was the other day:* "Mr. Disraeli at Oxford," *Examiner,* December 3, 1864, pp. 772–73. "Mr. Disraeli has taken advantage of the annual meeting of the Oxford Diocesan Society for augmenting small livings to hold forth on a wide range of topics which have nothing whatever to do with the objects of that Society," Presbyter Anglicanus protested. He then proceeded to attack Disraeli's flippancy as an unworthy attempt to "make some political capital in the mean season," charging him with "making mock of the religion which he professes to accept."

In his reply to Arnold's banter here, Presbyter Anglicanus argued that while he had indeed recognized that Mr. Disraeli was speaking in fun, the "joke" struck him as "contemptible." Arnold noted this retort in a letter to his mother: "There is a long letter in to-day's *Examiner* from 'Presbyter Anglicanus,' gravely arguing that I have done him injustice and that he does understand a joke." See *Letters,* I, 292.

The entire text of Disraeli's speech, delivered in the Sheldonian Theatre in Oxford on Friday, 25 November, 1864, was reported in the *Times* for 26 November, 1864, pp. 7–8. See also the *Saturday Review,* XVIII (December 3, 1864), 678–79.

247: 97   *Mr. Maurice:* Maurice had been deprived of his professorship in theology at King's College, London, in 1853 for openly denying the doctrine of eternal damnation. His name continued to be identified with this particular "heresy" of Liberalism. See, for example, his letter "On Punishments Here and Hereafter," *Spectator,* XXXVII (January 9, 1864), 38–39.

"Presbyter Anglicanus" had defended Maurice in the *Examiner* before. See "Dr. Pusey and the Oxford Declaration," *Examiner,* March 19, 1864, p. 180; and "A Question for Dr. Pusey," *Examiner,* October 22, 1864, p. 675.

247: 100   *"This passage":* See the *Examiner,* December 3, 1864, p. 773. Arnold condenses somewhat "Presbyter Anglicanus's" original indignant protestation.

The passage as it appeared in the *Times,* Saturday, November 26, 1864, is as follows: "or whether I read the lucubrations of nebulous professors (a laugh), who appear in their style to have revived chaos (much laughter); and who if they could only succeed in obtaining a perpetual study of their writings would go far to realise that eternity of punishment which they object to (continued laughter)," p. 8, col. 2. Mr. Disraeli was disparaging the "new [Liberal] party" in the Church, citing instances of its insufficiency.

That "eminently decorous clerical journal," the *Guardian,* however, did not take offense at Mr. Disraeli's high spirits: "Religious or charitable societies, if they obtain the assistance of an eminent speaker, do so on the implied condition that he shall speak what he has a mind to say, while they, on the other hand, derive the benefit of the larger gathering, wider popularity, and more ample donations, which the presence of an illustrious supporter commands." See the *Guardian,* November 30, 1864, p. 1153.

The *Saturday Review* scored Mr. Disraeli's superficiality and levity, his "peculiar" convictions and pragmatic use of a Church party as "a convenient weapon." See "Mr. Disraeli at Oxford," *Saturday Review,* XVIII (December 3, 1864), 678–79. In the same vein, a reviewer of the first edition of *Essays in Criticism* later remarked upon "Mr. Disraeli's late speech at Oxford" as "that wonderful specimen of the tone of the Pharisee and the spirit of the Sadducee, combined with the grossest clap-trap of modern Philistinism." See the *North British Review,* XLII (March, 1865), 173.

4: 43; 248: 123   *the young lions:* Arnold subsequently collected in *Friendship's Garland* letters first published in the *Pall Mall Gazette,* adding a dedicatory letter to Adolescens Leo, Esq., of the *Daily Telegraph.* For the subsequent history of this "feud," see Sidney M. B. Coulling, "Matthew Arnold and the *Daily Telegraph,*" *Review of English Studies,* XII, N.S. (May, 1961), 173–79.

248: 131   *the British College of Health:* See the note to "The Function of Criticism at the Present Time," at 26: 683.

248: 133   *the hare's stomach:* Arnold here refers to an amusing incident in the controversy over verbal inspiration of the Bible. In a letter to the *Times* Bishop Colenso challenged the position taken by the Bishop of Manchester, Dr. Prince Lee, at a meeting of the Church Missionary Society in Manchester, reported in the *Times,* March 18, 1863. Dr. Lee had protested against the tendency to question the reliability of the Scriptures, and Bishop Colenso, after quoting him at length, countered with the text from Leviticus (xi. 6) where the hare is described as "chewing the cud." Bishop Colenso pointed out that the hare is not, in fact, "a ruminant animal." See "The Bishop of Manchester and the Bishop of Natal," *Times,* April 2, 1863, p. 10, col. 6; "Dr. Colenso and the Hare," *Times,* April 4, 1863, p. 9, col. 3; and "The Bishop of Manchester and Dr. Colenso," *Examiner,* April 11, 1863, p. 288. See also F. D. Maurice, *The Claims of the Bible and of Science* (London, 1863), Letter XIII, "Opinions of Bishops on the Foundations of Our Hopes."

248: 135   *our intellectual deliverer, Mr. James Clay:* Clay was the author of *A Treatise on Short Whist,* by J. C., M. P., affixed to J. L. Baldwin's *Laws of Short Whist* (London, 1864). A review of Clay's treatise in the *Times,* November 19, 1864, probably accounts for Arnold's remark here. The reviewer quotes an extract from Clay's opening chapter: "Of short whist alone I propose to treat. I shall thus spare the reader the learning much in the old works that it is not necessary for him to know, and not a little which, if learned, should be at once forgotten" (p. 5, col. 2). See also the *Quarterly Review,* CXXX (January, 1871), 43–71, and, the *Saturday Review,* XVIII (November 12, 1864), 593–94, where Clay's allusion to Mr. Spurgeon and Demosthenes is reported.

For Arnold's serious use of the term "intellectual deliverer," a key expression in his discussion of the modern spirit, see his inaugural lecture as Professor of Poetry at Oxford, "On the Modern Element in Literature," *Macmillan's Magazine,* XIX (February, 1869), 304–14. This essay has been reprinted in *Essays in Criticism, Third Series,* ed. E. J. O'Brien (Boston, 1910), in *Essays by Matthew Arnold* (Oxford, 1914), and in *Matthew Arnold: On the Classical Tradition,* ed. R. H. Super (Ann Arbor, 1960).

248: 143   *a monograph by Mr. Lowe:* Arnold is here referring to a speech of Robert Lowe, representing the Committee of the Council of Education, delivered at Nottingham and reported in the *Times,* October 29, 1864, p. 5, cols. 3–6. After defending the utility of local examinations administered by the University of Oxford, Mr. Lowe proceeded to hold forth at great length on the disadvantages of including Latin and Greek in "modern middle-class education": "In the study of Greek and Latin we are not following classical examples. Words could not express the indignation with which an ancient Greek would have received a request that he would learn Persian; and the Greek language does not contain a word equivalent in sense to our word 'grammar.' . . . They were educated to understand [the] things about them, and allowing other countries to speak their own language, they classed them all with sovereign contempt under the name of barbarians" (p. 5, col. 5).

See also "Mr. Lowe's Last Effort," *Spectator,* XXXVII (November 5, 1864), 1262–63; and "Mr. Lowe on Examinations," *Saturday Review,* XVIII (November 5, 1864), 552–53.

249: 145   *Mr. Spurgeon:* Charles Haddon Spurgeon was a popular Baptist preacher whose audiences overflowed the Metropolitan Tabernacle, a building erected for his use which accommodated thousands. Both the *Times* and the *Saturday Review,* however, scorned him. See, for example, "Mr. Spurgeon's Tabernacle," *Saturday Review,* VIII (August 20, 1859), 218–19; "An Evening at the Tabernacle," *Saturday Review,* XV (April 25, 1863), 528–29; and "A Visit to the Tabernacle," *Saturday Review,* XVIII (December 3, 1864), 690–91.

In a letter to his mother, November 9, 1866, Arnold described what was evidently his first attendance at one of Mr. Spurgeon's lectures: "it is a most striking performance, and reminded me very much of Bright's. Occasionally there were bits in which he showed unction and real feeling; sometimes he was the mere dissenting Philistine; but . . . I am very glad I have heard him." *Letters,* I, 398–99.

249: 147–49   *Joyce's Scientific Dialogues, Mangnall's Questions, The Wide Wide World:* These were children's books popular in the early part of the nineteenth century. Joyce's *Scientific Dialogues for the Instruction and Amusement of Young People,* a book explaining and illustrating the first principles of natural and experimental philosophy, first appeared in 1807, while *Historical and Miscellaneous Questions for the Use of Young People,* a kind of catechetical handbook of "useful information" for children, was first published anonymously in 1800. *The Wide Wide World* was a novel for little girls written by Elizabeth Wetherell, a children's author, under the pseudonym Susan Warner.

249: 149   *D'Iffanger's Speeches:* See the note at 251: 229–30. The British Museum catalogue lists printed copies of eight of Ferrand's speeches, delivered in and out of Parliament between 1842 and 1866. His address to the Bradford Working Men's Conservative Association, 20 November 1866, is of the tone and temper which Arnold has in mind here.

249: 151   *Inspector Tanner:* Richard Tanner was the police agent instrumental in capturing the murderer Franz Müller to whom Arnold refers in a later portion of this preface.

4: 50; 249: 156   *such phrases as:* Arnold is quoting from Wright's *Letter to the Dean of Canterbury on the Homeric Lectures of Matthew Arnold, Esq.,* pp. 5–6, 12. 65 reads "his professional assault," evidently a misprint. Another notable assailant in this line had been Francis Newman, in his *Homeric Translation in Theory and Practice, a Reply to Matthew Arnold, Esq., Professor of Poetry at Oxford* (London, 1861). In both instances, however, Arnold had provoked the language, since he had attacked the two translators in his Oxford lectures. Fitzjames Stephen's article in the *Saturday Review* made the most of Arnold's connection with Oxford. See "Homeric Translators and Critics," *Saturday Review,* XII (July 27, 1861), 95–96.

In a letter captioned "The Bishop and the Professor," *Examiner,* January 10, 1863, p. 20, "Anti-Esotericus" identified Arnold with the Chair of Poetry at Oxford in censuring his treatment of Bishop Colenso. A later comment from the same source continued the attack upon the Professor of Poetry at Oxford. See also "Recent Homeric Critics and Translators," *North British Review,* XXXVI (May, 1862), 350. For protests against Arnold's ex cathedra pronouncements about hexameters, see "Translations of the Odyssey," *Blackwood's Magazine,* XCI (March, 1862), 345–59.

5: 59; 249: 165 *a title I share:* It was customary for all conjurors and magicians to assume the title "Professor." A satiric article in *Punch,* XXII (January-June, 1852), mocks the Emperor Louis Napoleon as "Professor of Political Sleight of Hand." See also the cartoon "A Native and Foreign Professor" on p. 44 of the same volume.

4: 59–60; 249: 165–66 *Professor Pepper:* John Henry Pepper (1821–1900) was a conjuror noted for his optical illusion known as "Pepper's Ghost." Hence Arnold's reference to the "play of a divine light." Pepper was a "Professor of Chemistry" at the Royal Polytechnic Institute, a popular metropolitan place of amusement. The author of a *True History of the Ghost,* Professor Pepper later developed another illusion called "Metempsychosis." See the *Times,* December 28, 1863, p. 8.

4: 60; 249: 166 *Professor Anderson:* John Henry Anderson (1814–74) performed in London at St. James Theatre, the Strand, and the Music Hall at Leeds. Anderson, who called himself "the Great Wizard of the North," was famed for two feats in particular, the "gun trick" and "second sight." Robert Houdin included several pages on Anderson in his *Memoirs.*

4: 60; 249: 166 *Professor Frickel:* Wiljalba Frikell (1818–1903) was born in Finland and educated in Munich. He practiced conjuring for some years in Europe, and later traveled to India to study the thaumaturgy of the fakirs. His first appearance in London was a performance before Queen Victoria and the Royal Family at Windsor Castle, in 1851. An innovator in the art of magic, he eliminated the necessity for elaborate mechanical apparatus. Frikell is mentioned in an article on magic in the *British Quarterly Review,* XLII (July, 1865), 94–95. In *The Unmasking of Robert Houdin* (New York, 1908), Harry Houdini includes photographs of Frikell with personal reminiscences of the famous conjuror.

For an account of all three "Professors," see Henry Ridgely Evans, *The Old and the New Magic* (Chicago, 1906).

249: 173–74 *an illustrious Chancellor:* The phrase which Arnold here quotes is noted in the Preface to Lord Derby's two-volume translation of the *Iliad:* "Numerous as have been the translators of the *Iliad,* or of parts of it, the metres which have been selected have been almost as various: the ordinary couplet in rhyme, the Spenserian stanza, the Trochaic or Ballad metre, all have had their partisans, even to that 'pestilent heresy' of the so-called English hexameter." *The Iliad of Homer Rendered into English Blank Verse,* 2 vols. (London, 1865), I, Preface, vii. Lord Derby had become Chancellor of the University in 1852.

5: 82-83 ; 250: 200   *Müller perpetrated his detestable act:* Arnold is here referring to a sensational murder which filled the papers from July to November, 1864. Thomas Briggs, Esq., a banking clerk, was murdered in a first-class carriage on the North London line, near Bow, July 9, 1864, by the vagrant, Franz Müller. Müller attempted to escape to America by boarding the *Victoria,* which after a tedious passage of six weeks docked on August 24, 1864. Inspector Tanner, who had crossed more quickly and arrived in New York on August 5, was on hand for the arrest. Müller was tried on October 27–29, and was hanged on November 14, 1864. See the *Times* for July 11–14, 1864, and the *Examiner* from July to December, 1864. A complete account of the case is contained in the *Annual Register* for 1864.

251: 229-30   *to hear Mr. D'Iffanger speak:* The name "D'Iffanger" defies all efforts at identification. Arnold has doubtless confused the name of William Busfield Ferrand, a member of the House of Commons since 1841, and very much the sort of figure suggested by Arnold's context here. Issues of the *Saturday Review* and of the *Illustrated London News* for November 12, 1864, both carried notices of Ferrand's speech to his constituents at Devonport. It can be demonstrated that Arnold had been reading both these papers.

The latter paper amused itself with "the peculiar qualities of Mr. Ferrand's eloquence" manifested on the occasions of his "delivering himself of one of those tremendous monologues with himself for the chief part of the audience, which once or twice in a Session the House of Commons allows him." Further comments on this "hurricane of a denunciator" very likely suggested him as prey for Arnold's preface: "Years ago when Sir Robert Peel—the Sir Robert—flourished as the greatest Member of Parliament that ever lived, we used to hear the roar and rattle of Mr. Ferrand's diatribes; and gigantic physical efforts they were. The lapse of sixteen or seventeen years does not seem to have toned down the capability of loud and blusterous talk which sounds so fierce and menacing, and which yet, after all, is born of the very good-nature and warm human feeling of the man. He is always denouncing what he conceives to be oppression, or misconduct, or intrigue, and he rushes at it like a hungry lion." See the *Illustrated London News,* November 12, 1864, p. 486.

Arnold may have been echoing mentally the name of Dr. Döllinger, Professor of Theology in the University of Munich, of whom his brother Thomas, then teaching in the Oratorian School in Birmingham, would have spoken frequently. The text of Ferrand's 1864 speech at Devonport was evidently not carried by the *Times.* That for 1863, however, appeared in the *Times* on 30 October (p. 5) and surveyed his "Parliamentary stewardship" during the previous session.

251: 231-32   *the amiable Dean of Ripon:* William Goode, D.D. (1801–68), was a vigorous champion of the Evangelical position in disputed issues concerning the Church of England. Arnold's description of the Dean as "amiable" appears to be somewhat facetious.

Arnold is here alluding to the storm aroused by Spurgeon's sermon entitled "Baptismal Regeneration," delivered in 1864. In it, Spurgeon openly reproved the Evangelical party for cowardly adherence to that Church whose professed doctrine on justification was antagonistic to the Evangelical position. Dean Goode's energetic reply to Spurgeon was his pamphlet: "Let Us Hear the Church. The Dean of Ripon's Letter on Mr. Spurgeon's Sermons with Some Reviews of the *Christian Observer, Furnishing Answers to the Query*——What Do the Ancient and Modern Reformers Say to Mr. Spurgeon's Charges?" (London, 1864).

Spurgeon's motto, *Cedo Nulli* ("I yield to none"), gives special point to Arnold's remark about "turning the other cheek."

6: 114; 251: 233   *his great dissected Master:* Jeremy Bentham authorized the dissection of his body in the interests of scientific research. His clothed skeleton is preserved in the museum of University College, London.

6: 122; 251: 241   *"There are our young barbarians":* This is an adaptation of Byron's description of the dying gladiator: "*There* were his young barbarians all at play." *Childe Harold's Pilgrimage,* IV, cxli.

6: 124-25; 243-44   *last enchantments of the Middle Age:* See Arnold's portrait of Cardinal Newman in the lecture on Emerson, where this phrase is applied to the character of Newman: "Somewhere or other I have spoken of those 'last enchantments of the Middle Age' which Oxford sheds around us, and here they were." Arnold, "Emerson," *Discourses in America* (London, 1889), p. 142.

6: 128; 251: 247   *Tübingen:* Arnold refers to the school of Biblical criticism headed by Christian Baur, who became Professor of Theology at Tübingen in 1826. In a review of R. W. Mackay's *The Tübingen School and Its Antecedents* (London, 1863), a critic characterized the school thus: "They might, we think, be called constructive rationalists, in opposition to the destructive rationalism of Strauss. The constructives are but little known in England, where the general mind has not yet got beyond their predecessors." See the *Athenaeum,* July 18, 1863, p. 78. See also "Tübingen in 1864," *Macmillan's Magazine,* X (October, 1864), 433–42, an article which Arnold was no doubt reading at this time.

To Arnold, Tübingen symbolized the scientific approach to theological questions, an approach which he strongly disliked. For his later comments on Baur and the Tübingen School, see *God and the Bible,* chapter 5.

7: 137; 251: 256   *was uns alle bändigt:* This is from Goethe's "Epilog zu Schillers Glocke," *Werke* (Stuttgart und Tübingen, 1829), XIII, 162:

"Indessen schritt sein Geist gewaltig fort
In's Ewige des Wahren, Guten, Schönen,
Und hinter ihm, in wesenlosem Scheine,
Lag, was uns Alle bändigt, das Gemeine."

THE FUNCTION OF CRITICISM AT THE PRESENT TIME

This essay first appeared in the National Review *for November, 1864.*

8: 3   *I said: 'Of the literature':* See "On Translating Homer," Lecture II, last paragraph; *Matthew Arnold: On the Classical Tradition,* ed. R. H. Super (Ann Arbor, 1960), p. 140.

8: 14–15   *a Mr. Shairp's excellent notice:* "Wordsworth: the Man and the Poet," *North British Review,* XLI (August, 1864), 1–54. On p. 32 of this article, Shairp commends Wordsworth's power of rendering "the inner truth of things, which Mr. Arnold has happily called the interpretative power of poetry." John Campbell Shairp had been a close friend of Arnold's at Balliol. See *The Letters of Matthew Arnold to Arthur Hugh Clough* (London, 1932), p. 104, n. 5, and index. Shairp himself became Professor of Poetry at Oxford in 1877.

See also George Knight, *Principal Shairp and His Friends* (London, 1888).

9: 18–19   *Wordsworth says in one of his letters:* See the letter to Bernard Barton, from Rydal Mount, January 12, 1816; Christopher Wordsworth, *Memoirs of William Wordsworth* (London, 1851), II, 53.

9: 24–25   *a more elaborate judgment:* The reporter was probably Lady Richardson. See *Memoirs,* II, 439. The quotation is also included in George Knight's *Life of William Wordsworth* (Edinburgh, 1899), III, 438 (chapter XLV, "Later Years at Rydal").

11: 123   *It has long seemed to me:* For other judgments of Arnold on the Romantic movements, including those of France and Germany, see the notes to "Maurice de Guérin" at 60: 281, and "Heinrich Heine," pages 107–8.

12: 140–41   *whom he disparaged without reading him:* Wordsworth spoke of Goethe as a "poetical sensualist," and disliked him on moral grounds. "There is a profligacy, an inhuman sensuality, in [Goethe's] works which is utterly revolting. I am not intimately acquainted with them generally." See Christopher Wordsworth, *Memoirs,* II, 478; Knight, *Life of Wordsworth,* II, 324. On another occasion Wordsworth is quoted as having insisted that Goethe "had not sufficiently clear moral perceptions to make him anything but an artificial writer." See Edith C. Batho, *The Later Wordsworth* (Cambridge, 1933), pp. 374–75.

13: 187   *'thrown quiet culture back':* Arnold is here quoting Epigramm 62 from "Vier Jahreszeiten: Herbst": "Franztum drängt in diesen verworrenen Tägen, wie ehmals Luthertum es getan, ruhige Bildung zurück." See *Goethe's Sämtliche Werke* (Stuttgart und Berlin, 1902–12), I, 242.

13: 203–4   *the old woman:* For an account of Jenny Geddes' exploit see Carlyle's *The Letters and Speeches of Oliver Cromwell,* ed. S. C. Lomas, 3 vols. (London, 1904), I, 85–86 (Part I, Letter II).

13: 207   *to count by tens:* Fitzjames Stephen had made great fun of this assertion of Arnold's in his reply to this essay upon its first appearance. See "Mr. Matthew Arnold and His Countrymen," *Saturday Review,* XVIII

(December 3, 1864), 683–85. Arnold's bantering footnote in the first edition, since deleted, does not escape notice in Stephen's subsequent review, "Mr. Matthew Arnold Amongst the Philistines," *Saturday Review,* XIX (February 25, 1865), 235–36. See pp. 330–31 and 334–35 below.

14: 211 *a decimal coinage:* This was actually a controversial subject at this time, as Arnold's footnote in the first edition indicates. A *Times* article described the English system as "dislocated, incoherent, and utterly inconsistent," while the French decimal system was favored by some members of Parliament as one which "afforded satisfaction" and "gave a constant triumph to the reason." See "The Decimal and Metric Systems in Practice," *Times,* July 9, 1863, p. 5, cols. 1–3.

14: 243 *'C'est la force':* *Pensées de Joseph Joubert,* ed. M. Paul Raynal (Paris, 1909), Titre XV, "De la liberté, de la justice, et des lois," ii (p. 178).

15: 270 *what distinguishes these writings:* In a letter of January, 1864, Arnold explained his enthusiasm for Burke to his sister: "What makes Burke stand out so splendidly among politicians is that he treats politics with his thought and imagination; therefore, whether one agrees with him or not, he always interests you, stimulates you, and does you good." *Letters,* I, 249.

15: 286 *'to party gave up':* See the epitaph "Good Edmund" in Oliver Goldsmith's poem "Retaliation."

16: 290 *some of the last pages:* See Herbert W. Paul, *Matthew Arnold* (London, 1902), p. 76, for an account of Arnold's "strange historical error" in this regard.

16: 293 *'The evil is stated':* See *The Works and Correspondence of the Right Honourable Edmund Burke* (London, 1852), IV, 591.

18: 374 *disinterestedness:* This major critical tenet of Arnold's derives from his reading in Goethe, Spinoza, and Sainte-Beuve. For evidence of the influence of Goethe and Spinoza in this regard, see Helen C. White, "Matthew Arnold and Goethe," *PMLA,* XXXVI (September, 1921), 439–40. Arnold acknowledges his indebtedness to Sainte-Beuve in this matter in a letter to Sainte-Beuve, January 6, 1854; see Louis Bonnerot, *Matthew Arnold, Poète: Essai de Biographie Psychologique* (Paris, 1947), Appendice, pp. 518–19. See also Sainte-Beuve's review of the *Lettres* of Mademoiselle de Lespinasse, *Causeries du Lundi,* II.

18: 399–400 *We have the Edinburgh Review:* Hazlitt makes the same point in his article entitled "The Periodical Press" which appeared in the *Edinburgh Review* for May, 1823. See *The Collected Works of William Hazlitt,* ed. A. R. Waller and Arnold Glover (London, 1904), X, 202–30. See also: "Remarks on the Periodical Criticism of England," *Blackwood's Edinburgh Magazine,* II (March, 1818), 670–79, and "On Critics and Criticism," *Blackwood's Edinburgh Magazine,* VIII (November, 1820), 138–40.

19: 413–14 *the extinction . . . of the Home and Foreign Review.* This quarterly was edited by Lord Acton, and, under his direction, became the "lay Catholic organ" in Victorian England. In 1858 Lord Acton had joined the staff of the *Rambler,* a bimonthly designed to stimulate Catholic literary production, succeeding Cardinal Newman as its editor in the next year. Although the *Rambler* nominally ceased publication in 1862, it actually continued as the *Home and Foreign Review*. Ecclesiastical opposition to its liberalism, however, increased during the next two years. One incident in particular profoundly influenced the fate of the *Review*.

In September, 1863, an Apostolic Brief on the subject of Catholic scholarship was officially promulgated. Although it contained no direct reference to the *Home and Foreign Review*, Lord Acton felt that the principles of submission to authority which it asserted were in total opposition to the design of his liberal Catholic organ. Since he could not in conscience operate in defiance of these principles, he dissolved the *Review* in 1864. The last issue of the *Home and Foreign Review* contains Lord Acton's vindication of Catholic liberalism as "an imperishable idea" of which his review had been only "a partial and temporary embodiment." See Lord Acton, *Essays on Church and State*, ed. Douglas Woodruff (London, 1952), pp. 16–34; Roland Hill, "Lord Acton and the Catholic Reviews," *Blackfriars*, XXXVI (December, 1955), 469–82; and Josef Altholz, *The Liberal Catholic Movement in England: "The Rambler" and Its Contributors, 1848–64* (London, 1962).

Arnold's brother Thomas, a convert to Roman Catholicism, had contributed several articles to the *Review*, among them "The Formation of the English Counties," "The Colonisation of Northumbria," "Hayti," and "Albania." His acknowledgment of these articles in the *Review* appears in his *Passages in a Wandering Life* (London, 1900), p. 177.

19: 437   *Sir Charles Adderley says* . . . '*Talk of the improvement':* Arnold is here quoting a speech which Adderley actually made at the annual meeting of the Warwickshire Agricultural Association, held at Leamington on September 16, 1863, and reported in the *Times* for the next day. Adderley commended the Association's contributions to society in the extravagant terms which so amused Arnold that he copied into his notebook for 1863 the excerpt which eventually found its way into this essay. See *The Note-Books of Matthew Arnold*, ed. H. F. Lowry, K. Young, and W. H. Dunn (London, 1952), pp. 21–22, and the *Times*, September 17, 1863, p. 5, col. 6.

19: 443–44   *Mr. Roebuck says* . . . '*I look around me':* Roebuck spoke at a dinner given by the Mayor of Sheffield in the Cutlers' Hall, August 18, 1864. A report of the event appeared in the *Times* for Friday, August 19, 1864, p. 4, cols. 4–5. Arnold also included this quotation in his notebook for 1864. See *Note-Books*, pp. 25–26. Roebuck actually used each of the inflated phrases which Arnold here quotes, but his tone was not altogether serious.

20: 452–53   '*Das wenige verschwindet':* This is from Goethe's *Iphigenie auf Tauris*, I, ii, 92–93.

20: 483–84   *A girl named Wragg:* An account of the trial of Elizabeth Wragg appeared in the *Times*, March 15, 1865, p. 12, col. 3. See Merle Bevington, *The Saturday Review: 1855–1868* (New York, 1941), p. 146. In his review of the first edition of *Essays in Criticism*, "Mr. Matthew Arnold Amongst the Philistines," which appeared in the *Saturday Review* for February 25,

1865, Stephen volunteered the latest information available concerning Wragg, replying in kind to Arnold's Preface. See p. 333 below.

21: 519–20   *the Indian virtue of detachment:* For evidence of Arnold's early attraction to the *Bhagavad-Gita*, see the *Letters to Clough*, pp. 69–71, 75. In a letter of March 4, 1848, for example, he wrote: "The Indians distinguish between meditation or absorption—and knowledge: and between abandoning practice, and abandoning the fruits of action and all respect thereto. This last is a supreme step, and dilated on throughout the Poem" (p. 71). Arnold's dictum of disinterestedness in criticism no doubt derives something from the "Indian virtue."

21: 522   *The mass of mankind:* Arnold is here making use of Spinoza's distinction between adequate and inadequate ideas. See the note to "Spinoza and the Bible," at 202: 750.

22: 553–54   *Lord Somers:* John Somers, Lord Somers (1651–1716), was a lawyer, statesman, and champion of the British Constitution, who supervised the drafting of the Declaration of Rights after the abdication of James II. Macaulay included a favorable sketch of Lord Somers in his *History of England from the Accession of James the Second,* IV (New York, 1879), chapter 20, 520–23.

23: 577   *intellectual delicacy, and the few and the many:* Arnold is here referring to the indignation aroused on so many sides by the line which he had taken in censuring the work of Bishop Colenso. His double criterion of information for the few, edification for the many, had provoked such heated protests as "Mr. Matthew Arnold on the Aristocratic Creed," *Spectator,* XXXV (December 27, 1862), 1438–39, and W. R. Greg's "Truth *Vs.* Edification," in the *Westminster Review* for April, 1863. Arnold's ideas on information and edification derive from Spinoza. See, for example, Spinoza's Preface to the *Tractatus Theologico-Politicus; The Chief Works of Benedict de Spinoza,* trans. R. H. M. Elwes I, (London, 1909), 11.

23: 585–86   *To act is so easy:* Arnold refers to a passage in Wilhelm Meister's "Lehrbrief": "Die Kunst ist lang, das Leben kurz, das Urteil schwierig, die Gelegenheit flüchtig. Handeln ist leicht, denken schwer; nach dem Gedachten handeln unbequem." See *Wilhelm Meister's Lehrjahre; Goethe's Sämtliche Werke,* Jubilaums-Ausgabe (Stuttgart und Berlin, 1902–12), XVIII, 259.

23: 590–91   *Perissons en résistant:* See E. P. de Senancour, *Obermann* (Paris, 1882), Supplement, Lettre XC, p. 412.

23: note 1:   *There is truth of science:* For Arnold's complete argument on this score see "Dr. Stanley's *Lectures on the Jewish Church,*" *Macmillan's Magazine,* VII (February, 1863), 327–36. This article was reprinted in *Essays in Criticism, with the Addition of Two Essays Not Hitherto Reprinted* (London, 1900?), 261–81 (New Universal Library edition).

24: 599–600   *the multitude . . . does really live by its true religion:* This argument is the basis of Arnold's reaction to Greg's article, "Truth *Vs.* Edification." See *Letters,* I, 219.

24: 604–5   *'Ignorance . . . in intellectual matters':* Pensées, ed. Raynal, Titre

XXIII, "Des qualités de l'écrivain, et des compositions litteraires," liv (p. 311).

24: note 1: *It has been said:* Arnold quotes Fitzjames Stephen in "Mr. Matthew Arnold and His Countrymen," *Saturday Review,* XVIII (December 3, 1864), 685. Arnold speaks of the importance of literary criticism to the diffusion of the higher culture in "The Bishop and the Philosopher," *Macmillan's Magazine,* VII (January, 1863), 245.

24; 626–27 *in her survey:* Frances Power Cobbe, *Broken Lights: an Inquiry into the Present Condition and Future Prospects of Religious Faith* (London, 1864). The book contains appendices on Renan and Colenso. Miss Cobbe borrowed her title from *In Memoriam:* "They ["our little systems"] are but broken lights of thee" (Prologue, 19).

The *Saturday Review* commended Miss Cobbe for her "frankness" and intelligibility, adding that this was "a remarkable book for any woman to have written, being calm, fair, and well-informed." See "Literature and Theology," *Saturday Review,* XVII (February 13, 1864), 187–88; "Miss Cobbe's *Italics,*" *Saturday Review,* XVIII (October 29, 1864), 540–42; "Miss Cobbe's Theology," *Spectator,* XXXVII (February 20, 1864), 213–15; "Contemporary Literature: Theology," *Westminster Review,* XXV, N.S. (April, 1864), 550–52; and *The Life of Frances Power Cobbe as Told by Herself* (London, 1904), pp. 400–407.

24: 627 *Bishop Colenso's book:* Arnold deprecates Colenso's pseudo-scientific approach to Biblical criticism, an approach which he regarded as neither constructive nor relevant to the problem "as now presented for solution." Arnold's own analysis and solution of the problem were to emerge in *Literature and Dogma.*

25: 647 *'Quiconque s'imagine':* See Claude Fleury, *Discours sur l'histoire écclesiastique* (premier discours servant de préface), new edition (Paris, 1763), p. 24. Arnold included this quotation in his notebook for 1863. See *Note-Books,* p. 22.

25: 656   *nemo doctus:* Cicero, *Ad Atticum,* XVI, 7, 3.

25: 659–60 *to find us:* Speaking of his perusal of the Old and New Testaments, Coleridge says: "I have found words for my inmost thoughts, songs for my joy, utterances for my hidden griefs, and pleadings for my shame and my feebleness. In short, whatever *finds* me, bears witness for itself that it has proceeded from the Holy Spirit." See Samuel Taylor Coleridge, *Confessions of an Inquiring Spirit.* Reprinted from the third edition, 1853, with the introduction by Joseph Henry Green and the note by Sara Coleridge. Ed. H. St. John Hart (London, 1956), Letter I, p. 42. Coleridge again uses the expression in Letter II.

26: 674 *her recent Religious Duty:* The second volume in a projected series, following the *Theory of Morals,* was *Religious Duty.* The former appeared in 1855, the latter in 1864: "As far as we have gathered opinions concerning it [*Religious Duty*] from religious persons, it is judged to be somewhat too severe in its exactions, and (what may be called) too stoical. . . . As we may say of her first treatise [*Theory of Morals*], that we never before read a book on morality which seemed to kindle one to a love of goodness;

so of the second we may say, that of the sermons we have heard, there are indeed few that have so purifying and invigorating a power." See "The Capacities of Women," *Westminster Review*, XXVIII, N.S. (October, 1865), 376. Pages 368–80 of this article are devoted to the works of Miss Cobbe.

26: 683   *Dr. Morrison and his disciples:* James Morrison (1770–1840), was a merchant who cured himself of illness by medication he himself had devised. "Morrison's Pills" were advertised as a universal cure-all; hence the title of a chapter in Carlyle's *Past and Present*. Morrison called himself "the Hygeist," and established himself in business in the "British College of Health."

During the first few months of 1852, advertisements appeared in the papers soliciting funds for a monument to Morrison. The humor of this did not escape the editors of *Punch*, who included a commentary on the proposed "Monument for the Man of Pills": "We think that a simple slab of stone erected in the churchyard fullest of the Doctor's late patients would be sufficient, with the well-known words: 'Si monumentum quaeris, circumspice!' " A subsequent thrust suggested the use of " 'monumental brass,' that being the material most in keeping with the intended object." See *Punch*, XXII (January-June, 1852), 118, 141.

28: 763   *Ab integro:* Virgil, *Eclogues*, IV, 5.

THE LITERARY INFLUENCE OF ACADEMIES

This essay first appeared in the Cornhill Magazine *for August, 1864.*

31: 1–2   *the history of the French Academy: Histoire de l'Académie Française,* par Pellisson et d'Olivet, avec une introduction, des éclaircissements et des notes par M. Ch.-L. Livet. 2 vols. (Paris, 1858). Arnold's account of the French Academy is taken in part from the first chapters of this book. Other sources are Sainte-Beuve's review of Livet's edition, reprinted in *Causeries du Lundi*, XIV, and Renan's essay, "L'Académie Française," in *Essais de Morale et de Critique* (Paris, 1903).

31: 9   *'It may safely be said':* See the twelfth and last of the "Letters from a Competition Wallah," *Macmillan's Magazine*, X (May, 1864), 3. This letter was entitled "Education of India since 1835 (with a Hitherto Unpublished Minute of Lord Macaulay)," the Minute being dated February 2, 1835. G. Otto Trevelyan reprinted the "Minute on Indian Education" in *The Life and Letters of Lord Macaulay* (London, 1876), I, 354. It also appears in the Oxford volume of *Speeches by Lord Macaulay* (London, 1935), p. 350.

32: 49   *Its statutes of foundation:* Livet reprints the statutes from the text of 1708 in an appendix, to supplement Pellisson's brief discussion of them in his second chapter. See *Histoire de l'Académie Française,* ed. Livet, I,

489–97. The article which Arnold here quotes, the twenty-fourth, appears also in Livet's introduction.

33: 67   *a literary tribunal:* "Mais ce que Richelieu voulait décidement . . . c'était de la faire juge des oeuvres d'éclat qui paraîtraient; de la constituer haut jury, comme nous dirions, haut tribunal littéraire tenu de donner son avis sur les productions *actuelles* les plus considérables qui partageraient le public." Sainte-Beuve, *Causeries,* XIV, 208.

33: 80   *[La Mésnardière] declared:* This was in a discourse at his reception into l'Académie Française. Quoted by Sainte-Beuve, *Causeries,* XIV, 207–8.

33: 95   *'a sovereign organ of opinion':* "Malgré le rôle brillant que l'Académie sut prendre dans la seconde moitié du dix-huitième siècle et qui fit d'elle un souverain organe de l'opinion . . . je ne crois pas qu'elle ait tout à fait et de tous point rempli le voeu de son fondateur; elle a fait plus et moins que ce qu'il voulait." *Causeries,* XIV, 205–6.

33: 95–34: 96   *'The duty of the Academy':* Renan, "L'Académie Française," *Essais de Morale et de Critique* (Paris, 1903), p. 350.

34: 98   *'maîtrise en fait de bon ton':* "L'Académie Française," p. 344.

34: 99   *'All ages':* "L'Académie Française," pp. 350–51.

34: 111–12   *'was uns alle bändigt':* "Epilog zu Schillers Glocke," *Werke* (Stuttgart und Tübingen, 1829), XIII, 162.

34: 122   *'quid sit ordo': De Officiis,* I, 4–5.

34: 134   *'In France': Causeries,* XIV, I, 4–5.

35: 138   *Those are very remarkable words:* In a letter to Alexis de Saint-Priest, November 28, 1848, however, Sainte-Beuve observed: "L'Académie, quoiqu'il en soit, me parait bien effacée; on n'y fait rien, on n'y fera rien, on manque de direction, de but de tout ce qu'il faut aux corps aussi bien qu'aux individus. Ce n'est qu'un salon, à ce titre du moins c'est quelque chose. Tâchons qu'elle reste un club littéraire de bonne compagnie." *Correspondance Générale de Sainte-Beuve,* ed. Jean Bonnerot (Paris, 1935), VII, 389.

In a note to this letter, the editor includes the following excerpt from a letter of Charles Brifaut to J. M. Frantin: "J'ai vu presque dans le sein de notre propre Académie Villemain, Villemain lui-même, déblatérer contre cette institution, qu'il jugeait, inutile et absurde, ajoutant qu'il n'existait point d'Académie anglaise, ce qui n'empêchait pas de parler très bien la langue de pays à Londres" (p. 390, n. 8).

35: 164   *energy and honesty:* Arnold again argues this point about the English national character in his essay "Equality." See Matthew Arnold, *Mixed Essays, Irish Essays, and Others* (London, 1883), p. 57.

38: 273   *Bernouilli:* In a critical essay on Arnold in the *British Quarterly Review,* this error in spelling does not escape caustic comment: Arnold, the critic complains, "holds that an English Academy would prevent the *Times* from misspelling 'diocese,' which it always spells 'diocess,' as if it were 'derived from Deus and census.' Perhaps an Academy might also teach Mr. Arnold how to spell Bernoulli's name." "Matthew Arnold, Poet and Essayist," *British Quarterly Review,* XLII (October 2, 1865), 249.

40: 340   *the Journal des Débats:* Founded in 1789, this newspaper in time be-

came an outstanding critical journal under the MM. Bertin, who directed
it from 1801 to 1807. Among its contributors were Geoffroy, Dussault,
Féletz, Delalot, Saint-Victor, and later Hoffman. In 1815 the name was
changed to the *Journal de l'Empire.* See Sainte-Beuve, "M. de Féletz et de
la Critique littéraire sous l'Empire," *Causeries,* I.

40: 352   *his Jashar:* In 1854 Dr. John W. Donaldson published at Berlin a
Latin work on the Book of Jashar, a hypothetical narrative reconstructed
from fragments which supposedly survived in the Old Testament. The
work, based upon two bits of evidence and a highly active imagination,
was unfavorably received as ingenious but unscholarly. See "Donaldson's
Book of Jashar," *London Quarterly Review,* V (January, 1856), 455–63;
"Contemporary Literature: Theology," *Westminster Review,* VII, N.S.
(April, 1855), 517–22; and "Dilettanti Society," *Edinburgh Review,* CV
(April, 1857), 512.

40: 354   *M. Renan calls it:* Renan uses this expression in *Études d'Histoire
Religieuse* (Paris, 1858), chapter 2, "L'Histoire du Peuple d'Israël," p. 83,
n. 1. "It is astonishing" etc. is a continuation of the same footnote.

40: 366–67   *'America and England':* See chapter 4, "Mahomet et les Origines de
l'Islamisme," p. 222. All this criticism is from the same section.

40: 368   *Irving's 'Life of Mahomet':* The Lives of Mahomet and His Successors,*
2 vols. (London, 1850).

41: 371   *Mr. Charles Forster published: Mahometanism unveiled: an inquiry
in which that arch-heresy, its diffusion and continuance, are examined on
a new principle tending to confirm the evidences and aid the propagation
of the Christian Faith,* 2 vols. (London, 1829); *The One Primeval
Language traced experimentally through ancient inscriptions in alphabetic
characters of lost powers from the four continents* (London, 1851).

41: 395   *urbanity:* Arnold borrows the word from Sainte-Beuve. In his review of
Livet's edition, Sainte-Beuve remarks: "Il y a, il y avait du temps de Pellisson deux sortes d'élégance et d'urbanité, soit en causant, soit en
écrivant," *Causeries,* XIV, 195. And again in "De la Critique littéraire
sous l'Empire," he describes M. de Féletz as "un veillard aimable, spirituel,
qui recouvrait sous les formes d'une politesse exquise et d'une parfaite
urbanité mondaine un caractère ferme, des opinions nettes et constantes,
bien de la philosophie pratique," *Causeries,* I, 293.

41: 402   *the note of so and so:* In a letter to his mother, November 9, 1866,
Arnold defends his use of this word: "As to 'note,' it is used in the sense
of the Latin word *nota* to mean a *mark.* It has long been used in theology,
and from thence I took it." *Letters,* I, 397.

41: 407   *provinciality:* Sainte-Beuve also used this term to describe the work of
Pellisson: "Mais si je crois sentir en lui une première couche legère de
provincialisme, ce n'est qu'au fond de certains de ses jugements et non
dans l'élégance accomplie de sa diction." *Causeries,* XIV, 197. Later, in
his Preface to *Culture and Anarchy* Arnold defined "provinciality" as
"narrowness, one-sidedness, and incompleteness." See *Culture and Anarchy,* ed. J. Dover Wilson (Cambridge, 1955), p. 12.

42: 432   *'So have I seen':* This passage is from "A Funeral Sermon Preached at the Obsequies of the Right Honourable and Most Virtuous Lady, the Lady Frances, Countess of Carberry," *The Practical Works of Jeremy Taylor,* 2 vols. (London, 1854), I, 440.

42: 449   *'Il ira':* This sermon was preached in a hospital in Paris, probably in 1659. See Bossuet, *Oeuvres Choisies,* ed. J. Calvet (Paris, 1917), p. 53. An English translation of the Panegyric of St. Paul appears in *Panegyrics of the Saints from the French of Bossuet and Bourdaloue,* ed. Rev. D. O'Mahoney (London, 1924), pp. 1–19.

43: 458   *'Blindfold themselves':* The *Works of the Right Honourable Edmund Burke* (London, 1852), IV, 348. The quotation is from "Reflections on the Revolution in France," and Burke is here indignantly censuring certain financial expedients employed by the French National Assembly.

43: 463   *'They used it':* This is from "A Letter to a Member of the National Assembly," *Works,* IV, 370. Burke refers to the tactics of the "usurpers" of French royal power.

43: 468   *'Without one natural pang':* This is from "Letter to a Member," *Works,* IV, 374. The discussion concerns the position of Rosseau as philosopher of the Revolution; Burke calls him "the insane Socrates of the National Assembly."

43: 472   *'I confess':* This is from "Reflections on the Revolution," *Works,* IV, 202. Burke is censuring the tendency of certain political theorists of the day to glorify the wrong aspects of the French Revolution.

44: 505   *'Those who delight':* "On the Means of Strengthening Faith," *Spectator,* no. 465, August 23, 1712. Arnold included this excerpt in his notebook for 1864. See *Note-Books,* pp. 29–30.

45: 519   *'L'expérience de beaucoup':* Pensées, Titre XVI, "Des Moeurs Publiques et Privées," xvii, p. 188. Arnold included this quotation in one of his general notebooks. See *Note-Books,* p. 543.

45: 544   *lenis minimeque pertinax:* Cicero, *De Officiis,* i. 134.

45: 547–48   *Goethe . . . about the immorality of Byron's poems:* "Byrons *Don Juan,*" *Werke* (Stuttgart und Tübingen, 1833), XLVI, 209. Goethe was defending himself against a possible charge of diffusing objectionable literature in Germany.

46: 569–70   *the critic who so disliked the Emperor of the French:* The *Saturday Review* regarded the position of the Emperor Napoleon as a threat to English national security, and nearly every issue contained an abusive leading article on the "Emperor of the French," even as late as 1864. See, for example, "The Advance of a Great Power," *Saturday Review,* V (February 13, 1858), 153–54; "The Emperor's Speech," *Saturday Review,* VII (February 12, 1859), 176–77; "The Duplicity of Louis Napoleon," *Saturday Review,* VII (April 30, 1859), 513; "Faithful Allies," *Saturday Review,* VII (May 14, 1859), 582–83; "The Liberator of Italy," *Saturday Review,* VIII (July 2, 1859), 7; and "Two Careers," *Saturday Review,* IX (May 5, 1860), 563–64.

For a study of the *Review's* political character, see Merle Bevington, *The Saturday Review: 1855–1868,* chapter 2.

46: 570–71   *who so disliked . . . academies:* This attitude was not characteristic of the "French Literature" column of the *Review* but rather of separate critical articles which appeared from time to time. See, for example, "The Elections to the French Academy," *Saturday Review*, XV (May 2, 1863), 544–45; and "The French Academy of Sciences," *Saturday Review*, XVIII (July 9, 1864), 62–63. In an article on the English Royal Academy this organization was described as "a close, self-elected, irresponsible body" with "a natural tendency towards corruption." See "Academicians *versus* Artists," *Saturday Review*, XV (May 9, 1863), 592.

46: 571–72   *so fond of the German element:* The critic to whom Arnold here refers is Edward Augustus Freeman (1823–92), author, historian, and voluminous contributor to the *Saturday Review*. See Hon. Lionel A. Tollemache, *Old and Odd Memories* (London, 1908), p. 306; and Merle Bevington, *The Saturday Review: 1855–1868*, p. 342.

A few of Freeman's articles illustrating the "Teuton crochet" are: "Dean Hoare's Exotics," *Saturday Review*, XVI (August 15, 1863), 227–29; a review of Charles Kingsley's *The Roman and the Teuton*, *Saturday Review*, XVII (April 9, 1864), 446–48; "The Landesgemeinden of Uri and Appenzell," *Saturday Review*, XVII (May 21, 1864), 622–23; and "Sion," *Saturday Review*, XVII (June 11, 1864), 715–16.

46: 591   *'Go out, in the spring-time':* Modern Painters, III, chapter xiv, "Of Medieval Landscape: First, the Fields."

47: 612   *'Of Shakespeare's names':* This is from *Munera Pulveris*, chapter 5, "Of Government."

47: 637   *The plan of arrangement:* Arnold is here referring to the Preface to Palgrave's *Golden Treasury*, where its editor had outlined a very elaborate scheme for arranging his selections: "Within each book the pieces have . . . been arranged in gradations of feeling or subject. The development of the symphonies of Mozart and Beethoven has been here thought of as a model, and nothing placed without careful consideration." See F. T. Palgrave, *The Golden Treasury of the Best Songs and Lyrics in the English Language* (London, 1861), Preface, p. iii.

48: 640   *those of Wordsworth and Shelley:* Arnold here refers to Wordsworth's "My Heart Leaps Up" and Shelley's lament beginning, "O World! O Life! O Time!"

48: 650   *this note on Milton's line:* This is a note on line 10 of Milton's sonnet "When the Assault was Intended to the City." See the *Golden Treasury*, p. 314.

48: 666   *the famous Handbook: Handbook to the Fine Arts Collections in the International Exhibition of 1862*, by F. T. Palgrave, Fellow of Exeter College, Oxford (London, 1862).

49: 692   *he quotes a criticism by M. Gustave Planche:* M. Planche was a critic and contributor to the *Revue des Deux Mondes*. In a letter to Sainte-Beuve, January 28, 1863, Arnold had remarked: "Planche est mort, et Planche est le seul contemporain qu'on eût pu vous opposer: et encore Planche se permettait-il trop souvent (ce vous ne vous permettez jamais) d'être cassant et peu élastique." Bonnerot, *Matthew Arnold*, p. 532.

The quotation which Arnold includes here is from Planche's article,

"Statue Equèstre de M. le Duc d'Orléans," *Revue des Deux Mondes*, XI, Nouvelle Série (August 15, 1845), 738. The entire article is an entertaining critique of Marochetti's work.

50: 718   *the first two volumes of Mr. Kinglake's Invasion: The Invasion of the Crimea: Its Origin and an Account of Its Progress Down to the Death of Lord Raglan.* By Alexander William Kinglake. Volumes I and II. Blackwood and Sons, Edinburgh and London, 1863. The entire work, in eight volumes, was completed in 1887.

Kinglake's *Invasion of the Crimea* aroused a storm of literary controversy on two chief counts: its alleged historical inaccuracy and its violent "over-charge" of style. A series of articles in the *Times* disparaged the book exhaustively. See the *Times*, January 21, 1863, p. 12; January 27, 1863, p. 6; February 9, 1863, p. 10; February 23, 1863, p. 5; March 23, 1863, p. 6; April 1, 1863, p. 5; and "Mr. Kinglake and the Quarterlies," *Times,* May 14, 1863, p. 12.

The *Saturday Review* endeavored to defend Kinglake against the *Times.* See the two articles entitled "Mr. Kinglake's Historical Accuracy," *Saturday Review*, XV (March 14, 1863), 332–33; and XV (March 28, 1863), 399–400.

In earlier versions of this essay Arnold included a mocking passage, deleted in 1875, which likened Kinglake to Pilate, "resolved . . . to stand by what he has written." A review of Kinglake's revised edition of the *Invasion* quotes the author at length on his policy of revision. See the *Guardian*, September 30, 1863, p. 918.

This amusing announcement in the *Illustrated London News* for 21 February, 1863, may well have caught Arnold's eye: "The circulation of the *Cornhill Magazine* has been prohibited in France, an article on Mr. Kinglake's 'History of the Crimea' having found disfavour in the eyes of the supreme authorities. We can scarcely wonder at it; yet it must not be thought that freedom of quotation in matters political is entirely tabooed within the limits of the French empire" (p. 191).

50: 724   *what he calls 'a good editorial':* Arnold should have said not a "good editorial," but a "clever editorial." In a review of *Marion* by Manhattan (London, 1864), Arnold had read the following excerpt: "After Monch and Gasper had failed in business, the light of Marion's or Manhattan's genius was kindled into a steady flame by the criticism and patronage of the *New York Herald.* 'One day you will be able to write a clever editorial, which is the highest style of composition known,' said Mr. Bennett encouragingly." See the *Saturday Review*, XVII (May 14, 1864), 600.

51: 756   *'dismissed from the presence':* Arnold quotes, but not exactly, from chapter 29 of Kinglake's text. See *The Invasion of the Crimea*, Tauchnitz edition (Leipzig, 1863), III, 35.

51: 784–85   *it can hardly begin . . . with an institution like the French Academy:* Arnold's conclusion regarding the establishment of an academy in England has been generally misunderstood. His later ultimatum, included in the Preface to *Culture and Anarchy*, serves to clarify his meaning here: "We are often supposed, when we criticise by the help of culture some imperfect doing or other, to have in our eye some well-known rival plan of doing, which we want to serve and recommend. Thus, for instance, because we have freely pointed out the dangers and inconveniences to which our literature is exposed in the absence of any centre of taste and authority like the French Academy, it is constantly said that we want to introduce here in England an institution like the French Academy. We have indeed expressly declared that we want no such thing; but let us notice how it is just our worship of machinery, and of external doing, which leads to this charge being brought." Arnold goes on to point out once more that the English national spirit is not academic, and that "an Academy such as we should be likely to get" would solve nothing. See *Culture and Anarchy,* ed. J. Dover Wilson, Preface, p. 7.

51: 786–87   *like that of Berlin:* Arnold refers to the Academy der Wissenschaften, founded by Leibnitz in 1700. Arnold had, of course, read Renan's estimate of the Berlin Academy in the latter's essay on the French Academy. See *Essais de Morale et de Critique,* p. 347.

51: 792   *a recent one of Spinoza:* Arnold is speaking of Spinoza's *Tractatus Theologico-Politicus,* translated by Robert Willis, and published anonymously in 1862. Arnold severely criticizes this work in his essay "Spinoza and the Bible." Willis subsequently published *Benedict de Spinoza: His Life, Correspondence, and Ethics* (London, 1870).

MAURICE DE GUÉRIN

This essay first appeared in Fraser's Magazine *for January, 1863. For an enthusiastic review of Arnold's essay see "French Thought," Saturday Review, XV (February 14, 1863), 196–97. A review of Maurice de Guérin: Journal, Lettres et Poèmes (Paris, 1862) was published in the Saturday Review, XV (February 21, 1863), 242–43.*

53: 5   *'Les dieux jaloux':* Maurice de Guérin: Journal, Lettres et Poèmes, ed. G. S. Trébutien (Paris, 1862), p. 385. Subsequent references are to this edition.

53: 11   *Madame Sand brought out . . . in the Revue des Deux Mondes:* George Sand, "Poètes et Romanciers Modèrnes de la France—XXXVIII: George de Guérin," *Revue des Deux Mondes,* XXII, Quatrième Série (May 15, 1840), 569–91. The article contains excerpts from fifteen letters written by Guérin to a close friend, Barbey d'Aurevilly, at whose instigation Madame Sand published this appreciation of an unknown poet. She also includes a favorable critique of *Le Centaure,* commending especially "la nouveauté de la forme, l'originalité non abrupte et sauvage, mais raisonnée et voulue, de la phrase, de l'image, de l'expression, et du contour" (pp. 573–74).

53: 13   *at the end of a volume of her novels:* The same article, but without the lengthy footnotes of the periodical version, appears at the end of the volume containing *La Dernière Aldini, Myrza, and Les Visions de la Nuit.*

54: 18   *At the end of 1860:* In September or October of 1860 a two-volume *Reliquiae* was published by Hardel at Caën by Trébutien. But the two-volume edition by Didier (Paris, 1861) is considered the original edition. The second edition, "revue et considérablement augmentée," appeared in a single volume, *Maurice de Guérin: Journal, Lettres et Poèmes* (Paris, 1862). In 1867 an English translation of the *Journal* "with an essay by Matthew Arnold and a memoir by Sainte-Beuve" was published in New York. See E. Decahors, *Maurice de Guérin: Essai de biographie psychologique* (Paris, 1932), Bibliographie, pp. 556–57.

54: 21–22   *a notice of Guérin by . . . M. Sainte-Beuve:* The biographical information about Maurice de Guérin included in Arnold's essay is drawn from two sources: from this notice by Sainte-Beuve and from the "Souvenirs et impressions de quatre années de la vie de Georges-Maurice de Guérin" by M. F. du Breil de Marzan, both of which appeared in the edition of Guérin's *Reliquiae* which Arnold was using. Actually, Arnold must have been using the edition of 1861, since that of 1860 did not contain the notice by Sainte-Beuve. Trébutien himself prepared the notice from two articles by Sainte-Beuve entitled "Oeuvres de Maurice de Guérin," published in the *Moniteur Universelle* for September 24 and October 1, 1860, and reprinted in *Causeries de Lundi,* XV. Several passages from Guérin's writings selected by Sainte-Beuve for his reviews appear also in Arnold's essay, and even Arnold's "lucida sidera" image echoes Sainte-Beuve's enthusiastic acclaim of Guérin's "rang d'étoile parmi les poètes de la France."

The "Souvenirs" of M. de Marzan, included in the edition of 1861, were reduced to a series of extracts for the revised edition in 1862. See Decahors, p. 559.

54: 22   *the first of living critics:* Arnold had sent Sainte-Beuve a copy of *Fraser's Magazine* containing his article on Maurice de Guérin immediately after its publication. In his letter of "remerciement," dated January 25, 1863, Sainte-Beuve disclaimed Arnold's high praise of himself, deferring to such other "living critics" as Carlyle, Renan, Villemain, and Gervinus. In his reply, January 28, 1863, Arnold insisted: "Je n'en rebattrai rien; vous êtes le premier; Carlyle est un esprit bizarre; M. Villemain est un grand écrivain, mais un peu trop borné et trop académique pour être un critique parfait; Gervinus a une forte dose de la pédanterie allemande; M. Renan est un esprit supérieur, mais il n'est pas *né critique*—son choix de sujets est trop restreint, et ses tendances personelles trop decidées. Vous seul avez la souplesse, la finesse, la curiosité désintéressée, qui donnent la pénétration et qui font en critique, le véritable maître." See Louis Bonnerot, *Matthew Arnold, Poète: Essai de Biographie Psychologique* (Paris, 1947), Appendice ("Lettres Inédites d'Arnold à Sainte-Beuve"), pp. 531–32.

See also Arnold's letter to his mother, March 20, 1861, in which he had used the same phrase to describe Sainte-Beuve; *Letters,* I, 155.

54: 53   *Of cold ablution:* Arnold here misquotes Keats' "Of pure ablution round Earth's human shores," from the so-called "Last Sonnet," on Shakespeare.

54: 55 *'Cette écorce blanche':* Obermann, Letter XI. Arnold again refers to this passage in the lectures on Celtic literature.

55: 61 *his poems in general take for their vehicle* . . . *the Alexandrine:* "La Sainte Thérèse de Gérard" and "Fragment" included in Trébutien's edition are in the Alexandrine, while an interesting experiment in freer measure is "Ma Soeur Eugénie" in the same volume. Abel Lefranc in his biography of Guérin prints several unpublished pieces, among which "Rêverie," "Maurice et François," "Les Bords de l'Arguenon," and "Entrétien" employ the Alexandrine while "Mélodie Automnale" and "Le Benarry" are more lyrical. See Abel Lefranc, *Maurice de Guérin* (Paris, 1910), pp. 262–89. In a letter to Eugénie, Maurice remarks that the Alexandrine "se prête de bonne grâce au ton de la causerie." See the letter of September 10, 1834; *Journal*, p. 321.

55: 88–89 *Gray,—hardly uses that couplet at all:* In *Fraser's* Arnold had said: "Gray,—does not use that couplet at all"; Gray does use it, however, in the fragments "Hymn to Ignorance" and "The Alliance of Education and Government," as well as in some epitaphs and translations.

56: 125 *Abbé Lamennais:* Arnold evidently derived most of the information in this narrative section from the "Souvenirs" of M. de Marzan. Felicité Robert de Lamennais (1782–1854), called M. Féli by the residents of La Chênaie, had been ordained a priest in 1816. In the next year he published his *Essay on Indifference in the Matter of Religion,* arguing that all authority rested with the Holy See. His prestige within the Church grew, and in 1824 he declined the honor of becoming a cardinal, which had been offered to him by Leo XIII. In 1830 he founded a liberal journal, *l'Avenir,* which was shortly thereafter suppressed by Gregory XVI. Lamennais' alienation from the ecclesiastical system continued beyond the dissolution of La Chênaie, and by his own request he was buried without the rites of the Church.

57: 155 *'but,' writes one of his hearers:* See the "Impressions et Souvenirs de M. du Breil de Marzan," appended to Trébutien's second edition, pp. 429–30.

58: 182 *'renovation without end':* Arnold is quoting from Wordsworth's "Address to My Infant Daughter, Dora," line 65. He quotes the same line in "Pagan and Mediaeval Religious Sentiment" (126:325).

58: 187 *Sainte-Beuve is inclined to pronounce even superior:* In his prefatory notice Sainte-Beuve speaks of the "soeur du poète, Eugénie de Guérin, son égale, sinon sa supérieure en talent et en âme." See the *Journal,* p. viii.

58: 193–94 *among the younger members of the Society:* M. de Marzan mentions, besides himself, Hippolyte de la Morvonnais and Élie de Kertanguy in particular.

58: 202 *'La Chênaie is a sort of oasis':* Journal, pp. 181–82.

59: 217 *'To-day (he writes in his journal):* See the entry for March 3, 1833, p. 9.

59: 227 *'It has snowed all night':* Journal, March 11, 1833, pp. 12–13.

59: 235 *'sitting in the sun':* Journal, April 5, 1833, p. 25.

59: 236 *'one can actually see':* Journal, May 3, 1833, pp. 36–37.

59: 244 *'the gloomy and bad days':* See the letter to M. de Bayne, May 16, 1833, p. 192. The following excerpt, 'This Brittany of ours,' is a continuation of the same letter. See also the entry of May 9, 1833, p. 38, where the same image occurs.

59: 253   *'What a difference'*: *Journal,* June 13, 1833, p. 41.

60: 259   *'What a sunshine'*: See the letter to Hippolyte de la Morvonnais, February, 1834, p. 280.

60: 268   *Hippolyte la Morvonnais:* A volume entitled *Thébaïde des Grèves* appeared anonymously in 1838, but a revised edition issued in 1864 contained a prefatory notice on its author, La Morvonnais. In a letter to La Morvonnais from Paris, November 8, 1838, Guérin expressed his impatience to see the volume, of which La Morvonnais had evidently already told him. See *Journal,* p. 370. La Morvonnais died in 1853 at the age of 51.

60: 275   *'Every poet'*: These are the concluding sentences of a letter to Eugénie dated April 29, 1833, p. 186.

60: 282   *'that youthful literature'*: See Guérin's letter to M. de la Morvonnais, February, 1834, p. 281. In "The Function of Criticism at the Present Time" Arnold passes a similar judgment upon the English Romantic School, and on substantially the same basis.

60: 287   *'whose name appears'*: This is from the same letter, pp. 281–82.

60: 292   *'the writers of books'*: This also is from the same letter, p. 282.

61: 296   *'invoking with his whole heart'*: This is from the same letter, p. 283.

61: 301   *'I want you to reform your system'*: See Guérin's letter of August 13, 1834, pp. 317–18. Guérin is here criticizing some verses which Eugénie had addressed to Louise de Bayne, warning his sister against repeating certain defects in her proposed "Enfantines."

61: 317   *'My God, what is my soul about'*: *Journal,* April 5, 1833, p. 25.

61: 325   *'Of what, my God, are we made'*: See Guérin's letter of May 8, 1833, p. 189. M. de Marzan had commented upon the apparent peacefulness of Guérin's life, and the latter here revealed the actual condition of restlessness and distraction he was then experiencing.

61: 331   *'Three days have passed'*: *Journal,* April 10, 1833, pp. 25–26.

62: 344   *Admiration for Lamennais:* Arnold here softens the account of Guérin's attitude toward Lamennais which M. de Marzan describes in his biographical study of Guérin. M. de Marzan suggests that Élie de Kertanguy had to act as a kind of mediator between Guérin and Lamennais, and of those letters and passages which appear to reveal Guérin as a devoted disciple of Lamennais, Marzan remarks: "C'est bien Guérin qui parle, mais ce n'est pas lui qui pense. C'est bien indubitablement Élie dont Maurice, en ces points, n'est que le traducteur et l'écho" (p. 453). In a later section of these "Impressions" Marzan contrasts Lamennais and Guérin as "deux natures qui ne s'offraient mutuellement ni points de contact, ni ressemblances" (p. 459).

62: 355   *'Do you know what it is'*: *Journal,* May 9, 1833, p. 39. The following quotation, 'If that clock knew,' is from the next paragraph.

62: 364   *'To-day M. Féli startled us'*: *Journal,* March 24, 1833, pp. 19–20.

63: 373–74   *'after a three weeks' close scrutiny'*: See the letter to M. François du Breil de Marzan, August 9, 1833, p. 205.

63: 380   *to Ploërmel:* They were transferred to a house of the Frères de l'Instruction Chrétienne, under the brother of Lamennais. See Guérin's letter to M. de la Morvonnais, November 7, 1833, pp. 218–20.

63: 381   *Lamennais, 'who had not yet ceased':* See the "Impressions," pp. 454–55.

63: 387–88   *'had need of the open air':* See Guérin's letter to M. de Bayne, from La Chênaie, Christmas Day, 1832, p. 180. Guérin was describing his new life at La Chênaie, particularly the philosophical study for which he felt himself naturally unfitted: "Je n'ai pas l'âme assez austère pour m'enfermer exclusivement dans les abstractions. J'ai besoin du grand air; j'aime à voir le soleil et les fleurs."

63: 393   *'to put in practice':* This and the following excerpt, *'garotté par un réglement,'* are from the "Impressions" of M. de Marzan, pp. 455–57. The letter from which Marzan quotes is that addressed to him, October 2, 1833, pp. 216–18.

64: 410   *'How full of goodness':* Journal, December 7, 1833, pp. 56–58.

64: 432–33   *'Never have I tasted':* Journal, December 20, 1833, pp. 62–64.

65: 472   *'All the sky':* Journal, January 20, 1834, pp. 69–70.

65: note   *White of Selborne:* Gilbert White (1720–93), the vicar of Selborne, was an ardent naturalist to whose noted *Natural History and Antiquities of Selborne* (London, 1850) Arnold is here referring. See the letter to the Hon. Daines Barrington, September 9, 1778: "The woodpecker sets up a sort of loud and hearty laugh" (p. 214).

66: 495–96   *'I enter the world':* Journal, January 20, 1834, p. 73.

66: 500   *One of his Brittainy acquaintances:* This was Paul Quemper, to whom several letters in Trébutien's edition are addressed. See also Sainte-Beuve's Prefatory Notice, p. xxxii.

66: 502   *his first essays:* In his letter of February 28, 1834, to M. de la Morvonnais, Guérin mentions three articles already accepted by French periodicals. The first of these, actually a letter which Guérin had addressed to La Morvonnais earlier in the same month, appeared in two parts in *La France Catholique.* See also *Journal,* pp. 273–83. The other two articles were on books, one on *Promenades dans Rome,* in *La France Catholique* for February 15, 1834, and another, "a page on Mon Portfeuille," in the *Revue Européenne.* See the *Journal,* p. 289.

Lefranc includes the texts of two other articles, "Martin de Gallardon" and "La Chapelle Expiatoire," in his first Appendix, pp. 223–32. The latter article appeared in *La France Catholique* for May 31, 1834.

For Guérin's further discussion of his literary endeavor at this time, see his letter to Eugénie, April 9, 1834, pp. 291–94. See also Decahors, Bibliographie, p. 556.

66: 505   *'Je n'ai qu'à écrire':* This phrase occurs in a letter to Eugénie, February 2, 1834, p. 269.

66: 516   *'scholars left':* See Guérin's letter to Eugénie, September 10, 1834, p. 318.

66: 518–19   *'The master of the fifth class':* See Guérin's letter to M. de la Morvonnais, October 19, 1834, p. 326.

67: 536   *'Destiny, who loves these surprises':* See Guérin's letter to M. de la Morvonnais, November 8, 1838, p. 370.

67: 539   *'the blind Fury':* The reference is probably to Milton's *Lycidas,* line 75.

67: 540   *'I pass my life':* See Guérin's letter to Eugénie, April 8, 1839, p. 372.

67: 549–50   *'To-night there will go forth':* See Guérin's letter to Eugénie, April 9, 1834, p. 292. The Encyclical *Singulari nos,* July 15, 1834, constituted the official condemnation of the liberal position Lamennais held. It was directed specifically against Lamennais' *Paroles d'un Croyant,* which had appeared in May, 1834.

67: 553   *'I assure you':* See Guérin's letter to his sister Marie, October 30, 1835, p. 357. Guérin was trying to reassure his family of his loyalty to them, and at the same time to defend himself against their suspicions that he was committing himself to dangerous political and religious systems.

67: 558   *'It has forgotten':* See Guérin's letter to M. de la Morvonnais, February, 1834, p. 283. This letter also contains Guérin's protest against charges of scepticism.

67: 560   *'deplorable revolution,' 'the bond of a common faith,' 'this inter-regnum':* The section of Marzan's "Impressions" which contained these phrases was deleted from the second edition of Guérin's works. See the note to the essay on Eugénie de Guérin, at 92: 609.

68: 568   *'disengaged from the social tumult':* Journal, June 26, 1834, p. 87.

68: 570   *M. Sainte-Beuve tells us:* See the Prefatory Notice, p. xxxiii.

68: 575–76   *'I owe everything to poetry':* Journal, August 13, 1832, pp. 5–6.

69: 607   *'I return':* See Guérin's letter to Barbey d'Aurevilly, April 11, 1838, which is included in Madame Sand's article on Guérin. The fragment appears also in the *Journal,* p. 467.

69: 615   *'My imagination welcomes':* Journal, June 25, 1834, p. 86.

69: 618   *'The longer I live':* Journal, August 20, 1834, pp. 92–93.

69: 628   *'When one is a wanderer':* See Guérin's letter to Eugénie, September 10, 1834, p. 320.

69: 630   *'The stream of travel':* See the journal entry for October 13, 1835. The same thought occurs in a letter to M. de la Morvonnais, written at the same time.

69: 636–37   *Lord Houghton has so gracefully written:* Richard Monckton Milnes, who was created first Baron Houghton in 1863. Arnold's connection with Milnes antedates this essay, for he had written to Milnes from Dover, August 3, 1859, to ask his "judicious" opinion of *England and the Italian Question.*

Arnold here refers to *The Luggie and Other Poems,* by David Gray, with a Memoir by James Hedderwick, and a Prefatory Notice by R. M. Milnes, M. P. (London, 1862). In his Introductory Notice Lord Houghton had likened the character and fortune of Gray to those of Keats.

Milnes himself contributed a review of this volume to the *Edinburgh Review.* See the *Edinburgh Review,* CXV (April, 1862), 567–76. A brief notice of Lord Houghton in the *Illustrated London News* for 16 February, 1865, commended his own poems as "marked by feeling and taste and a command of graceful versification" (p. 165).

69: 644 *'the sense profound': Journal,* May 7, 1834, p. 79.

69: 645 *'My inward misery': Journal,* May 18, 1834, p. 80. The sentence comprises Guérin's entire entry for this date.

70: 648 *'Craving, unquiet': Journal,* April 3, 1835, pp. 116–17.

71: 706 *'There is more power and beauty': Journal,* March 27, 1835, p. 115. Guérin is here paying tribute to the admirable character of Marie de la Morvonnais, who had died on January 22, 1835.

71: 708 *'My spirit':* See Guérin's letter to M. de la Morvonnais, December 5, 1835, p. 360.

72: 719 *'It seems to me intolerable': Journal,* March 23, 1834, pp. 76–77.

72: 724 *'High above my head': Journal,* May 7, 1834, p. 79.

72: 729 *'When I begin': Journal,* June 10, 1834, pp. 83–84.

72: 738–39 *The idea of this composition:* Sainte-Beuve discusses this in the Prefatory Notice, pp. xxxiv–xxxv.

72: 744 *a Bacchante:* In the periodical text of this essay, Arnold stated that the *Bacchante* had been lost, following Sainte-Beuve's assertion in the Notice: "Il avait aussi fait une *Bacchante* qui n'est point retrouvée, fragment anticipé de je ne sais quel poème en prose dont le sujet était *Bacchus dans l'Inde*" (p. xxxv). Since the *Bacchante* appeared in the second edition of the *Journal* (1862), Arnold deleted the phrase "which is lost" from the text of 1865.

Sainte-Beuve, in his review of the second edition of Guérin's remains, did not conceal his disappointment with the recovered poem. He speaks of the *Bacchante* as the "autre morceau de lui bien inférieur." See "Maurice et Eugénie de Guérin: Frère et Soeur," *Nouveaux Lundis,* III.

Quotations from *The Centaur*

72: 754 *'I had my birth': Journal* (Paris, 1862), pp. 375–77. Here, as in the succeeding extracts, Arnold condenses the French text considerably.

73: 791 *'O Melampus':* p. 378.

74: 800 *'The course of my youth':* p. 379.

74: 808 *'Wandering along':* pp. 381–83.

74: 829 *'Thou pursuest':* p. 383.

75: 837 *'O Macareus':* pp. 383–84.

75: 857 *'Such were the lessons':* p. 385.

75: 860 *'For me':* p. 386.

EUGÉNIE DE GUÉRIN

This essay first appeared in the Cornhill Magazine *for June, 1863.*

76: 3 *'There is nothing fixed': Eugénie de Guérin: Journal et Lettres* ed. G. S. Trébutien (Paris, 1862), September 17, 1844, pp. 443–44. Subsequent citations are from this edition; quotations from Maurice de Guérin are from the *Journal, Lettres et Poèmes,* ed. Trébutien (Paris, 1862).

This quotation was used by a writer in the *Saturday Review* to introduce an article entitled "Women's Friendships." See the *Saturday Review,* XVIII (August 6, 1864), 176–77.

76: 13   *'let what he did be lost':* See the letter to M. de la Morvonnais, March 10, 1841, p. 476. Eugénie wrote this letter to thank M. de la Morvonnais for his recently published article on Maurice written at her request to correct the impression conveyed in Madame Sand's article in the *Revue des Deux Mondes.* See Hippolyte de la Morvonnais, "Poètes Contemporains: Georges-Maurice de Guérin," *Université Catholique,* XI (January, 1841), 76.

In her letter Eugénie speaks of it thus: "J'ai dans le coeur cette précieuse Notice, si belle d'expression, de sentiment et de verité. Grâce à vous, notre Maurice est là dans sa vie de poésie et de foi, et sous l'auréole céleste qui lui convient et qui lui manquait jusqu'ici" (pp. 474–75).

77: 17   *'furnished to others':* See the letter to M. de la Morvonnais, July 2, 1842, p. 480. This letter is concerned with the progress of Guérin's *Reliquiae* toward publication. His sister's anxiety over some unexplained delay is evident. The phrase also occurs in a fragment of Eugénie's journal [1842, à Rivières], p. 447.

77: 20–21   *'il était leur vie':* This incident is described both in a letter to M. de la Morvonnais, July 2, 1842, p. 480, and in the fragment of Eugénie's journal, à Rivières, 1842, p. 447. In the former the phrase appears to refer to the family of the young girl, but in the latter to the Guérin family itself.

77: 21   *talent, exquisite as that of Keats:* In evaluating Arnold as a literary critic, Enrico Nencioni scored this particular estimate of Guérin as absurd, classing it with Arnold's celebrated remark about the prose of Shelley. See Enrico Nencioni, "Rassegna delle Letterature Straniere (Inglese)," *Nuova Antologia di Scienze, Lettere ed Arti,* XV, Serie III (May 16, 1888), 345.

77: 23–24   *'that winning, delicate, and beautifully happy turn':* This is an adaptation of a phrase in the journal, June 9, 1840, p. 383: Eugénie speaks of "cette douce, délicate et si fine façon de parler" which Maurice possessed.

77: 38–39   *She seemed hardly less gifted:* In March, 1863, Arnold received a letter from Trébutien, who had seen the article on Guérin in *Fraser's.* The volume to which Arnold here refers was sent to him by Marie de Guérin, then a nun at Toulouse, through M. Trébutien. Arnold's first impressions of Eugénie were soon altered: "After all they say about her, I am a little disappointed. I mean she is not comparable for genius, or at least for expression and poetical power, to her brother." And a few days later: "I have read through Eugénie de Guérin, and must fall to work and make my article upon her this next week. It will not be such a labour of love as I imagined beforehand it would be, though she is a truly remarkable person." With his essay nearly finished, Arnold observed: "I think the article will be interesting, but the sister is not so good a subject as her brother." *Letters,* I, 217, 221–22.

77: 42   *The book has made a profound impression in France:* Ten editions of the *Journal* were exhausted in the two years following its publication in 1862. A favorable review of Trébutien's edition appeared in the *Saturday Review*, XVI (August 15, 1863), 221. See also "Eugénie de Guérin: Journal et Lettres . . . Paris: 1863," *Edinburgh Review*, CXX (July, 1864), 249–67. Sainte-Beuve's review of the two Guérin volumes which appeared in 1862, "Maurice et Eugénie de Guérin: Frère et Soeur," is included in *Nouveaux Lundis*, III.

77: 46 *a writer in the National Review*: "Eugénie de Guérin: Reliquiae," *National Review*, XII (January, 1861), 145–51. This volume of *Reliquiae*, the work of d'Aurevilly and Trébutien, appeared in 1855 and was favorably reviewed by Sainte-Beuve in the *Athenaeum* for February 9, 1856. This review has since been included in *Causeries du Lundi*, XII. The *National Review* critic also praised the *Reliquiae* highly, even urging a general publication to neutralize the damaging effect upon English readers of "the nameless baseness and badness of their [French] novel-literature" (p. 148).

77: note *a volume of these*: Sainte-Beuve's review of this new volume of letters appears in *Nouveaux Lundis*, IX.

78: 59 *Her family*: See the "Notes sur la Famille et sur les Premières Années de Maurice de Guérin," written by Eugénie for Trébutien's edition of Maurice's *Reliquiae*. See *Maurice de Guérin: Journal*, etc. (Paris, 1862), 419–25.

78: 64 *'one may pass days there'*: See the journal entry for June 1, 1840, p. 382.

78: 86 *'We were . . . two eyes looking out of one head'*: See the letter to the Baroness de Maîstre, July 26, 1839, p. 462. This was Eugénie's first letter to the Baroness after the death of Maurice.

78: 90 *There is a trace*: See the journal entry for December 31, 1839, pp. 317–18. Her cousin Victor had died in Paris in 1829.

79: 95 *'to Maurice in heaven'*: Her entry for October 19, 1839, indicates that Eugénie planned to address her journal to M. de la Morvonnais, then in Paris, out of regard for his friendship with Maurice.

79: 104 *M. Sainte-Beuve's critical judgments*: Sainte-Beuve subsequently remarked upon Arnold's objection here, in a review of the volume of Eugénie's letters which appeared in 1865. Sainte-Beuve was content to reassert his claim of superiority for Eugénie, adding the caution: "Prenez *génie* dans le sens le plus naturel et le plus simple." See *Nouveaux Lundis*, IX, 250.

79: 108 *bring the intimate life of nature*: Sainte-Beuve had remarked upon this talent of Guérin's in his Prefatory Notice to Guérin's *Journal* (pp. xiv–xv). Madame Sand, in her article in the *Revue des Deux Mondes*, made similar observations (p. 576).

79: 116 *'It does one good'*: *Journal*, May 1, 1839, pp. 262–63.

79: 121–22 *'I have been along the Loire'*: See the letter to M. de la Morvonnais, from Paris, October, 1835; *Maurice de Guérin: Journal*, etc., pp. 351–52.

79: 129 *'ce beau torrent'*: *Journal*, December 10, 1834, p. 104.

80: 136–37 *'You will find in him'*: *Journal*, p. 345; in a letter from Paris, March 4, 1835, Maurice was urging Eugénie to address a letter of consolation to M. de la Morvonnais, whose wife, Marie, had died in January, 1835.

80: 149–50   *St. Theresa (it is Mdlle. de Guérin herself):* See her journal, August 21, 1835, p. 89.

80: 159–60   *'There are days':* Journal, February 12, 1838, p. 155.

80: 162   *'Poor soul':* Journal, May 12, 1838, p. 201.

80: 173   *the counsel of Fénelon: Lettres Spirituelles*, 37; *Oeuvres*, I, 473. The journal entry is that for May 22, 1835, p. 76.

81: 175   *'This morning I was suffering':* Journal, April 2, 1838, p. 181.

81: 194   *the severe, morbid Pascal:* See Goethe's review of Munter's history of Count Struensee: "Wir müssen es einmal sagen, weil es uns schon lang' auf dem Herzen leigt: Voltaire, Hume, La Mettrie, Helvetius, Rosseau und ihre ganze Schule haben der Moralität und der Religion lange nicht so viel geschadet als der strenge, kranke Pascal und seine Schule." *Goethe's Sämtliche Werke* (Stuttgart und Tübingen, 1830), XXXVI, 122.

81: 209   *'emptiness and nothingness':* Journal, March 14, 1836, p. 111. Another characteristic expression of this sentiment appears in the journal entry for April 10, 1839, pp. 247–48.

82: 217   *'I do not say':* See the letter from Maurice, June 21, 1833, p. 198.

82: 223   *'You see, my dear Tortoise':* See the letter from Maurice, February 2, 1834, p. 271. He concludes: "Adieu, mon poète malgré toi." Maurice again condemns these scruples in a letter of August 13, 1834, p. 318.

82: 231   *'It is the instinct of my life':* Journal, April 24, 1835, p. 64.

82: 236   *she had a great correspondence:* Besides Maurice and Louise de Bayne, the recipients of the published letters include Antoinette de Boisset, Irène Compayre, Madame la Baronne de Maître, Madame de Ste. Marie, Euphrasie Mathieu, M. Hippolyte de la Morvonnais, Count Xavier de Maître, M. Paul Quemper, and the Prince de Hohenlohe.

83: 268   *'Ceci n'est pas pour le public':* Journal, August 24, 1835, p. 91.

83: 271   *'We see things':* Journal, January 27, 1838, p. 144.

83: 281   *'I am furious':* Journal, November 18, 1834, p. 6.

83: 289   *Antiquities of the Anglo-Saxon Church:* This book was written by the Reverend John Lingard, later John Cardinal Lingard. First published at Newcastle in 1806, the book is an account of the origin and progress of Christianity in England from the conversion of Prince Lucius in A.D. 180 to the period of Anglo-Saxon missionaries to Denmark and Norway in A.D. 1027. A revised and enlarged edition incorporating additional historical material was published in London in 1845. A French translation of the earlier version appeared in Paris in 1828.

84: 304   *She sometimes complains:* See her journal, March 22, 1836, p. 114.

84: 306   *'The poetess':* Journal, January 3, 1835, p. 31. The "literary friend" was M. de la Morvonnais, from whom Eugénie had just received a letter.

84: 314   *'To-day,' she writes:* Journal, December 9, 1834, pp. 24–25.

84: 325–26   *the list of her library:* See her journal, May 30, 1835, pp. 81–82. The list itself is printed in Trébutien's edition, pp. 430–32.

84: 329   *'What then?':* Journal, May 7, 1837, p. 123. A French edition of these letters, by Migne, appeared in 1840.

85: 332   *Madame de Stael's book: De l'Allemagne* (London, 1813), by Anne-Louise-Germaine Necker, Baroness de Stael-Holstein, daughter of the famous minister of Louis XVI. In 1810 her *De l'Allemagne,* a book of observations on German manners, society, philosophy, and literature was confiscated by the imperial police shortly before its scheduled publication in Paris, and its author exiled from France as a political enemy. Her fortunes aroused great interest in England, and upon Madame de Stael's arrival there in 1813, the book was published both in French and in English. See the *Gentleman's Magazine,* LXXXIII (July, 1813), 40; *Edinburgh Review,* XXII (January, 1814), 198–238; and a series of articles in the *Monthly Review* for December, 1813, and January, April, and July, 1814.

85: 338   *to look out upon the sky: Journal,* November 24, 1834, pp. 12–13, and July, 1840, pp. 386–87.

85: 340–41   *'I find writing': Journal,* April 24, 1835, pp. 64–65.

85: 356   *'Would to God that my thoughts': Journal,* January 3, 1835, pp. 31–32.

85: 364   *'My journal has been untouched': Journal,* March 1, 1835, p. 35.

86: 372   *'It is from the Cross': Journal,* August 27, 1835, pp. 92–93. The friend was M. de la Morvonnais, whose wife had died earlier in the year.

86: 391   *'Cloaks, clogs, umbrellas': Journal,* November 29, 1834, p. 16.

87: 411   *'Christmas is come': Journal,* December 31, 1834, pp. 28–29.

87: 446   *the memoir and poems: Memoir of Emma Tatham, Author of the Dream of Pythagoras and other Poems, by Benjamin Gregory, with The Angels' Spell and other pieces not published during her lifetime.* (London, 1859).

88: 462   *'I pursue after God': Journal,* April 15, 1835, p. 61.

88: 463–64   *her quoting . . . the story of the ten disobedient children: Journal,* May 22, 1837, p. 138. See also *De Civitate Dei,* Book XXII, end of chapter 8.

89: 497   *she says twice in her journal:* April 28, 1835, p. 70, and March 12, 1836, p. 108.

89: 499   *'cher pèlerinage': Journal,* August 29, 1835, p. 94.

89: 500   *'laissé tant de misères': Journal,* March 12, 1836, p. 108.

89: 501   *'This morning': Journal,* November 28, 1834, pp. 15–16.

89: 513   *'the more the heart': Journal,* March 12, 1836, p. 109.

89: 518   *'What a grief': Journal,* March 12, 1836, pp. 107–8.

90: 531   *'To-day I am going': Journal,* April 24, 1839, p. 259.

90: 537   *She tells us:* See her journal, March 4, 1835, pp. 37–38. She did not, however, pray before "an image of the Virgin which hung in her room" but before a picture of Calvary in her father's room.

90: 542   *'Oh, how well': Journal,* July 31, 1835, p. 85.

90: 545   *'The mystery': Journal,* January 26, 1840, p. 336.

90: 552   *'My God, what have we done':* This is an entry without a date, following that of May 15, 1836, p. 118.

91: 570   *'Notwithstanding this': Journal,* May 14, 1838, p. 203.

91: 590   *'Oh, the agony': Journal,* July 30, 1840, p. 394. The reference is not to Maurice but to the recent burial of a suicide at Andillac.

91: 601   *'These six months with us':* This and the following excerpt are from the *Journal,* January 26, 1840, pp. 335–36.

92: 609   *his divergence from his sister:* After the death of her brother, Eugénie grew extremely sensitive regarding his "divergence" in matters of faith. In her journal entry for June 15, 1840 (p. 384) and later in a letter to Louise de Bayne (September 4, 1840), Eugénie spoke disapprovingly of Madame Sand's treatment of Maurice. She described the article in the *Revue des Deux Mondes* as "fort élevé, fort beau, mais incomplet et même faux sous le rapport religieux. Maurice y est montré presque comme un Werther ou un Byron, et des amis veulent donner de lui un portrait plus vrai." *Eugénie de Guérin: Lettres à Louise de Bayne,* ed. Émile Barthés (Paris, 1925), II, 302.

At Eugénie's request, M. Hippolyte de la Morvonnais published an article on Guérin more to his sister's liking in the *Université Catholique* for January, 1841.

With the publication of a second edition of Guérin's *Journal,* M. Trébutien found it necessary to insert a lengthy defense of Guérin's orthodoxy (pp. ii–v). M. Sainte-Beuve, on the other hand, in his review of this second edition, insisted upon a strong element of paganism in Guérin, arguing from the psychological structure of *The Centaur.* See *Nouveaux Lundis,* III, 156–62.

92: 627   '*God knows when we shall see': Journal,* May 3, 1839, pp. 264–65.

92: 646   '*He coughs': Journal,* May 21, 1839, p. 271.

93: 655   '*that beloved pale face,' 'that beautiful head': Journal,* January 22, 1840, p. 332.

93: 657   '*I have seen': Journal,* August 4, 1839, p. 280.

93: 670   '*Poor beloved soul': Journal,* July 21, 1839, p. 276. In the original text, Eugénie addresses Maurice directly.

93: 683   '*I am broken down': Journal,* August 20, 1839, pp. 283–84.

94: 701   '*this return': Journal,* May 1, 1840, p. 373.

94: 706   '*I am dying': Journal* [May], 1840, p. 375.

94: 716   '*So beautiful in the morning': Journal* [August], 1840, p. 401.

94: 723   *A day or two afterwards:* The last entry is that for December 31, 1840, but fragments written at Paris in 1841 and a note at Le Cayla in December, 1842, are included in the fragments at the end of Trébutien's edition.

95: 730–31   *letter of the 22nd of August, 1845:* This was a letter addressed to M. Paul Quemper, who had undertaken the task of collecting the various writings of Guérin for publication (pp. 492–93).

HEINRICH HEINE

This essay first appeared in the Cornhill Magazine *for August, 1863.*

96: 1   '*I know not': Reisebilder,* Part III, "Journey from Munich to Genoa," chapter XXXI, last paragraph. See *Heinrich Heines Sämtliche Werke* (Leipzig, 1912), IV, 305–6. All quotations are from this edition unless otherwise indicated.

In an article on Heine, Elsie M. Butler censures Arnold's inaccuracy here: "Heine had not italicized *sword*; he had not claimed that he was a hero, nor even that he was brave. He had only said that he had fought well. *Brav* and *brave* are not synonymous terms." See Elsie M. Butler, "Heine in England and Matthew Arnold," *German Life and Letters,* IX, N.S. (April, 1956), 159.

96: 12   *he is significant:* While preparing his lecture on Heine, Arnold wrote to Sir Mountstuart E. Grant-Duff declining the latter's offer of additional material on Heine: "My object is not so much to give a literary history of Heine's works, as to mark his place in modern European letters, and the special tendency and significance of what he did." See Arnold's letter of May 14, 1863; *Letters,* I, 224.

97: 22–23   *his labours on German literature:* Carlyle contributed a number of articles on German writers and German literature to the *Edinburgh Review,* the *Foreign Review,* and *Fraser's Magazine* from 1827 to 1832. See Thomas Carlyle, *Critical and Miscellaneous Essays* (New York, 1865), a volume which includes the essays on the state of German literature, Goethe, Novalis, and Jean Paul Richter.

97: 37–38   *continuator of . . . Goethe's varied activity:* Arnold's judgment of Heine as the continuator of Goethe thoroughly enraged Carlyle. In his essay on Arnold, Grant-Duff describes a conversation in which Carlyle vehemently attacked Arnold's estimate of Heine. See The Right Honourable Sir Mountstuart E. Grant-Duff, *Out of the Past* (London, 1903), II, 95–96. See also David A. Wilson and David W. Macarthur, *Carlyle in Old Age* (London, 1934), p. 23.

97: 40   *Goethe's mantle fell:* Miss Butler challenges Arnold's judgment about the influence of Goethe on Heine, arguing that Arnold's assertion here would have "startled" both Goethe and Heine. But Arnold is not concerned with the question of political liberalism, as Miss Butler assumes, but rather with "intellectual deliverance," accessibility to ideas and the application of "modern ideas" to life.

97: 41–42   *clearly risen above the horizon:* During the period in which Carlyle was producing his essays on German literature, Heine's *Buch der Lieder* (1827) and his *Reisebilder* (1826–31) appeared. His *Romantische Schule, Französische Zustande, Deutschland,* and *Romanzero* were yet to come.

For an account of the English attitude of "violent hostility" toward Heine during the 1830's, see Sol Liptzin, *The English Legend of Heinrich Heine* (New York, 1954), chapter 1: "Blackguard and Apostate."

98: 59   *'The wind of the Paris Revolution':* "Schlusswort," *Englische Fragmente; Werke,* V, 166–67. Arnold condenses Heine's text somewhat.

98: 72   *'If I were to say':* See "Noch ein Wort für junge Dichter," *Ferneres über deutsche Literatur,* in Goethe's *Sämtliche Werke* (Stuttgart und Tübingen, 1833), XLV, 426.

98: 96   *'Through me':* "Noch ein Wort," *Werke,* XLV, 426–27.

99: 131   *born at Hamburg:* Arnold is mistaken here. Heine explicitly states in the *Reisebilder* that he was born in Düsseldorf. See *Reisebilder,* Part II, "Ideen: Das Buch Le Grand," chapter VI; *Werke,* IV, 152. See also

"Schreiben an den Dekan in Göttingen," *Kleinere Schriften; Werke,* V, 461.

100: 153–54   *'respectability with its thousand gigs':* At the trial of John Thurtell for the murder of a Mr. Weare, a witness had defined the "respectable man" as one who "kept a gig." See "Two Years in New South Wales," *Quarterly Review,* LXXIII (January, 1828), 15, note. In "Richter Again," Carlyle cited this article as the source of his expression. See *Critical and Miscellaneous Essays* (New York, 1865), p. 208.

100: 160   *the term Philistine:* Heine employs the term in this sense in the early sections of the *Reisebilder:* "Im allgemeinen werden die Bewohner Göttingens eingeteilt in Studenten, Professoren, Philister, und Vieh." See "Die Harzreise," *Reisebilder,* Part I, second prose paragraph; *Werke,* IV, 6. See also "Reise von München nach Genua," *Reisebilder,* II, chapters 1 to 5; *Werke,* IV, 221–36.

Carlyle himself also used the term "Philistine." In "The State of German Literature," Carlyle traced the origin of the term to contemptuous opposition to the partisans of "political and philosophical Illumination." See *Critical and Miscellaneous Essays,* p. 29. Again, in a review of Taylor's *Historic Survey of German Poetry* Carlyle complained that for such an individual as Taylor, whose philosophy is utterly "sensual" and whose "only lamp of life" is logic, the Germans have a one-word epithet: "Philister." See *Critical and Miscellaneous Essays,* p. 291.

For Arnold's own later use of the term see the fourth of the lectures on Celtic literature.

101: 172   *'the French':* Englische Fragmente, "Die Befreiung," last paragraph; *Werke,* V, 164–65. Heine is here speaking of a phase in the "War of Liberation of humanity": "Die Freiheit ist eine neue Religion, die Religion unserer Zeit."

101: 180   *'I might settle':* See the poem "Jetzt wohin?" in the *Romanzero,* Book II, "Lamentationen"; *Werke,* III, 109. For other unfavorable treatments of England and the English, see "Die Englander" and "John Bull," from *Englische Fragmente* and *Kleinere Schriften* respectively; *Werke,* V, 90–96 and 343–49.

According to Lucy Duff-Gordon, however, Heine virtually retracted all his abusive remarks about England, expressing regret for them upon his deathbed. See Lord Houghton's *Monographs Personal and Social* (New York, 1873), p. 318.

101: 183   *'ächtbrittische Beschränktheit':* The expression Heine actually uses is "echtbrittischer Beschränktheit." See "Wellington," *Englische Fragmente,* X; *Werke,* V, 155.

101: 203   *The enthusiast for the idea:* Arnold probably found this expression in Heine's own writings. He used it, for example, in a letter to Moses Moser, July 1, 1825. Heine was speaking of Goethe who, unlike himself, was not an "enthusiast for the idea": "Ich hingegen bin von Haus aus ein Schwärmer, d. h., bis zur Aufopferung begeistert für die Idee und immer gedrängt." See *Heinrich Heines Briefwechsel* (München und Berlin, 1914–20), I, 367.

102: 216 *'While I translate'*: See "Die Schuld," *Englische Fragmente; Werke,* V, 126–27. The excerpt is from a speech of Cobbett's on national resources and private property.

102: 240 *'moving altogether'*: This is an adaptation of a line from Wordsworth's "Resolution and Independence" (XI, 7).

102: 251 *'What demon'*: See "Ludwig Borne: Eine Denkschrift," Book II; *Werke,* VIII, 383–84. The newspaper was the *Politische Annelen* which Heine, with L. Lindner as co-editor, directed during his stay in Munich, in 1827–28. Arnold translates Heine's "Michel" as "Hodge."

103: 263 *'The Emperor Charles'*: "Schlusswort," *Englische Fragmente; Werke,* V, 167–69. Actually this incident belongs to the life of the Emperor Maximilian I, the grandfather of Charles V. Anecdotes about Kunz or Conrad von der Rosen can be found in Karl Friedrich Flögel's *Geschichte der Hofnarren* (Liegniss und Leipzig, 1789), 190–203.

104: 324 *published in America:* Heinrich Heine, *Sämtliche Werke,* 6 Bde. (Philadelphia, 1857–59). The German edition which Arnold mentions in his note is that edited by Adolf Strodtmann: Heinrich Heine, *Sämtliche Werke,* 21 Bde. (Hamburg, 1861–68). A last volume of *Nachlässe* was added in 1869.

105: 345 *'Pouvez-vous siffler?'*: This and the two anecdotes which follow can be found in Adolf Strodtmann's biography of Heine. See *H. Heines Leben und Werke* (Berlin, 1869), II, Book 4, chapter 2, "Die Mattrazzengruft." See also *Skizzen über Heinrich Heine,* von seiner Nichte, Fürstin della Rocca (Leipzig, 1882).

105: 370 *'It is all of no use'*: In his book *Nach Fünf Jahren,* Adolph Stahr describes his visit to Heine in October, 1855. This incident is included in William Stigand's *The Life, Work, and Opinions of Heinrich Heine,* 2 vols. (London, 1880), II, 410–11.

106: 397 *A French critic of Heine:* Saint-René Taillandier, in "Poètes Contemporains de l'Allemagne: Henri Heine," *Revue des Deux Mondes,* XIV, Nouvelle Période (April 1, 1852), 5–36. The criticism to which Arnold here refers appears on p. 19; "Au bruit de ce joyeux tambour, les principes de 89 ont pénétré dans les lettres, les révenants du moyen-âge ont pris la fuite, et l'image de l'empereur, insultée chaque jour par tant de racunes furieuses, s'est relevée dans les imaginations tudesques comme le rude initiateur des temps nouveaux."

106: 408–9 *'When Candide'*: "Bäder von Lucca," *Reisebilder,* Part III, chapter X; *Werke,* IV, 377. The reference is to chapter XVII of Voltaire's *Candide.*

107: 420 *'Child of the French Revolution'*: See Heine's letter dated August 10, 1830, in "Ludwig Börne," Book II; *Werke,* VIII, 405.

107: 420 *an 'Initiator'*: See "Poètes Contemporains de l'Allemagne," *Revue des Deux Mondes,* XIV, Nouvelle Période (April 1, 1852), 22.

107: 424 *he declared that the great task:* In the last of the four wills which Heine made, dictated in 1851 to a M. Ducloux, Heine said: "La grande affaire de ma vie était de travailler à l'entente cordiale entre l'Allemagne et la France et à déjouer les artifices des ennemis de la démocratie, qui exploitent à leur profit les préjugés et les animosités internationaux." See *Der Prosa-Nachlass von H. Heine; Heines Werke* (Hamburg, 1921), XII, 246–47.

107: 437   *the modern spirit:* For Arnold's earlier discussion of the "modern spirit" see "On the Modern Element in Literature," Arnold's inaugural lecture as Professor of Poetry at Oxford, where the terms "intellectual deliverance" and "moral deliverance" are clearly defined.

107: 454   *literary movement of the beginning of the nineteenth century:* Arnold regarded the so-called "Romantic" movements in literature as failures precisely because they evaded reality, i.e., modern problems and "the application of modern ideas to life." See his comments on the English Romantic movement in "The Function of Criticism at the Present Time," pp. 11–12, and his analysis of the superiority of Goethe and Heine to the German Romantics, pp. 107–8.

108: 485   *stat magni nominis umbra:* Lucan, *Pharsalia,* I, 135.

109: 498–99   *keener wit:* Shortly after delivering his Heine lecture, Arnold wrote to his mother: "There was, nevertheless, one thing which even a wooden Oxford audience gave way to—Heine's wit. I gave them about two pages of specimens of it, and they positively laughed aloud." *Letters,* I, 226 (June 16, 1863).

109: 499   *his story of the French abbé:* See "Ideen: Das Buch Le Grand," *Reisebilder,* Part II, chapter VII; *Werke,* IV, 164–65.

109: 511   *'It is curious':* "Ideen: Das Buch Le Grand," chapter IX; *Werke,* IV, 173.

109: 515   *'The Englishman':* "Gespräch auf der Themse," *Englische Fragmente; Werke,* V, 81–82.

110: 545   *'Siehst sehr sterbeblässlich aus':* This is from the poem, "Sterbende," *Romanzero,* Part 2: "Lamentationen"; *Werke,* III, 116. Arnold translates this poem on pp. 115–16 of this essay.

110: 563   *'Ah, my child':* "Berg-Idylle," from "Aus der Harzreise," *Buch der Lieder; Werke,* I, 176–78. A French translation of the same portion which Arnold here quotes appeared in Saint-René Taillandier's article on Heine, pp. 17–18.

111: 592–93   *his latest poems . . . Matrazzen-gruft:* Heine's *Nachlässe* or posthumous poems included a section headed "Matrazzen-gruft," which contained a number of melancholy and bitter poems. See *Werke,* III, 399–440.

111: 602   *Spanish Atridae:* This is from the second book of the *Romanzero* "Lamentationen"; *Werke,* III, 89–99.

113: 659   *He has excellently pointed out:* See "Der Doktor Faust: Erläuterungen"; *Werke,* X, 70–71. In analyzing Goethe's treatment of the Faust legend, Heine indicates the existence of conflicting elements of "Hebraism" and "Hellenism": "Sonderbar! die beiden grossen Bücher der Menschheit, die sich vor einem Jahrtausend so feindlich befehdet und wie kampfmüde während dem ganzen Mittelalter vom Schauplatz zurückgezogen hatten, der Homer und die Bibel, treten zu Anfang des sechzehnten Jahrhunderts wieder öffentlich in die Schranken. Wenn ich oben aussprach, dass die

Revolte der realistischen, sensualistischen Lebenslust gegen die spiritualistische altkatholische Ascese die eigentliche Idee der Faustsage ist."

For an instance of Heine's contrast of these two elements in their religious context see "Ludwig Börne: Eine Denk-Schrifft," Book I; *Werke,* VIII, 360–61.

113: 669   *There lives at Hamburg':* "Die Bäder von Lucca," chapter IX, *Reisebilder,* Part III; *Werke,* IV, 365–66. The sentence with which the section concludes is evidently a parody of the words which Alexander the Great is said to have uttered on meeting Diogenes: "If I were not Alexander, I would be Diogenes."

114: 696   *Princess Sabbath:* This poem, together with the two which follow here, *Jehuda ben Halevy* and the "Dispute" comprise the whole of the third section of the *Romanzero,* the "Hebrew Melodies"; *Werke,* III, 135–88.

116: 778   *'Can it be?':* This is from the "Nachwort" to the *Romanzero,* written September 30, 1851; *Werke,* III, 199.

116: 798–99   *Goethe says that he was deficient in love:* Arnold is mistaken both here and in his elegy "Heine's Grave" (lines 98–100). The poet to whom Goethe referred was not Heine, but Count August Graf von Platen. Goethe's statement is recorded in later editions of Eckermann's *Gespräche mit Goethe,* 1825 (last paragraph): "Wir sprachen darauf über Platen, dessen negative Richtung gleichfalls nicht gebilliget wurde. 'Es ist nicht zu läugnen,' sagte Goethe, 'er besisst manche glänzende Eigenschaften; allein ihm fehlt—die Liebe—. Er liebt so wenig seine Leser und seine Mit-Poeten . . . Noch in diesen Tagen habe ich Gedichte von Platen gelesen und sein reiches Talent nicht verkennen können. Allein, wie gesagt, die Liebe fehlt ihm, und so wird er auch nie so wirken als er hätte müssen.' " See *Gespräche mit Goethe in den Letzten Jahren seines Lebens,* von Johann Peter Eckermann (Leipzig, 1909), p. 134.

In his *Matthew Arnold and Goethe,* J. B. Orrick refutes this identification of Goethe's bard with Heine. He cites the *Nachwort zu Eckermann,* where Eckermann's son includes a note of his father's stating that Platen was the poet meant. Platen's name thereafter replaced the three stars of omission which appeared in early editions of the *Gespräche.* For the text of this note of Eckermann's, see the edition of the *Gespräche mit Goethe* by H. H. Houben (Leipzig, 1925), pp. 712–13.

But the mistake was not original with Arnold. The source of the error was rather a review of Eckermann's *Conversations with Goethe* which appeared in the *Foreign Quarterly Review.* Here the reviewer twice associates the bard "deficient in love" with Heine. See the *Foreign Quarterly Review,* XVIII (October, 1836), 1–30. The Heine identifications appear on pp. 16–17.

117: 811–12   *Look at Byron:* Arnold's reference to Byron here is significant since Heine had acquired for himself in the 1840's the reputation of "the German Byron." See, for example, the *Dublin University Magazine,* XXVI (September, 1845), 283, and Julian Fane's "Heinrich Heine, Poet and Humorist," *Saturday Review,* I (November 3, 1855), 13–14. See also Sol Liptzin's *English Legend,* chapters 1–3.

Arnold's earliest reaction to Heine, disgust at the affectation of Byron's gloom and cynicism without Byron's social experience, appeared in a letter to his mother, May 7, 1848. See *Letters*, I, 11.

PAGAN AND MEDIAEVAL RELIGIOUS SENTIMENT

This essay first appeared in the Cornhill Magazine *for April, 1864.*

118: 1   *I read:* Arnold quotes from "The Catholic Congress of Malines," *Dublin Review*, I, N.S. (October, 1863), 488. He included this quotation in his notebook for 1863. See *Note-Books*, p. 23.

119: 25   *Mr. Spurgeon:* See the note to the 1865 Preface, 249: 145.

119: 27   *the collection of the Abbé Migne:* Jacques Paul Migne (1800–75) published an immense collection of historical and theological writings, including: *Scripturae Sacrae Cursus Completus*, 28 volumes; *Theologiae Patrologiae Cursus Completus*, 28 volumes; *Collection des Orateurs Sacrés*, 100 volumes; *Patrologiae Cursus Completus*, 383 volumes; and *Encyclopédie Théologique*, 171 volumes.

120: 68–69   *Quicquid agunt homines:* Juvenal, *Satires*, I, 85.

120: 73   *Dictionnaire des Apocryphes:* The various *Dictionnaires* to which Arnold refers are volumes of the *Encyclopédie Théologique*.

120: 81   *'The religious persecutions':* Arnold here quotes from the article on Anglicanism.

126: 325   *'Hope and a renovation':* This is from Wordsworth's "Address to My Infant Daughter Dora," line 65. He quotes the same line in the essay on Maurice de Guérin, at 58: 182.

127: 356   *St. Francis:* Early biographies of St. Francis were written by Thomas of Celano, a disciple of St. Francis, in 1229; by the so-called "three companions," Leo, Rufinus, and Angelus, in 1234; and by St. Bonaventure in 1263.

128: 379   *'I hear':* This quotation is taken from the first of Charles de Berthoud's articles on a German life of St. Francis of Assisi. See the review of Dr. Karl Hase's *Franz von Assisi*, in the *Revue Germanique et Française*, XXVI (July 1, 1863), 236.

128: 385   *the beginnings of the mundane poetry:* Arnold had been reading Antoine F. Ozanam's *Les Poètes Franciscains en Italie au Treizième Siècle* (Paris, 1852), as well as Charles de Berthoud on Dr. Hase's biography of St. Francis. Much of the material in this essay is derived from these two sources.

128: 390–91   *Canticle of the Sun:* In the second of de Berthoud's articles the text of the *Canticle* is given in Italian; a French translation appears in a footnote. See *Revue Germanique et Française*, XVII (September 1, 1863), 77–79. Arnold's English version presented in this essay is an exact translation of the French rendition included in de Berthoud's note.

130: 463   *the real Reformation:* For Arnold's earlier evaluation of "Luther's Reformation" see "Dr. Stanley's *Lectures on the Jewish Church,*" *Macmillan's Magazine,* VII (February, 1863), 327–36. In that article Arnold stated: "The greatness of a religious reformer consists in his reconciling [new ideas] with the religious life, in his starting this life upon a fresh period in company with them" (pp. 329–30). Arnold's estimate of Luther followed: "The critical ideas of the sixteenth century broke up the Church of the Middle Ages . . . But Luther was a great religious reformer, not because he made himself the organ of these ideas, themselves negative . . . but because he reconciled these ideas with the religious life, because he made the religious life feel that a positive and fruitful conclusion was to be drawn from them . . . [The religious reformer] is not he who rivets our minds upon the untruth of this [or that] proposition. . . . He is the man who makes us feel the future which undoubtedly exists for the religious life in the absence of it" (p. 335).

130: 474   *in his very last poem:* "Die Passionsblüme," or "Für die Mouche"; *Werke,* III, 430–35. Arnold here refers to the third-last verse of the poem:

> O, dieser Streit wird enden nimmermehr,
> Stets wird die Wahrheit hadern mit dem Schönen
> Stets wird geschieden sein der Menschheit Heer
> In zwei Partein: Barbaren und Hellenen.

130: 480   *'All through the Middle Age':* This is from *Zür Geschichte der Religion und Philosophie in Deutschland,* Book I; *Werke,* VII, 201.

131: 505   *'What pipes':* See Keats' "Ode on a Grecian Urn," line 10.

131: 516   *'The great pot':* This is from *Geständnisse; Werke,* X, 206. Arnold condenses Heine's text somewhat.

131: 530   *'In the year 1340':* This is from *Geständnisse,* last paragraphs; *Werke,* X, 207–8. Heine gives the date as 1480.

134: 619   *'Oh! that my lot':* This is from Sophocles' *Oedipus Tyrannus,* lines 863 ff.

A PERSIAN PASSION PLAY

This essay first appeared in the Cornhill Magazine *for December, 1871.*

135: 1-2   *the Ammergau Passion Play:* The *Guardian* for November 15, 1871, sketches the historical background of the play, and describes the performance in 1871: "More than two hundred years ago [i.e., in 1633] Oberammergau was afflicted with a plague by which many died. The monks of Ettal . . . induced the inhabitants to make a vow to perform the Passion of Our Lord every ten years, and tradition affirms that from that date not a villager died of the pestilence. The vow has been religiously kept from that time to this; and one year in ten, every Sunday from May to September, the Play is acted." The play itself consisted of *"tableaux vivants* representing Old Testament scenes, such as 'The Expulsion from Eden' and 'The Lifting Up of the Serpent in the Wilderness,' as types of the New Testament revelation, alternating with the acting of the scenes of the Passion itself" (p. 1362).

In 1870 the performance was interrupted by the Franco-Prussian War. For this reason, the year 1871, although not the scheduled decade year, saw the performance resumed, beginning on June 24 and concluding on September 24. The popularity of the play among the English at this time was due in part to Malcolm Maccoll's detailed descriptions of the 1870 performance which appeared in the *Times* for June 13 and June 23, 1870.

See also: "The Passion Play," *Catholic World,* XII (October, 1870), 81–89; "Miracle Plays," *Saturday Review,* XXXII (July 1, 1871), 9–10; "The Oberammergau Passion Play," *Guardian,* July 26, 1871, p. 899; "The Ammergau Passion Play," *Saturday Review,* XXXII (September 16, 1871), 361–63; "Recollections of the Passion Play at Oberammergau," by H. N. O., *Guardian,* October 4, 1871, pp. 1167–69; and *Malcolm Maccoll, Memoirs and Correspondence,* ed. G. W. E. Russell (London, 1914), pp. 29–32.

137: 61   *book on the present state:* Les Réligions et Philosophies dans l'Asie Centrale (Paris, 1865). A second edition appeared in 1866, a third in 1900. Subsequent references are to a fourth edition reprint (Paris, 1933).

137: 85   *'He desired':* See chapter VI, "Commencement du bâbysme," pp. 135–36.

138: 121–22   *Gibbon shall tell the rest:* Edward Gibbon, *The History of the Decline and Fall of the Roman Empire,* ed. J. B. Bury (New York, 1898), V, 388 (chapter 50). Gobineau himself refers readers interested in more detail to the "beau récit de Gibbon."

139: 143   *'In the fourth age':* This is a continuation of the quotation from Gibbon in the preceding paragraph of Arnold's text.

139: 166   *'O death,' cries the bandit-minstrel:* Kurroglou was a Turkman Tuka, a native of Northern Khorassan, who lived in the second half of the seventeenth century. His real name was Roushan, and that of his father Mirza-Serraf. In consequence of a cruel punishment inflicted upon his father by a tyrannical ruler, the Sultan Murad, Roushan assumed the name Kurroglou, "son of the blind one." The bandit-minstrel plundered caravans on the great commercial road between Persia and Turkey, gradually attaining the stature of national warrior and bard.

The passage which Arnold here quotes is taken from the last of Kurroglou's Improvisations, a chant on the death of the ideal warrior. See *Specimens of the Popular Poetry of Persia,* trans. Alexander Chodzko (London, 1842), p. 342.

139: 170   *'Hussein traversed . . . phrenzy of sorrow and indignation':* Gibbon, V, 390–92 (chapter 50).

141: 216   *Count Gobineau relates:* This is from chapter XIII, "Le Théatre en Pèrse," and chapter XIV, "Les Tekyèhs ou Théatres." His comparison with the Greek and the European drama appears in chapter XIII, pp. 321–22.

141: 232   *the Emperor Tamerlane:* See chapter XIII, pp. 329–30.

142: 257   *every one is in mourning:* See chapter XIII, pp. 335–36.

142: 289   *The tekyèhs, or theatres:* This is from chapter XIV, "Les Tekyèhs ou Théatres." In this section of his essay Arnold is condensing and rearranging the material on pp. 339–49 of Gobineau's book.

144: 357   *'The actor is under a charm':* See chapter XIV, p. 348.

145: 379   *'Nothing is more touching':* See chapter XIV, pp. 352–53.

145: 394—147: 467   See chapter XIV, pp. 352–53; pp. 345–50; and pp. 353–56.

147: 469—148: 501   See chapter XVI, "Autres Compositions Théatrales," pp. 392–94.

148: 502—151: 637   See chapter XV, "Les Noces de Kassem," pp. 359–86.

151: 639   *The narrative of Gibbon:* Gibbon, V, 391 (chapter 50, "Death of Hosein"). Arnold alters Gibbon's text slightly here.

152: 660–61   *the Christian Damsel:* See chapter XVI, "Autres Compositions Théatrales," pp. 397–400.

152: 687   *Another piece closes:* See chapter XVI, pp. 394–95.

153: 715   *Count Gobineau suggests:* See chapter XIII, p. 326.

154: 744   *Jaffer answered:* Jaffer was the son of Abu Talib. The incident which Arnold here describes appears in various biographies of Mohammed. See D. S. Margoliouth, *Mohammed and the Rise of Islam* (London, 1905), p. 160; and E. Lamairesse and Gaston Dujarric, *Vie de Mahomet d'après la Tradition* (Paris, 1897), pp. 191–94. The source from which Arnold took his narrative has not been found.

156: 831   *'The twelve Imams':* Gibbon, V, 392 (chapter 50, "Posterity of Mahomet and Ali").

156: 842   *'O brother,' said Hassan:* Arnold here quotes from Simon Ockley's *The History of the Saracens* (Cambridge, 1757), II, 83. The incident is also included in Washington Irving's *The Lives of Mahomet and His Successors* (Philadelphia, 1873), II, chapter XLIII, 361.

156: 845   *'God loved Hussein':* See Ockley, II, 181.

157: 881   *I have elsewhere often said:* See *St. Paul and Protestantism* and *Literature and Dogma*.

JOUBERT

This essay first appeared in the National Review *for January, 1864.*

160: 30   *M. Sainte-Beuve has given:* Sainte-Beuve wrote two appreciations of Joubert, one in 1838, on the private publication of the *Pensées* by Madame Joubert and Châteaubriand, later reprinted in *Portraits Littéraires*, II, and the second, in 1849, after the publication of the edition by Paul de Raynal, included in *Causeries du Lundi*, I.

160: 39–40   *by the Jesuits:* Arnold is mistaken here. In his Preface to the *Correspondance*, Paul de Raynal states that the Collège de Toulouse at this time was no longer directed by the Jesuits but by their successors, the "Pères de la Doctrine chrétienne." See the *Correspondance de J. Joubert,* ed. Paul de Raynal (Paris, 1895): "Notice sur la vie, le caractère, et les travaux de M. J. Joubert." Subsequent citations from the correspondence are from this volume; those from the *pensées* are from *Pensées de Joseph Joubert,* ed. M. Paul de Raynal (Paris, 1909).

160: 51   *'s'inquiétait de perfection':* See Raynal's "Notice," p. xiv.

161: 58   *'He has chosen':* During his journey in Italy Châteaubriand addressed three letters to Joubert. To one of these he later added a note describing Joubert as a man "d'un talent qui lui aurait donné une reputation meritée, s'il n'avait voulu cacher sa vie." See Raynal's "Notice," p. i.

161: 84   *after two distinguished names:* The names were those of M. de Bonald and M. de Beausset. See the "Notice," p. lxv. The incident is described on pp. lxv–lxvi.

162: 104   *'a great deal of sky':* Joubert wrote "Beaucoup de ciel se mêlait à peu de terre"; see the "Notice," p. xliv.

162: 105   *treasures of a library:* Joubert's library contained "few modern works," but many volumes of Plato, Homer, Virgil, Aristotle, and Plutarch, as well as books of ecclesiastical history and travel. There were even collections of fairy tales, "récits merveilleux et naïfs," to be read for relaxation. See the "Notice," pp. xlv–xlvi.

162: 107   *a complete Voltaire:* See the "Notice," p. xlv. See also Joubert's letter to Madame de Beaumont, May, 1797, in which he exclaims: "Dieu me préserve d'avoir jamais en ma possession un Voltaire tout entier!" *Correspondance,* Letter XV, p. 32.

163: 157   *a short notice of him:* This notice appeared in the *Journal des Débats* for May 8, 1824. Raynal included the notice in his Preface, pp. lxxxii– lxxxiii.

163: 175   *M. Sainte-Beuve gave of it:* See "Écrivains Moralistes et Critiques de la France: VI. M. Joubert," *Revue des Deux Mondes,* XVI, Quatrième Série (December 1, 1838), 666–81. The essay was reprinted in *Portraits Littéraires,* II.

165: 229   *M. de Rémusat, indeed, reproaches Coleridge:* See "Des Controverses Religieuses en Angleterre: Deuxième Partie—Coleridge—Arnold," *Revue des Deux Mondes,* V, Seconde Période (October 1, 1856), 492–529. M. de Rémusat discusses the influence of German philosophy upon Coleridge's religious thought, and notes with some irritation the latter's tendency to disparage French intellectualism: "Il dit que les opinions de nos philosophes ont été les dents du dragon de Cadmus; il les redoute, mais il s'en moque. Il nous trouve trop speculatifs dans le monde politique et trop peu dans le monde intelligible." Such *saugrenu* judgments M. de Rémusat traces to the German element in the development of Coleridge's thought (pp. 511–12).

165: 235   *as M. Sainte-Beuve remarks:* See "Anciens Poètes Français—Du Bartas," *Revue des Deux Mondes,* XXIX, Quatrième Série (February 15,

1823), p. 102, adding: "Chaque nation est, ce semble, le premier juge des siens; si grand que soit Goethe, cela ne le rend pas un arbitre plus sûr des vers français" (pp. 555–56). Goethe also censured the French indifference to Du Bartas in his commentary on "Rameau's Neffe": "Die Französen haben einen Poeten Du Bartas, den sie gar nicht mehr, oder nur mit Verachtung nennen"; *Werke* (Stuttgart und Tübingen, 1830), XXXVI, 170.

165: 245   *the high estimate:* See Joubert's letter to M. Molé, January 9, 1805: "Il n'y a point de livre où la langue française soit si brillante. . . . Cet homme aura, plus que tout autre, révélé à la langue française ses richesses et ses couleurs" (pp. 138–39).

166: 264   *'It is a dangerous mistake':* This passage appeared in Châteaubriand's first Preface to *Atala, ou les Amours de Deux Sauvages dans le Désert,* and it was quoted by Sainte-Beuve in *Châteaubriand et son Groupe Littéraire* (Paris, 1878), I, chapter 7, 199–200. Châteaubriand said the same thing again in an article on Shakespeare, which appeared in the *Mercure,* June 14, 1802. See also *Note-Books,* p. 482.

166: 279   *'Mon Dieu':* This is quoted by Sainte-Beuve in *Châteaubriand et son Groupe Littéraire,* II, "Châteaubriana," 399. The words appear in a fragment of a letter beginning: "Il m'a dit souvent que l'homme devenait meilleur en veillissant." See also *Note-Books,* p. 475.

166: 283   *Châteaubriand is most ignorantly underrated:* Perhaps Arnold had in mind Macaulay's estimate of the *Génie du Christianisme* which he had bought in France in 1857: "I was astonished . . . at the utter worthlessness of the book, both in matter and manner. The French may be beautiful, as far as mere selection and arrangement of words go. But in the higher graces of style—those graces which affect a foreigner as much as a native —those graces which delight us in Plato, in Demosthenes, and in Pascal— there is a lamentable deficiency. As to the substance, it is beneath criticism. Yet I have heard men of ten times Châteaubriand's powers talk of him as the first of French writers. He was simply a great humbug." See G. Otto Trevelyan, *The Life and Letters of Lord Macaulay* (New York, 1876), II, 345.

166: 290–91   *Coleridge's judgments on French literature:* M. de Rémusat had taken particular exception to an essay of Coleridge's on "The Grounds of Morals and Religion, and the Discipline of the Mind Requisite for a True Understanding of the Same," the "printed philosophical essay" to which Arnold subsequently refers. In a note appended to this essay Coleridge first defined genius as "the faculty which adds to the existing stock of power and knowledge by new views, new combinations," and again as "originality in intellectual construction." He immediately proceeded to deny "genius" to the mind of France, granting it "cleverness" instead: "By cleverness . . . I mean a comparative readiness in the invention and use of means, for the realizing of objects and ideas—often of such ideas, which the man of genius only could have originated, and which the clever man perhaps neither fully comprehends nor adequately appreciates." If it is genius at all, he continues, it is "a sort of genius for instrumentality."

As a parting thrust, and one which especially grieved M. de Rémusat, Coleridge asserted that to Germany belong the Past and the Future, to England the Past and the Present, but to France only the Present. See *The Complete Works of Samuel Taylor Coleridge*, ed. W. G. T. Shedd (New York, 1884), II, *The Friend*, second section, "On the Ground of Morals and Religion," Essay I, note. Quotations here are from pp. 384–87.

167: 301   *'As to your Milton'*: See Joubert's letter to M. Molé, February 18, 1805, p. 143. In an earlier letter to the same, January 9, 1805, Joubert also praised the Abbé Delille at Milton's expense. The Abbé's translation is admirable, but in fact it is only "imperfect poets" who can be translated at all. See *Correspondance*, p. 139.

167: 310   *a deliberate proposition:* See the note to 166: 290–91.

167: 327-28   *as Coleridge treats his Jeffrey:* Coleridge attacked Jeffrey in a letter dated May 23, 1808, and again in chapter 21 of the *Biographia Literaria*. See Jeffrey's scathing review of the *Biographia* in the *Edinburgh Review*, XXVIII (August, 1817), 488–515. This review included a lengthy footnote in which Jeffrey addressed himself to Coleridge personally.

See also Walter Graham, *English Literary Periodicals* (New York, 1930), pp. 233–39.

167: 329   *'Geoffroy in this article':* See Joubert's letter to Madame de Beaumont, August 1, 1801, p. 58. The article had appeared in the *Journal des Débats* for this date.

168: 357   *'The true science':* Titre XII, "De la philosophie," xxiii, p. 154.

168: 362   *'Distrust':* Titre XII, xxv, p. 154.

169: 395   *'It is by means':* Titre XXII, "Du style," xcix, p. 293.

169: 415   *'Be profound':* Titre XXIII, "Des qualités de l'écrivain," xxxvi, p. 308.

170: 420   *'spirits, lovers of light':* Titre IV, "De la nature des esprits," lxiii, pp. 62–63.

170: 441   *'I cannot build':* Titre Préliminaire, "L'Auteur peint par lui-même," p. 10.

170: 442   *'I have tried':* Titre Préliminaire, p. 8.

170: 443   *'If there is a man':* Titre Préliminaire, p. 8.

170: 445   *'I can sow':* Titre Préliminaire, p. 5.

171: 459   *'One should be fearful':* Titre I, "De la religion," xci, p. 26.

171: 462   *'There is a great difference':* Titre I, lxxxv, p. 25.

171: 470   *'May I say it':* Titre I, vi, p. 12.

171: 472   *'Do not bring':* Titre XI, "De la vérité," xxxvii, p. 143.

171: 487   *'Why is even':* Titre I, "Des livres saints et des prêtres," cxix, p. 31.

171: 493   *'You may do':* Titre I, cxx, p. 31.

172: 497   *'The only happy people':* Titre I, "De la piété," lii, p. 20.

172: 503   *'Piety is not':* Titre I, "De la religion," lxi, p. 21.

172: 508   *'Religion is neither':* Titre I, "De la religion," lxii, pp. 21–22.

172: 513   *'The pomp':* Titre I, lxviii, pp. 22–23.

172: 528   *'The Old Testament':* Titre I, "Des livres saints," cxxix, p. 33.

173: 537   *'The austere sects':* Titre I, lxxv, pp. 23–24.

173: 545   *'We ought to lay stress':* Titre I, cxxx, pp. 33–34.

173: 563   *'The Jansenists erect "grace" ':* Titre I, cxxxv, pp. 35–36.

173: 571   *'The Jansenists tell men'*: Titre I, cxxxii, p. 35. The original reads: "La doctrine de ceux-ci est remplie d'inexactitudes et d'erreurs peut-être," etc.

173: 575   *'The Jansenists have carried'*: Titre I, cxxxi, pp. 34–35.

174: 595   *'Ignorance'*: Titre XXIII, "Des qualités de l'écrivain," liv, p. 311.

174: 599   *'With the fever'*: Titre XXIII, cxxviii, p. 325.

174: 605   *'Fiction has no business'*: Titre XXIV, section VI, "Sur quelques romans du temps," third-last paragraph, pp. 389–90.

175: 619   *'Whether one is an eagle'*: Titre XXIII, "Des qualités de l'écrivain," ccxviii, p. 339.

175: 642   *'Plato shows us'*: Titre XXIV, section I, "Écrivains de l'antiquité," xii, p. 344.

175: 649   *'Plato loses himself'*: Titre XXIV, xiv, p. 344.

175: 650   *'It is good'*: Titre XXIV, x (last sentence), p. 343.

175: 654   *'Nicole is a Pascal'*: Titre XXIV, section II, "Écrivains religieux," vi, p. 351.

176: 661   the *'declaimer' Bossuet*: Arnold was perhaps thinking of this passage from Macaulay's *History*: "In literature [France] gave law to the world. The fame of her great writers filled Europe. No other country could produce a tragic poet equal to Racine, a comic poet equal to Molière, a trifler so agreeable as La Fontaine, a rhetorician so skilful as Bossuet." *A History of England from the Accession of James the Second* (New York, 1879), I, chapter 3, 365. The tone is not so severe, however, as Arnold indicates, and several other references to Bossuet in the *History* are likewise respectful enough.

176: 663   *'Bossuet employs'*: Titre XXIV, section V, "Écrivains religieux," x, pp. 351–52.

176: 677   *'Those who find Racine'*: Titre XXIV, section V, "Poètes et Romanciers," xiii, p. 378.

176: 684   *'The talent of Racine'*: Titre XXIV, xi, p. 378.

176: 685   *'Of Racine'*: Titre XXIV, ix, pp. 377–78.

176: 693–94   *'Racine est le Virgile'*: Titre XXIV, section V, "Poètes et Romanciers," xv, p. 379.

176: 695   *'Boileau is a powerful poet'*: Titre XXIV, xiv, p. 378.

177: 697   *'Neither Boileau's poetry'*: Titre XXIV, xv, p. 378.

177: 707   *'Voltaire's wits'*: Titre XXIV, section IV, "Philosophes." Arnold here combines maxims xxii, xxvi, xxix, xxxii, and xxxiii, pp. 364–66.

177: 729   *'That weight'*: Titre XXIV, combining maxims xxxv and xxxviii, p. 367.

178: 738   *'Rosseau imparted'*: Titre XXIV, xlii, p. 368.

178: 744   *'Life without actions'*: Titre XXIV, combining maxims xlviii, xlix, and l, pp. 369–70.

178: 758   *'The ancients'*: Titre XVII, "De l'antiquité," i, p. 203.

178: 769   *'A great many words'*: Titre XVII, iii, p. 204.

179: 777   *'Let your cry'*: Titre XV, "De la liberté," combining maxims v and xiv, pp. 178 and 180.

179: 784   *'Liberty'*: Titre XV, xv, p. 180.

179: 792   *'Notre vie'*: Titre VII, "De la vie," lxii, p. 95.

179: 793   *'les dettes':* Titre VII, lxxiii, p. 96.
179: 793   *'celui qui a':* Titre IV, "De la nature des esprits," xxxix, p. 58.
179: 803   *'le bonheur':* Titre V, "Des passions et des affections de l'âme," xxx, p. 67.
179: 804   *'toute vérité':* Titre XI, "De la vérité," xxxvi, pp. 142–43.

SPINOZA AND THE BIBLE

This essay is a composite of two articles which appeared originally in Macmillan's Magazine, *"The Bishop and the Philosopher," in January, 1863, and "A Word More About Spinoza," in December, 1863.*

183: 1   *'By the sentence of the angels':* This is taken from the anathema pronounced against Spinoza, reproduced in part from Van Vloten's *Supplementum.* See J. Van Vloten, *Ad Benedicti de Spinoza Opera Quae Supersunt Omnia Supplementum* (Amsterdam, 1862), pp. 290–93.
184: 21   *in 1656:* Van Vloten offers the correct date in the *Supplementum,* p. 290. See also *The Chief Works of Benedict de Spinoza,* trans. R. H. M. Elwes, 2 vols. (London, 1887), I, Introduction, p. xii.
184: 25-26   *Of Voltaire's disparagement and Bayle's detraction:* There is a long and inimical article on Spinoza in the *Dictionnaire Historique et Critique* by M. Pierre Bayle. See the fourth edition (Paris, 1730). Bayle's censures were directed against Spinoza's alleged "atheism" and "impiety."

In "Le Philosophe Ignorante: XXIV—Spinosa," Voltaire admits the "justice" but scores the "harshness" of Bayle's attack upon Spinoza. Spinoza was an atheist, Voltaire concedes, and employed religious terminology in his writings only to avoid scandalizing his readers. See *Oeuvres Complètes de Voltaire,* Nouvelle Edition, 52 vols. (Paris, 1877), XXVI, 66–67. Voltaire criticized Bayle's method of attack upon Spinoza in "Dieu, Dieux," *Oeuvres,* XVIII, 367.

Voltaire also manifested a certain contempt for the philosophy of Spinoza in the opening lines of the second part of his "Poème sur la Loi Naturelle," *Oeuvres,* IX, 446 ff. See also "Causes Finales," *Oeuvres,* XVIII, 98.

But Voltaire did not devote all his energy to "disparagement" of Spinoza. In the tenth of a series of letters "on authors accused of having spoken ill of the Christian religion," Voltaire defended both the character and the works of Spinoza. See *Oeuvres,* XXVI, 522. See also his tribute to Spinoza's character as "homme sans reproche, ami serviable, bon citoyen" in "Le Système Vraisemblable: III—de Spinosa," *Oeuvres,* XXXI, 167.

184: 33-34   *An avowed translation: Tractatus Theologico-Politicus: A Critical Inquiry into the History, Purpose, and Authenticity of the Hebrew Scriptures, etc.* By Benedict de Spinoza. From the Latin, with an Introduction and notes by the editor (London, 1862). See the note to "The Literary Influence of Academies," at 51: 792.

Arnold first criticized this translation of the *Tractatus Theologico-Politicus* in "A Word More About Spinoza," *Macmillan's Magazine*, IX (December, 1863), 136–42. The opening section of the present essay is from this article.

184: 36   *his book on ethics:* Benedict de Spinoza Opera Posthuma, containing the *Ethica, Politica, De Emandatione Intellectus, Epistolae,* and *Compendium of Hebrew Grammar* was published in 1667. Robert Willis, whose translation of the *Tractatus* Arnold is here criticizing, published *Benedict de Spinoza: His Life, Correspondence, and Ethics* in 1870.

184: 39   *one such passage:* This is from Spinoza's Preface to the *Tractatus*. The English version which Arnold here quotes is from the 1862 English edition, p. 25.

185: 62   *'to Bayle':* "To Bayle, indeed, may be traced the frequent, though by no means universal, disfavour among the learned in which the name of Spinoza was so long held." See the Translator's Introduction, p. 15.

185: 65   *that advanced school:* Typical of the attitude expressed in the Introduction is this reference to "our own days of freer individual thought and of greater general enlightenment, when authority and prescription in matters of faith no less than in subjects of science are ignored by the truly educated in all classes of society"; Introduction, p. 4.

185: 81   *Spinoza sees:* See, for example, the opening section of the seventh chapter of the *Tractatus*, "Of the Interpretation of Scripture." Spinoza describes his method in detail in his Preface and in chapter 7, "Of the Interpretation of Scripture."

186: 97   *The comments of men:* The section from here to 194: 421 constitutes the first of Arnold's interpolations from "The Bishop and the Philosopher." In this paragraph Arnold summarizes the principal points in Spinoza's Preface to the *Tractatus*.

186: 109   *all the learning:* For demonstrations of Spinoza's technical knowledge see chapter 7, "Of the Interpretation of Scripture," and chapter 9, "The Last Reviser of Historic Books."

186: 112   *In what then:* In this paragraph Arnold summarizes chapter 1, "Of Prophecy."

186: 123   *The prophets:* This paragraph and the two which follow summarize chapter 2, "Of Prophets." See also chapter 15, "Theology Not Subservient to Reason."

188: 177   *To know and love God:* This is from chapter 4, "Of the Divine Law." See also the *Ethics,* IV, xxviii; Elwes, II, 205–6.

188: 183   *In the case of the Jews:* The remainder of this paragraph summarizes chapter 3, "Of the Vocation of the Hebrews."

188: 201   *vera vita:* Arnold here refers to an expression which Spinoza used in reference to "the well-spring of life" (Prov. XVI, 22): "Life being taken to mean the true life . . . the fruit of the understanding consists only in the true life, and its absence constitutes punishment." *Tractatus,* chapter 4, "Of the Divine Law"; Elwes, I, 66.

188: 206   *Christ came:* This is from chapter 4, "Of the Divine Law."

189: 219   *And the apostles:* In the remainder of this paragraph Arnold summarizes chapter 11, "Of the Apostolic Mission."

189: 245   *'turned the Church':* Arnold quotes from chapter 13, "Of the Simplicity of Scripture." See Elwes, I, 175–76. Spinoza complains again of this kind of sectarian fury in the opening of chapters 7 and 14 and in the end of chapter 11.

189: 247   *What, then:* This is from chapter 13, "Of the Simplicity of Scripture," and chapter 15, "Definitions of Faith."

190: 289   *'as it is only':* Arnold quotes from the concluding sentences of chapter 15, "Theology Not Subservient to Reason." See Elwes, I, 199.

190: 293   *It follows:* With the exception of the last sentence, which derives from chapter 20, "Of Freedom of Thought and Speech," this paragraph summarizes chapter 14, "Definitions of Faith," and chapter 15, "Theology Not Subservient to Reason."

191: 308   *The truest speculative opinion:* Spinoza argued in chapter 14 that faith allows one to think what he likes without blame, "only condemning as heretics and schismatics, those who teach opinions which tend to produce obstinacy, hatred, strife, and anger; while, on the other hand, only considering as faithful those who persuade us, as far as their reason and faculties will permit, to follow justice and charity." See Elwes, I, 189. This is essentially the argument which Arnold raises against Colenso's examination of the Pentateuch, in "The Bishop and the Philosopher," and from which he derives his norms of "truth" and "edification."

191: 313   *But the multitude:* In this paragraph Arnold summarizes chapter 6, "Of Miracles."

191: 328   *Jeremiah declares:* Arnold cites this from the last section of chapter 6, "Of Miracles." Spinoza first argued against the possibility of miracles on a purely philosophical basis, concluding with "evidence" from Scripture itself to fortify his contention. See Arnold's objection to Spinoza's interpretation here on p. 196.

191: 329   *Scripture, however:* This is from chapter 7, "Of the Interpretation of Scripture."

191: 330   *Scriptura definitiones:* "Denique Scriptura rerum, de quibus loquitur, definitiones non tradit, ut nec etiam Natura"; Elwes, I, 100–101. Spinoza was outlining his method here; he had determined "to admit no principles for interpreting Scripture and discussing its contents save such as [we] find in Scripture itself"; Elwes, I, 99.

192: 345   *It is demonstrable:* Arnold here briefly summarizes the arguments of chapters 8–10: "The Authorship of the Pentateuch," "The Last Reviser of Historic Books," and "Of the Prophetic Books."

192: 366   *the learned men:* Spinoza asserted: "It is thus abundantly clear that men expert in the law summoned a council to decide which books should be received into the canon, and which excluded." The statement here regarding the New Testament canon, however, is Arnold's insertion; Spinoza expressly declined to examine the New Testament. See chapter 10, "Of the Prophetic Books," Elwes, I, 155–56 (and note 23, p. 275).

193: 391   *He points out:* Arnold cites this and the following examples from the beginning of chapter 8, "The Authorship of the Pentateuch."

193: 403   *non est cur circa:* This is from chapter 9, "The Last Reviser of Historic Books." See Elwes, I, 139. The following quotation, *"nolo taediosa,"* is from the same chapter (p. 143).

194: 416   *he calls urgently:* See chapter 20, "Freedom of Thought and Speech"; Elwes, I, 265.

194: 420   *anticipating Mr. Gladstone:* In 1838 Gladstone published *The State in Its Relations with the Church,* defending the principle of Church Establishment against advocates of the Voluntary system. Gladstone regarded the state as a person with moral responsibility; hence its strict obligation to maintain and propagate religious truth. The book has been described as "an argument along Tractarian lines," but this is not strictly true, since the Tractarian position was vehemently anti-Erastian, whereas Gladstone envisioned the Church simply as the religious aspect of the civil power.

Macaulay energetically attacked the book in the *Edinburgh Review,* LXIX (April, 1839), 231–80. The review is reprinted in Thomas Babington Macaulay, *Critical and Historical Essays Contributed to the Edinburgh Review* (London, 1848), II, 430–503.

194: 424   *he nowhere distinctly gives:* Such remarks as these occur frequently in the *Tractatus:* "We are at work not on the truth of passages but solely on their meaning"; "Therefore such a tradition should be received with extreme suspicion; and although, according to our method, we are bound to consider as uncorrupted the tradition of the Jews . . . we may accept the latter while retaining our doubts about the former." See chapter 7, "Of the Interpretation of Scripture"; Elwes, I, 101, 107.

194: 426   *Revelation differs:* See chapter 1, "Of Prophecy"; Elwes, I, 13–14.

194: 429   *'of which the laws':* Chapter 1, "Of Prophecy"; Elwes, I, 14.

194: 431   *verum nec nobis:* Chapter 1; Elwes, I, 25.

194: 447   *a vera vox:* Chapter 1; Elwes, I, 15: "Voce enim vera revelavit Deus Mosi leges, quas Hebraeis praescribi volebat."

194: 452   *nisi Scripturae:* Chapter 1; Elwes, I, 16. By confining himself to his method of explaining Scripture only by Scripture itself, Spinoza evaded the necessity of revealing what he himself thought. See especially chapter 7, "Of the Interpretation of Scripture," and chapter 15, "Theology Not Subservient to Reason."

195: 463   *'This revelation':* This passage occurs near the end of chapter 6, "Of Miracles." See Elwes, I, 95–96.

195: 473–74   *a spurious addition:* See chapter 6, "Of Miracles"; Elwes, I, 92: "And if anything is there set down which can be proved in set terms to contravene the order of nature . . . we must believe it to have been foisted into the sacred writings by irreligious hands."

195: 488   *the epicurean Solomon:* See chapter 4: "Of the Divine Law"; Elwes, I, 66–67.

195: 491   *he uses promiscuously:* See chapter 3, "Of the Vocation of the Hebrews."

196: 495   *He is capable:* See the note to 191: 328.

196: 518   *Mr. Mill:* Arnold here refers to *Representative Government,* chapter II, third-last paragraph. Mill speaks of the "inestimably precious unorganised institution—the Order (if so it may be termed) of Prophets. Under the protection, generally, though not always, effectual, of their sacred character, the Prophets were a power in the nation, often more than a match for kings and priests, and kept up, in that little corner of the earth, the antagonism of influences which is the only real security for continued progress." There is much more to the same effect. See John Stuart Mill, *On Liberty and Considerations on Representative Government,* ed. R. B. McCallum (Oxford, 1948), p .134. Mill's *Representative Government* first appeared in 1861.

196: 519   *Dr. Stanley:* Arnold is referring to Lecture XX, "On the Nature of the Prophetical Teaching," in Dr. Stanley's *Lectures on the History of the Jewish Church* (London, 1862). Arnold reviewed Dr. Stanley's work in *Macmillan's Magazine* for February, 1863.

196: 522   *one of her main elements:* Spinoza maintained that the prophets "rather irritated than reformed mankind by their freedom of warning, rebuke, and censure," concluding that "religion gained more harm than good by such freedom," so that "if the prophets had retained their rights, great civil wars would have resulted"; Elwes, I, 239–40.

196: 530   *in his letters:* The *Opera Posthuma* (1677) contained a selection of Spinoza's letters. Van Vloten included several more of them in a section of his *Supplementum* (pp. 295–350).

197: 562–63   *'He spoke of God':* Arnold quotes, but not exactly, from Maurice's "Spinoza and Professor Arnold," *Spectator,* XXXVI (January 3, 1863), 1474. Maurice replied to this stricture of Arnold's in a note to his article, "Christmas Thoughts on Renan's *Vie de Jésus,*" *Macmillan's Magazine,* IX (January, 1864), 197. Maurice also included a chapter on Spinoza in his *Modern Philosophy* (1862), a book which reappeared as Volume II of Maurice's *Moral and Metaphysical Philosophy* (London, 1882).

197: 570   *his denial of final causes:* This is one of the "misconceptions" which Spinoza brought "before the bar of reason" in his Appendix to Part I of the *Ethics.* After asserting that "Nature has no particular goal in view," Spinoza proceeded to demonstrate that men invented a necessity for final causes, "having persuaded themselves that everything which is created is created for their sake." See Elwes, II, 77, 79.

197: 570   *his stoicism:* See the note to 198: 597 below.

198: 589   *'Deus naturam':* This is from chapter 6, "Of Miracles"; Elwes, I, 88. Arnold alters the text somewhat.

198: 597   *'Non studemus':* This is from chapter 6, "Of Miracles"; Elwes, I, 88. Arnold is here adapting Spinoza's remarks about the reasoned assurance of those philosophers "who aim at obeying nature, rather than being obeyed by her." In Spinoza's text this passage immediately precedes the one which Arnold has just quoted concerning denial of final causes.

198: 609   *'Ipsa hominis':* **Ethics,** Part IV, proposition xviii, first sentence of the demonstration; Elwes, II, 200. Arnold alters the original slightly.

198: 610 *'Virtus hominis':* Ethics, IV, proposition xx; Elwes, II, 202. Arnold alters the original text considerably.

198: 611 *'Felicitas in eo':* Ethics, IV, proposition xviii, note; Elwes, II, 201.

198: 612–13 *'Laetitia . . . Tristitia':* Ethics, Part II, "Definitions of the Emotions," II and III; Elwes, II, 174.

199: 632 *'remarries us to God':* Purgatorio, canto XXIII, lines 80–81, where Dante speaks to Forese about the latter's sudden death. Arnold quoted these lines in one of his general notebooks. See *Note-Books*, p. 483.

199: 634 *the fundamental diversity:* This "diversity" consists essentially in the different meanings attached to the concept of God. In a letter to Henry Oldenburg, November, 1675, Spinoza confessed: "I acknowledge that I have a notion of God and Nature very different from that of modern Christians. I believe that God is the immanent, and not the transient cause of all things." This passage is quoted by John Colerus, *The Life of Benedict de Spinoza* (London, trans. 1706), 64–65. See also Robert Willis, *Benedict de Spinoza: His Life, Correspondence, and Ethics*, p. 260.

199: 637–38 *in the knowledge of God:* See the note to 188: 177 above.

200: 656 *several lately found works:* Van Vloten's *Supplementum* also contains the "Tractatus Brevis de Deo et Homine Ejusque Valetudine," the "Iridis Computatio Algebraica," both in Latin and in Dutch versions. Some letters and fragments in Latin only are also included.

200: 663 *'It is a great mistake':* This is from the concluding paragraph of Van Vloten's Preface to the *Supplementum*, pp. iv–v.

200: 679 *Unction, indeed:* The section from here to p. 202 constitutes Arnold's second interpolation from "The Bishop and the Philosopher." See the textual notes, pp. 456–57.

200: 688 *Strauss has treated:* See his *Leben Jesu* (Tübingen, 1835), Part II, chapter 9, "The Miracles of Jesus."

201: 697 *'The love of God':* Tractatus, chapter 4, "Of Divine Law"; Elwes, I, 60.

201: 698 *The supreme reward: Tractatus,* chapter 4; Elwes, I, 62.

201: 703 *the Masora: Masora* is derived from a Hebrew word meaning "to bind" or "to hand down." The term refers to the textual tradition of the Hebrew Bible, consisting of an official registration of its words and phonology for the purpose of fixing definitely the Hebrew text.

201: 704 *'What,' he cries:* See the *Tractatus,* opening of chapter 12, "Of the Sacredness of Scripture." Arnold is expressing Spinoza's attitude here, but not quoting directly.

201: 719 *he was poor:* Colerus relates these incidents in his *Life of Spinoza,* pp. 43–44, 47–48.

202: 750 *his distinction:* Adequate ideas, for Spinoza, are those which correspond to the total reality of the thing in question, as opposed to "inadequate, fragmentary, or confused ideas," false because of their incompleteness. See *Ethics,* II, propositions XXXII–XLIII; Elwes, II, 108–15; *Ethics,* III, postulate II; Elwes, II, 130–31; *Ethics,* V, proposition IV and note; Elwes, II, 248–49. See also Spinoza's letter to Tschirnhausen, January, 1675; Elwes, II, 395–96.

202: 752   *sentence of Heracleitus:* In the *Metaphysics* (IV, 3, 7), Aristotle quotes Heracleitus: "Being and non-Being are the same; everything is and yet is not." Hegel developed from this idea his system of truth as the unity of distinct opposites. See Georg Wilhelm F. Hegel, *Lectures on the History of Philosophy,* trans. E. S. Haldane, 3 vols. (London, 1892), I, 282.

202: 757–58   *much-criticised expression:* Arnold greatly enjoyed the commotion his expression had created. In the fourth of his Homer lectures, "On Translating Homer: Last Words," he attempted to define the expression, in deference to the "sincere" perplexity of some of his critics: "The grand style arises in poetry, when a noble nature, poetically gifted, treats with simplicity or with severity a serious subject." See *On the Study of Celtic Literature* and *On Translating Homer* (New York, 1909), pp. 264–65.

A few articles attacking Arnold's use of the expression "grand style" are: Fitzjames Stephen's "Homeric Translators and Critics," *Saturday Review,* XII (July 27, 1861), 95–96; "On Translating Homer," *Westminster Review,* XXI, N.S. (January, 1862), 161–62; "The Bishop and the Professor," *Examiner,* January 10, 1863, p. 20; and Wright's *Letter to the Dean of Canterbury on the Homeric Lectures of Matthew Arnold* (London, 1864).

202: 762   *'There is no possible view':* This is quoted from the noted conversation between Lessing and Friedrich Jacobi in Jacobi's *Über die Lehre des Spinoza in Briefen an den Herrn Moses Mendelssohn* (Breslau, 1785), p. 13. The incident took place during a visit with Lessing at Wolfenbüttel in July, 1780, when Jacobi introduced the subject of Goethe's poem, "Prometheus." See also Willis, *Benedict de Spinoza: His Life, Correspondence, and Ethics,* pp. 149–60.

202: 763   *Goethe has told us:* Arnold refers to Goethe's *Aus Meinem Leben: Dichtung und Wahrheit.* In Book XIV Goethe attributes his first acquaintance with the philosophy of Spinoza to the influence of Fritz Jacobi. In the opening of Book XVI, he defends Spinoza against Bayle's detraction. See *Goethe's Autobiography: Poetry and Truth,* trans. R. O. Moon (Washington, D.C., 1949), pp. 553–54; 591 ff.

202: 767–68   *Hegel's influence:* In his "Confessions" Heine admits that he had never been a convinced disciple of Hegel, but only temporarily attracted by the idea of personal "divinity." For Heine's mocking renunciation of Hegel, see *Geständnisse; Werke,* X, 173–77.

202: 768   *'I have seen Hegel': Geständnisse; Werke,* X, 171. Heine is describing his impressions after hearing his first lecture by Hegel. The "eggs" refer to Hegel's atheism.

202: 770   *'How easily': Geständnisse; Werke,* X, 173.

202: 772   *'His life':* See *Zur Geschichte der Religion und Philosophie in Deutschland,* Book II; *Werke,* VII, 255.

MARCUS AURELIUS

This essay first appeared in the Victoria Magazine *for November, 1863.*

204: 1   *'Christian morality':* "Christian morality (so called) has all the characters of a reaction; it is, in great part, a protest against Paganism. Its ideal is negative rather than positive; passive rather than active . . . 'thou shalt not' predominates unduly over 'thou shalt.' " Mill is here arguing that not even the "received principles" of Christian morality, or rather "theological morality" are exempt from the necessity of "diversity of opinion" and "fair play to all sides of the truth," since "they contain, and were meant to contain, only a part of the truth." John Stuart Mill, *On Liberty* (London, 1864), chapter II, "Of the Liberty of Thought and Discussion," pp. 87–91. Arnold's opening quotations are from the eighth-last paragraph of this chapter.

205: 19   *'Vita sine proposito':* This is not from the *Imitation* but from Seneca: "Vita sine proposito vaga est: quod si proponendum est, incipiunt neces- saria esse decreta." See *Epistulae Morales*, XV, 3, 46.

205: 20   *'Omni die renovare':* Imitation, I, 19, vv. 9, 13–14. See *Note-Books*, p. 3 *et passim*.

205: 22   *'Secundum propositum':* I, 19, v. 15. See *Note-Books*, p. 5 *et passim*.

205: 22–23   *'Raro etiam':* I, 11, vv. 15–17. See *Note-Books*, p. 3 *et passim*.

205: 24   *'Semper aliquid':* I, 19, v. 36. See *Note-Books*, p. 5 *et passim*.

205: 24–25   *'Tibi ipsi violentiam':* I, 24, v. 23. Arnold alters the text slightly here.

205: 35   *the great masters of morals,—Epictetus or Marcus Aurelius:* In a note to a quotation from the *Enchiridion* in the *Quarterly Review,* a critic re- marked: "May we express a wish that Mr. Matthew Arnold, whose beauti- ful criticism on Antoninus published lately in one of the Magazines, gives proof also of his skill and taste as a translator, would render the little Handbook of Epictetus into scholarly and readable English?" See the re- view of Alexander Gilchrist's *Life of William Blake* in the *Quarterly Re- view,* CXVII (January, 1865), 17. See also Arnold's letter to his mother, January 21, 1865, in which he refers to this suggestion; *Letters,* I, 286. Long's two-volume edition of Epictetus, including the *Enchiridion,* ap- peared in 1877.

206: 60   *'Lead Me, Zeus and Destiny':* This passage, quoted from the *Enchi- ridion,* chapter 52, is itself a quotation from the Stoic Cleanthes:

> Duc me, O Jupiter, et tu, Fatum,
> Quocunque a vobis sum destinatus,
> Quippe, qui impiger sequar. Quod si noluero
> Improbus, factus, nihilominus sequar.

206: 75   *'Every matter':* Enchiridion, chapter 43.

207: 100   *Mr. Long has recently published: The Thoughts of the Emperor Mar- cus Aurelius Antoninus,* trans. George Long (London, 1862). An edition of Long's *Thoughts* to which Arnold's essay was appended appeared in 1913. All citations are from this edition.

207: 111   *his notes on Plutarch's Roman Lives:* Plutarch, *The Civil Wars of Rome, Select Lives,* translated, with notes, by G. L., 1844.

207: 114   *his remarks and essays:* Long's edition includes an introductory essay, "M. Aurelius Antoninus" (pp. 1–26), another essay, "The Philosophy of Antoninus" (pp. 27–62), as well as editorial commentary.

207: 116   *'example of life':* This is from the Sixth Article of Religion, "On the Sufficiency of the Scriptures," in the Book of Common Prayer.

207: 125   *'a most coarse and vulgar copy':* See Long's Introductory Essay, p. 22.

207: 129   *knew him through Jeremy Collier:* Collier's edition was *The Emperor Marcus Antoninus, His Conversation with Himself* (London, 1701).

208: 140   *'In the morning':* V, 1, p. 107.

208: 154   *'No longer wander':* III, 14, p. 91.

209: 180   *Marcus Antoninus instead of Marcus Aurelius:* In the opening paragraph of his introductory essay, "M. Aurelius Antoninus," Mr. Long describes the various stages in the development of the future Emperor's name: his original name was Marcus Annius Verus, the son of Annius Verus; after his adoption by Antoninus Pius, himself the protégé of Hadrian, the youth became M. Aelius Aurelius Verus, Aelius being the name of Hadrian and Aurelius that of Antoninus Pius; in A.D. 139 the title Caesar was added, and on his succeeding to the throne, he dropped the names of Aelius and Verus, assuming that of Antoninus instead. He was thenceforth known as M. Aurelius Antoninus.

209: 185   *to make Marcus Aurelius's work as popular as the Imitation:* Later, in his Preface to *Culture and Anarchy,* Arnold couples the work of Marcus Aurelius with the *Maxims* of Bishop Wilson: "The *Maxims* were never meant to be printed, and have on that account, like a work of, doubtless, far deeper emotion and power, the *Meditations* of Marcus Aurelius, something peculiarly sincere and first-hand about them." Matthew Arnold, *Culture and Anarchy,* ed. J. Dover Wilson (Cambridge, 1955), Preface, p. 4.

209: 189   *Volitare per ora virûm:* This is quoted from Ennius in Cicero's *Tusculanarum Disputationum,* I, 15, 34. Arnold alters the syntax slightly.

209: 203–4   *the seventh chapter of the tenth book:* This chapter deals with the philosophic concept of change, which, Marcus Aurelius states, is at once an "evil" and a "necessity." "The Emperor here maintains that the essential part of man is unchangeable, and that the other parts, if they change or perish, do not affect that which really constitutes the man" (Long's note, p. 182).

209: 215–16   *an old Lyons commentator:* "Marci Philosophi scriptio abscissa et horrida est sed firma et potens quae sapit Imperatorem." See the Preface to the edition by Franciscus de la Bottière (Lyons, 1626): *Marci Antonini Imperatoris et Philosophi, de vita sua, Libri XII.*

210: 243   *Trajan talks of 'our enlightened age':* The reference is to Trajan's celebrated reply to Pliny the Younger, who had written to ask how he was to interpret Nero's decree concerning the treatment of Christians in a province of Asia Minor. See Pliny, *Letters,* X, xcvii.

210: 249 *the Saturday Review critic:* Edward Augustus Freeman. See the note to "The Literary Influence of Academies" at 46: 571–72 above.

210: 253 *the record of the outward life:* Arnold derives his information here from Long's introductory essay, "M. Aurelius Antoninus," and from Renan's "Marc-Aurèle," in *Les Origines du Christianisme.*

211: 267–68 *the record of his inward life:* The real title of the book is unknown. The first edition, published in Zurich by Xylander in 1558 in Greek and Latin, was entitled: Μάρκου ʼΑντωνίνου Αὐτοκράτορος τῶν εἰς ἑαυτὸν βιβλία ιβ (*Marci Antonini Imperatoris ad seipsum, Libri xii*). The manuscript from which Xylander's edition was printed has since disappeared, and the only other manuscript, now in the Vatican Library, has no title. See Long's introductory essay, p. 21.

211: 278–79 *'From my mother':* I, 3, p. 65.

211: 282 *the sixth satire of Juvenal:* This satire, a bitter tirade against the vices and follies of Roman women, is almost twice the length of any of the others. Dryden, in an introduction to his version of the satire, called it the wittiest of Juvenal's satires.

211: 282 *'From my tutor':* I, 5, pp. 65–66.

211: 292 *from the private memoranda:* I, 16, pp. 70–73. This is by far the longest section of the acknowledgments which constitute the first book of the *Meditations,* and a tribute to the memory of his adoptive father, the Emperor Antoninus Pius.

212: 295–96 *'caret quia vate sacro':* Horace, *Odes,* IV, ix, line 28. Arnold alters the syntax slightly.

212: 301 *he was sorry:* This incident is included in the life of Avidius Cassius by Vulcatius Gallicanus. See *Historiae Augustae Scriptores VI* (Lugd. Batavo. 1671), I, 457–58.

212: 321 *the persecution at Lyons:* An account of this persecution (A.D. 177) is contained in the Epistle of the Churches of Lyons and Vienne to the Churches of Asia and Phrygia, in Eusebius' *Historia Ecclesiastica,* V, chapter 1. See the edition in the Fathers of the Church series of Eusebius Pamphili, *Ecclesiastical History,* trans. Roy J. Defarrari, 2 vols. (New York, 1953–55).

Renan also devotes considerable space to this persecution in his *Marc-Aurèle.* Long mentions it in his essay, pp. 6, 18.

212: 322 *the persecution at Smyrna:* See the Epistle of the Church of Smyrna to the Church sojourning at Philomelium, *Historia Ecclesiastica,* IV, chapter 15. The persecution probably took place in A.D. 167. Long treats this incident in great detail, with much scholarly annotation (pp. 12–13).

212: 327 *the letter:* See *Historia Ecclesiastica,* IV, chapter 13. Long refers to it as "one of the most stupid forgeries of the many which exist, [which] cannot be possibly founded even on the genuine report of Antoninus to the Senate" (p. 10). Again, the "style and tenor" of the letter, supposedly written after the war with the Quadi (A.D. 174), indicate that it is nothing more than a "clumsy forgery" (p. 16). Several external evidences for such a judgment are also supplied by Long.

212: 329 *his alleged answer:* This was in reply to an official at Lyons, who had asked for instructions regarding the fate of an imprisoned Christian. The Emperor is supposed to have directed him that those Christians who denied might be released, but those who persisted were to be punished. See Long, p. 6.

212: 334 *'A man,' he says:* In his Introductory Essay, p. 7, Long continues: "But he who rejects it may still admit that such a letter may be founded on real facts; and he would make this admission as the most probable way of accounting for the existence of the letter: but if, as he would suppose, the writer has stated some things falsely, he cannot tell what part of his story is worthy of credit" (p. 7).

213: 344–45 *They imagine Trajan:* See Long's essay, pp. 13–20, where the historical situation is treated very carefully. Long admits, as does Arnold, that "it would be unfair not to state all that can be urged against a man whom his contemporaries and subsequent ages venerated as a model of virtue and benevolence" (p. 20).

213: 362 *exitiabilis superstitio: Annals,* XV, 44. Tacitus is describing the cruel treatment of captive Christians in Rome, a placation of the gods after the fire in Rome during the reign of Nero.

214: 393 *Who can doubt:* Long remarks that it is difficult to determine "how far popular clamour and riots went in this matter, and how far many fanatical and ignorant Christians, for there were many such, contributed to excite the fanaticism on the other side and to embitter the quarrel between the Roman government and the new religion" (p. 18).

214: 409–10 *the moderate and sensible Fleury:* See M. Fleury, *Histoire Ecclésiastique* (Paris, 1758), I, Book 4, chapter 45: "Ainsi M. Aurèle persecuta les chrétiens: quoiqu'il se piquât de clémence, et qu'il eut accoutumé de punir au-dessous de la rigeur des loix. S'il ne fit pas d'édit pour ordonner la persecution générale, du moins il souffrit des persécutions particulières et violentes en plusieurs provinces" (p. 367). An earlier section of the same chapter deals with Antoninus Pius.

215: 429 *if the story is true:* This story is contained in Renan's *Marc-Aurèle,* chapter XXVII, "Mort de Marc-Aurèle—la Fin du Monde Antique." See *Oeuvres Complètes de Ernest Renan,* ed. Henriette Psichari (Paris, 1947–55), V, 1053.

215: 453 *'Not frequently':* I, 12, p. 68. This was the teaching of Alexander the Platonic.

216: 459 *'The idea of a polity':* I, 14, p. 69, in the acknowledgment of his indebtedness to his "brother" Severus.

216: 463 *'drive at practice':* This is quoted from Jeremy Collier's translation of III, 14; see 208: 165 above.

216: 465 *'The greatest part':* IV, 24, p. 99.

216: 471 *'We ought to check':* III, 4, p. 86.

216: 482 *Let nothing be done:* IV, 2, p. 93: "Let no act be done without a purpose, nor otherwise than according to the perfect principles of art" (Long's translation).

216: 493 *'One man':* V, 6, p. 109.

217: 505   *'What more dost thou want':* IX, 42, p. 177.

217: 523   *'cheerfulness in all circumstances':* I, 15, p. 69.

217: 531   *'Figs, when they are quite ripe':* III, 2, p. 85.

218: 545   *'Thou sayest':* V, 5, p. 108.

218: 565   *'Suppose that thou hast':* VIII, 34, p. 158.

218: 574   *'Men seek retreat':* IV, 3, pp. 93–94.

219: 590   *'I have to thank Heaven':* I, 17, pp. 73–74. Arnold alters the text here.

220: 619   *'A black character':* IV, 28, p. 100.

220: 622   *'About what':* V, 11, p. 112.

220: 630   *'When thou hast assumed':* X, 8, pp. 182–83.

220: 642–43   *'between two infinities':* IV, 50, pp. 105–6: "For look to the immensity of time behind thee, and to the time which is before thee, another boundless space. In this infinity then, what is the difference between him who lives three days and him who lives three generations?"

220: 651   *'Consider, for example':* IV, 32, pp. 100–101.

221: 662   *'The things which are much valued':* V, 33, p. 118. The verse quoted is from Hesiod's *Works and Days,* V, 197.

221: 669   *'Look down':* IX, 30, p. 173.

221: 677   *'the prime principle':* VII, 55, p. 144.

221: 681   *'When thou wishest':* VI, 48, pp. 132–33.

221: 689   *'within ten days':* IV, 16, p. 97.

222: 694   *'But if thou requirest':* IX, 3, pp. 167–68.

222: 708   *'Short is the little':* X, 15, p. 186.

222: 717   *'whatever happens':* VI, 45, p. 132 *et passim.*

222: 720   *'even if it seems':* V, 8, p. 110.

222: 722   *'all other things':* VII, 55, p. 144.

222: 732   *'The ruling part':* IV, 1, p. 93.

223: 735   *'What else':* X, 31, pp. 189–90.

223: 739   *'Thou wilt not cease':* X, 33, p. 190. Arnold here alters the text.

223: 773   *'obstinacy of the Christians':* XI, 3, p. 195. This is the only mention of the Christians in the *Meditations.*

224: 776   *'tendentemque manus':* Aeneid, VI, 314: "tendebantque manus," etc. Arnold alters the syntax to fit the sense here.

CONTEMPORARY REVIEWS OF
MATTHEW ARNOLD'S *ESSAYS*

CONTEMPORARY REVIEWS OF
MATTHEW ARNOLD'S *ESSAYS*

Mr. Matthew Arnold and His Countrymen

A Review by Fitzjames Stephen from the Saturday Review, *XVIII*
(December 3, 1864), 683–85

Mr. Matthew Arnold has contributed to the first number of the new series of
the *National Review* a paper on the functions of criticism at the present time,
which is an excellent specimen of that peculiar turn, both of style and thought,
with which of late years he has so often amused and rather surprised his readers.
Few readers of the better class of periodical literature need to be told that Mr.
Arnold is a very clever man, possessed in an unusual degree of some very
uncommon gifts. He is always brilliant, good-natured, entertaining, and even
instructive. There is generally a certain degree of truth in what he says, and,
whatever its nature may be, there can never be any doubt about its good faith.
Mr. Arnold's utterances may not be the result of any profound meditation, but
they at least represent genuine likes and dislikes. He does really work himself,
at any rate for the time being, into an esoteric enthusiasm for the particular
point which he enforces. It is also to be noticed that his points are always of the

same kind. His self-imposed mission is to give good advice to the English people as to their manifold faults, especially as to their one great fault of being altogether inferior, in an intellectual and artistic point of view, to the French. He is so warm upon this subject that he has taught himself to write a dialect as like French as pure English can be. Indeed, it is a painful duty to admit that his turn for French is so strong that the undefiled well is sometimes very near defilement. Take such a sentence, for instance, as the following: —"But Burke is so great because, almost alone in England, he brings thought to bear upon politics, he saturates politics with thought; it is his accident that his ideas were at the service of an epoch of concentration, not of an epoch of expansion." We can almost hear the head-voice, with its sharp nasal ring, and see the eloquent hands gracefully turned outwards, as if to point first to the epoch of concentration and then to the epoch of expansion, with which a French lecturer would hand us this neat little sentence. The exquisite French-English in which Mr. Thackeray so much delighted is only a very little more of a caricature.

Mr. Arnold's present object is to make English criticism ashamed of itself and conscious of its own contemptible character. Like all that he writes, his article is very pretty reading, but from the first to last it appears to us to be fundamentally wrong, and, in particular, it totally fails to apprehend that against which it is directed. The truth is that, like his French models, Mr. Arnold has quick sympathies and a great gift of making telling remarks; but, also like them, he has hardly any power of argument. At least, if he has, he rarely shows it. His general object in the paper before us is to defend some observations which he had made elsewhere on the functions of criticism; but the greater part of it is composed of illustrations of the poverty and vulgarity of the modern English mind, with an attempt to explain the cause and the remedy. The cause of our unfortunate condition is, he says, our constant anxiety about immediate practical results. The remedy is that criticism, and thought in general, ought to be disinterested. "And how is it to be disinterested? By keeping aloof from practice; by resolutely following the law of its own nature, which is to be a free play of the mind on all subjects which it touches; by steadily refusing to lend itself to any of those ulterior political practical considerations about ideas which plenty of people will be sure to attach to them, which perhaps ought to be attached to them, which, in this country at any rate, are certain to be attached to them quite sufficiently, but which criticism has really nothing to do with. Its business is simply to know the best that is known and thought in the world, and, by in its turn making this known, to supply a current of new and fresh ideas."

In illustration of his meaning, he tells us that the French live by ideas. Speaking of the French Revolution, he says, "That a whole nation should have been penetrated with an enthusiasm for pure reason" (can Mr. Cobden have been looking at the *National Review*?), "and with an ardent zeal for making its prescriptions triumph, is a very remarkable thing . . . The French Revolution derives from the force, truth, and universality of the ideas which it took for its law, and from the passion with which it could inspire a multitude for those ideas, an unique and still living power." It failed in practice by attempting to give an immediate practical application to those "fine ideas of the reason;" but we English, who are great in practice, never ascend to ideas at all. A member of Parliament blasphemously said to Mr. Arnold, "That a thing is an anomaly I consider to be no objection to it whatever." We think ourselves a wonderful people—*teste* Mr. Adderley, who made a speech to that effect to the Warwickshire farmers, and Mr. Roebuck, who said so to the Sheffield cutlers; but criticism ought to see how short we fall of anything like ideal beauty. Mr. Roebuck spoke of the "unrivalled happiness" of England. Mr. Adderley spoke of "the Anglo-Saxon race . . . the best breed in the whole world." Mr. Arnold, representing the higher criticism, read in a newspaper that a woman named Wragg was in custody at Nottingham for child murder. Of this the higher criticism says:—"Wragg! If we are to talk of ideal perfection, has any one reflected what a touch of grossness in our race, what an original shortcoming in the most delicate spiritual perceptions, is shown by the natural growth amongst us of such hideous names—Higgenbottom, Stiggins, Bugg . . . and the final touch, *Wragg is in custody?* The sex lost in the confusion of our unrivalled happiness." Criticism ought to show that Wragg should have been called (say) Fairfax; and that, instead of saying "Wragg is in custody," the brutal journalist should have said, "And so, on that cold November night, the door of Nottingham gaol was shut behind our sinful sister." To the general public this way of putting it may not seem to make much difference, but Mr. Arnold thinks otherwise: —"Mr. Roebuck will have a poor opinion of an adversary who replies to his defiant songs of triumph only by murmuring under his breath, 'Wragg is in custody,' but in no other way will these songs of triumph be gradually induced to moderate themselves." We do not envy the higher criticism if it has to go about "murmuring *Wragg is in custody,*" till all after-dinner speeches rise to the level of ideal beauty.

More serious functions, however, do present themselves for criticism in the other illustrations given by Mr. Arnold. He tells us, for instance, that "the British Constitution, seen from the speculative side, sometimes looks a colossal machine for the manufacture of Philistines." Then criticism, looking at the Divorce Court, "in which the gross, unregenerate British Philistine has indeed stamped an image of himself" . . . "may be permitted to find the marriage theory of Catholicsm refreshing and elevating." Some parts of the marriage theory of Catholicism, as expressed in Suarez' *De Matriminio,* would, by the way, form an appropriate appendix to the *Times'* report of the Codrington case. Dr. Colenso is a mere Philistine of rather a contemptible kind, though M. Renan (with whom Mr. Arnold by no means agrees) is quite the reverse: —"Bishop Colenso's book reposes on a total misconception of the essential elements of the religious problem as that problem is now presented for solution. To criticism, therefore . . . it is, however well meant, of no importance whatever. M. Renan's book attempts a new synthesis of the elements furnished to us by the four Gospels," and such a synthesis "is the very essence of the religious problem as now presented." The higher criticism, of course, knows what the religious problem is, and how it is presented, and therefore it treats M. Renan with respect, and Bishop Colenso with the most curious kind of contempt—the contempt of a benevolent elder sister for the little girl who thinks that the world is a sham because she has discovered that her doll is stuffed with straw.

Mr. Arnold's theory, diffused over more than twenty pages, may be shortly expressed thus, for the most part in his own words: —

"The prescriptions of reason are absolute, unchanging, of universal validity."

It is the function of the higher criticism to discover and state these prescriptions of reason, leaving to others the inferior task of adapting them to practice.

English criticism is deficient in caring only for immediate practical results, putting on one side the prescriptions of reason.

Unless by some means this is remedied, the nation's spirit "must in the long run die of inanition."

Let us now consider what this theory is worth. Mr. Arnold overlooks two considerations which dispose of his whole argument about the present state of English criticism. These are, first, that there is in England a school of philosophy which thoroughly understands, and on theoretical grounds deliberately rejects, the philosophical theory which Mr. Arnold accuses the English nation of neglecting, and that the practical efforts of the English people, especially their practical efforts in the way of literary criticism, are for the most part strictly in accordance with the principles of that philosophy. Secondly, that whereas, according to his own system, practice and theory form different spheres —practice to be regulated by a view to immediate results, theory by a view to pure reason (whatever that may be)—and whereas practical objections only ought to be applied by him to practical inquiries, and objections drawn from pure reason to theoretical inquiries, yet again and again he objects to specific practical measures on theoretical grounds.

First, there is in England a school of philosophy which perfectly understands, and on theoretical grounds deliberately rejects, the philosophical theory which Mr. Arnold accuses the English of neglecting. Mr. Arnold's whole essay assumes the truth of the transcendental theory of philosophy. Englishmen are merely practical, they have no philosophy in them at all, because they set on one side "prescriptions of reason, absolute, unchanging, and of universal validity." This is just like saying a man has no religion because he is not a Roman Catholic. Mr. Arnold surely cannot be ignorant of the fact that, from the days of Hobbes and Locke to those of Mr. Mill and Mr. Bain, the most influential of English thinkers have utterly denied the truth of transcendentalism, and have constantly affirmed that all knowledge is based upon experience and sensation. This may be true, or it may be false, but it is just as much entitled to be called philosophy as anything else. Now the commonest acquaintance with this view of things will show that in principle, though of course not in detail, it justifies the common run of English criticism—that is, of the remarks which English people make on passing events for practical or literary purposes. Take, for instance, Mr. Arnold's member of Parliament who did not object to anomalies. What Mr. Arnold viewed as his blasphemy really amounts to this: —Political institutions exist for the purpose of producing a maximum of happiness, in the wide sense of the word. Experience alone can show what institutions, in a given case, will produce that result. Experience is either in the inductive or in the deductive stage. It is in the inductive stage until its results have fallen into the shape of general principles, like those of mathematics, which can be applied at once to particular cases. When they have, it is in the deductive stage. Our political experience has not yet reached the deductive stage. It is still inductive. But, in considering institutions inductively, it can be no objection to them that they are anomalies—*i.e.* that they vary from some principle asserted to be true, for induction considers them only as facts, and does not, and by its very nature cannot, recognise the truth of the principles which they are said to contradict. Before Mr. Arnold lectures the English nation on their want of logic, he ought to understand that a man may deny his major without denying the force of syllogisms in general. The member of Parliament meant, "Your general principles being false, it is no objection to any institution that, judged by them, it is anomalous." No man out of a madhouse ever says, Admitting the truth of your premises and the form of your syllogism, I deny the truth of the conclusion.

In fact, no nation in the world is so logical as the English nation. Once get it well convinced of the truth of a general principle—which is, as it ought to be, considering how hard it is to state general principles correctly, a very hard task—and it will do anything. For instance, the English nation believes in political economy, and the consequence is that it is the only nation in the world which has established free trade. The new Poor Law and the Bank Charter Act were based upon the principles of the same science. Bentham persuaded the English nation that the greatest happiness of the greatest number was the true rule for legislation, and every part of the law has been reformed by degrees by the application, more or less skilful and complete, of that abstract principle. Newton persuaded the English nation that the force of gravity varies inversely as the square of the distance, and this doctrine with its consequences, was accepted and worked out to its practical results by the English nation before any other people fully took it in. Mr. Mill has persuaded the English nation that men ought to argue, not from universals to particulars, but from particulars to particulars, and the practical influence of this highly abstract principle is seen in that state of criticism to which Mr. Arnold objects. Our modern Indian policy has been governed by the abstract principle that the natives ought to be civilized on the English pattern. When abstract principles like these are embraced by and do influence the English people most deeply, is it just, or even decent, to talk about "British Philistines" because we English do not choose to recognise as eternal truths a set of platitudes which may be proved to be false? And is it better than sophistry to try to bolster up the credit of these platitudes, in the face of their notorious failure, by saying that they are true in the sphere of absolute reason, and that, in order to purge our grossness, we ought to go and live in that sphere, murmuring under our breaths "Wragg is in custody"? Our English notion is, that the only test by which you can judge of the truth of a general principle is its application to facts. If it will not open the lock, it may be a very pretty key, but it is certainly not the true one. It is from facts only that principles can be got, and it is by facts only that their truth, when they are got at, can be tested. Mr. Arnold is like a man who says to a painter or a sculptor, "What a gross Philistine you are to pass your time in chipping at that hideous stone, dabbling with that nasty clay, or fiddling about with oil-paints and canvas! Why do you not at once rise to the sphere of pure reason, and produce, as I do in my dreams, statues and pictures of eternal and absolute beauty?"

Mr. Arnold, like other transcendentalists, is very shy of giving us an eternal truth to look at. He does, however, try his hand at one, and a better illustration of that great maxim, "I never heard of an eternal truth without thinking of an infernal lie," has seldom been seen:—"The prescriptions of reason are absolute, unchanging, of universal validity. *To count by tens is the simplest way of counting.* That is a proposition of which every one from here to the antipodes feels the force; at least, I should say so if we did not live in a country where it is not impossible that any morning we may find a letter in the *Times* declaring that a decimal coinage is an absurdity." This is a marvellous passage. The Decimal Coinage Commissioners declared against the scheme. One of them was Lord Overstone. Imagine Mr. Matthew Arnold asserting that Lord Overstone is incapable of abstract thought on his own subjects! Apart from this, Mr. Arnold is not only wrong, but so clearly wrong that there is probably little hope of convincing him of it. What he calls a self-evident proposition is, in the first place, not abstract; in the second place, it is not true; and in the third place, if it were both abstract and true, it would not prove the consequence connected with it. First, it is not abstract. The abstract proposition is that, if any system of notation whatever be given, there will be some convenience in making the base of that system the unit of tables of weights, measures, and coinage. This is, no doubt, true. But some other abstract propositions are also true, one of which is that to be a multiple of many factors is a convenience to which regard should be had in choosing a base of notation. Now the number ten has but two factors, two and five, both of which are prime numbers, and ten is therefore a very inconvenient base for a system of any kind. Twelve, on the other hand, is highly convenient, being divisible by four factors, of which two only are primes. Hence there is a balance of advantages. To count by tens has the advantage of taking as your unit the base of an established system of notation. To count by twelves has the advantage of taking as your unit a number in itself far more convenient for that purpose. The advantage of counting by twelve is principally felt in small calculations done in the head. The advantage of counting by ten is principally felt in large calculations done on paper, and is not felt till you get past twenty. Hence a system of pounds reckoned on the decimal basis, and shillings and pence reckoned on the duodecimal basis, combines two sets of advantages. On the other hand, the decimal system is notoriously inconvenient for small transactions.

To sum up—our transcendentalist supposes himself to be stating an abstract proposition when he is stating a concrete one. Instead of saying "to count by tens," he should say, "to take as your unit an established base of notation." He supposes himself to be stating a true proposition when he is stating a false one. It is not true that to count by tens is the simplest way of counting, or that it is the most convenient, unless you add the very material clauses—"ten being given as the basis of notation," and "except for numbers under twenty." Lastly, he supposes himself to be stating a complete proposition when he is stating one which is incomplete; for it does not follow that, because a particular way of counting is the simplest, any special system of coinage ought to be adopted. To count by ones, to have a separate name for each number, would no doubt be simpler than to count by tens, but no one advocates such a system. Let it be observed that each of these objections is theoretical. Mr. Arnold may call his countrymen gross Philistines as much as ever he pleases, but they will always be able to reply—We object to what you call your theories not because they are theories, but because they are not true theories, but arbitrary generalities, which we can show to be rash, false, or at best incomplete.

The second objection to Mr. Arnold's theory is that, according to his own view, theory and practice form different spheres—practice to be regulated by a view to immediate results, theory by pure reason. Yet he constantly objects to practical measures on theoretical grounds. Thus, he says that the Divorce Court is a hideous institution, and that it is refreshing to turn from it to the Catholic marriage theory. What relation, on his principles, is there between the two things? By his own rule, he cannot inquire into, and has no right to notice, the hideousness of the Divorce Court. That is a practical question, a matter of business to be decided on common earthly grounds. The Catholic marriage theory, we suppose, is a matter of pure reason. Let each have its sphere, but unless and until pure reason can work out its marriage theory in a sufficiently definite shape to solve every practical question connected with the marriage law, those who hold it have no other right to call the Divorce Court hideous than the authors of the Divorce Act have to call them visionary. If theorists are not sure enough of the truth of their theories to take the responsibility of putting them in practice, they have no right to depreciate the rule of thumb. When Don Quixote refused to try his sword on the second edition of his helmet, he surely renounced the right to sneer at less romantic wares. When Mr. Arnold has got a theory which will fully explain all the duties of the legislator on the matter of marriage, he will have a right to abuse the Divorce Court.

Much the same may be said of Mr. Arnold's criticism on Dr. Colenso. His book, he says, is "of no importance whatever" to criticism. It "reposes on a fundamental misconception of the essential elements of the religious problem." M. Renan's book, on the other hand, deals with the very essence of the religious problem. "For saying this" (in *Macmillan's Magazine*), says Mr. Arnold, "I was greatly blamed, because I was told that I was a liberal attacking a liberal; yet surely I had a right to say that a man in pursuit of truth had taken a false method." Certainly some of Mr. Arnold's readers thought, and still think, that, considering how desperately hard the lower criticism was on Dr. Colenso, the higher criticism might have chosen some other victim, or some other time for scourging that particular victim. It was not, however, for this alone that Mr. Arnold was blamed, but for something very different. It was for the way in which he argued that it was a crime against literary criticism and the higher culture to attempt to inform the ignorant. He was blamed for saying much which was summed up in these words, "Knowledge and truth, in the full sense of the words, are not attainable by the great mass of the human race at all." In reference to the matter in hand, this meant, "Ordinary English people have no business to have any opinion on the question whether or not the whole of the Pentateuch is true. The higher minds have, but the great bulk of the nation ought to leave such matters to M. Renan and a few others, and it is bad taste, a low vulgar thing, to address them on the question." This was very different from saying that Dr. Colenso's method was false. It said that his object was bad. Granting the goodness of the object and the truth of the assertions, it was simply absurd to deny their relevancy. Indeed, Mr. Arnold did not deny it. His point was, that the book ought not to have been written. This is altogether inconsistent with his present view, which is, that practice and theory ought to be divorced. Theory ought to sit on a hill retired, and argue high about a new synthesis of the four Gospels, and care nothing for practice. Let it, then, care nothing for practice, but do not let it attack practical men for making practical remarks. Dr. Colenso wrote *ad populum*. Mr. Arnold denied his right to do so, but it is very hard now to change the charge, and to blame him for having addressed the higher culture of Europe in a popular way. Dr. Colenso's book may or may not repose on a false conception of the religious problem, though it is a strong thing to assert that a critical inquiry into the Old Testament must, under all circumstances, be simply worthless; but Mr. Arnold's criticism certainly reposes on a false conception of Dr. Colenso's book. Indeed, his two criticisms "repose" on conflicting conceptions, and, as in the case of other attempts to sit on two stools at once, the result is grotesque.

The way in which Mr. Arnold treats Dr. Colenso is an excellent illustration of the fundamental weakness which affects all that he writes. With all his ability, he sometimes gives himself the airs of the distinguished courtier who shone so bright and smelled so sweet when he had occasion to talk with Hotspur about the prisoners. He is always using a moral smelling-bottle, like those beloved countrymen who, at foreign *tables d'hôte,* delight to hold forth on the vulgarity of "those English." Dr. Colenso condescended to do a sum about the "800 and odd pigeons." Mr. Arnold is almost ready to faint, till he is consoled by the thought of M. Renan and his sublime synthesis. He reads or looks at the Codrington case (which certainly had a strong scent about it), and murmuring under his breath, "Gross unregenerate British Philistines," flies in despair to the Catholic marriage theory, which purifies the country of Rabelais, Diderot, Faublas, Montépin, and M. Dumas *fils.*

Mr. Matthew Arnold Amongst the Philistines

A Review by Fitzjames Stephen from the Saturday Review, *XIX*
(February 25, 1865), 235–36

Two or three months ago we made some observations on an article of Mr. Matthew Arnold's, in the *National Review,* on the functions of criticism. Mr. Arnold has republished that and some other essays in an excellent little volume, which contains, amongst other things, a preface replying in the most good-humoured manner imaginable to his various critics, and several notes levelled at our article. We have, on former occasions, remarked upon most of the essays thus republished, and we do not mean to return to them. They have very good points. Some of them are exceedingly interesting, and all of them display a remarkable power of appreciation. Thus the essays on Heine, on Marcus Aurelius, on the Pagan and Mediaeval Moral Sentiment, and two others on Maurice and Eugénie de Guérin, are all full of interest, and will introduce the great bulk of Mr. Arnold's readers to topics with which they are not likely to have been familiar previously, and to a mode of treatment which he is certainly right in considering as uncommon in English periodical writing. We heartily wish them success. They form a most agreeable volume, written in excellent taste by a refined and highly cultivated man. There are, however, other matters in the book on which we should wish to say a word or two in a tone, if possible, as good-humoured as that of Mr. Arnold himself. His retorts upon our criticisms are in perfect good temper, and some of them are very happy. His Preface is a curiosity, coming as it does from a man who has suffered many things from many reviewers, and is determined to be no better, but rather to become worse, and to go on not only repeating, but even exaggerating, the sins for which it was their painful duty to take him to task. Like the early Christians exposed to wild beasts in the arena, Mr. Arnold has been baited by reviewers. For instance, he is attacked by Mr. Wright, the translator of Homer, and by one "Presbyter Anglicanus," whom he accuses of writing, not merely in the *Examiner,* but in "half a dozen of the daily newspapers" as well. The *Guardian* has acted toward him the part of a "kind monitor," and has charged him with making jokes. He stands in awe of the "magnificent roaring of the young lions of the *Daily Telegraph,*" though whether they have actually assailed him or not does not appear; and the *Saturday Review* has treated him most unkindly. His attitude in the midst of this storm of censure, is almost as peaceful as that of Daniel in the den of lions, seated, as the showman observed, on his three-legged stool and reading the *Times* newspaper. He returns blessings for curses, gently reproves the *Examiner,* gravely exonerates the *Guardian* from the faintest suspicion of levity, suggests for the Editor of the *Saturday Review* the honour of a statue in a temple dedicated to Philistinism, and asks Mr. Wright—who, it appears, lives at Mapperley—for information about Wragg, the young woman whose arrest Mr. Arnold so feelingly deplored in his remarkable contribution to the *National Review.* We will not object to the statue which he proposes for us, and let him have all the honours of the small war which we have carried on; nay, we will even tell him something about Wragg. She is still in custody in Nottingham Gaol and will be tried at the assizes to be held there sometime between the 9th and the 13th of next month. The only objection to Mr. Arnold's Preface is that it is too good-natured. There is no pleasure in hitting a man who will not hit you back again; who says meekly that it is not his nature to "dispute on behalf of any opinion . . . very obstinately"; who cares little for argument, and "has a profound respect for intuitions"; who thinks that truth is something to be seen, and not to be proved; and who, strong in that conviction, sees exclusively by his own inner light, and, like the humming-bird when pressed in the chase (to quote the showman a second time), retires into his interior by creeping down his own throat, whence, illuminated by the inner light, he smiles benignantly on his baffled pursuers.

Admitting that it is not easy to argue with any one who takes such an ethereal view of things, and has such a pleasant way of slipping through every difficulty, we must notice one or two of his replies, inasmuch as they illustrate the texture of his mind and the principles which pervade every word that he writes. In our former notice we observed upon Mr. Arnold's passion for eternal truths, and remarked that, after all, he specified only one eternal truth, which appeared to us to be false. The great principle in question, reiterated in the present volume, was and is as follows:—

> To count by tens is the simplest way of counting; that is a proposition of which every one from here to the antipodes feels the force—so at least I should say if we did not live in a country where it is not impossible that any morning we may find a letter in the *Times* declaring a decimal coinage an absurdity.

On this we observed that the proposition in question is not true; that counting by tens is not the simplest way of counting, though there is a certain degree of convenience in taking the base of an established system of notation, whether it happens to be ten or anything else, as the unit of tables of coinage or weights and measures. We further observed that the number ten is a very inconvenient base, especially for low numbers, and that twelve is far more convenient. Hence we argued that, to make his proposition true, it ought to have been stated thus: —It is convenient to take an established base of notation as the unit of tables of coinage, weights, and measures. If ten is given as the established base of notation, then to count by tens is the simplest way of counting for numbers above twenty. If Mr. Arnold looks back to the article in question, he will see that this was the result of our criticism. He has followed our statement hastily, and has ascribed to us the following strange piece of nonsense:—

> To take as your unit an established base of notation, ten being given as the base of notation, is, except for numbers under twenty, the simplest way of counting.

We said nothing of the sort. Indeed the words have no meaning. He then goes on to make the following remark: —

> The mass of Frenchmen, by legislating as they did, showed a keen susceptibility to purely rational intellectual considerations. On the other hand, does my reviewer say that we keep our monetary system unchanged because our nation has grasped the intellectual proposition, which he puts in his masterly way thus: "to count by twelves has the advantage of taking for your unit a number in itself far more convenient than ten for that purpose"? Surely not; but because our system is there, and we are too practical a people to trouble ourselves about its intellectual aspect.

Mr. Arnold has again done our statement injustice. The two lines which he quotes as an "intellectual proposition" form one step in an argument which fills a paragraph of twenty-two lines, and which we think Mr. Arnold will not find it easy to condense into a smaller compass. It would be absurd to say that our monetary system is upheld because it is duodecimal. It is neither purely duodecimal nor purely decimal, but a mixture of the two; and, whatever Mr. Arnold may think, we said before, and now repeat, that the reason why the English people keep the system unchanged is that the Decimal Coinage Commissioners proved, on purely theoretical grounds, that it is a more convenient one than the decimal system. The "mass of Frenchmen" no doubt trusted the opinion of some Commission of their own, and the difference between the two countries is a difference of theory. This is the very point which we tried to establish, and which Mr. Arnold is apparently quite unable to understand. Does he deny that there ever was a Decimal Coinage Commission, or that it reported in favour of the existing system, or that it gave reasons for so reporting, or that it was on account of that report that the system was maintained? Unless he can deny one at least of these propositions, he must admit that the question is between theory and theory, not between theory and neglect of theory. To say that "we are too practical a people to trouble ourselves about the intellectual aspect" of the question is really to talk without a meaning. In proportion as people are practical they act in a reasonable manner. What could be less practical than to refuse to substitute a rational and convenient for an irrational and inconvenient system of coinage? And how can a system of coinage be rational unless and except in so far as it is convenient?

Another of Mr. Arnold's observations is even more curious. He said, and says again, "When one looks at the English Divorce Court . . . which in the ideal sphere is so hideous . . . one may be permitted to find the marriage theory of Catholicism elevating and refreshing." Upon this we observed that Mr. Arnold had no right to object to practical measures on theoretical grounds, and that he ought to wait to abuse the Divorce Court till he had got a theory which would fully explain all the duties of the Legislature in the matter of marriage. Upon this Mr. Arnold remarks:—"My critic wants me to produce a plan for a new and improved Divorce Court before I call the present one hideous. But God forbid that I should thus enter into competition with the Lord Chancellor!" God forbid, indeed, for Mr. Arnold's own sake; but his critic wanted no such thing. We carefully avoided saying what Mr. Arnold puts into our mouths. Our demand was, not for a working plan, but for "a theory which will fully explain all the duties of the Legislature on the subject of marriage." A Court which has to deal with adultery cannot of course be ornamental. The question therefore is, whether the Divorce Court is more hideous than it ought to be. This depends on the question, what is the theory on which a legislator ought to deal with marriage? And unless Mr. Arnold can state such a theory and defend it, he has no right to condemn the existing Court. Not only is he unable to state such a theory, but he does not seem to see the necessity for it. He says, indeed, that he condemns the Divorce Court because "it is not the result of any legislator's meditations on the subject of marriage. Rich people had an anomalous privilege of getting divorced; privileges are odious, and we said everybody should have the same chance. There was no meditation about marriage here; that was just the mischief." It is amusing to hear Mr. Arnold say that impatience of an "anomaly" was the reason why the Divorce Court was established. It is one of the counts in his indictment against the gross British

Philistine that he does not care for anomalies. A few pages before, he had said, "For a thing to be an anomaly we consider to be no objection to it whatever." Where, however, did he learn that "no meditation about marriage" preceded the legislation which produced the Divorce Court? The subject had been discussed in England for a great length of time, and from every point of view, and it is quite easy to state the theory upon which the final legislation proceeded. The people of this country had gradually come to the conclusion that there ought to be a way of judicially dissolving marriage in certain cases. The "idea" of the Court, to use Mr. Arnold's own phraseology, is not hard to describe. It is that *in foro humano* marriage ought to be considered as a condition founded on a contract in which the public are interested, and which therefore ought not to be dissolved without the intervention of the law, and for causes legally defined; and that the rights and duties of the married state *in foro divino,* be they what they may, ought to be enforced by the conscientious and not by the legal, sanction. He will find, if he turns to the Statute-Book, that this theory, not of marriage itself, but of the relation of the English Legislature to marriage (which is a very different thing) influenced many other Acts of Parliament besides the one in question—for instance, the Marriage Act of 1836, which it would be absurd to ascribe to impatience of an anomaly. This theory may be true or false, but it is just as much a theory as any other; and Mr. Arnold, in this as in all other cases, shows himself perfectly unable to conceive that any one can hold any theory at all which is not expressed in some short smart phrase, like "the Catholic idea of marriage which exhibits marriage as indissoluble," "that Protestant idea of marriage which exhibits it as a union terminable by mutual consent."

Unable or unwilling to comply with what we think was a very reasonable demand—the demand for a theory of the relations between the Legislature and marriage as a condition precedent to the condemnation of a practical measure— Mr. Arnold does give us some sort of advice, if he gives us no guidance:—

> If my practical critic will himself accompany me, for a little while, into the despised world of ideas;—if, renouncing any attempt to patch hastily up, with a noble disdain for transcendentalism, our present Divorce law, he will but allow his mind to dwell a little, first on the Catholic idea of marriage, which exhibits marriage as indissoluble, and then upon that Protestant idea of marriage, which exhibits it as a union terminable by mutual consent,—if he will meditate well on these, and afterwards on the thought of what married life, according to its idea, really is, of what family life really is, of what social life really is, and national life, and public morals,—he will find, after a while, I do assure him, the whole state of his spirit quite changed; the Divorce Court will then seem to him, if he looks at it, strangely hideous; and he will at the same time discover in himself, as the fruit of his inward discipline, lights and resources for making it better, of which he does not dream.

Mr. Arnold, of course, has gone through all this "inward discipline" himself; for if he has not, how can he possibly know what effect it will produce? Why then does he not comply with our request, and give us, as the fruit of his reflections and of the lights and resources which they have produced in him, a theory of the relations of the Legislature to marriage? No one asks him for practical details, but we have a right to ask for a statement of general principles. If he has them, why not state them? If he has them not, his contemplations have produced no effect. As matters stand, we cannot but suspect the real truth to be that Mr. Arnold, like every other decent person, has been much disgusted by the reports of the Divorce Court trials; that he knows little or nothing about jurisprudence, or about the way in which law-makers ought to deal with marriage or with the other great interests of life; and that he feels pleasure in using vague and big phrases about "the Catholic idea" and "the Protestant idea" "married life according to its idea," etc., etc., without attaching any particular meaning to those words.

It is no reproach to any one to be a man of taste and not a man of thought, but he ought not to deny to the whole English nation the power of thinking, merely because their thoughts do not happen to be expressed in a way which suits his taste. He ought also to try to understand that people may be influenced by difficult as well as by easy theories, and that in this complicated world the difficult theories are very often the true ones.

Matthew Arnold's Essays

An unsigned review from the Reader, *V*
(April 8, 1865), 391–93

This volume contains various articles which Mr. Arnold has contributed to our magazines. The subjects have no obvious connexion with each other. Yet the book leaves on the reader's mind an impression of completeness and unity which is equally rare and delightful. The opening essay in part explains the secret. Mr. Arnold desires to reform English criticism. Every one of his articles has been written to illustrate his conception of its true nature. Each one, therefore, helps to interpret the rest; the greater the diversity of topics, the more they conduce to the general object. And every essay being written with this design, is a far more elaborate composition than it could be under any other conditions. The workmanship is too skilful ever to betray itself. Mr. Arnold's style is so graceful, so perfect, that it has all the appearance of being the most natural and spontaneous expression of his thoughts.

After a preface which must have been meant as a foil to the beauty of the volume which it introduces, or to illustrate by example the errors of taste which that volume denounces, Mr. Arnold proceeds at once to his main business. As his essay 'On the Function of Criticism at the Present Time' is to teach us our own duties, we are bound to notice it first. In spite of a natural dislike to a judge, we have every motive to hear this judge. He has the highest notion of the grandeur of our craft. There may come a time of creative energy. At present the critics must account themselves the real lords and dictators of the world. On the way in which they shall use this tremendous power is dependent the condition of the next age—what poets, philosophers, theologians shall be hereafter will be decided by the conduct of critics now.

How then ought we to behave? We wish we could answer the question in Mr. Arnold's language. But the passage to which we would refer our readers (pp. 18–20), is too long for extraction. We can only give its substance in our feeble words. The English people are given up to facts. They abhor ideas. They are given up to parties. Criticism has indulged these habits. It has stooped to facts. It has been Whig, or Tory, or Radical. It has paid homage to the habits and tastes of our own race. It must become 'disinterested.' It must hold itself aloof from all facts. It must simply aim at 'creating a current of true and fresh ideas.' No application of these ideas, in one way or another, must be attempted. 'The best' must be sought everywhere and in every department. There must be no preference for English writers or thinkers; on the contrary, a deliberate preference for those whom Englishmen are least likely to care for, are most likely to overlook or despise. Mr. Arnold remarks:

> It is because criticism has so little kept in the pure intellectual sphere, has so little detached itself from practice, has been so directly polemical and controversial, that it has so ill-accomplished, in this country, its best spiritual work, which is to keep man from a self-satisfaction which is retarding and vulgarising, to lead him towards perfection, by making his mind dwell upon what is excellent in itself, and the absolute beauty and fitness of things.

This 'retarding and vulgarising' self-satisfaction is illustrated by extracts from speeches of Mr. Adderley and Mr. Roebuck, in which the English are eulogised 'as the best breed in the world.' Their statements are confronted by the case of a girl who murdered her illegitimate child at Nottingham, and whose name was Wragg. 'In Ionia and Attica,' exclaims our critic, 'they were luckier in this respect than the best race in the world; by the Ilissus there was no Wragg.'

Now it seems to us that self-satisfaction of the kind which Mr. Arnold denounces, or of any kind, is very odious; that British orators, like the orators in Athens, are tempted to flatter Demus, panegyrizing their own race as the best in the world, and denouncing other races from which they might learn much; that critics may confirm, and have confirmed, this evil habit; that they ought to fight against it; that we should be most thankful to any person like Mr. Arnold, who raises his voice against it; still more to any person who, like Mr. Arnold, teaches us to know and admire men not of our race. We admit all that tendency to worship facts and scorn ideas which he attributes to Englishmen; we admit that the party spirit of our journals is connected with that tendency; we admit that there should be a strenuous effort to counteract both the effect and the cause. But we are as strongly convinced that the remedy which Mr. Arnold proposes would not cure or alleviate the disease, but would strengthen it; that all remedies against it which have been effectual have been exactly of the opposite character; that what he calls 'a current of true and fresh ideas' has been most created by those Englishmen who have most stooped, even against their inclination, to their countrymen's love of facts; that the wisest teachers and critics—those whom Mr. Arnold himself reverences most—have sought for ideas in the facts, instead of bringing them from their own minds to the facts, or letting them stand aloof from the facts; that our history, our science, our literature, all alike prove this to be the method which we must follow if we would work any reform in the English faith or the English practice.

Take one signal instance. Mr. Arnold is a sincere, even a passionate admirer of Burke. He owns that this great man lived 'in the world of ideas, not the world of catchwords and party habits.' No sentence can be more just or more happily expressed. But Burke was emphatically, from the beginning of his life to the end of it, from the publication of his thoughts on the 'Sublime and Beautiful,' to the publication of his 'Letters on a Regicide Peace,' a man who sought for the idea in the fact, a man who was impatient of all ideas that were not deduced from the study of facts. This is what reconciles his earliest political treatises with those which are supposed to contradict them; this is what vindicates him from Goldsmith's charge, which Mr. Arnold so justly repudiates. He did not like the pedantry of those who opposed the American war, merely by talking about the necessary connexion of representation with taxation, any more than the pedantry of those who talked about the rights of man. Both seemed to him doctors who idealised out of their own minds, instead of seeking a far deeper, larger, grander idea in history—God's idea, not their own. He pleaded for actual relations between the mothercountry and her colonies, for duties which she owed to them, apart from all formulas. And when in a passage which Mr. Arnold has quoted with great honour, but which he pronounces quite 'unEnglish,' Burke confesses that hereafter some of the ideas of the French Revolution against which he protested, might establish themselves, it was precisely because he believed that facts might come to light of which he had not taken account.

What, again, is all experimental science but the search for the idea in the fact, in the particular instance? Against what did Bacon protest, but against the school habit of bringing forth ideas either to control the facts, or to exist apart from them? . . .

To this law, we believe, English criticism, the criticism of this day, must conform itself. If it does not—if a set of men called critics, or men of letters, or children of light, form themselves into a caste, and try to spread certain ideas through society, looking down upon facts, and resigning them to the custody of an inferior Sudra caste, whom they call hodmen or Philistines—we believe that the ordinary Englishman will wrap himself more and more closely in his hatred of all ideals—of all that is graceful and beautiful—and that the so-called idealists, differing from them in all things else, will be like them in that self-satisfaction which Mr. Arnold feels to be so retarding and vulgarising. . . .

The able article following the one on which we have commented, 'On the Literary Influence of Academies,' is in the strictest harmony with it. That Mr. Arnold has alleged many ingenious arguments against our chartered libertinism, —in favour of an organised opinion to control the taste and promote the urbanity of authors—no one will deny. The real weight of his argument, however, depends on our admission of his suppressed premiss, that it is desirable to have a caste of writers and critics who shall keep up a certain tone and habit of thought and feeling distinct from that of general society, and shall hold itself aloof from the common movements of the world. As we do not wish to see such a caste, as we think the nearest approximation ever made to it was in that body of highly-accomplished men whom the world has called the *sophists,* whom Mr. Grote perhaps more rightly calls the *professors* of Greece, who might bear the name of *Critics* more properly than either; as we hold that these men, who diffused ideas upon all possible subjects among the young men of the finest race in the world, were, most happily for those young men, resisted and defeated by a man who had an Anglo-Saxon love for facts, who put all propounders of theories to a horrible torture: as we believe that out of this pursuit of facts, this persecution of theorists, was developed the most lofty and effectual idealism which the world has ever seen, and a style even more exquisite (can we say more?) than Mr. Arnold's—we may doubt whether an Academy, which all admit must have had a number of inconveniences, can be desirable merely for the creation and support of a literary guild, probably much inferior to its Greek prototype. Since its main function would be to cultivate prose— poetry being in Mr. Arnold's judgment better without such an influence—we may venture to ask whether the prose of Bossuet was not formed to meet the necessities of the pulpit, and of ecclesiastical controversy; whether the prose of Pascal was not forged amidst hard mathematical and theological studies, because a very sharp weapon was needed to cut through the webs of the Jesuit fathers; whether the prose of Rousseau was not fashioned amidst the hills about the Lake of Geneva, and developed by political controversies; whether Voltaire's prose was not sharpened and perfected by continual attrition with the debates, serious and trifling, of the eighteenth century; whether the Academy can be really credited with the strength, or delicacy, of fervour, or wit, of any one of the four.

An admirable essay on 'Maurice de Guérin' is far more likely than this to cultivate our affection for Frenchmen, and to abate our Anglo-Saxon conceit. It is pleasant to observe that Mr. Arnold can sympathise heartily with a man who had no ambition to be a critic, who loved nature more than a book; who had an unsatisfied yearning for spiritual treasures, who, if he could have followed Lamennais, would willingly have shared his best thoughts with the people. The biography of such a man, illuminated by translations which are a study in English as well as in French, is a real gift to us all. There, indeed, Mr. Arnold shows us the true function of a critic. Through a special instance he unfolds ideas which Englishmen and Frenchmen may prize equally.

Eugénie de Guérin, the sister of Maurice, presents us with another, also a very striking, type of character. We grudge no admiration which Mr. Arnold bestows on the graceful saint in the Château of Languedoc. But was he not aware that he was spoiling the effect of his portrait, and disclosing too evidently his purpose in painting it, when he introduced an unknown lady of Margate, whose biography he had happened to meet with, because she seemed to him a very ordinary and vulgar person, as the parallel representative of English female devotion? We ask him, as an honest critic, with a high sense of his functions and responsibility, whether he sincerely believed that this lady was the best specimen he could find for such a comparison—whether he did not know from personal experience and from reading that she was not? If so, may there not be something 'vulgarising and retarding' in the wish to discover and expose whatever is weakest and least attractive in his own land, as well as in the wish to glorify it at the expense of every other?

That question we will repeat in reference to the next and very different subject of the next sketch. We pass from France to Germany, from Eugénie de Guérin to Heinrich Heine. The leap, we need not say, is prodigious; the contrast serves to display the comprehensiveness of Mr. Arnold's taste. Of Heine himself and his genius we would gladly have heard more. Mr. Arnold regards him merely as *par excellence* the antagonist of Philistines or idealess men. His three qualifications for the task are apparently these: 1. He disliked his own country. 2. He hated England. 3. He considered France the holy land of Europe. We should have listened willingly to some apology for Heine's want of patriotism and his incapacity for sympathy with a country which has produced Shakespeare and one or two eminent men besides. If we had been reminded of his Jewish birth—his want of a proper home in any European country—we should have felt we had no right to treat him harshly for these intellectual infirmities, even though they had some relation to that immorality in act and word which Mr. Arnold deplores. But if they are produced as signs of a vocation, proofs of his right to take place among the liberators of humanity, we must pause. The liberators would, it strikes us, turn out to be the haughtiest and most mischievous tyrants the world has yet seen.

The entire freedom of Joubert from such disagreeable characteristics makes the sketch of him one of the most satisfactory in the volume. Mr. Arnold does not merely use him to expose the pretensions of the best breed in the world. He compares Joubert with Coleridge, treating his own countryman, on the whole, with much respect and appreciation. To us the suggestion of a likeness between the two men is most instructive and edifying. Coleridge was always in danger of becoming a mere idealist. He was kept, in spite of himself, in perpetual contact with the facts of life, being a vehement politician in youth—still busy with politics, though under a new phase, when he had returned from Germany, and was writing his 'Friend,'—compelled in later days by contrition and the consciousness of moral weakness to seek for a practical faith. Mr. Arnold shows us that Joubert had more of this useful counteraction to the natural habit of his mind than Coleridge; that he had a healthy dislike of scholastic phraseology, for which our philosopher had a dangerous affection; that he submitted more to the ordinary demands of duty and of social life. Surely he was a greater enemy of Philistines than Heine, because he did not confront their arrogance with a worse kind of arrogance.

Spinoza, to whom Mr. Arnold has devoted an inadequate and superficial, but, of course, graceful essay, is another specimen of a man who lived in a world of ideas, and was cut off from the world of facts; but who was always exhibiting his discontent with those who regarded ideas as products of their own intellects, who reverenced them as substantial and divine. Mr. Arnold is satisfied, and thinks Goethe was satisfied, with considering Spinoza as an enemy of final causes. A true, possibly, but a most feeble estimate of a noble man, who was ever struggling after light—of a man who fell into ten thousand confusions, which we fall into without knowing it, because he could not find the God in whom he was sure that he was living, and moving, and having his being. Mr.

Arnold treats with lofty superiority certain Christians who have thought that Spinoza meant by love of God what they mean by it, and a Hegelian critic who boasted of him as one that banished God altogether, and substituted an idea in His place. Might he not have been nearer the truth if he had done justice to both the Christian and the Hegelian critic; if he had believed that Spinoza intended love when he spoke of love, and not at all less because he speaks as St. Paul does, of knowing love, and that he was never able to find, much as he often tried to find, how the idea passes into reality?

Was it otherwise with the greatest heathen emperor, who is the subject of a more satisfactory essay than that on the excommunicated Jew? The worth of Marcus Aurelius as the pursuer of an ideal, Mr. Arnold has perceived and not exaggerated; his intense conviction that the idea must have fact to dwell in and sustain it, he has not understood nearly as well. If he had, he would have found a far better apology than he has found for his conduct to the Christian Church. Unless this Church proclaims that the highest ideal is embodied in fact, it is nothing. Had Marcus Aurelius accepted the Cross as the reconciliation of Idea and Fact, he would have been what Mr. Mill wishes he had been, the precursor of Constantine, who merely saw that the Cross was stronger than the Eagle. As he did not, he was obliged by the devoutness of his mind to take the old fictions as attempts to embody some conception of the divinity; his duty as the head of the Roman State obliged him to persecute a rival kingdom.

The praises of Philistines cannot be acceptable to Mr. Arnold. But for the sake of our readers, and for the satisfaction of our own consciences, we must say that he has given us a remarkable book, which ought to benefit all its readers, specially those who reject as cordially as we do its fundamental maxim.

BIBLIOGRAPHY
INDEX

BIBLIOGRAPHY

BOOKS

General

Baker, Joseph, ed. *The Reinterpretation of Victorian Literature*. New York: Russell and Russell, 1962 (reprint).

Buckley, Jerome H. *The Triumph of Time: A Study of the Victorian Concepts of Time, History, Progress, and Decadence*. Cambridge, Mass.: Harvard University (Belknap) Press, 1966.

———— *The Victorian Temper: A Study in Literary Culture*. London: George Allen and Unwin, 1952.

Ford, George. *Keats and the Victorians*. London: Archon Books, 1962.

Holloway, John. *The Charted Mirror*. New York: Horizon Press, 1962.

Houghton, Walter E. *The Victorian Frame of Mind, 1830-1870*. New Haven: Yale University Press, 1957.

Miller, J. Hillis. *The Disappearance of God*. Cambridge, Mass.: Harvard University (Belknap) Press, 1963.

Wellek, René. *A History of Modern Criticism*. Vols. 3-4. New Haven: Yale University Press, 1965.

Williams, Raymond. *Culture and Society*. New York: Columbia University Press, 1958.

On Matthew Arnold and Essays in Criticism

Alexander, Edward. *Matthew Arnold and John Stuart Mill*. New York: Columbia University Press, 1965.

Anderson, Warren. *Matthew Arnold and the Classical Tradition*. Ann Arbor: University of Michigan Press, 1965.

Arnold, Matthew. *The Complete Prose Works*. Edited by R. H. Super. 6 vols. Ann Arbor: University of Michigan Press, 1960-67. Vol. 3, *Lectures and Essays in Criticism*.

Bonnerot, Jean. *Matthew Arnold, Poëte: Essai de Biographie Psychologique*. Paris: Didier, 1947.

Brown, E. K. *Matthew Arnold: A Study in Conflict*. Chicago: University of Chicago Press, 1948.

———— *Studies in the Text of Matthew Arnold's Prose Works*. Paris: Pierre André, 1935.

Buckler, William E. *Matthew Arnold's Books: Toward a Publishing Diary*. Geneva: Librairie E. Droz, 1958.

Buckley, Vincent. *Poetry and Morality: Studies on the Criticism of Matthew Arnold, T. S. Eliot, and F. R. Leavis*. London: Chatto and Windus, 1959.

Campos, Christophe. *The View of France from Arnold to Bloomsbury*. New York: Oxford University Press, 1965.

345

Culler, A. Dwight. *Imaginative Reason: The Poetry of Matthew Arnold.* New Haven: Yale University Press, 1966.

Dawson, W. H. *Matthew Arnold and His Relation to the Thought of Our Time.* New York: G. P. Putnam's Sons, 1904.

Fairclough, G. Thomas. *A Fugitive and Gracious Light: The Relation of Joseph Joubert to Matthew Arnold's Thought.* University of Nebraska Studies, n. s. no. 23. Lincoln, Nebraska: University of Nebraska Press, 1961.

Garrod, H. W. *Poetry and the Criticism of Life.* Cambridge, Mass.: Harvard University Press, 1931.

Gottfried, Leon. *Matthew Arnold and the Romantics.* London: Routledge and Kegan Paul, 1963.

Harding, F. J. W. *Matthew Arnold the Critic and France.* Geneva: Librairie Droz, 1964.

Holloway, John. *The Victorian Sage.* New York: Macmillan Company, 1953.

James, D. G. *Matthew Arnold and the Decline of English Romanticism.* Oxford: Clarendon Press, 1961.

Lowry, Howard Foster, ed. *The Letters of Matthew Arnold to Arthur Hugh Clough.* London: Oxford University Press, 1932.

Neiman, Fraser, ed. *Essays, Letters and Reviews by Matthew Arnold.* Cambridge, Mass.: Harvard University Press, 1960.

Orrick, J. B. *Matthew Arnold and Goethe.* London: Publications of the English Goethe Society, n. s., no. 4, (1928).

Raleigh, John H. *Matthew Arnold and American Culture.* Berkeley and Los Angeles: University of California Press, 1961.

Robbins, William. *The Ethical Idealism of Matthew Arnold.* Toronto: University of Toronto Press, 1959.

Russell, George W. E., ed. *The Letters of Matthew Arnold, 1848-1888.* 2 vols. London: Macmillan Company, 1895.

Sells, Iris. *Matthew Arnold and France.* Cambridge: Cambridge University Press, 1935.

Stange, G. Robert. *Matthew Arnold: The Poet as Humanist.* Princeton: Princeton University Press, 1967.

Temple, Ruth. *The Critic's Alchemy: A Study of the Introduction of French Symbolism into England.* New York: Twayne Publishers, 1953. (Reprinted by College and University Press, Hamden, Connecticut, n.d.)

Trilling, Lionel. *Matthew Arnold.* New York: Columbia University Press, 1949.

Whitridge, Arnold, ed. *Unpublished Letters of Matthew Arnold.* New Haven: Yale University Press, 1923.

ARTICLES

Angell, J. W. "Matthew Arnold's Indebtedness to Renan's *Essais de Morale et de Critique.*" *Revue de Literature Comparée,* XIV (1934), 714-33.

Arnold, Matthew. "Sainte-Beuve." *The Academy,* November 13, 1869. Reprinted in *The Complete Prose Works,* edited by R. H. Super, V, 304-10.

———— "Charles-Augustin Sainte-Beuve." *Encyclopedia Britannica,* 9th ed. (1886).

Armytage, W. H. G. "Matthew Arnold and Thomas Huxley: Some New Letters: 1870-80." *Review of English Studies,* n. s., IV, (1953), 346-53.

Bateson, F. W. "The Function of Criticism at the Present Time," *Essays in Criticism,* III (1953), 1-27.

Buckler, William E. "Studies in Three Arnold Problems." *PMLA,* LXIII (1958), 268-69 (Section III: "The Method of Arnold's *Essays in Criticism:* A Supplementary Note").

Butler, Elsie M. "Heine in England and Matthew Arnold." *German Life and Letters,* n. s., IX (1956), 157-65.

Carnall, Geoffrey. "Matthew Arnold's 'Great Critical Effort.'" *Essays in Criticism,* VII (1958), 256-68.

Coulling, Sidney M. B. "The Background of 'The Function of Criticism at the Present Time.'" *Philological Quarterly,* XLII (1963), 36-49.

———— "Matthew Arnold's 1853 Preface: Its Origin and Aftermath." *Victorian Studies*, VII (1963-64), 233-63.

———— "Renan's Influence on Arnold's Literary and Social Criticism." *Florida State University Studies*, V (1952).

De Laura, David J. "Arnold and Carlyle." *PMLA*, LXXIX (1964), 104-29.

———— "Matthew Arnold and John Henry Newman: The 'Oxford Sentiment' and the Religion of the Future." *Texas Studies in Language and Literature*, VI supplement (1965), 573-702.

Donovan, Robert A. "The Method of Arnold's *Essays in Criticism*." *PMLA*, LXXI (1956), 921-31.

Ebel, Henry. "Matthew Arnold and Marcus Aurelius." *Studies in English Literature*, III (1963), 555-66.

Feltes, N. N. "Matthew Arnold and the Modern Spirit: A Reassessment." *University of Toronto Quarterly*, XXXII (1962), 27-36.

Garrod, H. W. "Matthew Arnold's 1853 Preface." *Review of English Studies*, XVII (1941), 310-21.

Harris, Alan. "Matthew Arnold: The Unknown Years." *Nineteenth Century and After*, CXIII (1933), 498-509.

Hipple, Walter J., Jr. "Matthew Arnold, Dialectician." *University of Toronto Quarterly*, XXXII (1962), 1-25.

Hunt, Everett Lee. "Matthew Arnold and His Critics." *Sewanee Review*, XLIV (1936), 449-67.

James, Henry. "Matthew Arnold." *English Magazine*, I (1884), 241 ff. (Reprinted in *Literary Reviews and Essays by Henry James*, edited by Albert Mordell. New York: Vista House, 1957.)

Knickerbocker, W. S. "Matthew Arnold at Oxford: A Natural History of a Father and Son." *Sewanee Review*, XXXV (1927), 399-418.

Leavis, F. R. "Arnold as Critic." *Scrutiny*, VII (1938), 319-32.

———— "The Responsible Critic: or, The Function of Criticism at Any Time." *Scrutiny*, XIX (1952-53), 162-83.

Le Roy, Gaylord C. "Ambivalence in Arnold's Prose Criticism." *College English*, XIII (1952), 432-38.

Liptzin, Sol. "Heine, the Continuator of Goethe: A Mid-Victorian Legend." *Journal of English and Germanic Philology*, XLIII (1944), 317-25.

Loring, M. L. S. "T. S. Eliot on Matthew Arnold." *Sewanee Review*, XLIII (1935), 479-88.

Lubell, A. J. "Matthew Arnold: Between Two Worlds." *Modern Language Quarterly*, XXII (1961), 248-63.

Madden, William A. "The Divided Tradition of English Criticism." *PMLA*, LXXIII (1958), 69-80.

Mott, Lewis F. "Renan and Matthew Arnold," *Modern Language Notes*, XXXIII (1918), 65-73.

Mulhauser, F. L. "The Tradition of Burke." In *The Reinterpretation of Victorian Literature*, edited by Joseph Baker. New York: Russell and Russell, 1962 reprint, pp. 153-68.

Muller, Herbert. "Matthew Arnold: A Parable for Partisans." *Southern Review*, V (1940), 551-58.

Neiman, Fraser. "The *Zeitgeist* of Matthew Arnold." *PMLA*, LXXII (1957), 977-96.

Perkins, David. "Arnold and the Function of Literature." *ELH*, XVIII (1951), 287-309.

Raleigh, Walter. "Matthew Arnold." In *Some Authors*. Oxford: Clarendon Press, 1923, pp. 300-10.

Shumaker, Wayne. "Matthew Arnold's Humanism: Literature as a Criticism of Life." *Studies in English Literature*, II (1962), 385-402.

Super, R. H. "Documents in the Matthew Arnold-Sainte-Beuve Relationship." *Modern Philology*, LX (1963), 206-10.

———— "Arnold's Oxford Lectures on Poetry,." *Modern Language Notes*, LXXX (1955), 581-84.

———— "Vivacity and the Philistines." *Studies in English Literature,* VI (1966), 629-37.

Templeman, W. D. "Arnold's 'The Literary Influence of Academies,' Macaulay, and Espinasse." *Studies in Philology,* XLIII (1946), 89-92.

Tillotson, Geoffrey. "Matthew Arnold: The Critic and the Advocate." In *Criticism and the Nineteenth Century.* London: University of London, Athlone Press, 1951, pp. 42-60.

White, Helen C. "Matthew Arnold and Goethe." *PMLA,* XXXVI (1921), 436-53.

Whitridge, Arnold. "Matthew Arnold and Sainte-Beuve." *PMLA,* LIII (1938), 303-13.

Wickelgren, Florence L. "Matthew Arnold's Literary Relations with France." *Modern Language Review,* XXXIII (1938), 200-14.

INDEX